PRAISE FOR *THE FLAT WORLD AND EDUCATION: HOW AMERICA'S COMMITMENT TO EQUITY WILL DETERMINE OUR FUTURE*

"We are so fortunate that Linda Darling-Hammond has provided this roadmap for educational excellence for all children in today's flat world. She thoughtfully emphasizes the basic strengths—standards, assessment, teaching, etc.—that we need in these changing times, and then she outlines what our schools must do to respond to these 21st-century learning needs. Linda is one of the education researchers whom I most respect. I am so pleased that she clearly designates equity as the priority for educating our current and future students. 'All children' must mean *all children*, and this book shows us how to do it."

Richard W. Riley, Former U.S. Secretary of Education,
and Former Governor of South Carolina

"When Linda Darling-Hammond speaks, America's teachers listen! I listened and learned from her as together we led the National Board for Professional Teaching Standards and created the National Commission on Teaching and America's Future. Excellent schools are the key to America's economic future—and superb teaching is the key to great schools. This book makes clear as a bell how to organize schools for successful teaching and what state and national policies are required to support it."

James B. Hunt, Former Governor of North Carolina,
and President of the Hunt Institute

"Darling-Hammond has provided readers with a thorough and insightful explanation of what it will take to create the schools we need in the United States. In addition to providing a powerful critique of current policy to explain why we are still leaving so many children behind, she uses examples taken from nations that have experienced a greater degree of educational success to make the case for the kinds of policies that should be pursued here. Her ideas are clear and compelling and her arguments are sound, rooted in evidence and unencumbered by the kinds of ideological partisanship that characterizes too much of current debates on education. After reading this book, one will understand why it was that candidate Obama, when seeking advice from the sharpest minds in education, turned to Dr. Linda Darling-Hammond."

Pedro A. Noguera, Ph.D., Peter L. Agnew Professor of Education,
Steinhardt School of Culture, Education and Development,
and Executive Director, Metropolitan Center for Urban Education,
New York University

"Anyone who desires a quantum leap in the educational achievements of American students—as opposed to the 'quick fix'—must address the issues raised in this carefully argued and well-documented work."

Howard Gardner, Hobbs Professor of Cognition and Education,
Harvard Graduate School of Education

"Once again, Linda Darling-Hammond brings clarity to complexity, thoughtful analysis to politically charged issues, and sound policy recommendations to the hysteria of what to do to save America's public schools. In this volume, the macro meets the micro on terms that let all democratically minded citizens breathe a sigh of relief."

Gloria Ladson-Billings, Kellner Family Chair of Urban Education,
University of Wisconsin-Madison

"Linda Darling-Hammond has written the definitive description of the problems that drag down the quality and equity of our educational system. Writing with passion, solid scholarship, and compassion, she presents a vision of the changes that are necessary to build a better education system and a brighter future for all our children and our nation."

Diane Ravitch, Research Professor of Education, New York University,
and author of *The Death and Life of the Great American School System*

"Linda Darling-Hammond's latest is a profoundly important book. She provides both a powerful rationale and a clear, detailed roadmap for how public education must be transformed to meet the challenges of teaching, learning, and assessment in the 21st century. It is a 'must-read' for educators, policymakers, and others concerned about the future of our country in a 'flat' world."

Tony Wagner, co-director, Harvard Change Leadership Group,
and author of *The Global Achievement Gap*

MULTICULTURAL EDUCATION SERIES

James A. Banks, Series Editor

THE
FLAT
WORLD
AND
EDUCATION

HOW AMERICA'S COMMITMENT TO
EQUITY WILL DETERMINE OUR FUTURE

LINDA DARLING-HAMMOND

TEACHERS COLLEGE, COLUMBIA UNIVERSITY
NEW YORK AND LONDON

Published by Teachers College Press, 1234 Amsterdam Avenue, New York, NY 10027

Library of Congress Cataloging-in-Publication Data

Darling-Hammond, Linda, 1951–
    The flat world and education : how America's commitment to equity will determine our future / Linda Darling-Hammond.
        p. cm. — (The multicultural education series)
    Includes bibliographical references and index.
    ISBN 978-0-8077-4962-3 (pbk. : alk. paper)
    ISBN 978-0-8077-4963-0 (hardcover : alk. paper)
        1. Educational equalization—United States. 2. Multicultural education—United States. 3. Students with social disabilities—United States. I. Title.
LC213.D37 2010
379.2'60973—dc22   2009043075

ISBN 978-0-8077-4962-3 (paper)
ISBN 978-0-8077-4963-0 (hardcover)

Printed on acid-free paper
Manufactured in the United States of America

17   16   15   14   13   12   11   10   8   7   6   5   4   3   2   1

Contents

Series Foreword

Linda Darling-Hammond is one of the world's most eloquent, authoritative, compassionate, and prolific voices for equity, social justice, and the transformation of schools and teacher education. She has amassed her myriad gifts in *The Flat World and Education: How America's Commitment to Equity Will Determine Our Future*. In this book, which has all the marks of a magnum opus, Darling-Hammond presents indisputable and chilling statistics that document the extent to which the United States faces a national crisis because students in other nations such as South Korea, Finland, Japan, and the United Kingdom are outperforming U.S. students in math and science achievement. She also presents compelling evidence that the United States will be unable to meet its scientific and technical needs in the present and future unless it makes a national commitment to improve schools and teacher education for the nation's most vulnerable and neglected students. Darling-Hammond points out that the significant achievement gap between students in the United States and in other developed nations is widening rather than closing.

American classrooms are experiencing the largest influx of immigrant students since the beginning of the 20th century. About a million immigrants are making the United States their home each year (Martin & Midgley, 2006). The U.S. Census (2007) projects that ethnic minorities will increase from one-third of the nation's population in 2006 to 50 percent in 2042 (Roberts, 2008). Ethnic minorities made up 100 million of the total U.S. population of just over 300 million in 2006. Between 1997 and 2006, roughly 9 million immigrants entered the United States (U.S. Department of Homeland Security, 2007). Only 15 percent came from nations in Europe. Most came from Mexico and from nations in Asia, Latin America, Central America, and the Caribbean (U.S. Department of Homeland Security, 2007). A large but undetermined number of undocumented immigrants also enter the United States each year. In 2007, the *New York Times* estimated that there were 12 million illegal immigrants in the United States (Monday, June 4, 2007, p. A22). The influence of an increasingly ethnically diverse population on U.S. schools, colleges, and universities is and will continue to be enormous. The Progressive Policy Institute estimated that 50 million Americans (out of 300 million) spoke a language other than English at home in 2008.

Our schools are more diverse today than they have been since the early 1900s, when a flood of immigrants entered the United States from Southern, Central, and Eastern Europe. In the 30-year period between 1973 and 2004, the percentage of students of color in U.S. public schools increased form 22 to 43 percent. If current trends continue, students of color will equal or exceed the percentage of White students in U.S. public schools within two decades. Students of color already exceed the number of Whites students in six states: California, Hawaii, Louisiana, Mississippi, New Mexico, and Texas (Dillon, 2006).

Darling-Hammond describes how the national achievement scores of students in the United States are significantly influenced by the academic performance of low-income students and students of color. The scores of Asian and White students are above the Organization for Economic Cooperation and Development (OECD) average in each subject area. However, when the scores of African Americans and Hispanic students are added, the U.S. national average "plummets to the bottom tier of the rankings." As students of color and English Language Learners (ELLs) become an increasingly large percent of the U.S. student population, the country's educational destiny will become more tightly connected to the academic status and achievement of these students, most of whom are structurally excluded and marginalized within our society and schools. Students of color in the United States are the canaries in the coalmine. Their status and destiny are a harbinger of the future of the country. That is why it is imperative, as Darling-Hammond persuasively argues, that we attain equity in our schools and close the widening gap in educational achievement between U.S. students and those in other developed nations.

One of the most painful and disturbing findings that Darling-Hammond reveals is how high rates of incarceration in the United States are tied to undereducation, race, and unemployment. The United States has 5 percent of the world's population and 25 percent of its prison inmates. Most U.S. prison inmates are high school dropouts, and many are functionally illiterate and have learning disabilities. A highly disproportionate percentage are individuals of color and from the lowest rungs of the social ladder. The nation's prison population is increasing, and states' prison budgets are growing almost three times faster than education budgets.

This sobering but hopeful book was written to mobilize the nation to action, to challenge pervasive myths and misconceptions about education and schooling, and to present a blueprint for reforming educational policy, schooling, and teacher education. The stark statistics, forthright descriptions of how the future of the nation is tied to the fate of our most neglected youth, and the declining status of U.S. schools in the world context should motivate policy makers and practicing educators to act decisively and thoughtfully. Darling-Hammond describes specific policies and school reforms that must be implemented to halt the nation's academic decline and re-establish it as a global educational leader. These include: (1) meaningful learning goals; (2) intelligent, reciprocal accountability systems; (3) equitable and adequate resources; (4) strong professional standards; and (5) the organization of schools for student and teacher learning.

Darling-Hammond candidly documents the educational crisis in the United States. She depicts a dismal scenario if we fail to act and describes specific actions that school districts, states, and the federal government can take to actualize educational equity and close the widening gap between our democratic ideals and realities. If we can improve race relations and help all students acquire the knowledge, attitudes, and skills needed to participate in cross-cultural interactions and in personal, social, and civic action, we will create a more democratic and just society.

The major purpose of the Multicultural Education Series is to provide preservice educators, practicing educators, and graduate students with an interrelated and comprehensive set of books that summarizes and analyzes important research, theory, and practice related to the education of ethnic, racial, cultural, and linguistic groups in the United States and the education of mainstream students about diversity. The books in the Series provide research, theoretical, and practical knowledge about the behaviors and learning characteristics of students of color, language minority students, and low-income students. They also provide knowledge about ways to improve academic achievement and race relations in educational settings. Multicultural education is consequently as important for middle-class White suburban students as it is for students of color who live in the inner-city. Multicultural education fosters the public good and the overarching goals of the commonwealth. I hope this timely, trenchant, and significant book will have the influence on educational policy makers and practitioners that it deserves.

—James A. Banks

REFERENCES

Banks, J. A. (2004). Multicultural education: Historical development, dimensions, and practice. In J. A. Banks & C. A. M. Banks (Eds.). *Handbook of research on multicultural education* (2nd ed., pp. 3–29). San Francisco: Jossey-Bass.

Banks, J. A. (Ed.). (2009). *The Routledge international companion to multicultural education.* New York and London: Routledge.

Banks, J. A., & Banks, C. A. M. (Eds.) (2004). *Handbook of research on multicultural education* (2nd ed.). San Francisco: Jossey-Bass.

Dillon, S. (2006, August 27). In schools across U.S., the melting pot overflows. *The New York Times,* vol. CLV [155] (no. 53,684), pp. A7, A16.

Martin, P., & Midgley, E. (1999). Immigration to the United States. *Population Bulletin, 54*(2), pp. 1–44. Washington, DC: Population Reference Bureau.

Progressive Policy Institute (2008). *50 million Americans speak languages other than English at home.* Retrieved September 2, 2008, from http://www.ppionline.org/ppi_ci.cfm?knlgAreaID=10 8&subsecID=900003&contentID=254619

Roberts, S. (2008, August 14). A generation away, minorities may become the majority in U.S. *The New York Times*, vol. CLVII [175] (no. 54,402), pp. A1, A18.

Suárez-Orozco, C., Suárez-Orozco, M. M., & Todorova, I. (2008). *Learning a new land: Immigrant students in American society.* Cambridge, MA: Harvard University Press.

U.S. Census Bureau (2003, October). *Language use and English-speaking ability: 2000.* Retrieved September 2, 2008, from http://www.census.gov/prod/2003pubs/c2kbr-29.pdf

U.S. Census Bureau (2008, August 14). *Statistical abstract of the United States.* Retrieved August 20, 2008, from http://www.census.gov/prod/2006pubs/07statab/pop.pdf

U.S. Department of Homeland Security (2007). *Yearbook of immigration statistics, 2006.* Washington, DC: Office of Immigration Statistics, Author. Retrieved August 11, 2009, from http://www.dhs.gov/files/statistics/publications/yearbook.shtm

Acknowledgments

This book has, in a manner of speaking, been nearly a lifetime in the making, and there are more people to thank for my learning about the ideas reflected here than can possibly be named. Nonetheless, I must make an attempt.

I want to thank James Banks, who gently insisted over many years that I write this book and who has been a leader in our field for decades. His work and colleagueship paved the way for this effort.

In my own learning journey, I want to mention especially the influence of my mentor Dr. Bernard Charles Watson, who literally pulled me into graduate school and taught me how to understand and confront issues of social justice. Along the way, many others schooled me and supported my work. Special thanks are due to former D.C. schools superintendent Floretta Mackenzie; extraordinary school reformers and leaders Deborah Meier, James Comer, Ted Sizer, Ann Cook, George Wood, Tony Alvarado, Eric Cooper, and Charla Rolland; my research colleagues Arthur Wise, Barnett Berry, Gloria Ladson-Billings, Carol Lee, Jeannie Oakes, Ann Lieberman, Kris Gutierrez, Angela Valenzuela, Rachel Lotan, Ed Haertel, Lee Shulman, Rich Shavelson, Ray Pecheone, Martin Carnoy, Prudence Carter, Milbrey McLaughlin, Kenji Hakuta, Guadalupe Valdés, and Arnetha Ball; courageous policymakers Thomas Sobol, Gerry Tirozzi, former governor of South Carolina James B. Hunt, and former U.S. Education Secretary Richard Riley; and my colleagues in the struggle for more equitable schools, Sharon Porter Robinson, Fred Frelow, Diana Daniels, Claude Mayberry, Benjamin Todd Jealous, Marion Wright Edelman, Ray Bacchetti, Hugh Price, Susan Sandler, John Affeldt, and Michael Rebell, who have never stopped fighting for what children need to secure a genuine right to learn.

The book draws on research funded by the Ford Foundation, the Rockefeller Foundation, the Spencer Foundation, the Wallace Foundation, the Carnegie Corporation of New York, the Bill and Melinda Gates Foundation, the Flora Foundation, the Morgan Family Foundation, Justice Matters, Atlantic Philanthropic Services, and the U.S. Department of Education. I am grateful to all of these sources of support over many years.

My research was conducted with many extraordinary colleagues. From New York City and Teachers College, Columbia University: Jacqueline Ancess, Jon Snyder, Susanna Ort, Beverly Falk, Maritza Macdonald, and Velma Cobb, among many others. From California and Stanford University: Ash Vasudeva, Ruth Chung Wei, Nikole Richardson, Julian Vasquez Heilig, Diane Friedlaender, Laura Wentworth, Ken Montgomery, Michael Milliken, Peter Ross, and Olivia Ifill-Lynch. In the course of preparing this manuscript, research assistance was also provided by Sarah Nash, Jillian Hamma, Fagan Harris, and Sergio Rosas.

Jessica Gimenez was heroic in her extensive bibliographic and editorial assistance, and the team at Teachers College Press—especially Carole Saltz, Susan Liddicoat, and Shannon Waite—was unfailingly supportive and helpful in every imaginable way.

Of course, I thank my husband Allen and my children Kia, Elena, and Sean for being the motivation and primary support for my work. The children fortunate enough to be taught by Kia and Elena are among the beneficiaries of the kind of well-prepared and deeply committed teachers all young people deserve.

I dedicate this book to all of the children and families in communities across this country and the world who fight for an education that should be their birthright and whose efforts, with those of their advocates, will someday produce a right to learn for every human being. Their struggles require great courage and conscience. As Martin Luther King Jr. reminded us in 1968:

> On some positions, Cowardice asks the question, "Is it safe?" Expediency asks the question, "Is it politic?" And Vanity comes along and asks the question, "Is it popular?" But Conscience asks the question "Is it right?" And there comes a time when one must take a position that is neither safe, nor politic, nor popular, but he must do it because Conscience tells him it is right.

CHAPTER 1

The Flat World, Educational Inequality, and America's Future

The best employers the world over will be looking for the most competent, most creative, and most innovative people on the face of the earth and will be willing to pay them top dollar for their services. . . . Beyond [strong skills in English, mathematics, technology, and science], candidates will have to be comfortable with ideas and abstractions, good at both analysis and synthesis, creative and innovative, self-disciplined and well organized, able to learn very quickly and work well as a member of a team and have the flexibility to adapt quickly to frequent changes in the labor market as the shifts in the economy become ever faster and more dramatic. If we continue on our current course, and the number of nations outpacing us in the education race continues to grow at its current rate, the American standard of living will steadily fall relative to those nations, rich and poor, that are doing a better job. The core problem is that our education and training systems were built for another era, an era in which most workers needed only a rudimentary education. It is not possible to get where we have to go by patching that system. We can get where we must go only by changing the system itself.

—The New Commission on the Skills of the American Workforce, 2007

The 21st century is characterized by the availability of abundant information, advanced technology, a rapidly changing society, greater convenience in daily lives, and keener international competition. In response to these changes, our Education Reform should aim at nurturing in the new generation characteristics and abilities capable of meeting the challenges of the new century. . . . Education Reform must be student-focused . . . to develop the potential and personalities of students. This student-focused spirit underlines the education and curriculum reforms, improvement to the learning environment, and enhancement of teacher training.

—Hong Kong Education Commission, June 2003

In the last decade, mountains of reports have been written in countries around the world about the need for more powerful learning focused on the demands of life, work, and citizenship in the 21st century. The process of managing decisions and solving social and scientific problems in contemporary democracies is growing ever more complex. At least 70% of U.S. jobs now require specialized knowledge and skills, as compared to only 5% at the dawn of the last century, when our current system of schooling was established. These new skills include the capacity to:

- Design, evaluate, and manage one's own work so that it continually improves
- Frame, investigate, and solve problems using a wide range of tools and resources
- Collaborate strategically with others
- Communicate effectively in many forms
- Find, analyze, and use information for many purposes
- Develop new products and ideas[1]

Furthermore, the nature of work will continue to change ever more rapidly. During much of the 20th century, most workers held two or three jobs during their lifetimes. However, the U.S. Department of Labor estimates that many of today's workers will hold more than 10 jobs before they reach the age of 40.[2] The top 10 in-demand jobs projected for 2010 did not exist in 2004.[3] Thus, the new mission of schools is to prepare students to work at jobs that do not yet exist, creating ideas and solutions for products and problems that have not yet been identified, using technologies that have not yet been invented.

Is our society ready to take on this challenge? Are we able to provide education that will develop these more complex skills—not just for a small slice of students who have traditionally been selected for the kind of ambitious learning represented in elite schools and advanced programs, but for the vast majority of children in communities across the country? Or will we be waylaid by our long-standing tradition of unequal education coupled with our inability, thus far, to move from a factory model approach to education designed at the end of the 19th century to one that is pointed clearly and unambiguously at the demands of the 21st?

This book takes on these questions, arguing that the United States needs to move much more decisively than it has in the last quarter century to establish a purposeful, equitable education *system* that will prepare *all* our children for success in a knowledge-based society. This means moving beyond a collection of disparate and shifting reform initiatives, only occasionally related to what we know about teaching and learning, to a thoughtful, well-organized, and well-supported set of policies that will enable students to learn how to learn, create, and invent the new world they are entering. It also means finally making good on the unmet American promise that education will be made available to all on equal terms, so that every member of this society can realize a productive life and contribute to the greater welfare.

During his recent historic campaign for the presidency, Barack Obama described the large race- and class-based achievement gaps we experience as "morally unacceptable and economically untenable." At a time when three-quarters of the fastest-growing occupations require postsecondary education, our college participation rates have slipped from 1st in the world to 16th, and only about one-third of our young people receive a college degree.[4] Meanwhile, in many European and some Asian nations, more than half of young people are becoming college graduates. At a time when children of color comprise a majority in most urban districts, and will be a majority in the nation as a whole by 2025,[5] we face pernicious achievement gaps that fuel inequality, shortchanging our young people and our nation. Today, in the United States of America, only 1 in 10 low-income kindergartners becomes a college graduate. A greater number join the growing ranks of inmates in what the *New York Times* recently dubbed our "prison nation."[6]

At a time when high school dropouts are unlikely to be able to secure any job at all, our high school graduation rates—stuck at about 70%—have dropped from first in the world to the bottom half of industrialized nations. At a time when advances in science and technology fuel economic growth in East Asian and European nations, our students rank near the bottom of industrialized countries in math and science achievement. If these trends continue, by 2012, America will have 7 million jobs in science and technology fields, "green" industries, and other fields that cannot be filled by U.S. workers who have been adequately educated for them.[7]

As Americans seek to deal with the effects of the monetary meltdown that became an economic tsunami by the time President Obama was inaugurated, it is critical to realize that financial responses alone won't ultimately safeguard our economic and social well-being, and that substantial, strategic investments in education are essential to our long-term prosperity and to our success as a democracy. We cannot just bail ourselves out of this crisis. We must teach our way out. How we can and must do that is the subject of this book.

EDUCATION IN OUR FLAT AND CHANGING WORLD

The world is changing, and as Tom Friedman has demonstrated, it is increasingly flat.[8] Globalization is changing everything about how we work, how we communicate, and, ultimately, how we live. Employers can distribute their activities around the entire globe, based on the costs and skills of workers in nearly any nation that has built an infrastructure for transportation and communications. Customers in the United States buy their clothes from China and the Philippines, and have their questions about the new computer they bought answered by workers in India.

As manufacturing jobs have become automated or moved overseas, the entire structure of the U.S. economy has drastically changed. Whereas in 1967, more than half (54%) of the country's economic output was in the production of material goods and delivery of material services (such as transportation, construction, and retailing), by 1997, nearly two-thirds (63%) was in the production of information products (such as computers, books, televisions, and software) and the provision of information services (such as telecommunications, financial services, and education). Information services alone grew from about one-third to more than half of the economy during that 30-year period.[9]

Meanwhile, knowledge is expanding at a breathtaking pace. It is estimated that five exabytes of new information (500,000 times the volume of the Library of Congress print collection) was generated in 2002, more than three times as much as in 1999. Indeed, in the 3 years from 1999 to 2002, the amount of new information produced nearly equaled the amount produced in the entire history of the world previously.[10] The amount of new technical information is doubling every 2 years, and it is predicted to double every 72 hours by 2010.[11] As a consequence, education can no longer be productively focused primarily on the transmission of pieces of information that, once memorized, comprise a stable storehouse of knowledge. Instead, schools must teach disciplinary knowledge in ways that focus on central concepts and help students learn how to think critically and learn for themselves, so that they can use knowledge in new situations and manage the demands of changing information, technologies, jobs, and social conditions.

These are not new skills, but they were not envisioned for most students in the school system we designed between 1900 and 1920. That system was based on the factory model then made popular by Henry Ford's assembly line. The notion was that one could organize all of the facts needed into a set body of knowledge and divide it up neatly into the 12 years of schooling, doling out the information through graded textbooks and testing it regularly. By the 1950s, "modern" methods allowed the accrual of knowledge to be evaluated with multiple-choice tests that could be scored exclusively by machine, without the involvement of teachers or the complications of asking students to produce and defend their own ideas.

This transmission-oriented curriculum was designed to be delivered in large, impersonal factory-model schools that passed students off from one teacher to the next from year to year and, by junior high school, from subject area to subject area every 50 minutes. Tracking systems were invented to provide a basic skills curriculum to the children of the poor, and a more thinking-oriented curriculum to the more affluent, who were taught in separate "lanes," "tracks," or "streams," or in small elite private schools and public schools in wealthy districts. And while efforts to change this "one best system"[12] have been the object of reforms over several decades, these features remain substantially in place in most U.S. schools—often reinforced by the very reforms that were launched to change them, but that reverted to old paradigms along the way.

Meanwhile, other nations around the world are transforming their school systems to meet these new demands. They are expanding educational access to more and more of their people, and they are revising curriculum, instruction, and assessment to support the more complex knowledge and skills needed in the 21st century. Starting in the 1980s, for example, Finland dismantled the rigid tracking system that had allocated differential access to knowledge to its young people and eliminated the state-mandated testing system that was used for this purpose, replacing them with highly trained teachers and curriculum and assessments focused on problem solving, creativity, independent learning, and student reflection.[13] These changes have propelled achievement to the top of the international rankings and closed what was once a large, intractable achievement gap.[14]

In the space of one generation, South Korea moved from a nation that educated less than a quarter of its citizens through high school to one that now ranks third in college-educated adults, with most young people now completing postsecondary education.[15] Starting in the 1970s, Singapore began to transform itself from a collection of swampy fishing villages into an economic powerhouse by building an education system that would ensure every student access to strong teaching, an inquiry curriculum, and cutting-edge technology.[16] These countries have created high and equitable achievement, despite high levels of poverty and growing ethnic and linguistic diversity among their citizens.

In Singapore, for example, 80% of families live in public housing, yet its 4th- and 8th-grade students scored first in the world in both mathematics and science on the TIMSS (Trends in International Mathematics and Science Study) assessments in 2003.[17] When children leave the tiny, spare apartments they occupy in concrete high-rises throughout the city, they arrive at colorful, airy school buildings where student artwork, papers, projects, and awards are displayed throughout; libraries and classrooms are well stocked; instructional technology is plentiful; and teachers are well trained and well supported.

With few natural resources, Singapore recognizes that its human capital will determine its future. Building on its ongoing efforts, former prime minister Goh Chok Tong led the tiny nation in adopting a system-wide reform in 1997 called "Thinking Schools, Learning Nation." The Ministry of Education explains that this initiative is meant to create:

a nation of thinking and committed citizens capable of meeting the challenges of the future, and an education system geared to the needs of the 21st century. Thinking schools will be learning organizations in every sense, constantly challenging assumptions, and seeking better ways of doing things through participation, creativity and innovation. Thinking Schools will be the cradle of thinking students as well as thinking adults and this spirit of learning should accompany our students even after they leave school. A Learning Nation envisions a national culture and social environment that promotes lifelong learning in our people. The capacity of Singaporeans to continually learn, both for professional development and for personal enrichment, will determine our collective tolerance for change.[18]

This spirit of creativity and innovation is visible throughout the schools, which are encouraged to engage both students and teachers in experiential and cooperative learning, action research, scientific investigations, entrepreneurial activities, and discussion and debate.

A visit to Nan Chiau Primary School, for example, finds 4th- and 5th-grade students eagerly displaying the science projects they have designed and conducted in an "experience/investigate/create" cycle that is repeated throughout the year. Students are delighted to show visitors their "Innovation Walk," displaying student-developed projects from many subject areas along a long corridor.

The school brochure describing its "Curriculum Innovations" notes that "Traditional teaching . . . with a focus on rote-learning, contributes as one of the main reasons for unmotivated students. . . . Nan Chiau Primary School has adopted an active learning model that leverages experiential learning [which] allows students to experience the lesson, investigate, and create new knowledge." Students study plants, animals, and insects in the school's eco-garden; they run their own recycling center; they write and edit scripts for the Internet radio program they produce; and they use handheld computers to play games and create mathematical models that develop their quantitative abilities.

In a 4th-grade language arts lesson, I watched as students completed brief essays analyzing an aspect of a piece of literature they had just read. They then called up another student's essay on their computer and wrote a response and critique to their peer. As they worked intensely at their tables of four, periodically sharing their ideas with one another and getting feedback, the teacher called up all of the essays on her own computer to carefully choose those she would use in a few moments as models for a brief lesson on both the critical thinking students were developing and elements of their written expression. After seeing and discussing work displayed on the classroom projector, students would have the opportunity to work further on their analyses, with the benefit of insights into other students' efforts. The use of self- and peer assessments, along with active engagement in creating their own products, is one of the many ways the school seeks to "empower pupils to take ownership of their learning so they may grow into independent, inquisitive, life-long learners, confident of managing changes in the future."[19] Teachers, meanwhile, engage in action research, sponsored by the government, to continually improve their teaching.

Certainly there are schools that look like this in the United States, but they are not the norm. What distinguishes systems like Singapore's is that this quality of education—aimed intently at empowering students to use their knowledge in inventive ways—is replicated throughout the entire nation of 4 million—a jurisdiction with a population about the size of Kentucky, the median U.S. state. Furthermore, Singapore is not alone. The pace at which many nations in Asia and Europe are pouring resources into forward-looking education systems that educate all of their citizens to much higher levels is astonishing. And the growing gap between the United States and these nations—particularly in our most underfunded schools—is equally dramatic.

Contrast the above picture of a typical Singaporean school with the description below of a California school, from a lawsuit filed in 2002 on behalf of low-income students of color in schools like it throughout the state, nearly 50 years after *Brown v. Board of Education*:

> At Luther Burbank, students cannot take textbooks home for homework in any core subject because their teachers have enough textbooks for use in class only. . . . For homework, students must take home photocopied pages, with no accompanying text for guidance or reference, when and if their teachers have enough paper to use to make homework copies. . . . Luther Burbank is infested with vermin and roaches and students routinely see mice in their classrooms. One dead rodent has remained, decomposing, in a corner in the gymnasium since the beginning of the school year. The school library is rarely open, has no librarian, and has not recently been updated. The latest version of the encyclopedia in the library was published in approximately 1988. Luther Burbank classrooms do not have computers. Computer instruction and research skills are not, therefore, part of Luther Burbank students' regular instruction. The school no longer offers any art classes for budgetary reasons. . . . Two of the three bathrooms at Luther Burbank are locked all day, every day. . . . Students have urinated or defecated on themselves at school because they could not get into an unlocked bathroom. . . . When the bathrooms are not locked, they often lack toilet paper, soap, and paper towels, and the toilets frequently are clogged and overflowing. . . . Ceiling tiles are missing and cracked in the school gym, and school children are afraid to play games in the gym because they worry that more ceiling tiles will fall on them during their games. . . . The school has no air conditioning. On hot days classroom temperatures climb into the 90s. The school heating system does not work well. In winter, children often wear coats, hats, and gloves during class to keep warm. . . . Eleven of the 35 teachers at Luther Burbank have not yet obtained regular, nonemergency teaching credentials, and 17 of the 35 teachers only began teaching at Luther Burbank this school year.[20]

Under these kinds of circumstances, it is impossible even to begin to talk about developing the deep knowledge and complex skills required of young people in to-day's and tomorrow's society. If Maslow's hierarchy of needs were applied to schools, this kind of institution would be at the basic survival level, lacking the rudiments needed to begin to focus on the quality of learning and teaching or the development of higher-order thinking and performance skills.

Of course, one could argue that California is in many ways a worst case, as the state has allowed its school funding base to decline continuously as the result of the Proposition 13 property tax rollback passed 20 years before this lawsuit was filed. But far from being an anomaly, this school in San Francisco represents a growing number of "apartheid" schools across the United States—schools that serve racial/ethnic minority students exclusively, where political clout is nonexistent and re-sources are extraordinarily impoverished. Although the terrible conditions at Lu-ther Burbank are also not the norm for U.S. schools, they represent an unconscio-nable share of the total, and many other urban schools are just a step or two away from these totally dysfunctional conditions.

Although many U.S. educators and civil rights advocates have fought for higher-quality and more equitable education over many years—in battles for desegregation, school finance reform, and equitable treatment of students within schools—progress has been stymied in many states over the last 2 decades as segregation has worsened, and disparities have grown. While students in the highest-achieving states and dis-tricts in the United States do as well as those in high-achieving nations elsewhere, it is our continuing comfort with profound inequality that is the Achilles heel of American education.

HOW AMERICA IS LOSING GROUND

These disparities have come to appear inevitable in the United States; however, they are not the norm in developed nations around the world, which fund their education systems centrally and equally, with additional resources often going to the schools where students' needs are greater. As I describe later, the more equitable investments made by high-achieving nations are also more steady and more focused on critical elements of the system: the quality of teachers and teaching, the development of curriculum and assessments that encourage ambitious learning by both students and teachers, and the design of schools as learning organizations that support continuous reflection and improvement. With the exception of a few states that have had en-lightened long-term leadership, the United States, by contrast, has failed to maintain focused investments in a stable, well-prepared teaching force; has allowed the direction of learning to be whipsawed by unproductive "curriculum wars"; and has spent millions creating innovative schools that, although promising, remain at the margins of a system that has not been redesigned to support a 21st-century schooling enterprise.

Lagging Achievement

The results have been that the United States is standing still while more focused nations move rapidly ahead. This inertia is not due to a lack of hand-wringing or high-blown rhetoric. In 1983, *A Nation at Risk* decried a "rising tide of mediocrity" in education and called for sweeping reforms. In 1989, President George H.W. Bush and the 50 governors announced a set of national goals that included ranking first in the world in mathematics and science by the year 2000. However, by 2006, on the most recent international assessments conducted by the Program in International Student Assessment (PISA), the United States ranked 21st of 30 countries in the Organization for Economic Cooperation and Development (OECD) in science, and 25th of 30 in mathematics—a drop in both raw scores and rankings from 3 years earlier (see Figure 1.1).[21] When non–OECD members from Eastern Europe and Asia are added to the list, the U.S. rankings drop to 29th out of 40 developed countries in science, sandwiched between Latvia and Lithuania, and 35th out of 40 in mathematics—between Azerbaijan and Croatia (see Table 1.1 on next page).

Figure 1.1. U.S. PISA Scores, 2003 and 2006.

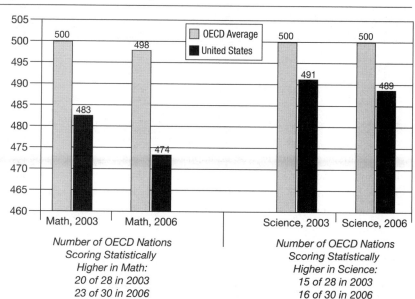

Source: OECD, 2007.

Table 1.1. PISA Scores and Rankings, 2006.

Science Rank	Country	Science Score	Math Rank	Country	Math Score
1	Finland	563	1	Chinese Taipei	549
2	Hong Kong—China	542	2	Finland	548
3	Canada	534	3	Hong Kong-China	547
4	Chinese Taipei	532	4	South Korea	547
5	Japan	531	5	Netherlands	531
6	Estonia	531	6	Switzerland	530
7	New Zealand	530	7	Canada	527
8	Australia	527	8	Liechtenstein	525
9	Netherlands	525	9	Macao-China	525
10	South Korea	522	10	Japan	523
11	Liechtenstein	522	11	New Zealand	522
12	Slovenia	519	12	Australia	520
13	Germany	516	13	Belgium	520
14	United Kingdom	515	14	Estonia	515
15	Czech Republic	513	15	Denmark	513
16	Switzerland	512	16	Czech Republic	510
17	Austria	511	17	Iceland	506
18	Macao-China	511	18	Austria	505
19	Belgium	510	19	Slovenia	504
20	Ireland	508	20	Germany	504
21	Hungary	504	21	Sweden	502
22	Sweden	503	22	Ireland	501
—	OECD average	500	—	OECD Average	498
23	Poland	498	23	France	496
24	Denmark	496	24	United Kingdom	495
25	France	495	25	Poland	495
26	Croatia	493	26	Slovak Republic	492
27	Iceland	491	27	Hungary	491
28	Latvia	490	28	Norway	490
29	United States	489	29	Luxembourg	490
30	Lithuania	488	30	Latvia	486
31	Slovak Republic	488	31	Lithuania	486
32	Spain	488	32	Spain	480
33	Norway	487	33	Russian Federation	476
34	Luxembourg	486	34	Azerbaijan	476
35	Russian Fed.	479	35	United States	474
36	Italy	475	36	Croatia	467
37	Portugal	474	37	Portugal	466
38	Greece	473	38	Italy	462
39	Israel	454	39	Greece	459
40	Chile	348	40	Turkey	424

Source: OECD (2007).

Importantly, the PISA assessments require more advanced analysis and knowledge use than most U.S. tests, going beyond the question "Did students learn specific facts?" to ask, "What can students do with what they have learned?" PISA defines literacy in mathematics, science, and reading as students' ability to *apply* what they know to new problems. It is focused on the kind of learning for transfer that is increasingly emphasized in other nations' curriculum and assessment systems, but often discouraged by the kind of textbooks and testing most often used in the United States. Indeed, U.S. students fall furthest behind on PISA tasks that require complex problem solving.[22]

Inequality has an enormous influence on U.S. performance. As Figure 1.2 shows, the distance between the average PISA scale score for Asian and White students, on the one hand, and African American and Hispanic students, on the other, is equal to the distance between the U.S. average and that of the highest-scoring countries.[23] Indeed, White and Asian students in the United States score above the OECD average in each subject area, but African American and Hispanic students score so much lower that the national average plummets to the bottom tier of the rankings.

Of nations participating in PISA, the United States is among those where two students of different socioeconomic backgrounds have the largest difference

Figure 1.2. U.S. PISA Results by Subgroup, Compared to OECD Average, 2003.

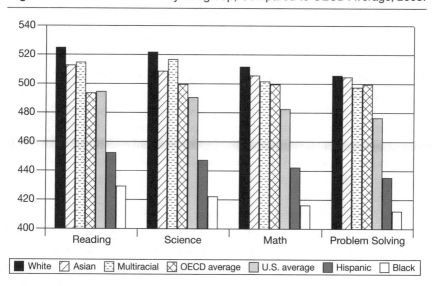

Source: Stage, 2005.

in expected scores. On this measure of equity, the United States ranked 45th out of 55 countries, just above Brazil and Mexico.[24] Thus, the United States's poor standing is substantially a product of unequal access for underserved students of color to the kind of intellectually challenging learning measured on these international assessments.

International studies continue to confirm that the U.S. educational system is also one of the most unequal in terms of inputs. In contrast to European and Asian nations that fund schools centrally and equally, the wealthiest school districts in the United States spend nearly 10 times more than the poorest, and spending ratios of 3 to 1 are common within states.[25] These disparities reinforce the wide inequalities in income among families, with the greatest resources being spent on children from the wealthiest communities and the fewest on the children of the poor, especially in high-minority communities. This creates huge inequalities in educational outcomes that ultimately weaken the very fabric of our nation.

It is worth noting that our poor and declining standing in mathematics and science also results from the lack of sustained, serious attention to improving teaching in these areas, where shortages of skilled teachers have been recurrent since the 1950s and where struggles over the curriculum have caused giant pendulum swings in classroom tactics over the same period of time. With teacher salaries typically lagging those for math and science careers by 40% overall and by more in low-wealth districts, coupled with meager investments in teacher preparation and few incentives for entering teaching, the nation has repeatedly created avoidable shortages that have undermined progress.

Meanwhile, in the wars between "new math"—aimed at mathematical reasoning, communication, and problem solving—and a "back to the basics" approach—favoring the use of memorization and algorithms for computation—political forces have repeatedly pushed most mathematics teaching in the United States back to drill-and-practice methods at odds with what research shows are the most effective strategies for developing high levels of mathematical competence.[26] Implemented by a disproportionate number of teachers without the combination of pedagogical training and content knowledge needed for highly skillful teaching, these decisions have created a math-phobic nation that has consistently failed to produce enough people interested and skilled in quantitative fields to fill the growing demands for these abilities.

The algorithmic methods found in most American classrooms are also at odds with what higher-achieving nations do. Although Asian nations, in particular, have had a reputation for fostering rote learning, close studies of mathematics teaching in countries such as Japan, China, and Singapore reveal instead a robust and disciplined approach to teaching mathematical reasoning and complex problem solving where knowledge is continually applied to real-world problems and students are asked to go beyond routines to use mathematics flexibly in new situations.[27] Furthermore, high-achieving nations teach about half as many topics each year as American schools do, treating them more deeply, with greater opportunity to work on a range of solution strategies and to engage students in applying what they are learning.[28]

Scholars of teaching, such as James Stigler of UCLA, have shown how teachers in countries like Japan and China will often pose a single well-chosen problem to students, contextualized in a real-world situation, which they will spend the entire class lesson reasoning through together.[29] Students will individually and collectively develop and present a variety of potential solutions for class discussion and further evaluation until everyone understands the concept from multiple perspectives. At the end of this process, the students may derive a formula or set of principles to characterize what they have learned, rather than having blindly applied a set of rules learned by rote to a group of problems they never truly understood. As students learn more deeply, they are able to build a more solid foundation for their later learning.

Interestingly, the United States ranks better in reading, where the PIRLS (Program in International Reading and Literacy Studies) assessments showed American fourth graders performing above the international average in 2006, ranked 18th out of 40 nations.[30] This relatively better showing, even given a slight decline in performance between 2001 and 2006, may be linked to the substantial investments in improving the preparation of teachers to teach reading that occurred during the 1990s. During that time, federal, state, and local investments in professional development for literacy grew, new models of teacher support and coaching were developed, and much higher standards for new teachers' reading preparation were established for teacher education and licensing in many states.

Although reading curricula have also been disrupted by recurrent battles between reading for comprehension and an emphasis on phonics, the expertise developed in this field has led most states to a balanced approach that recognizes that good teachers use a range of strategies supporting both decoding and comprehension, as they are appropriate to the needs of students. Although there are still unfortunate battles over curriculum in some places and skirmishes over whether all teachers need training to teach reading,[31] the relatively greater investments in professional development for teaching reading mean that, in most places, practice has improved since the 1980s, and students learn more. This suggests that when we are organized about building stronger teaching for more students, it can be done.

In this field, as others, however, constant progress has been difficult to maintain. For example, after the passage of No Child Left Behind (NCLB) in 2002, some well-researched reading programs were sidelined as the administration of the Reading First initiative required districts receiving federal funds to adopt specific commercial programs and abandon other approaches such as Reading Recovery, Success for

All, and integrated literacy approaches organized around trade books and writing. While the adopted programs brought structured reading approaches to many communities that had previously lacked coherence, and improved decoding skills in the early grades in a number of districts, they were also sometimes less successful than the previously used programs, especially for developing deeper comprehension and acquiring academic literacy in the content areas, key skills needed for meaningful reading in later grades. A federal evaluation eventually found that the Reading First initiative had no effect on elementary students' reading comprehension, although it improved decoding in the first grade.[32] In the years following the passage of NCLB, while reading scores improved somewhat at the 4th-grade level on NAEP (though at a slower pace than in the 1990s), they declined at the 8th-grade level and on international tests like PIRLS, suggesting the trade-offs that might have resulted from the government's prescriptions. Reading First, in its original form, was ended, and a new program will offer a broader range of successful program models.

Such U-turns in education policy and practice are not unusual in U.S. education. Local, state, and, sometimes, federal policies frequently force schools to change course based on political considerations rather than strong research about effective practice. In the long run, the fact that these battles must be continually refought means that we make less headway on student learning than we could and should—and the students most harmed are the most vulnerable students in urban and poor rural schools where the political currents are strongest and changes of course most frequent.

Stagnating Educational Attainment

We must also be concerned about lagging educational attainment. In the past, Americans have had a more democratically accessible education system than other nations, making it possible for more young people to complete high school and go to college. This, too, has changed dramatically. As other countries have been pouring resources into education, both their achievement and graduation rates have been climbing for all of their students, including recent immigrants and historical minorities. Meanwhile, the current generation of young Americans may be the first to be less well educated and less upwardly mobile than the one before.

Many of the top-scoring nations—including nations that were previously low-achieving—now graduate more than 90% of their students from high school, showing tremendous increases from 20 years ago. During the same period, U.S. graduation rates have been virtually stagnant, and now fall significantly below those of many other countries. (see Figure 1.3).[33] While the demands for an educated workforce increase, only about 69% of U.S. high school students graduated within 4 years with a standard diploma in 2000, down from 77% in 1969.[34] Including

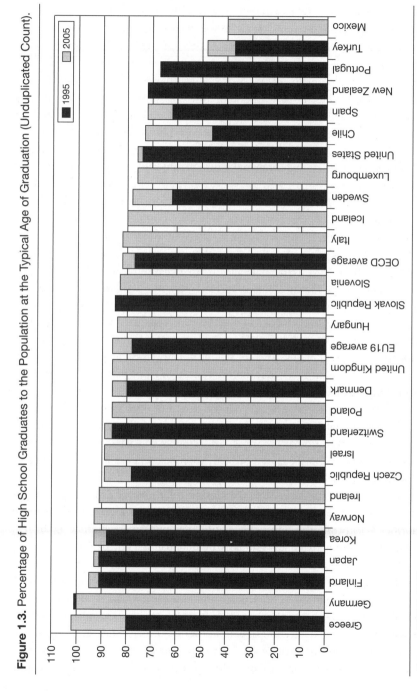

Figure 1.3. Percentage of High School Graduates to the Population at the Typical Age of Graduation (Unduplicated Count).

Source: OECD, 2008.

students who receive nonstandard diplomas (GEDs and other kinds of certificates) increases U.S. graduation rates to about 75%; however, this is still far below the rates of most advanced nations and leaves many young people without access to the economy or a living wage.

Many nations have also created higher education systems that are quickly becoming equally productive. Whereas the United States was an unchallenged first in the world in higher education participation, it had slipped to 14th by 2007 as college participation for our young people was declining,[35] and to 16th by 2008.[36] Although about 60% of U.S. high school graduates go off to college, only about half of these are well enough prepared educationally and well enough supported financially to graduate with a degree—far too few for the knowledge economy in which we now operate. In the end, about 35% of an age cohort in the United States gains a college degree, as compared to about 50% in European countries, and over 60% in Korea.[37] Other countries in Southeast Asia are also rapidly increasing the proportion of their citizens attending college by expanding higher education institutions at home and subsidizing their studies abroad.

For students of color in the United States, the pipeline leaks more profusely at every juncture. Only about 17% of African American young people between the ages of 25 and 29—and only 11% of Hispanic youth—had earned a college degree in 2005, as compared to 34% of White youth in the same age bracket.[38] Although these young people of color will be a majority of public school students by 2025, investments in their education remain highly unequal and inadequate to meet today's demands for the kinds of learning needed in the labor market. The schools they attend are both more segregated than they were 25 years ago[39] and less adequately resourced.[40] International studies confirm that the U.S. educational system not only lags most other industrialized countries in academic achievement by high school, but it is also allocates more unequal inputs and produces more unequal outcomes than its peer nations.[41]

The implications of these trends are important for national economies. A recent OECD report found that for every year the average schooling level of the population is raised, there is a corresponding increase of 3.7% in long-term economic growth,[42] a statistic worthy of note while the United States is going backward in educating many of its citizens, and most of the rest of the world is moving forward.

This is partly because state contributions to higher education have declined, causing increases in tuition, as the federal commitment to financial aid also dipped. In 1979, for example, the maximum federal Pell Grant award covered about 75% of the cost of a 4-year college education, but 30 years later, the share had dropped to 33% of college costs.[43] The situation is growing worse. In 2009, as a full-fledged fiscal crisis set in across the nation, state after state announced large cutbacks in higher education. In California alone, the state university system has cut more than 20,000 seats, while the number of young people prepared for college and needed for high-technology jobs increases steadily.

Our great university system is now increasingly the training ground for students from other countries who, unlike American students, are fully subsidized by their governments. A recent report of the National Science Foundation notes that the pipeline into America's Ph.D. programs is now dominated by graduates of Chinese universities.[44] In 2006, for the first time ever, the top producers of students coming into U.S. doctoral programs were Tsinghua and Beijing universities, with the University of California at Berkeley coming in third. The two Chinese universities nearly quadrupled the number of students they sent to U.S. doctoral programs over the course of a decade. Of the top 10 sources of doctoral students, only six are U.S. schools, and of all U.S. doctoral recipients in science and engineering, more than one-third come from other countries.

This continues a long-standing decline in the number of Americans pursuing advanced degrees in science and engineering, even as the proportion of jobs requiring such advanced training increases. As Intel's director of research, Andrew Chien, commented, advanced degrees in these fields "hold the keys to the kingdom in terms of unleashing what is possible in the world and driving change."[45] The good news, he notes, is that U.S. universities are still among the top in the world and a magnet for students from overseas, many of whom say they would like to stay in the United States and work here on visas. The bad news is that both these visas and U.S. citizens trained for these high-tech jobs are in short supply.

The results of the lack of investment in American youth are highly visible in my home community in the heart of Silicon Valley, where shortages of individuals adequately trained for the growing number of high-tech science and engineering jobs are a source of grave concern. As just one example, on April 4, 2007, a *San Jose Mercury News* headline screamed: "H-1B demand exceeds limit." The article noted that, on the very first day that companies were eligible to apply for H-1B visas for high-tech workers, a record 150,000 applications had been filed for the only 65,000 visas available for all of 2008. Anxiety was rampant among technology companies, which would have to participate in a lottery to determine who would receive these visas designated for engineers, computer programmers, and other technically skilled workers.

Meanwhile, all around Silicon Valley, poorly educated California children are dropping out of school in increasing numbers—recent statistics show the on-time graduation rate having declined to about 67% in 2006—and the state's prisons are bursting at the seams, filled largely with dropouts and functionally illiterate young men who were the victims of the state's declining investments in education in the years since a tax cap caused disinvestments in public education.[46]

HOW POLICY CAN MATTER

These declines are not inevitable. We have made strong headway on educational achievement in the past and can do so again. At this moment in history, it is easy to forget that during the years following *Brown v. Board of Education*, when desegregation and school finance reform efforts were launched, and when the Great Society's War on Poverty increased investments in urban and poor rural schools, substantial gains were made in equalizing both educational inputs and outcomes. Gaps in school spending, access to qualified teachers, and access to higher education were smaller in the mid- to late 1970s than they had been before and, in many states, than they have been since.

Driven by the belief that equal educational opportunity was a national priority, the Elementary and Secondary Education Act of 1965 targeted resources to communities with the most need, recognizing that where a child grows up should not determine where he or she ends up. Employment and welfare supports reduced childhood poverty to levels about 60% of what they are today,[47] and greatly improved children's access to health care. Congress then enacted the Education for All Handicapped Children Act, which opened educational doors to children with special education needs, and the Elementary and Secondary Assistance Act, which supported desegregation, the development of magnet schools, and other strategies to improve urban and poor rural schools. These efforts to level the playing field for children were supported by intensive investments in bringing and keeping talented individuals in teaching, improving teacher education, and investing in research and development.

These investments began to pay off in measurable ways. By the mid-1970s, urban schools spent as much as suburban schools, and paid their teachers as well; perennial teacher shortages had nearly ended; and gaps in educational attainment had closed substantially. Federally funded curriculum investments transformed teaching in many schools. Innovative schools flourished, especially in the cities.

Improvements in educational achievement for students of color followed. In reading, large gains in Black students' performance throughout the 1970s and early 1980s reduced the achievement gap considerably, cutting it nearly in half in just 15 years (see Figure 1.4). The achievement gap in mathematics also narrowed sharply between 1973 and 1986.[48] Financial aid for higher education was sharply increased, especially for need-based scholarships and loans. For a brief period in the mid-1970s, Black and Hispanic students were attending college at rates comparable to those of Whites, the only time this has happened before or since (see Figure 1.5).

However, this optimistic vision of equal and expanding educational opportunity, along with the gains from the "Great Society" programs, was later pushed back. Most targeted federal programs supporting investments in college access and K–12 schools in urban and poor rural areas were reduced or eliminated during the Reagan administration in the 1980s. Meanwhile, childhood poverty rates, homelessness,

Figure 1.4. Differences in Black and White Students' Reading Scores on the National Assessment of Educational Progress (NAEP), 1971–2004.

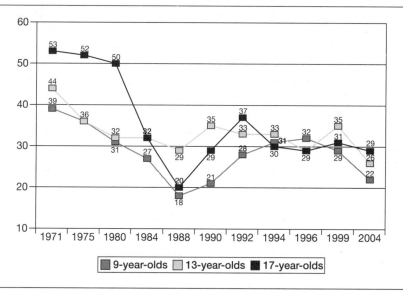

Source: U.S. Department of Education, National Center for Education Statistics, NAEP long-term trend data.

Figure 1.5. College Enrollment Rates as a Pecentage of High School Graduates, by Race/Ethnicity (1972–2005).

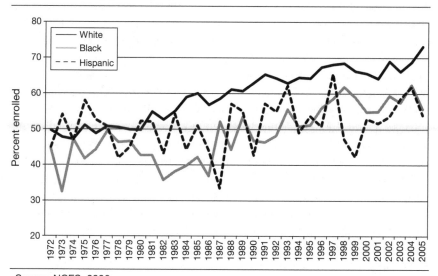

Source: NCES, 2006

and lack of access to health care also grew with cuts in other federal programs supporting housing subsidies, health care, and child welfare.

As states picked up more and more of the responsibility for these programs, and state school funding failed to keep pace, urban and poor rural schools fell behind their counterparts in resources. Over time, they began to experience growing teacher shortages and increasingly poor teaching and learning conditions. Most of the programs supporting educational innovation and investment in high-need communities were cut when the federal share of funding shrank from 12% to 6% during the 1980s. The situation in many urban schools deteriorated over the decade. Drops in real per pupil expenditures accompanied tax cuts and growing enrollments. Meanwhile, student needs grew with immigration, concentrated poverty and homelessness, and increased numbers of students requiring second-language instruction and special educational services.

By 1991, when Jonathan Kozol wrote *Savage Inequalities,* stark differences had re-emerged between segregated urban schools and their suburban counterparts, which generally spent twice as much. This included places like Goudy Elementary School, which served an African American student population in Chicago, using "15-year-old textbooks in which Richard Nixon is still president" and "no science labs, no art or music teachers . . . [and] two working bathrooms for some 700 children," in contrast with schools in the neighboring town of New Trier (more than 98% White), where students had access to "superior labs . . . up-to-date technology . . . seven gyms [and] an Olympic pool."[49]

By the end of the 1980s, the achievement gap had begun to grow again. Although it has fluctuated from year to year, after 1988 the reading achievement gap grew sharply again at all grade levels, and, except for a recent improvement for 9-year-olds, has never been as narrow since. In 2005, the average Black or Hispanic twelfth grader was reading at the level of the average White eighth grader (see Figure 1.6). The gap in mathematics achievement also widened for Blacks and Latinos after 1988, and although there has been progress since the mid-1990s at the 4th-grade level, that gap has remained a yawning chasm for students at the 8th- and 12th-grade levels.

The investments in the education of students of color that characterized the school desegregation and finance reforms of the 1960s and 1970s have never been fully re-established in the years since. Ironically, had the rate of progress achieved in the 1970s and early 1980s been continued, the achievement gap would have been fully closed by the beginning of the 21st century. Unfortunately, that did not occur. While nations that are now high-achieving and equitable built on the progressive reforms they launched in the 1970s (more on this in Chapter 6), the United States undid much of this progress in the Reagan years. Conservatives introduced a new theory of reform focused on outcomes rather than inputs—that is, high-stakes testing

Figure 1.6. Reading Trends on the National Assessment of Educational Progress (NAEP), 1994–2007.

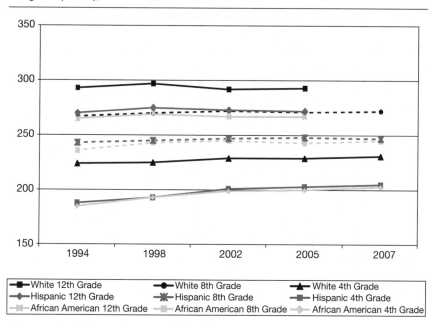

Source: National Center for Education Statistics, NAEP Trend Data.

without investing—that drove most policy initiatives. Although some federal support to high-need schools and districts was restored during the 1990s, it was not enough to fully recoup the earlier losses, and after 2000, inequality grew once again.

By 2003, for example, more than a decade after *Savage Inequalities* was written, school spending in New Trier, at nearly $15,000 per student, still far exceeded the $8,500 per student available in Chicago for a population with many more special needs. Chicago's smaller budget has to stretch to provide food and health care for students, before- and afterschool programs so that children will not be unsupervised when their parents must work long hours, extra assistance for large numbers of new English language learners and students who come to school without yet having the basic vocabulary and world knowledge other children have acquired, and more resources to ensure learning progress for students who receive fewer assists at home.

The added instructional costs that are concentrated in segregated high-poverty schools—the need for language supports, more extensive special education services, remedial education, constant training and supervision of new teachers because of rapid turnover, social work and counseling for students from severely troubled families, health emergencies, frequent moves and school transfers in mid-year, and many other problems—mean that equal dollars cannot produce equal opportunities.[50] Yet, perversely, our society not only constructs substantial income inequality with fewer social supports for poor children, but it also funds the schools these children attend much more inadequately.

Nationwide, most cities now spend far less than what their much wealthier suburbs can spend. The fact that the suburban district of Lower Merion, Pennsylvania, can spend $17,000 compared to Philadelphia's $9,000, and Manhassat, New York, can spend $22,000 compared to New York City's $11,000,[51] means that they can offer higher salaries and better teaching conditions to attract the best-qualified and most experienced teachers. Higher-spending districts also have smaller classes, more specialists, and greater instructional resources, as well as better facilities; more up-to-date texts, libraries, computers, and equipment; and a wider range of high-quality course offerings. Thus, the continuing segregation of neighborhoods and communities intersects with the inequities created by property tax revenues, funding formulas, and school administrative practices to create substantial differences in the educational resources made available in communities serving White as compared to "minority" children. And the students least likely to encounter a wide array of educational resources at home are also least likely to encounter them at school.[52]

Recent analyses of data prepared for school equity cases in more than 20 states have found that on every tangible measure—from qualified teachers and class sizes to textbooks, computers, facilities, and curriculum offerings—schools serving large numbers of students of color have significantly fewer resources than schools serving more affluent, White students.[53] Many such schools are so severely overcrowded that they run a multi-track schedule offering a shortened school day and school year, lack basic textbooks and materials, do not offer the courses students would need to be eligible for college, and are staffed by a parade of untrained, inexperienced, and temporary teachers.[54]

Clearly, students do not experience a right to learn under these circumstances. This is not a new problem, of course. Throughout 200 years of slavery, a century of court-sanctioned discrimination based on race, and a half-century of differential access to education by race, class, language background, and geographical location, we have become accustomed in the United States to educational inequality. While politicians and pundits bemoan the dramatically unequal educational outcomes announced each year in headlines focused on the achievement gap, we often behave, as a nation, as though we are unaware of the equally substantial inequalities in access to educational opportunity that occur from preschool through elementary and secondary education, into college and beyond. Indeed, most ordinary Americans *are* unaware of these disparities, believing that in the United States of America, schools must be equitably funded, and that the schools they have seen their children attend are the norm everywhere else.

But the children who experience the downside of these inequalities notice. As one New York City 16-year-old observed of his school, where holes in ceilings exposed rusty pipes and water poured in on rainy days, in comparison with others:

> You can understand things better when you go among the wealthy. You look around you at their school, although it's impolite to do that, and you take a deep breath at the sight of all those beautiful surroundings. Then you come back home and see that these are things you do not have. You think of the difference.[55]

His classmate added:

> If you . . . put white children in this building in our place, this school would start to shine. No question. The parents would say: "This building sucks. It's ugly. Fix it up." They'd fix it fast—no question. . . . People on the outside may think that we don't know what it is like for other students, but we visit other schools and we have eyes and we have brains. You cannot hide the differences. You see it and compare.[56]

The disparities in physical facilities are just the tip of the iceberg. Measurable and compounded inequalities leave most students of color without many of the basic tools for learning. It all adds up.

THE LEGACY OF EDUCATIONAL INEQUALITY

The result of these trends is that, while the United States must fill many of its high-tech jobs with individuals educated overseas, more and more of its own citizens are unemployable and relegated to the welfare or prison systems, representing enormous personal tragedy, as well as a drain on the nation's economy and social well-being, rather than a contribution to our national welfare. With a more educationally demanding economy, the effects of dropping out are worse than they have ever been before. In the years from 2001 to 2006, a 21-year-old high school dropout who was Black had less than a one-in-four chance of being employed full-time, and the odds for his White counterpart were less than 45%.[57] Even recent high school graduates struggle to find steady jobs. Among African American high school graduates not enrolled in college at 21, only 46% were employed full-time, as compared to 59% of White graduates at 21. Nearly one-fourth of high school graduates not in college were not employed at all. Those who do not succeed in school are increasingly becoming part of a growing underclass, cut off from productive engagement in society.

Because the economy can no longer absorb many unskilled workers at decent wages, lack of education is increasingly linked to crime and welfare dependency. Women who have not finished high school are much more likely than others to be on welfare, while men are much more likely to be in prison. Most inmates are high school dropouts, and more than half of the adult prison population is functionally illiterate—with literacy skills below those required by the labor market.[58] Nearly 40% of adjudicated juvenile delinquents have treatable learning disabilities that were often undiagnosed and unaddressed in the schools.[59] Some states are said to predict the number of prison beds they will need in a decade based on 3rd-grade reading scores.[60]

This is substantially, then, an educational problem associated with inadequate access to the kinds of teachers and other resources that could enable young people to gain the skills that would enable them to become gainfully employed. States that would not spend $10,000 a year to ensure adequate education for young children of color spend over $30,000 a year to keep them in jail. The strong relationship between under-education, unemployment, and incarceration creates a vicious cycle, as lack of adequate investment in education increases the need for prisons, which now compete with the funding available for education.

Since the 1980s, national investments have tipped heavily toward incarceration rather education. During the 1980s, incarceration rates doubled, and by 1993, there were more African American citizens on probation, in jail, in prison, or on parole (1,985,000) than there were in college (1,412,000).[61] Since then, prison enrollments have continued to climb. With 1 out of every 100 Americans—more than 2.3 million—now behind bars, the United States imprisons far more people—both proportionately and absolutely—than any country in the world, including China.[62] Representing only 5% of the world's population, America has 25% of the world's inmates.

States now spend about $44 billion annually on corrections. As the number of prisoners has quadrupled since 1980, state budgets for corrections grew by over 900%, three times faster than funds for education (see Figure 1.7).[63] These rising costs increasingly cut into resources for schools. Between 1987 and 2007, state spending on higher education increased only 21% in real dollar terms while spending on corrections grew by 127%. By 2007, five states were spending as much as or more on corrections than they spent on public colleges and universities.[64]

Ironically, many states also find prison costs eating into the funds they want to spend on early childhood education, an investment that has been found to dramatically increase graduation rates and reduce participation in juvenile and adult crime.[65] As Michigan governor Jennifer Granholm noted, "It's not good public policy to take all of these taxpayer dollars at a very tough time and invest them in the prison system when we ought to be investing in the things that are going to transform the economy, like education."[66]

Figure 1.7. Increase in State and Local Expenditures, 1977–1999.

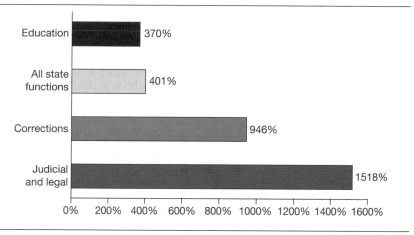

Source: Gifford, 2002.

So the United States finds itself in a catch-22 situation from which it cannot long sustain the healthy democracy and high-tech economy it needs to create a strong standard of living for most citizens. The failure of many states to invest adequately in the education of low-income children and new immigrants, to provide them with effective teachers and the necessary curriculum and learning materials, results in growing numbers leaving school without the skills needed to become a part of the economy. While the highest-achieving nations are making steep, strategically smart investments in education, the United States is squandering much of its human capital.

The implications of these social choices for our national well-being are enormous. Dropouts cost the country at least $200 billion a year in lost wages and taxes, costs for social services, and crime.[67] With only three potential workers for every one person on Social Security in 2020 (as compared to 20 workers for every retiree in 1950), having one-third on the nonproductive side of the equation will undermine the social compact on which the nation depends.

The United States must shift course if it is to survive and prosper as a First World nation in the 21st century. We can ill afford to maintain the structural inequalities in access to knowledge and resources that produce persistent and profound barriers to educational opportunity for large numbers of our citizens. There is no doubt that the long-term survival and success of individuals and societies increasingly depend on a top-flight education system. Our future will be increasingly determined by our capacity and our will to educate all children well—a challenge men—and women—are "created equal and entitled to life, liberty, and the pursuit of happiness." Furthermore, according to the 14th Amendment, all are entitled to equal protection under the law. However, the realization of these ideals has required long struggle, in education and in other arenas of national life.

That struggle has concerned not only access to schooling but access to an empowering form of education—one that can enable people to think critically and powerfully, to take control of the course of their own learning, and to determine their own fate—rather than merely to follow dictates prescribed by others. These tensions were articulated most clearly in the great debates between Booker T. Washington and W.E.B. DuBois about how African Americans should be educated, with some philanthropists and politicians advocating training for menial jobs while educators like DuBois, Carter G. Woodson, and Anna Julia Cooper sought access to a classical education that would allow Blacks to become leaders.[3] This struggle has played out in each historical era for racial/ethnic minority groups, new immigrants, and the poor, surfacing in decisions about whom to educate, with what resources, where and how, and toward what ends. The debate is even more relevant today, as preparation for thinking work is the prerequisite for productive engagement in our economy and society.

Enormous energy is devoted in the United States to discussions of the achievement gap. Much less attention, however, is paid to the opportunity gap—the accumulated differences in access to key educational resources—expert teachers, personalized attention, high-quality curriculum opportunities, good educational materials, and plentiful information resources—that support learning at home and at school. Compounded inequalities in all of these resources, reinforced over generations, have created what Gloria Ladson-Billings has called an "educational debt," owed to those who have been denied access to quality education for hundreds of years.[4]

Indeed, institutionally sanctioned discrimination in access to education is older than the American nation itself. In his history of 18th-century colonial education, Lawrence Cremin wrote:

> For all of its openness, provincial America . . . distributed its educational resources unevenly, and to some groups, particularly those Indians and Afro-Americans who were enslaved and even those who were not, it was for all intents and purposes closed. . . . For the slaves, there were few books, few libraries, [and] few schools . . . the doors of wisdom were not only not open, they were shut tight and designed to remain that way. . . . [B]y the end of the colonial period, there was a well-developed ideology of race inferiority to justify that situation and ensure that it would stand firm against all the heady rhetoric of the Revolution.[5]

The legacy of discrimination did persist. From the time Southern states made it illegal to teach an enslaved person to read, throughout the 19th century and into the 20th, African Americans faced *de facto* and *de jure* exclusion from public schools throughout the nation, as did Native Americans and, frequently, Mexican Americans.[6] Even in the North, the problems were severe: "While [19th-century] publicists glorified the unifying influence of common learning under the common roof of the common school, black Americans were rarely part of that design."[7] In 1857, for example, a group of African American leaders protested to a New York State investigating committee that the New York board of education spent $16 per White child and only one cent per Black child for school buildings. While Black students occupied schools described as "dark and cheerless" in neighborhoods "full of vice and filth," White students had access to buildings that were "splendid, almost palatial edifices, with manifold comforts, conveniences, and elegancies."[8]

Over a century later, after the Supreme Court had already declared "separate but equal" education to be a violation of the 14th Amendment, James Bryant Conant's *Slums and Suburbs* documented continuing disparities in educational opportunity, including spending in suburban districts that was twice that of segregated inner-city schools.[9] These disparities, although somewhat reduced in the 1960s and 1970s, have returned in full force and characterize U.S. education for many students today, just as they did more than 50 years ago. This is especially true for the children of those who did not squeak through the door of opportunity when it opened a crack in the late 1960s, before it slammed shut again in the 1980s.

These inequities are in part a function of how public education in the United States is funded. In most cases, education costs are supported primarily by local property taxes, along with state grants-in-aid that are somewhat equalizing, but typically not sufficient to close the gaps caused by differences in local property values. Rich districts can spend more, even when poorer districts tax themselves at proportionally higher rates. In Texas, for instance, when school finance litigation was under way in 1989, the 100 wealthiest districts could raise more than twice as much per pupil at tax rates that were nearly 50% lower than those being levied in the 100 poorest districts.[10]

These same differences exist among states, with per pupil expenditures ranging from nearly $13,000 in New Jersey to just $5,000 in Utah in 2004.[11] And, while states generally make some effort to provide aid that has some equalizing effect on spending among districts, the federal government thus far plays no such role with respect to differential wealth among states. In fact, the largest federal education program, Title I of the Elementary and Secondary Education Act, allocates funds in part based on levels of state per pupil spending, thus reinforcing rather than ameliorating these wealth-based inequalities.[12]

It is true that there are many great schools in this country that offer every possible opportunity to learn in empowering and engaging ways. And more of them are open to a wider range of children than was once the case. This leads many to assume that inequality has been eliminated from the national landscape. And precisely

Figure 2.2. Child Poverty Rates, Before and After Governmental Transfers.

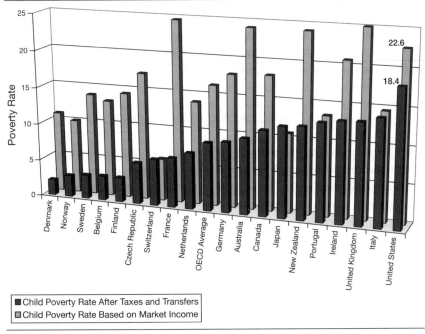

Source: Bell, Bernstein, & Greenberg (2008), p. 85.

after governmental transfers of any of these nations (see Figure 2.2). These transfers occur through tax policies, cash benefits, housing and health-care subsidies, and child care assistance. American children living in poverty have a much weaker safety net than their peers in other industrialized countries, where universal health care, housing subsidies, and high-quality childcare are the norm.

Because of both the large income disparities and our shredded safety net, in 2004, 38.2 million Americans lived in households experiencing hunger, an increase of more than 20% since 1999 and more than 50% since 1985.[16] The per person allocation for food stamps each month is less than half of what would be needed to purchase low-cost food that meets the Surgeon General's guidelines for a healthy diet.[17] Ironically, while research has shown how strongly food insecurity influences childhood illness, the average total cost for a single hospitalization for pediatric illness would purchase almost 5 years of food stamps for an average family.[18]

Meanwhile, in a growing number of households, poor families are forced to make choices between paying rent and buying food or medicine, and more are losing their homes in the greatest economic crisis since the 1930s. In 2004, of more than 3 million Americans experiencing homelessness, 40% were families with children and an additional 5% were unaccompanied children.[19] And with 46 million Americans lacking health-care coverage in 2005, 11% of children under 18 had no coverage, including 19% of children in poverty and 22% of Hispanic children.[20] With the deep job losses in 2009, these numbers are now growing too rapidly to keep count.

The devastating effects of these realities of contemporary American life were brought home poignantly in a recent congressional briefing by then-Superintendent John Deasy of the Prince Georges County Public Schools, an urban district bordering on Washington, D.C., who described a 9-year-old child in his district, living within sight of the Capitol, who had recently died of sepsis from an infected cavity that had gone untreated because the child lacked dental insurance. As this story suggests, child mortality is higher in the United States than in any other wealthy country.[21]

In other developed countries, schools can focus primarily on providing education, rather than also having to provide breakfasts and lunches, help families find housing and health care, and deal with constant mobility due to evictions, the effects of untreated physical and mental illness, and the large gaps in children's readiness that exist at entry to school.

LIMITED EARLY LEARNING OPPORTUNITIES

A growing body of research suggests that learning opportunities before children enter school also substantially predict their success or failure. However, many children do not have the kinds of experiences at home or in a preschool setting that enable them to develop the communication and interaction skills, motor development, cognitive skills, and social-emotional skills that enable them to be independent learners when they arrive in school. This undermines their academic success both in the short and longer run.

An estimated 30 to 40% of children enter kindergarten without the social and emotional skills and language experiences needed to be initially successful in school.[22] Studies have found that the size of the working vocabulary of 4-year-old children from low-income families is approximately one-third that of children from middle-income families,[23] which makes it much more difficult for them to read with comprehension or to engage in academic learning relying on that vocabulary, even when they can decode text. By first grade, only half as many first graders from poor families are proficient at understanding words in context and engaging in basic mathematics as first graders from nonpoor families.[24]

Nobel Prize–winning economist James Heckman notes: "Compared to 50 years ago, a greater fraction of American children is being born into disadvantaged families where investments in children are smaller than in advantaged families."[25] These lower investments in early education and health care negatively affect later school success and adult outcomes; yet, he argues, there is convincing evidence that if interventions occur early enough, they can improve children's health, welfare, and learning significantly. The earlier the intervention, the greater the social returns, since

> Skills beget skills and capabilities foster future capabilities. All capabilities are built on a foundation of capacities that are developed earlier. Early learning confers value on acquired skills, which leads to (a) self-reinforcing motivation to learn more and (b) early mastery of a range of cognitive, social and emotional competencies making learning at late ages more efficient, and therefore easier and more likely to continue.... Early interventions promote economic efficiency and reduce lifetime inequality.[26]

High-quality preschool programs, such as the Perry Preschool Program and the Abecedarian Program, have been found to reduce the probability of students being retained in grade, needing special education, dropping out of school, being unemployed, and being incarcerated. They have also shown gains in educational attainment, with more graduates going onto postsecondary education, which boosts later earnings. As a consequence of all of these benefits, studies have estimated returns to investment in preschool education of about $4 to $10 for every dollar invested.[27] High-quality programs that produce these kinds of benefits have relied on highly qualified teachers with a bachelor's or master's degree in early childhood education, small class sizes, rich hands-on learning materials, and parent outreach and education.[28]

Although pre-kindergarten enrollment has been growing in recent years, low-income children continue to participate in early education at much lower rates than children from higher-income families. In 2000, 65% of children ages 3 to 5 (not yet in kindergarten) whose parents earned $50,000 or more were enrolled in pre-kindergarten, but only 44% of children the same age with family incomes below $15,000 were enrolled.[29] These children rely heavily on publicly funded programs, which serve more than three-quarters of those from families with incomes below $35,000.[30] Yet, as the demands for educational success increase, the supports for children in and out of school have not kept pace.

Ironically, as more and more middle-income children receive preschool education that poor children lack, the gap in cognitive skills, vocabulary, and learning experiences the children bring with them to school is further exacerbated. In racially and economically integrated environments, the differentials present teachers with an even wider range of developed abilities among entering children than was once the case. The parents of those who have had high-quality preschool for several years and enriched home environments often demand a more academically accelerated curriculum while students without these advantages still need to learn their colors, numbers, and other basic concepts. These disparities can influence both teachers' perceptions of the potential of less-prepared children and students' own self-confidence and perceived abilities, all of which have cumulative effects on motivation and learning. In cases where teachers cannot manage this wide range, it can create a reverberating cycle of discouragement and failure for less experienced children who soon perceive that they are behind before they even begin. In racially and economically segregated environments, this often leads to lowered expectations of low-income children and few models of success to be emulated.

RESEGREGATION AND UNEQUAL SCHOOLING

As Heckman notes, "the advantages gained from effective early interventions are best sustained when they are followed by continued high quality learning experiences."[31] However, beyond the large and growing inequalities that exist among families, profound inequalities in resource allocations to schools have been reinforced by the increasing resegregation of schools over the decades of the 1980s and 1990s. During that 20-year span, desegregation policies were largely abandoned by the federal government and the courts, and state governments generally followed suit.[32] With the abandonment of funding for federal desegregation assistance to schools in the 1980s and a spate of court decisions that ended judicial oversight of desegregating districts in the 1990s, there were fewer and fewer levers to counterbalance residential segregation.

While desegregation has clearly made it possible for many students of color to attend schools they could never before have accessed, the nation's limping progress has left many behind. Many Americans presume that school desegregation happened immediately and completely after *Brown v. Board of Education;* however, by 1964, fully a decade later, 98% of African American students in Southern schools were still enrolled in all-Black schools, and over 70% of Northern Black students were still enrolled in predominantly minority schools.[33] Progress made after the passage of the 1964 Civil Rights Act was steady for only about a decade. Although the percentage of African American students in predominantly minority schools declined in the 1960s, it remained virtually unchanged between 1972 and 1986, while the share of Hispanic students located in such schools actually grew from 55% in 1968 to 71% by 1986.[34]

During the 1990s, segregation increased further across both schools and classrooms. Classroom-based segregation increased as a function of additional tracking within schools,[35] a strategy that created largely segregated experiences for many students within "integrated" schools. By 2000, 72% of the nation's Black students attended predominantly minority schools, up significantly from the low point of 63% in 1980. The proportion of students of color in intensely segregated schools also increased. Nearly 40% of African American and Latino students attend schools with a minority enrollment of 90 to 100% (see Table 2.1). Thus, with respect to school segregation, America stood at the gateway to the 21st century, almost exactly where it stood 30 years earlier—having lost in a giant tug-of-war much of the ground it gained during the 1970s.

Table 2.1. Percentage Distribution of Public Elementary and Secondary School Students of Each Racial/Ethnic Group, by Percent Minority of School, Fall 2000.

Race/Ethnicity	< 10%	10–24%	25–49%	50–74%	75–89%	> 90%
Total	28	19	19	13	8	14
White, non-Hispanic	43	26	20	8	2	1
Black, non-Hispanic	2	7	19	21	13	37
Hispanic	2	7	15	20	19	38
Asian/Pacific Islander	7	15	23	22	18	15
American Indian/Alaska Native	9	19	27	17	8	20

Source: National Center for Education Statistics, Common Core of Data, 2000–2001.

The situation threatens to become worse, since the Supreme Court's 2007 ruling in a case brought by parents from Jefferson County, Kentucky, and Seattle, Washington, which found that local school authorities could no longer use race as a basis for decision making in school assignments, even if it was the only way to maintain integrated schools.[36] More than 550 scholars signed onto a social science review that was filed as an amicus brief—something that has happened only five times in the history of the court. The first time was the social science statement signed by a few dozen researchers about the harms of segregated schools prior to the landmark *Brown v. Board of Education* in 1954.

In this brief, scholars summarized an extensive body of research showing the educational and community benefits of integrated schools for both White and minority students, documenting the persisting inequalities of segregated minority schools, and examining evidence that schools will resegregate in the absence of race-conscious policies. The scholars concluded that

> More often than not, segregated minority schools offer profoundly unequal educational opportunities. This inequality is manifested in many ways, including fewer qualified, experienced teachers, greater instability caused by rapid turnover of faculty, fewer educational resources, and limited exposure to peers who can positively influence academic learning. No doubt as a result of these disparities, measures of educational outcomes, such as scores on standardized achievement tests and high school graduation rates, are lower in schools with high percentages of nonwhite students.[37]

Part of the achievement effect is that, for all groups except Whites, racially segregated schools are almost always schools with high concentrations of poverty.[38] Nearly two-thirds of African American and Latino students attend schools where most students are eligible for free or reduced price lunch (see Table 2.2). A number of studies have found that this concentration of poverty has an independent influence on student achievement, beyond the individual students' own socioeconomic status,

Table 2.2. Percentage Distribution of 4th-Grade Public School Students of Each Racial/Ethnic Group, by Percentage of Students in School Eligible for Free or Reduced-Price Lunch, Fall 2000.

Race/Ethnicity	0%	1–5%	6–10%	11–25%	26–50%	51–75%	76–99%	100%
Total	6	11	11	14	20	20	11	6
White, non-Hispanic	7	14	15	18	23	17	5	1
Black, non-Hispanic	2	2	2	7	14	28	32	13
Hispanic	4	4	7	9	16	26	16	17
Asian/Pacific Islander	7	27	16	9	13	10	17	2
American Indian/ Alaska Native	3	2	1	9	25	32	16	12

Source: National Center for Education Statistics, Common Core of Data, 2000–2001.

confirming the 1966 Coleman Report finding that "the social composition of [a school's] student body is more highly related to student achievement, independent of the student's own social background, than is any school factor."[39]

All kinds of students, both poor and nonpoor, have lower achievement in high-poverty elementary schools. Indeed, students who are not low-income have lower achievement in high-poverty schools than do low-income students attending more affluent schools.[40] And a recent study of Southern high schools found that the socioeconomic status of students' high schools had as much independent impact on their achievement growth as their own socioeconomic status.[41]

Concentrated poverty is shorthand for a constellation of inequalities that shape schooling. These schools not only typically have less qualified and less experienced teachers and fewer learning resources, but they also have lower levels of peer group support and competition, more limited curricula taught at less challenging levels, more serious health and safety problems, much more student and family mobility, and many other factors that seriously affect academic achievement.[42]

With respect to peer effects, for example, having a critical mass of students from higher-income families with better-educated parents may mean that there are more role models in classrooms who model successful learning strategies. They may bring academic know-how to study groups, cooperative work groups, and other settings where students work together. For new immigrant students, being in classes with English speakers is critical to mastering a new language. High levels of segregation produce linguistic isolation in schools with many native Spanish speakers and few fluent native speakers of academic English. The lack of opportunity for ongoing conversation with native English speakers impedes the acquisition of academic English, which students must acquire to be successful in high school and college.[43] Higher-income parents may also have more social capital and clout, insisting on higher levels of services from the central administration and stronger accountability for performance from schools.

Deepening segregation tied to dwindling resources has occurred as African American and Hispanic American students are increasingly concentrated in central city public schools, many of which have become majority "minority" over the past decade while their funding has fallen further behind that of their suburbs. In 2005, students of color comprised 71% of those served by the 100 largest school districts.[44] By the late 1990s, in cities across the nation, a group of schools emerged that might be characterized as "apartheid schools"—schools serving exclusively students of color in low-income communities. Whether in Compton, California; Chicago, Illinois; or Camden, New Jersey, these schools have featured crumbling, overcrowded buildings, poor libraries and few materials, old and dilapidated texts so scarce that students must share them in class and cannot take them home for homework, and a revolving-door teaching force with little professional expertise.

In part, these conditions arose as taxpayer revolts pulled the bottom out of state education funding, and the distribution of funds became more unequal. The extent to which urban and poor rural schools serving high proportions of low-income students of color could be abandoned without major outcry was in part a function of their intense segregation. This, indeed, was one of the reasons civil rights advocates sought desegregation in the first place. Their long struggle to end segregation was not motivated purely by a desire to have Black children sit next to White children. Instead, there was strong evidence that the "equal" part of the "separate but equal" principle enunciated by the Supreme Court in its 1896 *Plessy v. Ferguson* decision had never been honored, and that predominantly White schools offered better opportunities on many levels—more resources, higher graduation and college attendance rates, more demanding courses, and better facilities and equipment. Furthermore, there was a belief that such schools, once integrated, would continue to be advantaged by the greater public commitment occasioned by the more advantaged community they serve. This belief seems borne out by the rapid slide of resegregated schools in cities that were turning black and brown during the 1980s and 1990s into conditions of severe resource impoverishment comparable to those in undeveloped nations.

This connection between inadequate funding and the race and social status of students exacerbates the difficulties of creating either integrated schools or adequately funded ones. The vicious cycle was described early on in the fight for school funding reform:

> School inequality between suburbia and central city crucially reinforces racial isolation in housing; and the resulting racial segregation of the schools constantly inhibits progress toward funding a therapeutic answer for the elimination of school inequality. If we are to exorcise the evils of separateness and inequality, we must view them together, for each dimension of the problem renders the other more difficult to solve—racially separate schools inhibit elimination of school inequality, and unequal schools retard eradication of school segregation.[45]

The differences in resources that typically exist between city and suburban schools can strongly influence school outcomes. For example, an experimental study of African American high school youth randomly placed in public housing in the Chicago suburbs rather than in the city found that, compared to their city-placed peers, who started with equivalent income and academic attainment, the students who were enabled to attend better-funded, largely White suburban schools with higher-quality teachers and curriculum had better educational outcomes across many dimensions: They were substantially more likely to have the opportunity to take challenging courses, receive additional academic help, graduate on time, attend college, and secure good jobs.[46]

Finally, not only do funding systems and other policies create a situation in which urban districts receive fewer resources than their suburban neighbors, but schools with high concentrations of low-income and "minority" students typically receive fewer resources than other schools within these districts. This occurs both because upper-income parents lobby more effectively for academic programs, computers, libraries, and other supports—and tolerate less neglect when it comes to building maintenance and physical amenities—and because more affluent schools generally secure more experienced and educated teachers through initial assignments and seniority transfers.

One recent study of five urban districts found that the official disparities in funding between schools in the highest-poverty quartile and those in the lowest-poverty quartile ranged from 10% to 23% of a school's overall budget.[47] In another study of the 50 largest California districts, high-poverty schools spent an average of $2,576 per teacher less on salaries than low-poverty schools within the same district.[48]

The New America Foundation notes that, while the Elementary and Secondary Education Act once included very detailed requirements for ensuring comparability of funding, staffing, services, and salary costs among Title I (low-income) and non–Title I schools, enforcement of the comparability provisions essentially ended in 1981, during President Reagan's administration. The previous requirement that districts demonstrate comparability through both staff-student and salary-student ratios was relaxed to allow districts to submit written assurances in lieu of actual data reports, asserting that they had a district-wide salary schedule and policies to ensure equivalence among schools in staffing and materials.[49]

These assurances have often masked or ignored the differential allocation of resources to schools by student race, class, language background, and zip code. And these official disparities do not even include the much more substantial private fundraising more affluent parents can accomplish for the schools their students attend. In some communities, these privately raised funds—in the tens and even hundreds of thousands of dollars—purchase music and art programs, library books and computers, and even teachers that these schools (both public and private) would otherwise be unable to afford, further expanding inequality.

UNEQUAL ACCESS TO QUALIFIED TEACHERS

More important even than the contrasts between up-to-date and dilapidated buildings, or between overflowing libraries and empty shelves, are the differences in teachers different children encounter. In the United States, teachers are the most inequitably distributed school resource. When I worked in New York City during the 1990s, the city hired nearly half of its new teachers each year without full preparation, while losing about that same proportion of new teachers at the end of each year as they burned out and gave up or moved on. Meanwhile, the minimum qualification to get hired in a wealthy district like suburban Scarsdale was 5 years of successful teaching experience and at least a master's degree from a highly respected school like Columbia University's Teachers College. During those years, New York City could not manage to hire even the qualified teachers who applied (including many from Teachers College), because of a combination of dysfunctional hiring practices and noncompetitive salaries. In 2003, median teacher salaries in New York City were $53,000, as compared to $95,000 in Scarsdale—a function of dramatically different salary schedules as well as levels of teacher experience and education.

To understand the import of these differences, consider this description by Jonathan Kozol of teaching conditions at that time in a middle school in Harlem serving African American and Hispanic students, 70% of whom scored at the lowest level on the state's achievement tests:

> The school ... turned out to be a bleak and grimy institution on the top floor of an old five-story building in East Harlem.... Class size averaged 30 students....Thirteen of the 15 teachers were "provisionals," which meant they were not fully certified to teach. Supplies were scarce. "Three of my classes don't have textbooks," said the principal. "I have to fight and scratch for everything we get." ... "If we had the money, ideal class size for these kids would be 15 to 20," said a teacher. "Many are in foster care—their parents may have died of AIDS or are in jail." But even if they had the money for more teachers, said the principal, "we wouldn't have the space," and he unlocked a door to show me that his social studies teacher had to use a storage closet as her office. Standards posters, lists of numbered mandates, lists of rubrics lined most of the classroom walls. I asked a mathematics teacher if these lists had pedagogic value for his students. "District wants to see it, wants to know I'm teaching this," the teacher answered, rather dryly. When I asked him how he'd found a job in this academy, he told me he had been in "real estate, insurance" for nine years, then for some reason (I believe he lost his job) he needed to find work. "A friend said, 'Bring your college transcript in.' I did. They sent me to the district. The next day I got the job."[50]

The "bleak and grimy" conditions Kozol describes are closely related to the shortages of qualified teachers. Studies have found that working conditions are at least as powerful as salaries in predicting whether schools can recruit and retain teachers who have other options.[51] As in New York, increasing numbers of underqualified teachers have been hired in many cities since the late 1980s, when teacher demand began to increase while resources were declining. In 1990, for example, the Los Angeles City School District was sued by students in predominantly minority schools because their schools were not only overcrowded and less well funded than other schools, but they were also disproportionately staffed by inexperienced and unprepared teachers hired on emergency credentials.[52] The practice of lowering or waiving credentialing standards to fill classrooms in high-minority, low-income schools—a practice that is unheard of in high-achieving nations and in other professions—became commonplace in many U.S. states during this period of time, especially in states with large minority and immigrant populations, such as California, Texas, Florida, and New York, which allocated such teachers almost exclusively to these students.

A decade later, California was sued again as disparate access to well-qualified teachers had grown even worse. In 2001, for example, students in California's most segregated minority schools were more than five times as likely to have uncertified teachers as those in predominantly White schools. As standards were lowered, nearly 50% of the state's new teachers entered without training, virtually all of them assigned to teach in high-need schools. In the 20% of schools serving almost exclusively students of color, more than 20% of teachers were uncertified, and in some schools they comprised the majority of the teaching force[53] (see Figure 2.3).

Figure 2.3. Distribution of Unqualified Teachers in California, 2001.

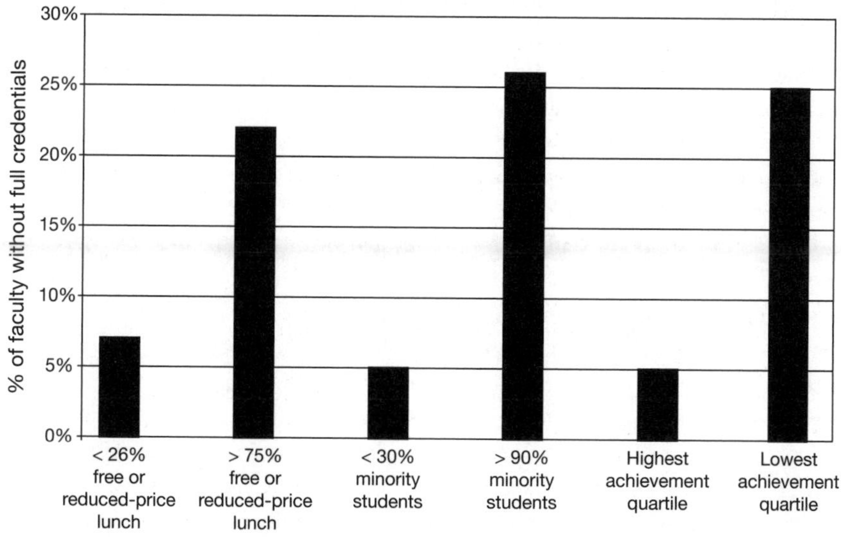

Source: Shields et al. (2001).

During this era in California, an episode of the Merrow Report[54] illustrated how debilitating these policies had become for a group of students in Oakland—although the segment could as easily have been about schools in Philadelphia, Los Angeles, Chicago, Newark, Atlanta, or New York City. Zooming into a portable classroom in a middle school comprised entirely of African American and Latino students, Merrow interviewed the students in an 8th-grade math class that had been without a regular math teacher for most of the year, asking, "How many math teachers have you had this year?" One young man with an obviously good memory started off the count: "Let's see, there is Mr. Berry, Miss Gaines, Mr. Lee, Mr. Dijon, Mr. Franklin. . . . Coach Brown was one of our substitutes one day." A studious-looking girl chimed in: "We had Miss Nakasako; we had Miss Gaines; we had Miss Elmore; we had this other man named . . . he had like curly hair. His name was Mr. umm . . ." Merrow noted: "So you've had so many teachers you can't remember all their names?" The children nodded in agreement.

A few miles away at Oakland High School, a 9th-grade science class had had nothing but substitutes all year long, spending the entire year without a certified science teacher. Merrow asked what it was like having so many teachers during the year. Students' frustration was evident as they answered. Said one boy: "It's just weird. It's like we have to get used to a new teacher every couple of weeks or so." Echoed another, "I'm feeling short-handed, because this is the third year . . . ever since I got into junior high school, I haven't had a science teacher. . . . [I've had] substitutes all three years." A young Latina observed: "All we learn is like the same thing all over again. When a new teacher comes, sometimes we've got to skip chapters and start all over again; and it's difficult." When Merrow asked, "Have you learned much science this year?" the students shook their heads. A Black student, laying his hand on the book in front of him as though it were a life raft, shook his head sadly and answered, "Not really. We haven't had the chance to."

The reporter went on to interview several fully certified science teachers who had applied to teach in the district and had not received a call back from the personnel office. As in some other underresourced urban districts, uncredentialed teachers and temporary staff were hired in lieu of more expensive teachers with preparation and experience in order to save money. In recent years, Oakland's new leadership has worked heroically to change these historic practices and to seek out and hire teachers who will become better-prepared and stay in the district. Yet the district, like many others in the state, still struggles with the inadequate funding and low salaries that create an uphill climb to staff its schools each year.

Similar inequalities have been documented in lawsuits challenging school funding in Massachusetts, New Jersey, New York, South Carolina, and Texas, among other states. In Massachusetts, for example, students in predominantly minority schools were five times more likely in 2002 to have uncertified teachers than those in the quartile of schools serving the fewest students of color.[55] In South Carolina and Texas the ratio was four to one.[56]

By every measure of qualifications—certification, subject-matter background, pedagogical training, selectivity of college attended, test scores, or experience—less-qualified teachers are found in schools serving greater numbers of low-income and minority students.[57] In Jeannie Oakes's nationwide study of the distribution of mathematics and science opportunities, students in high-minority schools had less than a 50% chance of being taught by math or science teacher who held a degree and a license in the field they teach.[58] As Kati Haycock has noted, these statistics on differentials in credentials and experience, as shocking as they are, actually *understate* the degree of the problem in the most impacted schools:

> For one thing, these effects are additive. The fact that only 25% of the teachers in a school are uncertified doesn't mean that the other 75% are fine. More often, they are either brand new, assigned to teach out of field, or low-performers on the licensure exam. . . . There are, in other words, significant numbers of schools that are essentially dumping grounds for unqualified teachers—just as they are dumping grounds for the children they serve.[59]

The Influence of Teacher Quality on Student Achievement

All of these aspects of teacher quality matter. Studies at the state, district, school, and individual level have found that teachers' academic background, preparation for teaching, and certification status, as well as their experience, significantly affect their students' achievement.[60] These findings appear to extend around the world as well. For example, Motoko Akiba and colleagues found that the most significant predictors of mathematics achievement across 46 nations included teacher's certification, a major in mathematics or mathematics education, and at least 3 years of teaching experience.[61]

In combination, teachers' qualifications can have very large effects. For example, a recent study of high school students in North Carolina found that students' achievement was significantly higher if they were taught by a teacher who was certified in his or her teaching field, fully prepared upon entry, had higher scores on the teacher licensing test, graduated from a competitive college, had taught for more than 2 years, and was national board certified.[62] While each of these traits made teachers more effective, the combined influence of having a teacher with most of these qualifications as compared to one having few of them was larger than the effects of race and parent education combined. That is, the difference in student achievement between having a very well-qualified teacher rather than a poorly qualified one was larger than the average difference in achievement between a typical White student with college-educated parents and a typical Black student with high school–educated parents. The achievement gap would be much reduced if low-income minority students were routinely assigned such highly qualified teachers rather than those they most often encounter.

A similar study of teachers in New York City[63] also found that teachers' certification status, pathway into teaching, teaching experience, graduation from a competitive college, and math SAT scores were significant predictors of teacher effectiveness in elementary and middle grades mathematics. A student's achievement was most enhanced by having a fully certified teacher who had graduated from a university pre-service program, who had a strong academic background, and who had more than two years of experience. Students' achievement was hurt most by having an inexperienced teacher on a temporary license—again, a teaching profile most common in high-minority, low-income schools. In combination, improvements in these qualifications reduced the gap in achievement between the schools serving the poorest and most affluent student bodies by 25%.

Changes in the teacher qualifications available to students strongly influence student achievement, suggesting that policies that tackle the twin problems of inadequate and unequally distributed teacher quality may help improve school outcomes.

Indeed, because of public attention to these disparities and to the importance of teacher quality,[64] Congress included a provision in the No Child Left Behind Act of 2002 that states should ensure that all students have access to "highly qualified teachers," defined as teachers with full certification and demonstrated competence in the subject-matter field(s) they teach. This provision was historic, especially since the students targeted by federal legislation—students who are low-income, low-achieving, new English language learners, or identified with special education needs—have been in many communities those least likely to be served by experienced and well-prepared teachers.[65]

At the same time, reflecting a key Bush administration agenda, the law encouraged states to expand alternative certification programs, and regulations developed by the U.S. Department of Education allow candidates who have just begun, but have not yet completed, such a program to be counted as "highly qualified"—a ruling that caused parents of low-income, minority students taught by such teachers in California to sue the Department of Education. The parents claimed that the department's rule sanctioned inadequate teaching for their children and masked the fact that they were being underserved, thus reducing pressure on policymakers to create the incentives that would have given their children access to fully prepared teachers.

The alternative programs created in the field vary widely. Some of these programs are well-designed routes for mid-career entrants that provide a tailored pathway that wraps relevant coursework around a carefully supervised practicum over the course of a year under the wing of an expert teacher. Given the emphasis in most states on 4-year undergraduate preparation programs, these routes have created a useful pathway into teaching for those who already earned a bachelor's degree, and have allowed the schools to benefit from a more mature pool with useful work experience—and sometimes parenting experience—that provides a strong foundation for teaching. Other programs—generally targeted for high-turnover urban schools—offer only a few weeks of training before teachers step into the classroom on their own, with variable access to mentoring or support. These efforts to address shortages in high-need schools by reducing training rather than increasing the incentives to teach have, in many cases, actually exacerbated staffing problems and undermined efforts to raise student achievement.

The Effects of Alternative Certification

The effects on achievement of nonselective alternative certification programs were illuminated by a recent Mathematica study[66] of such programs. The researchers found only 12 states that had such routes allowing elementary teachers to enter without having completed training; some of these, such as Wisconsin and Michigan, allow the practice only in a single high-need district, such as Milwaukee or Detroit. In the high-minority, low-income schools that hire many such teachers, candidates from "low-coursework" and "high-coursework" alternative programs were compared to counterpart teachers of similar experience in the same schools. "High-coursework" programs usually cover most or all of the same courses as traditional programs, but allow candidates to start teaching before they have completed the courses and sometimes without having had student teaching. "Low-coursework" programs usually skip student teaching and reduce the overall amount of training prospective teachers are exposed to, sometimes by as much as two-thirds.

This means that teachers get little training in areas such as child development and learning; how to construct curriculum and develop assessments; how to teach reading, mathematics, or other subjects; how to manage a classroom productively; and how to teach special education students or those who are learning English for the first time. These teachers generally also take coursework while they are teaching, but much less of it, and they generally enter teaching without studying under the wing of a successful veteran teacher. Advice from a mentor who visits the classroom periodically is intended to offset these reductions in pre-service training. Most of the "low-coursework" teachers in the sample were from Texas, a state that had lowered its requirements for teacher education training for all teachers more than a decade earlier, and then reduced still further the requirements for alternative route entrants, who teach primarily in low-income, minority schools.

Even though the traditionally certified (TC) teachers in the hard-to-staff sample schools were also less well prepared than most elementary teachers nationally, the study found that their students gained more on achievement tests than those of the alternatively certified (AC) teachers who were still taking coursework, as well as those of AC teachers in their third and fourth years. Most important, though, a careful look at the test score data shows that the reading and math achievement of students taught by teachers from what the study called "low-coursework" alternative programs actually *declined* by nearly two normal curve equivalent (NCE) points between fall and spring of the academic year.[67] Students taught by their traditional route counterparts, who started further behind in the fall, declined by a smaller amount, and ended up roughly comparable to those of the alternative route teachers by spring—not a reassuring finding for any of the children in these high-need schools (see Figure 2.4).

Teachers from the "high-coursework" programs did somewhat better, and their traditional route counterparts did better still, suggesting that more comprehensive programs can lead to better outcomes for students. However, these teachers added only one to two NCE points in achievement for their students over the course of the year, not nearly enough to begin closing the achievement gap for their students who were already scoring well below the norm. While the researchers who conducted the study interpreted their findings as suggesting that the alternative route candidates who teach in these difficult contexts do not much more harm than other teachers in their schools, these poor outcomes are not an acceptable standard. They

Figure 2.4. Fall-to-Spring Test Score Gains/Losses of Students Taught by Alternative-Route and Traditional-Route Teachers.

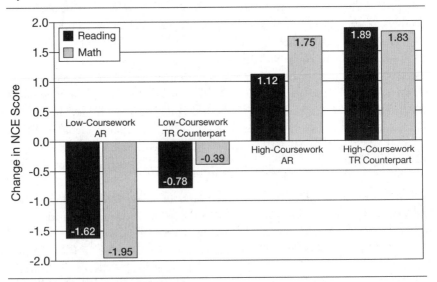

Source: Darling-Hammond (2009).

represent a race to the bottom for the students and schools in these communities, rather than the race to the top we need to create substantially higher levels of teacher effectiveness, especially for children who have been left furthest behind.

These findings are similar to those in other studies. In the North Carolina study cited above, the largest negative effects on student achievement were found for inexperienced teachers and for teachers who had entered teaching on the state's "lateral entry" program, an alternate route that allows entry for mid-career recruits who have subject-matter background but no initial training for teaching. In addition, three large, well-controlled studies, using longitudinal individual-level student data from New York City and Houston, Texas, found that teachers who entered teaching without full preparation—as emergency hires or alternative route candidates—were significantly less effective when they started than fully prepared beginning teachers working with similar students, especially in teaching reading.[68] This is not surprising, given the sophisticated knowledge and skills needed to teach beginning reading, especially to students who have few literacy experiences outside of school and those who are new English language learners.

On the more positive side, all of these studies found that, among the alternate route teachers who stayed in teaching long enough to complete their required coursework for certification, the gap in effectiveness closed. Indeed, in two of the studies, students of Teach for America (TFA) alumni who became certified after a couple of years of teaching had larger than average gains in mathematics. However, this represented a small minority of these recruits, as more than 80% of the TFA entrants and half of other alternatively prepared teachers had left the profession by year 4, as compared to about one-third of traditional entrants. Since less effective teachers tend to leave sooner, it is likely that these findings are both because the better teachers stayed and because they had gained in effectiveness as they completed their training and gained experience.

Even if those who stay in teaching catch up to their peers later, however, students who have had such teachers when they were novices suffer and may never catch up, especially if the students have a revolving door of such beginners year after year. In reading, for example, the negative differential for upper elementary students taught by underprepared novices was estimated to be the loss of about one-third of a grade level.[69] When children in hard-to-staff schools experience several such teachers in a row, it is easy for the students to fall further and further behind. And when teachers who quit are replaced by other new, underprepared teachers, the achievement level within a school or district remains depressed.

This high turnover for those who enter without having complete preparation is not unusual. A nationwide study by the National Center for Education Statistics (NCES) found, for example, that, among recent college graduates, 49% of those who entered teaching without certification left the profession within 5 years, as compared to only 14% of certified entrants who entered at the same time.[70] An analysis of another NCES database showed attrition rates for new teachers who lacked student teaching and teacher education coursework at rates double those of those who had had student teaching[71] (see Figure 2.5). Ironically, efforts to address shortages of teachers through fast-track programs that offer a few weeks of preparation before a sink-or-swim entry can ultimately add to the churn in urban schools.

This high turnover is often linked to teachers' sense of effectiveness. Although many people believe they do not need much specialized preparation before they enter, most learn quickly that teaching is much more difficult than they thought, and they either desperately seek out additional training, construct a teaching style that focuses on control—often by "dumbing down" the curriculum to what can be easily managed—or leave in despair.[72]

For example, a report in the St. Petersburg *Times* in January 2001 reported on the loss of nearly 100 area recruits in the first few months of that school year, many of them mid-career alternative certification candidates who had entered without education training and were supposed to learn on the job. Microbiologist Bill Gaulman, a 56-year-old African American former Marine and New York City firefighter, left before mid-year; his comments reflected the experiences of many: "The word that comes to mind is 'overwhelmed,'" said Galman. "People told me 'Just get through that first year.' I was like, 'I don't know if I can get through this week.' I didn't want to shortchange the kids. I didn't want to fake it. I wanted to

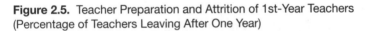

Figure 2.5. Teacher Preparation and Attrition of 1st-Year Teachers (Percentage of Teachers Leaving After One Year)

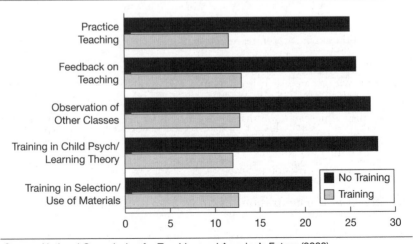

Source: National Commission for Teaching and America's Future (2003).

do it right." Erika Lavrack, a 29-year-old psychologist without education training, was assigned to teach special education resigned on her second day. "The kids were nice enough," Lavrack said, "but they were running all over the place. There was no way I could teach them anything if I couldn't get them to sit down. I didn't know what to do."[73]

Some, like this recruit who entered teaching after a few weeks of summer training, find that they end up blaming the students for their own lack of skills:

> I stayed one year. I felt it was important for me to see the year out but I didn't necessarily feel like it was a good idea for me to teach again without something else. I knew if I wanted to go on teaching there was no way I could do it without training. I found myself having problems with cross-cultural teaching issues—blaming my kids because the class was crazy and out of control, blaming the parents as though they didn't care about their kids. It was frustrating to me to get caught up in that.

Other teachers understand that they will ultimately carry the burden of the students who are undereducated by teachers who are underprepared. A teacher in a California school with a revolving door of underprepared teachers explained:

> Teachers who had not been through [preparation] programs had more concerns about classroom management and about effective methods for delivering instruction to the student population at our school than teachers who had been through credential programs. It was a topic that was discussed at the lunch table . . . the fact we had a class that had had so many substitutes and had had an uncredentialed teacher who was not able to handle the situation and ended up not returning, and that the kids were going to struggle and the teachers who received them the next year would probably have a difficult time with those students because of what they had been through.[74]

Some studies confirm what this teacher suggests: that the negative effects of an ineffective teacher persist into future years, lowering children's academic achievement, and two or three such teachers in a row create a substantial deficit. One analysis indicates, for example, that students who receive three ineffective teachers in a row may achieve at levels that are as much as 50 percentile points lower than students who receive three highly effective teachers in a row[75]—a differential large enough to distinguish students who may struggle to graduate from high school from those who go on a competitive college or university (see Figure 2.6).

The Effects of Concentrations of Underprepared Teachers

Beyond the effects of individual teachers on students, there are additional effects on student learning of teacher expertise across a school or district. The more

Figure 2.6. Cumulative Effects of Teacher Effectiveness. Student Test Scores in 5th-Grade Math by the Effectiveness Levels of Their Teachers (Low, Average, High) Over a 3-Year Period, for Two School Systems.

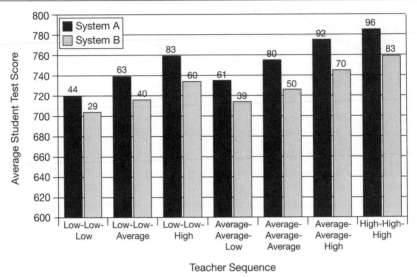

Source: Sanders & Rivers (1996).

expert and experienced teachers there are in a school, the more professional knowledge they can share and bring to bear on making good curriculum decisions. In addition, the greater the continuity in instructional practice from class to class and from year to year, the larger the cumulative effects of good teaching. The converse is also true. Studies have found that, at the school, district, and even state levels, the proportion of teachers who are inexperienced, underprepared, or uncertified has a significant negative effect on student achievement after controlling for student characteristics like poverty and language background.[76]

This is partly because high levels of turnover and staff instability create additional problems for schools beyond the effects of individual teachers who may be weak. As a study by Stanford Research International found, in the many low-income, high-minority schools with large shares of inexperienced, underprepared teachers, high turnover drains both financial and human resources. Schools that hire a parade of novices and short-term teachers must constantly pour money into recruitment and professional support for new teachers, without reaping benefits from the investments. Like filling a leaky bucket, these schools are forced to repeat this waste of energy and resources over and over again. Other teachers, including the few who could serve as mentors, are stretched thin by the needs of their colleagues as well as their students, increasing the chance they will burn out.[77] Scarce resources are wasted trying to reteach the basics each year to teachers who arrive with few tools and leave before they become skilled. Most important, the constant staff churn consigns a large share of children in high-turnover schools to a parade of relatively ineffective teachers, with all of the long-term costs of remediation, grade retention, and dropping out experienced by the society at large.

LACK OF ACCESS TO HIGH-QUALITY CURRICULUM

In addition to being taught by less expert teachers than their White counterparts, students of color face stark differences in courses, curriculum programs, materials and equipment, as well as in the human environment in which they attend school. High-quality instruction—which is shaped by all of these factors—has been found to matter more for school outcomes than students' backgrounds. For example, when sociologist Robert Dreeben studied reading instruction for 300 Black and White first graders across seven schools in the Chicago area, he found that differences in reading achievement were almost entirely explained not by socioeconomic status or race, but by the quality of curriculum and teaching the students received:

> Our evidence shows that the level of learning responds strongly to the quality of instruction: having and using enough time, covering a substantial amount of rich curricular material, and matching instruction appropriately to the ability levels of groups. . . . When Black and White children of comparable ability experience the same instruction, they do about equally well, and this is true when the instruction is excellent in quality and when it is inadequate.[78]

However, the study also found that the quality of instruction received by African American students was, on average, much lower than that received by White students, thus creating a racial gap in aggregate achievement by the end of first grade. In fact, the highest ability group in Dreeben's sample at the start of the study was in a school in a low-income African American neighborhood. These students, though, learned less during first grade than their White counterparts because their school was unable to provide the quality instruction this talented group deserved—a story replicated over many decades in many communities across the country.

Allocating Knowledge

Unequal access to knowledge is structured in a variety of subtle and not-so-subtle ways. In U.S. schools, far more than those in high-achieving nations around the world, this occurs through the allocation of different programmatic and coursetaking opportunities to different students very early in their school experience. Sorting and tracking often begin as early as kindergarten or 1st grade, with decisions about which students will be placed in remedial or "gifted" programs and with differentials among affluent and poor schools in what is offered. For example, wealthy districts often offer foreign languages early in elementary school whereas poor districts offer few such courses even at the high school level; richer districts typically provide extensive music and art programs, project-based science, and elaborate technology supports, while poor districts often have none of these, and offer stripped down drill-and-practice approaches to reading and math learning, rather than teaching for higher-order applications.

Research has found that schools serving African American, Latino, and Native American students are "bottom heavy"—that is, they offer fewer academic and college preparatory courses and more remedial and vocational courses that tend to train specifically for low-status occupations, such as cosmetology and sewing.[79] For example, in 2005, only 30% of California's highly segregated schools (serving more than 90% students of color) had a sufficient number of the state-required college preparatory courses to accommodate their students. In these schools, constituting one-quarter of all schools in the state, a substantial number of the college-required courses were taught by teachers lacking certification in their subject areas.[80] As a result of these conditions, in 2003, only 6% of the state's African American and Latino high school graduates had taken and passed both the courses and the tests required to be eligible for admission to the state university system.[81]

In racially mixed schools, curriculum tracks are generally color-coded. Honors or advanced courses are reserved primarily for White students, while the lower tracks (basic, remedial, or vocational) are disproportionately filled with students of color.[82] Unequal access to high-level courses and challenging curriculum explains much of the difference in achievement between minority students and White students, as coursetaking is strongly related to achievement, and there are large race-based differences among students in coursetaking from an early age, especially in such areas as mathematics, science, and foreign language.[83]

By contrast, there is very little curriculum differentiation in the education offerings for students in contemporary high-achieving European and Asian nations, such as Finland, Sweden, Korea, Japan, and Hong Kong, which have sought, as part of their reforms, to equalize access to a common, intellectually ambitious curriculum.[84] These nations typically do not track or sort most students until the end of high school, when, in the last 2 years, there is often differentiation of courses by interest and aptitude, and matriculation examinations influence college admissions. By comparison, European countries such as France and Germany that have continued a tradition of sorting students much earlier are, like the United States, lagging in international assessments.

Historical Origins

The historical origins of tracking systems in the United States were beliefs in differential intelligence held by eugenicists and some education reformers in the early 1900s, which translated into grouping systems that would lead to specific vocations assigned by socioeconomic status. In 1909, Stanford University Education School dean Ellwood P. Cubberly described the problem as it was then conceptualized with the arrival of Italians, Poles, Czechs, and other new immigrants:

> These southern and eastern Europeans are of a very different type from the north Europeans who preceded them. Illiterate, docile, lacking in self-reliance and initiative, and not possessing the Anglo-Teutonic conceptions of law, order, and government, their coming has served to dilute tremendously our national stock, and to corrupt our civic life. . . . Our city schools will soon be forced to give up the exceedingly democratic idea that all are equal and our society devoid of classes . . . and to begin a specialization of educational effort along many lines in an attempt to adapt the school to the needs of these many classes. . . . Industrial and vocational training is especially significant of the changing conception of the school and the classes in the future expected to serve.[85]

Psychologist and IQ test developer Lewis Terman, also a professor at Stanford, found that 80% of the immigrants he tested appeared to be "feeble-minded," and he concluded in his book *Intelligence Tests and School Reorganization,* published in 1922:

> Their dullness seems to be racial, or at least in the family stock from which they come. The fact one meets this type with such extraordinary frequency among Indians, Mexicans, and negroes suggests quite forcibly that the whole question of racial differences in mental differences will have to be taken up anew. . . . Children of this group should be segregated in special classes. . . . They cannot master abstractions, but they can often be made efficient workers.[86]

Schools were designed to be mechanisms for efficient sorting of manpower in the industrialized economy. As educator W. B. Pillsbury wrote in *Scientific Monthly* in 1921:

> We can picture the educational system as having a very important function as a selecting agency, a means of selecting the men of best intelligence form the deficient and mediocre. All are poured into the system at the bottom; the incapable are soon rejected or drop out after repeating various grade and pass into the ranks of unskilled labor. . . . The more intelligent who are to be clerical workers pass into the high school; the most intelligent enter the universities whence they are selected for the professions.[87]

The conception of schools as selecting only a few for thinking work rather than as developing the talents of all to a high level has remained, even as educational expectations in the society and the labor market have changed dramatically. As a result of the work of the scientific managers in the early 1900s, tracking in U.S. schools starts much earlier and is much more extensive than in many other countries. The result of this practice is that challenging curricula are rationed to a very small proportion of students, and far fewer U.S. students ever encounter the kinds of learning opportunities students in high-achieving countries typically experience.[88]

Indeed, access to high-quality curriculum—that is, a combination of ambitious, well-sequenced goals for learning enacted through intellectually challenging assignments, strong instruction, and supportive materials—is relatively rare in the United States. The story of inadequate curriculum is one that has two important dimensions: One is the disparity between the kind of curriculum to which more and less advantaged students have access in this country—a gap that is much greater in the United States than in higher-achieving countries around the world that have been consciously reducing differences in access to knowledge. The second dimension is what Tony Wagner calls the global gap—"the gap between what even our best suburban, urban, and rural public schools are teaching and testing versus what all students will need to succeed as learners, workers, and citizens in today's global knowledge economy."[89] I discuss this gap further in Chapter 6 where I describe the reforms under way in high-performing nations that have transformed their education systems.

Wagner describes the skills that students need in terms very similar to those others have outlined in reform reports around the world: critical thinking and problem solving; collaboration; agility and adaptability; initiative and entrepreneurialism; effective oral and written communication; accessing and analyzing information; curiosity and imagination. The kind of curriculum that supports these qualities has typically been rationed to the most advantaged students in the United States—a strategy that is increasingly problematic as demand for these skills becomes universal.

Curriculum Opportunities and Learning

The curriculum rationing system we have inherited was justified on the grounds that it was best for students, so that they could be educated in the most appropriate ways, at their own "levels," and find their way into society. However, a substantial body of research over the last 40 years has found that the combination of teacher quality and curriculum quality explains most of the school's contribution to achievement, and that access to curriculum opportunities is a more powerful determinant of achievement than initial achievement levels. That is, when students of similar backgrounds and initial achievement levels are exposed to more and less challenging curriculum material, those given the richer, more demanding curriculum opportunities ultimately outperform those placed in less challenging classes.[90] For example, a rigorously designed experimental study which randomly assigned 7th-grade "at-risk" students to remedial, average, and honors mathematics classes found that at the end of the year, the at-risk students who took the honors class offering a pre-algebra curriculum outperformed all other students of similar backgrounds.[91]

Similarly, a study by Jeannie Oakes in a California city found that, for students scoring at about the median on the district's standardized test, those placed in low-track classes lost an average of two normal curve equivalents (NCEs) after 1 year and sustained these losses for 3 years, while those who were placed into an accelerated course gained 6.5 NCEs after 1 year and 9.6 NCEs after 3 years. These patterns held true for students who were initially much lower in the achievement distribution (for example, near the 20th percentile) and for those much higher in the achievement distribution (for example, near the 80th percentile)—a finding reinforced by other studies.[92] In these ways, tracking exacerbates the achievement gap.

Tracking is associated with curriculum differences that can dramatically restrict students' encounters with knowledge and their opportunities to learn. Decades of research have shown that teachers who produce high levels of learning for initially lower- and higher-achieving students alike provide active learning opportunities involving student collaboration and many uses of oral and written language, connect to students' prior knowledge and experiences, provide hands-on learning opportunities, and engage students' higher-order thought processes, including their capacities to approach tasks strategically, hypothesize, predict, evaluate, integrate, and synthesize ideas.[93]

However, many studies have found that students placed in the lowest tracks or in remedial programs tend to experience instruction geared only to rote skills, working at a low cognitive level on fill-in-the-blank worksheets and test-oriented tasks that are profoundly disconnected from the skills they need to learn. Teacher interaction with students in lower-track classes is less motivating and less supportive, more likely to focus on behavioral criticisms, especially for minority students,[94] and less focused on higher-order reasoning and responses.[95] In these classes, students are rarely given the opportunity to talk about what they know, to read real books, to research and write, to construct and solve problems in mathematics, science, or other subjects.[96] Yet, these practices are essential to the development of higher-order thinking skills and to sustained academic achievement.

Differential Goals

Students in the more advantaged tracks and programs not only encounter more curricular material; they are also typically asked to learn the material differently. They have opportunities to think, investigate, and create. They are challenged to explore. In *Keeping Track*, Jeannie Oakes describes the ways in which teachers differently frame their work for students in different tracks.[97]

Teachers of high-track classes described their class goals in terms of higher-order thinking and independent learning, for example: "Logical thought processes"; "Ability to think and use information"; "Scientific reasoning and logic"; "Self-reliance." Students' views of what they learned in class reflect these goals. High-track students said they learned: "To understand concepts and ideas and experiment with them, and to work independently"; "How to think and reason logically and scientifically"; "How to express myself through writing and compose [my] thoughts in a logical manner [and] express my creativity"; "To search and find out answers to questions."

Conversely, in low-track classes, teachers described few academic goals for their students and none related to thinking logically, critically, or independently. They often focused on compliance and low-level skills, for example: "Better use of time"; "Punctuality and self-discipline"; "Content—minimal. Develop goals they can achieve"; "Good work habits." And low-track students said they had learned how to: "Behave in class"; "How to shut up"; "[A]bout being quiet when the teacher is talking"; "[H]ow to listen and follow the directions of the teacher"; "[How to] do my questions for the book when he asks me."[98]

The contrasts between these experiences can be stark. As African American parent Mark Roberts observed of his daughter's "gifted" classroom in contrast to that of her lower-income friend, Tiffany:

> [In the gifted classrooms], children with the proper pedigrees . . . enjoyed the best teachers, smaller classes, an enriched curriculum, exciting field trips, challenging assignments, and the protective watch of the principal. They would never be assigned a teacher like Mrs. Simmons, who screamed at her students, kept a brick on her desk, and made frequent calls on her cell phone.[99]

The principal's response to questions about these differences in Tiffany's classroom was telling: "Remember who we are talking about," said the principal. "There's only so much we can do for these kids."

This phenomenon is widespread. In his research in New York City, Jonathan Kozol described how, within ostensibly integrated schools, minority children were disproportionately assigned to remedial or special education classes that occupy small, cramped corners and split classrooms, while gifted and talented classrooms—primarily White with a few Asian students—occupied the most splendid spaces, filled with books and computers, where they learned, in the children's words, "logical thinking," "problem solving," "respect for someone else's logic," and "reasoning." Students were recommended for these classes by their teachers and parents as well as by their test scores. Kozol wrote in his notes, "Six girls, four boys. Nine white, one Chinese. I am glad they have this class. But what about the others? Aren't there ten black children in the school who could enjoy this also?"[100]

Three thousand miles away in Alameda County, California, a high school student described the same kind of situation:

> Well, at [my school] . . . it is bad, but they have like another school system inside of it called Phi Beta, like all the smart kids, and it's like no minorities in there. And they get all the good instruments and all the other stuff like engineering. . . . And they split them up from the rest of [my school]. They've got their own side of the school. So it's just kind of scandalous how they put everyone else on the other side of the school or [in] different classes.[101]

Tracking, Race, and Class

Although test scores and prior educational opportunities provide the rationale for differential placements, race and income play a distinct role. Even after test scores are controlled, studies have found that race and socioeconomic status determine assignments to high school honors courses, as well as vocational and academic programs and more or less challenging courses within them.[102] Oakes's research demonstrated how students with the same standardized test scores were tracked "up" and "down" at dramatically different rates by race.[103] Latino students, for example, who scored near the 60th percentile on standardized tests were less than half as likely as White and Asian students to be placed in college preparatory classes. And even those who scored above the 90th percentile on such tests had only about a 50% chance of being placed in a college preparatory class, while their White and Asian peers were virtually assured of such placements (see Figure 2.7). Oakes's team found similar patterns for African American and Hispanic students in the Midwestern and East Coast cities they studied.

These patterns are in part a function of prior placements of students in tracked courses and schools of different quality in earlier grades, in part due to counselors' views that they should advise students in ways that are "realistic" about their futures, and in part because of the greater clout of higher-SES parents. For all of these reasons, as well as the influence of achievement scores and teacher recommendations, students of color are strongly underrepresented in academic courses, gifted and talented programs, honors and Advanced Placement programs (see Figure 2.8) and overrepresented in special education courses, where the curriculum is the most watered down and often teachers are least well qualified (see Figure 2.9).

The accumulated benefits of more challenging curriculum and effective instruction open up—or, in their absence, close off—a long string of opportunities for students. For example, in an "integrated" Maryland elementary school I visited which used a gifted and talented magnet program to bring White students into a school community that was just over 50% African American, I noted that the primary grade classrooms were distinctly identifiable by race. Although most classrooms were

Figure 2.7. Likelihood of Placement in a College Preparatory Course, Controlling for Standardized Test Scores (9th Grade).

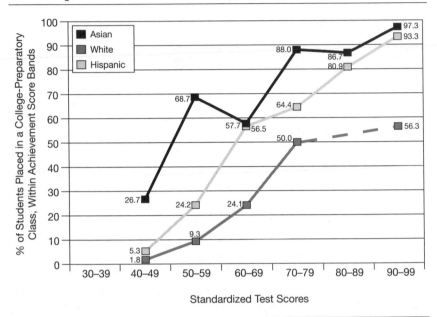

Source: Oakes (1993).

Figure 2.8. Participation in Advanced Placement Courses, 2003.

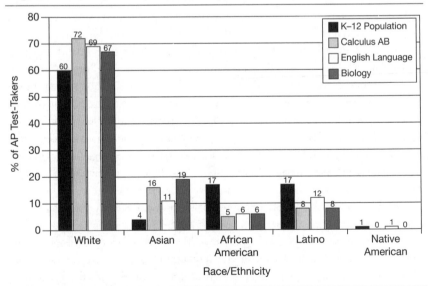

Source: The College Board, AP Summary Reports (2003).

Figure 2.9. Placement in Special Programs, 2000.

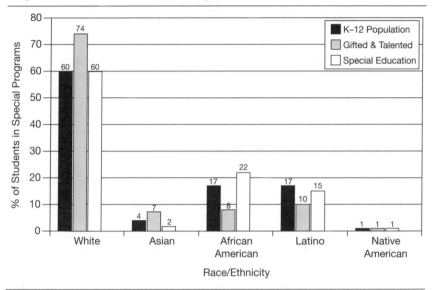

Source: U.S. Department of Education, Office for Civil Rights, 2000 Elementary and Secondary School Civil Rights Compliance Report, 2003. Calculations by the Education Trust (Education Watch).

predominantly Black, classes for "gifted and talented" students were almost entirely White. But the mathematics classes were most distinct. In two classrooms teaching a highly conceptual curriculum—the Comprehensive School Mathematics Program (CSMP)—there were no students of color. In the remaining classes, a mechanical, rote-oriented curriculum was being taught. It was clear even in first grade which students were being prepared for algebra, trigonometry, and calculus.

I learned from the principal, that the CSMP curriculum was reserved for "highly gifted" students who tested into the program in kindergarten. When I told her it had been developed by researchers for untracked urban students and should be available to them all, she agreed. She later secured resources so that the curriculum could be offered to all students the next year. And it was. But 3 years later, when I returned to the school, the old tracking system had been reinstated. When I asked what happened, the principal replied that, with only a few days of professional development to start them off, most of the teachers found the more conceptual curriculum too difficult to teach; they lacked the content and teaching skills needed to use it well with a diverse group of learners. And so, tracking for students was revived, primarily as a means for dealing with limitations in teachers' skills.

Thus, tracking persists in the face of growing evidence that it does not substantially benefit high achievers and tends to put low achievers at a serious disadvantage,[104] in part because of these long-standing beliefs about the role of schools in selection, and in part because good teaching is a scarce resource and thus must be allocated. Scarce resources tend to get allocated to the students whose parents, advocates, or representatives have the most political leverage. This typically results in the most highly qualified teachers offering the most enriched curricula to the most advantaged students. Evidence suggests that teachers themselves are tracked, with those judged to be the most competent, experienced, or with the highest status assigned to the top tracks, and those with the least experience and training assigned to the lower tracks.[105]

The disequalizing effects of early tracking continue throughout the remaining years of school. For example, only those students who attended the magnet program in the elementary school described above had the preparation needed to attend a magnet program in mathematics and science located within the feeder junior high school—which, in turn, fed into a magnet program within the feeder high school. In the junior high school of about 1,000 students, also predominantly African American, this special magnet program of about 100 students was also virtually all White, with the exception of a couple of African American children who prepared for it during the "reform period" that the elementary school principal had managed to open up for a couple of years.

The group of 100 students in the magnet encountered an enriched and rigorous math, science, and technology curriculum featuring plentiful computers, frequent science investigations, and access to algebra courses as early as seventh grade. These courses were taught by highly trained teachers with master's and doctoral degrees in their content fields as well as in education. For the other 900 students in the school, there were few computers, no science labs, and only a single mathematics teacher certified in his field and able to teach algebra. Because he was the department chair and needed to spend most of his time supervising other teachers, only one section of about 30 students out of the 900 in the "regular" program had the opportunity to take algebra in junior high school. The rest were tracked into general mathematics until they reached high school, far too late to qualify for the magnet program there—or the upper-level courses—that would have allowed them to catch up in the quest for knowledge.

School pathways locking in inequality can be found in most districts today, as high-quality education is rationed to a relative few. It can also be found in the ways that students of different racial and socioeconomic groups who attend elementary schools of differing quality are slotted into distinctive tracks when they reach larger, more "integrated" middle and high schools. The tracks typically reinforce segregation by race and class.

Tracking and Language Background

An additional form of tracking that reduces access to knowledge has occurred as schools serve a growing number of new English language learners (ELLs). Many schools engage in the common practice of segregating students in what has sometimes been called the "ELL ghetto"—a sequence of courses for English language learners that keeps them together for multiple years in classes that do not enable them to complete prerequisites for higher tracks or college. This clustering of students is a well-intentioned alternative to the extreme "immersion" strategy that often throws immigrant students into regular classes with no language supports at all, where many fail and give up. Yet it creates other problems when students discover at the end of high school that all of their ESL courses have failed to qualify them for college.

The learning opportunities created for English language learners in the United States are highly variable. As Laurie Olson describes of California schools in *Made in America*,

> Most high schools offer two types of classes to LEP (limited English proficient) students: English as a second language and selected electives in the mainstream taught in English, such as physical education or music. Beyond the two common elements, schools vary widely in the program they offer to LEP students.... One common pattern is of a partial program: a few classes available, sprinkled throughout all the core subject areas. There are insufficient class slots to accommodate all LEP students who need all the core content classes. And so, some LEP students receive a short schedule of classes. The remainder of the school day is spent in study halls, additional elective courses, or classes that they cannot comprehend in which they ... sink or swim.[106]

The quality of staffing is also variable, with teacher assignment to LEP classes a "highly political issue" that is resolved through seniority and clout within the faculty hierarchy, as such courses are often considered undesirable assignments by most teachers, both because of the students and the lack of materials and training needed to meet their needs.[107] "Sheltered" courses, taught using methods to make content accessible to English language learners, are viewed by many as a desirable solution, but they require the resource of trained teachers and linguistically appropriate materials; hence, most schools do not offer a full menu of such courses to their students, and many students do not get the academic courses, the language instruction, or the trained teachers they need.

Finally, and not a minor point, cross-school segregation and within-school tracking reduce the extent to which different kinds of students have the opportunity to interact with one another and gain access to multiple perspectives. In *Democracy and Education*, John Dewey noted that "a democracy is more than a form of government; it is primarily a mode of associated living."[108] He stressed the importance of creating circumstances in which people share a growing number of interests and participate in a growing number of associations with other groups, noting that,

> In order to have a large number of values in common, all the members of the group must have an equitable opportunity to receive and to take from others. There must be a large variety of shared undertakings and experiences. Otherwise, the influences which educate some into masters educate others into slaves. And the experience of each party loses in meaning, when the free interchange of varying modes of life experiences is arrested.[109]

In this respect, too, separate schools and tracks undermine democracy by segregating students by race, language, and social class, and by encouraging silence and separation where communication and connections are needed. These practices heighten divisions among groups and prevent many young people from becoming active social participants in the life of their school—and later in the broader community where, ultimately, we must all learn to work and live together.

DYSFUNCTIONAL LEARNING ENVIRONMENTS

Many of these practices are inherited from a century ago, and our system has not yet managed to transform itself. Like manufacturing industries that have struggled and gone under in recent decades, modern schools were designed at the turn of the last century as highly bureaucratic organizations—divided into grade levels and subject matter departments, separate tracks, programs, and auxiliary services—each managed separately and run by carefully specified procedures engineered to yield standard products.

The school structure created to implement the predominant conception of teaching and learning as the transmission of predetermined bits of information was designed to be impersonal. With the advice of scientific managers in the early 1900s, the United States adopted the Prussian age-grading system and developed the "platoon system" for moving students along a conveyer belt from teacher to teacher, grade to grade, and class period to class period, to be stamped with a lesson before they pass on to the next. They have little opportunity to become well known over a sustained period of time by any adults who can consider them as whole people or as developing intellects. Secondary school teachers may see 150 students or more each day—currently more than 200 in Los Angeles—precluded by this structure from coming to know most students well.

U.S. teachers also work in isolation from one another with little time to plan with others or share their knowledge. In the factory conception of the school, in which practice is made routine, there is little need for professional expertise or teacher collaboration to develop curriculum and solve problems of practice. Students, too, work alone and passively, listening to lectures and memorizing facts and algorithms at separate desks in independent seatwork. Rarely will teachers have the opportunity to work with any group of students for longer than that daily 45-minute period or for more than a year of their school careers. This is an important difference from many European and Asian schools where teachers often stay with their students for more than 1 year and may teach them multiple subjects, even at the high school level.[110] These strategies help them to know their students well enough to teach them effectively. Students in typical U.S. schools see nearly twice as many teachers over the course of their careers as those in many other countries.

Close connections between students and their teachers are most markedly absent in the large urban schools most low-income students of color attend. These schools are run like huge warehouses, housing 3,000 or more students in an organization focused substantially on the control of behavior rather than the development of community. With a locker as their only stable point of contact, young people cycle through a series of seven to nine overloaded teachers and rarely get to see the school counselor who struggles to serve the "personal needs" of hundreds of students. In this setting, students struggling to find connections have little to connect to. Heavily stratified within, and substantially dehumanized throughout, most students are likely to experience such high schools as noncaring, even adversarial environments where "getting over" becomes important when "being known" is impossible. Students perceive that the system is structured for not caring. A New York city dropout from a large, comprehensive high school described his experience this way: "At one time school was important to me. I liked getting good grades and making my parents proud of me. (But in high school) I never felt part of the school. It didn't make no difference if I was there or not. The teachers just threw me aside, probably because I was Spanish. I felt like I was being ignored, like I wasn't important." Another dropout offered this sophisticated analysis of the problem:

> I had passing grades when I decided to drop out, but nobody tried to stop me. Nobody cared.... None of the counselors paid any attention to me. The only time I ever saw the principal was when I got sent to him, which I never stayed around for. The individual classes were too big for students to learn. Students should have longer exposure to individual teachers. If students could have the same subject teachers throughout their high school careers, this would allow teachers to get to know students better.... No high school should have more than four hundred students max and all on one floor. Who needs seven floors in a school?[111]

A California high school student put it more succinctly: "This place hurts my spirit."[112] An administrator in the same school voiced the poignant dilemma of caring educators caught in the squeeze between mandates and children: "Yes, my spirit is hurt, too, when I have to do things I don't believe in."[113] In this study in which teachers and students shared their views of schooling, the dilemma emerged in full relief. The researchers note:

> Teachers perceive themselves to be very caring people who went into teaching to give something to youth. Teachers were initially shocked at the degree to which students felt adults inside schools did not care for them. Teachers struggled as they read student comments, trying to articulate how their attention had been focused away from students. Teachers felt they were pressured to cover the curriculum, meet bureaucratic demands and asked to do too many activities unrelated to the students in their classrooms. There is little time in the day to actually relate with students. Teachers and others felt the size of their classes and numbers of students they saw each day, particularly in middle and high schools, made it difficult to care.[114]

When teachers have little opportunity to come to know their students well, and students have little opportunity to relate to any adult in the school on an extended, personal level, it should not be surprising that factory model high schools create virtual chasms of the cracks into which students can fall. It is not unusual for such schools to graduate fewer than half of the students who enter them.

As concerns about the outcomes of urban comprehensive high schools have intensified, initiatives to launch small schools and small learning communities within large buildings have been launched. These efforts are built upon long-standing studies which have found that, other things equal, smaller schools appear to produce higher achievement, lower dropout rates, lower rates of violence and vandalism, more positive feelings about self and school, and more participation in school activities.[115] In New York, Chicago, Philadelphia, and elsewhere, initiatives to create small, personalized urban schools have been able to produce higher achievement and substantially better graduation and college-going rates for low-income students of color and recent immigrants.[116]

Although a "small schools movement" has been under way since the 1990s, spurred by major philanthropic investments such as the Annenberg Challenge and the efforts of the Bill and Melinda Gates Foundation, there have been considerable difficulties in lassoing the political will, financial support, and professional expertise to develop high-quality new-model schools in all the places they are needed. Long-term funding for such initiatives has been difficult to secure. Communities have difficulty changing their images of what high school means and how it should look. Reflexive responses to violence in schools often lead to investments in metal detectors and security guards rather than more personalized environments with effective human touch points for youth. More affluent parents continue to want their students cordoned off in special tracks. School officials struggle to find teachers and school leaders who can create these environments and the rich curriculum that is needed within them. Policies often create a hostile environment for school models that deviate from traditional structures that mountains of regulations have held in place.

Research suggests that successful new models of schooling require strong teaching faculties who work in organizational structures that create more coherence and a "communal" orientation, in which staff see themselves as part of a family and work together to create a caring environment. These schools reduce curriculum differentiation and tracking, increase instructional authenticity and rigor, and enhance the extent to which students are well known by adults through systems such as advisories and team teaching.[117] Smaller schools may provide the opportunity for important educational conditions such as stronger relationships, greater student involvement, and greater academic press, but they do not, by themselves, guarantee that those conditions will exist.

At the end of the day, both staff and structures need to support student learning. Beyond all of these tangible elements of successful schooling, young people have to believe that they can succeed in order to put forth the effort to do so. This means addressing the negative psychologies that an unequal and highly racialized society has often constructed for both teachers and students. For example, dozens of studies have found that teachers typically hold more negative attitudes about Black children's personality traits, ability, language, behavior, and potential than they do about White children, and that most Black students have fewer favorable interactions with their teachers than White students.[118] Studies have also found that children of color are more likely to be treated differently in the classroom—neither pushed academically nor praised as much as White students—and more often punished for offenses that White students commit without consequence; they are also more likely to be suspended from school than Whites who commit the same infractions.[119]

Young people are very observant. They note these patterns, and they understand when they have been identified as not deserving a high-quality, humane education. It is little wonder that in settings like these, students of color may come to doubt their academic ability and distrust the school, ultimately rejecting what it has to offer.[120] The psychology of doubt about academic ability has been found to exert measurable negative effects on achievement. People who think that ability is innate rather than developed with effort are less efficacious and less able to rebound from difficulties.[121] Furthermore, in dozens of experimental studies, researchers have found that students of all ages perform more poorly under conditions of "stereotype threat," when expectations are low and when stereotypes about their group's expected performance are triggered.[122] The good news is that, when these triggers are explicitly removed, achievement is found to be much higher.

Thus, overcoming inequality will require not only equalizing tangible resources, but also dealing with educators' views and behaviors, developing environments with strong supports and high expectations, and helping students reconceptualize their possibilities and responsibilities, so that they can commit to themselves and their learning.

New Standards and Old Inequalities: How Testing Narrows and Expands the Opportunity Gap

"I'm calling to inquire about one of your students, a young Mr. Henry Lamb. . . . What I would like to find out, Mr. Rifkind, is what *kind* of student Henry Lamb is." "What *kind?*" "Let me ask you this. How does he do on his written work?" Mr. Rifkind let out a whoop. "Written work? There hasn't been any written work at Rupert High for fifteen years! Maybe twenty! They take multiple-choice tests. Reading comprehension, that's the big thing. That's all the Board of Education cares about."

—Tom Wolfe, *The Bonfire of the Vanities*[1]

I encountered a student just a week ago, and he is 16 years old; this is his first year in the 9th grade. His chances of graduating are slim. . . . If he does not make it to the 10th grade, he is going to be 17 years old and he is going to be a dropout. . . . No school is going to want to take him. He is going to screw up their test scores. There are no incentives [to keep him in school] unless you have a principal that is willing to work with these kids. These kids move from school to school and then dropout.

—School Administrator, "Brazos City" School District, Texas[2]

While inequalities in educational opportunity in the United States continue—and have actually grown worse in many states over the last 2 decades—recognition of the increasing importance of education to individual and societal well-being has spawned an education reform movement focused on the development of new standards for students. Virtually all states have created new standards for graduation, new curriculum frameworks to guide instruction, and new assessments to test students' knowledge. Many have put in place high-stakes testing systems that attach rewards and sanctions to students' scores on standardized tests. These include grade retention or promotion, student graduation, merit pay awards or threats of dismissal for teachers and administrators, and closure or reconstitution for schools.

The federal No Child Left Behind Act (NCLB), enacted at the start of the Bush administration in 2001, reinforces such systems, requiring all states receiving funding to test students annually and to enforce penalties for schools that do not meet specific test score targets each year both for students as a whole and for groups defined by race/ethnicity, language, socioeconomic status, and disability. Civil rights advocates have supported NCLB for its emphasis on improving scores for students of color, those living in poverty, new English learners, and students with disabilities, and, indeed, the law contains some major breakthroughs. First, by flagging differences in student performance by race and class, it shines a spotlight on long-standing inequalities and has triggered attention to the needs of students neglected in many schools. Second, by insisting that all students are entitled to qualified teachers, the law has stimulated some productive recruitment efforts in states where low-income and minority students have experienced a revolving door of inexperienced, untrained teachers. This first-time-ever recognition of students' right to qualified teachers is historically significant.

However, the press for greater accountability through testing has proved to be a double-edged sword. The creation of state standards to guide student learning has clarified goals, and in cases where standards are well designed, has usefully upgraded expectations for knowledge and skills. Where assessments have been thoughtfully constructed and where standards-based reform has been implemented as intended— with greater investments in high-quality learning materials and teaching—education for underserved students has improved. However, where low-quality tests have driven a narrow curriculum disconnected from the higher-order skills needed in today's world, educational quality has languished, especially for the least affluent students whose education has come increasingly to resemble multiple-choice test prep, instead of the skills students desperately need. Furthermore, where high-stakes testing has occurred in lieu of investing, discouraged students and overwhelmed schools have produced higher dropout rates rather than higher standards, leaving the society to contend with a greater number of young people placed into the growing school-to-prison pipeline.[3] I explore these complex dynamics below.

THE PROSPECTS AND PITFALLS OF STANDARDS-BASED REFORM

The logic of "standards-based" reforms is compelling. Students cannot meet the demands of the new economy if they do not encounter much more challenging work in school, and schools are unlikely to improve unless the real accomplishments—and deficits—of their students are illuminated and become the focus of attention. Furthermore, the requirement that schools report and attend to the disparate outcomes of more and less advantaged students is intended to bring attention to the education of often-neglected students. There is merit to these arguments, and indeed considerable attention has been focused on achievement trends and the achievement gap. The problematic issue, once attention is focused, is what to do about it.

Using Standards for Improvement

The original theory of standards-based reform—introduced by Marshall Smith and Jennifer O'Day in the early 1990s—anticipated that learning standards and assessments for students would be tied to investments in better-prepared teachers, higher-quality and better-aligned learning materials, and stronger supports for struggling students.[4] This has, in fact, occurred in some states, especially in the first wave of standards-based reform during the 1990s. Studies have found that teachers and principals became more focused on state standards and, in some places, paid greater attention to students who need support, while investing in increased professional development.[5] In some states, high-quality assessments have been used to help educators figure out what aspects of the curriculum need improvement and to direct resources toward those areas.[6]

Early on, some of the most productive approaches occurred in states such as Colorado, Connecticut, Kentucky, Maine, North Carolina, and Vermont, that increased investments in teaching while they developed more thoughtful assessments of student learning.[7] In many cases, these assessments asked students to analyze texts and information in a variety of formats; write persuasive essays and literary critiques; find, evaluate, synthesize, and use information; conduct and present the results of scientific investigations; and solve complex mathematical problems in real-world settings, showing their solution strategies and explaining their reasoning.

States like Kentucky and Vermont created structured portfolios of student work in writing and mathematics; others, like Connecticut and Maryland, created complex performance tasks, such as science investigations, for teachers to administer according to standard specifications in their classrooms. The states convened and trained teachers to score this work according to common standards, often in moderated settings where they could calibrate their scoring, much as teachers do in other high-achieving countries. Although there were some early challenges in developing these assessments, states learned to create valid assessments and score students' work reliably and consistently. Over time, states such as New Hampshire, Oregon, and Rhode Island incorporated technology-based assessments as well as performance tasks. Others, such as Connecticut, Delaware, Massachusetts, and New Jersey, incorporated essays and other open-ended items into their state tests. As I describe further in Chapters 6 and 9, these assessments resemble those used in high-achieving countries around the world.

States that developed performance assessments found that teachers assigned more writing and more complex mathematical problem solving, and that achievement on these higher-order skills improved.[8] In addition, teachers who were involved in scoring these assessments with other colleagues felt they became smarter about student learning and about how to teach effectively as they examined student work and thinking directly and talked with their colleagues about what constitutes good work and how to produce it.[9]

This is consistent with the aspirations of advocates of standards-based reform, who have hoped that the use of tests to focus teaching will improve educational quality and access to important knowledge. It is well known that tests can exert powerful influences on curriculum and instruction, mimicking not only the content, but also the format and cognitive demands of tests.[10] If this influence supports more purposeful teaching toward strong forms of learning for more students, it may improve the quality of education students receive.

Indeed, a number of studies have found achievement gains for students in classrooms that offer a well-taught problem-oriented curriculum featuring performance assessment. For example, a study of more than 2,000 students in 23 restructured schools found much higher levels of achievement on complex performance tasks for students who experienced instruction focused on active learning in real-world contexts calling for higher-order thinking, consideration of alternatives, extended writing, and an audience for student work.[11] A larger-scale study found that students in restructured schools where this kind of instruction was widespread also experienced greater achievement gains on conventional tests.[12] Studies of well-designed projects culminating in assessments of what students can actually do—such as design a computer program, develop an engineering solution, collect and analyze data about a scientific problem, research and write an historical account—have generally found that students demonstrate comparable performance on basic skills tests as other students and much stronger achievement on tests of complex knowledge and skills.[13]

Similar results have occurred in states where intellectually challenging assessments were used by skillful teachers to guide instruction toward higher-order thinking and complex performance skills, to diagnose student learning needs, and to revise curriculum. A study of state achievement at the end of the 1990s found that the highest-achieving states—after controlling for student poverty, language background, and race/ethnicity—were those with the best-qualified teachers and with assessment systems used primarily to inform teaching and curriculum reform, rather than to allocate rewards and sanctions to students and schools.[14]

For example, the National Goals Panel and several teams of researchers attributed the steep increase in achievement in Connecticut during the 1990s to the way in which state level policymakers upgraded standards, preparation, and assessments for teachers as well as for students, creating more performance-based measures along with highly developed systems for using these to improve teaching and learning in both K–12 schools and colleges of education.[15] By 1998, the state was ranked at the top nationally and internationally in reading, math, science, and writing, even while its share of low-income, minority, and new immigrant students was increasing. Because the state explicitly prohibited the use of student tests for denying diplomas, it could set higher standards that drove more intellectually challenging work. Studies found that dramatic gains in student achievement, accompanied by increases in graduation rates and progress in closing the achievement gap, were a function of both investments in well-qualified teachers and the guidance provided by thoughtful assessments used to provide data to districts about student performance, analyzed by race, class, topic, and school, long before other states had developed systems for doing so. (See Chapter 5 for more on Connecticut's story.)

In states with less enlightened assessments, the results have been different. Researchers consistently find that instruction focused on memorizing unconnected facts and drilling skills out of context produces inert rather than active knowledge that does not transfer to real-world activities or problem-solving situations.[16] Most of the material learned in this way is soon forgotten and cannot be retrieved or applied when it would be useful later. Students lose ground over time when they are taught in this way, falling behind as intellectual demands increase. Thus, a critical issue for learning is the extent to which assessments focus on valuable content and generative skills that enable transfer of what is learned to new problems and settings, rather than focusing on lower-level skills of recall and recognition alone. Also, teachers' ability to learn from the assessment information determines whether results translate into more productive teaching or simply produce more failure and stigma for struggling students. These understandings have been a driving force for assessment reforms in high-achieving countries in Europe and Asia, as well as in some U.S. states, but they have been overlooked by many American policymakers.

Challenges of Contemporary Test-Based Accountability

Despite the positive outcomes for student learning of performance assessments, many U.S. state and local initiatives of the 1990s have either been scaled back or abandoned.[17] In 2001, Education Week's *Quality Counts* found only eight states using extended response items outside of writing tests. Since the passage of No Child Left Behind in 2001, some additional states have scaled back performance components and reverted to multiple-choice tests in order to comply with new federal requirements for annual testing and to meet the demands of the U.S. Department of Education, which frequently refused to approve performance-based assessments.[18]

Unfortunately, when used in high-stakes contexts, more narrow tests, limited to a multiple-choice format, have been found to exert strong pressures to reduce the curriculum to subjects and modes of performance that are tested, and to encourage less focus on complex reasoning and performance.[19] Studies in states using narrow high-stakes tests, such as Arizona, Florida, and Texas, have found that, under pressure to show improved performance, teachers often prepare students by spending substantial instructional time on exercises that look just like the test items, reverting to worksheets filled with multiple-choice questions and drill based on recall and recitation that they feel will prepare students for the tests. In the process, instructional strategies such as extended writing, research papers, investigations, and computer use are de-emphasized.[20]

Untested subjects are also neglected. A national survey of more than 1,000 public school teachers found that 85% reported their school gives less attention to subjects that are not on the state test.[21] One Texas teacher noted, "At our school, 3rd- and 4th-grade teachers are told not to teach social studies and science until March."[22] Teachers in high-stakes testing states have reported that not only do they no longer teach science or social studies, but also they do not use computers, because the state test requires handwritten answers,[23] impeding the acquisition of both writing skills and computer skills.[24] In 2007, a study by the Center on Education Policy found that nearly half of all elementary schools had reduced time for science, social studies, arts, music, and physical education in response to the emphasis on reading and mathematics tests under No Child Left Behind.[25]

A recent national survey of teachers found that teachers in high-stakes testing states were more likely than those in other states to report that the curriculum is distorted by tests and that they feel pressured to use test formats in their instruction and to teach in ways that contradict their ideas of sound instructional practice.[26] As two Florida teachers observed:

> Before FCAT I was a better teacher. I was exposing my children to a wide range of science and social studies experiences. I taught using themes that really immersed the children into learning about a topic using their reading, writing, math, and technology skills. Now I'm basically afraid to NOT teach to the test. I know that the way I was teaching was building a better foundation for my kids as well as a love of learning. Now each year I can't wait until March is over so I can spend the last two and a half months of school teaching the way I want to teach, the way I know students will be excited about.

> I believe that the FCAT is pushing students and teachers to rush through curriculum much too quickly. Rather than focusing on getting students to understand a concept fully in math, we must rush through all the subjects so we are prepared to take the test in March. This creates a surface knowledge, or many times very little

knowledge, in a lot of areas. I would rather spend a month on one concept and see my students studying in an in-depth manner.[27]

Interestingly, while U.S. teachers feel pressured to rush through topics, covering them superficially, international assessments have shown that higher-scoring countries in mathematics and science teach *fewer* concepts than most U.S. schools do each year, but teach them more deeply, so that students have a stronger foundation to support higher-order learning in the upper grades.[28] Ironically, states that test large numbers of topics in a grade level may encourage more superficial coverage leading to less solid learning. Furthermore, increases in test scores on rote-oriented tests do not stimulate increases on assessments that look for analytic thinking and application of knowledge.[29] As a Texas teacher noted in a survey:

> I have seen more students who can pass the TAAS but cannot apply those skills to anything if it's not in the TAAS format. I have students who can do the test but can't look up words in a dictionary and understand the different meanings. . . . As for higher quality teaching, I'm not sure I would call it that. Because of the pressure for passing scores, more and more time is spent practicing the test and putting everything in TAAS format.[30]

This reduction of the curriculum to test prep happens most frequently and intensely in schools serving low-income and minority students where meeting test score targets is a greater struggle, leaving these students with the least access to the kind of learning that will prepare them for college and contemporary careers.

Teachers often attribute test score gains to test preparation rather than to improved learning.[31] Nationally, 40% of teachers report that teachers in their school can raise test scores without improving learning, and three-fourths believe that scores and school rankings do not accurately portray the quality of education.[32] The possibility that test score increases may not always reflect general improvements in teaching and learning is consistent with evidence that while tests often induce adaptations from teachers, especially in the content and format of the tasks they give, they do not as often generate substantial improvements in the quality of teaching.[33] Beyond the nature of the tests themselves, this appears to be a function of teacher knowledge and curriculum resources. As Jennifer O'Day notes in a discussion of different approaches to accountability:

> Not all information leads to learning and change. . . . For information to be useful, members of the system must first have access to it. . . . Moreover, if they are to incorporate the information into their cognitive maps or repertoire of strategies, they must attend to it and must have sufficient knowledge and stability to interpret it. Action does not necessarily follow, even once learning occurs, as this step often requires motivation and resources beyond those necessary for the learning itself. . . . These elements—

access, attention, knowledge, motivation, and resources—are all essential. A breakdown in any one of them may disrupt the connection between information and change.[34]

To improve education through the use of standards and assessments, it is critically important to invest not only in well-designed assessments, but also in teacher expertise—through professional development, instructional assistance, and improved hiring and retention of teachers—and well-designed and plentiful curriculum resources. These factors have a great deal to do with whether testing policies improve the quality of education for underserved students or increase dropouts and pushouts without improving achievement for the most vulnerable students.

TESTING WITHOUT INVESTING

When investments in teacher knowledge, curriculum resources, and school supports are absent, testing can produce very different outcomes than when these resources are available. Indeed, the two different approaches to standards-based reform that have emerged are linked to very different theories of change. On the one hand, some states and districts have acted on the theory that improvements depend on greater teacher, school, and system learning about more effective practice, combined with more equal and better-targeted resource allocation. On the other are those who believe the major problem is a lack of effort and focus on the part of educators and students, and that standards and tests will motivate change if they are used to target punishments to those who fail to meet them. Policymakers who endorse the latter view have emphasized high-stakes testing as the primary policy tool. Indeed, some politicians learned that responding to low performance with more testing tied to greater sanctions was a cheap and easy way to appear to "reform" schools, without making the systemic transformations needed to truly change the conditions of learning for most vulnerable students. This approach has proved disastrous for these students.

When the national standards movement was first launched with the Goals 2000 Act in the Clinton administration, concerns about resources were squarely on the table. The report of the National Council on Education Standards and Testing (NCEST) argued both for national performance standards for students and for "school delivery standards," which would ensure the investments needed to meet the standards. The Council's Standards Task Force noted:

> If not accompanied by measures to ensure equal opportunity to learn, national content and performance standards could help widen the achievement gap between the advantaged and the disadvantaged in our society. If national content and performance standards and assessment are not accompanied by clear school delivery standards and policy measures designed to afford all students an equal opportunity to learn, the concerns about diminished equity could easily be realized.

Standards and assessments must be accompanied by policies that provide access for all students to high quality resources, including appropriate instructional materials and well-prepared teachers. High content and performance standards can be used to challenge all students with the same expectations, but high expectations will only result in common high performance if all schools provide high quality instruction designed to meet the expectations.[35]

However, it soon became clear that school delivery standards—or "opportunity to learn" standards as they were also called—were a no-win proposition in Congress, when governors and state representatives realized that outlining the resources expected for students would pave the way for more successful school funding lawsuits. So standards for students moved ahead without standards for what schools, districts, or states should provide.

Nearly 2 decades later, there is plentiful evidence that—although standards and assessments have been useful in clarifying goals and focusing attention on achievement—tests alone have not improved schools or created educational opportunities without investments in curriculum, teaching, and school supports. Ironically, low-income students of color have been the primary victims of high-stakes testing policies that determine promotion, placements, and graduation, and base school rankings and sanctions on student test scores. In fact, as I describe below, in some of the states offering the harshest sanctions for students' failures to pass tests, inequality in access to resources has grown, fewer well-qualified teachers are available and willing to teach in the schools that are labeled failures, and more students are held back and pushed out of school. The school-to-prison pipeline has been the greatest beneficiary of this approach, especially in states that serve large numbers of students of color and new immigrants in systems that are extremely unequal.[36]

Although many policymakers believe schools must be sanctioned if they don't perform, it is virtually impossible to punish underresourced high-needs schools without punishing the students who attend them. A growing body of research has linked increases in dropout rates in California, Georgia, Florida, Massachusetts, New York, South Carolina, Texas, and elsewhere to the effects of grade retention, student discouragement, and school exclusion stimulated by high-stakes testing.[37]

Punishing Students: Grade Retention and Exit Exams

Since the 1980s, a growing number of states have begun to use tests as the basis for grade promotion and graduation decisions. By 2009, 25 states serving more than two-thirds of all U.S. students had exit exams determining student graduation in place or planned.[38] Many of these states, or districts within them, use tests for decisions about promotion at key grade levels, and some have used scores to reward or sanction schools. State-level evidence on the effects of high-stakes testing is mixed. For example, in studies tracking state average trends on state and national tests, Carnoy and Loeb[39] found higher achievement and narrowing of achievement gaps as a result of what they called "strong accountability"; Hanushek and Raymond[40] found higher achievement but widening of achievement gaps; Lee and Wong[41] found no achievement gains and no changes in the achievement gap; and Amrein and Berliner[42] found no gains and some losses in achievement associated with high-stakes testing policies.

None of these studies, however, used individual student- or school-level data to track what happens to students as a result of policy incentives. Studies that look at what happens where the rubber hits the road have consistently found higher rates of retention and dropping out for the most vulnerable students in states and cities that have instituted test-based promotion and graduation requirements.[43] Using individual-level data from the National Educational Longitudinal Survey, Brian Jacobs found that graduation tests increased the probability of dropping out among the lowest ability students.[44] With a similar longitudinal data set, the Chicago Consortium for School Research found that, although some students' scores improved in response to a high-stakes testing policy tied to grade promotion, the scores of the 20,000 low-scoring students who were retained in grade actually declined relative to those of similarly achieving students who had been promoted, and their dropout rates increased substantially.[45] The researchers concluded, as other studies have:

> Chicago has not solved the problem of poor performance among those who do not meet the minimum test cutoffs and are retained. Both the history of prior attempts to redress poor performance with retention and previous research would clearly have predicted this finding. Few studies of retention have found positive impacts, and most suggest that retained students do not do better than socially promoted students. The CPS [Chicago Public Schools] policy now highlights a group of students who are facing significant barriers to learning and are falling farther and farther behind.[46]

The Chicago study noted that the failure to invest in improved teaching was a central problem in the city's reform strategy, which had tried to rely on a highly scripted curriculum and grade retention as its major tools. The authors noted: "The administration has sought to raise test scores among low-performing students without having to address questions regarding the adequacy of instruction during the school day or spend resources to increase teachers' capacity to teach and to meet students' needs more successfully."[47]

Generally, the premise of grade retention as a solution for poor performance is that the problem resides in the child, rather than in the school. Rather than looking carefully at classroom practices when students are not achieving, schools send students back to repeat the same experience over again. Very little is done to ensure that the experience will be higher in quality or more appropriate for the individual needs of the child. In short, grade retention provides little accountability for the quality of the educational experience students receive.

The Chicago story replicates both earlier and later experiences in New York City—which introduced an "end to social promotion" twice during the space of 20 years—and in Los Angeles, Atlanta, and other urban areas. After the first go-round in New York during the 1980s, a district study found that nearly half of the students retained in seventh grade had dropped out within 4 years, much higher than the rate of a comparison group with similar achievement levels.[48] The policy was repealed in 1989, but in September 1999, with no sense of irony or institutional memory, the *New York Times* reported that 21,000 students would be held back under the city's "new" policy that would "finally" end social promotion.[49]

Shortly thereafter, the city's Division of Assessment and Accountability concluded that a 25% increase in dropout rates between the classes of 1998 and 2000 was a function of both the "new" promotional standards and the state's new test-based graduation requirements, noting that "whenever standards are raised without the necessary academic and social supports, graduation rates tend to decline and dropout rates increase."[50] The 19% dropout rate reported by the Division excluded the even larger number of students "discharged" by the district before graduating. By 2000–2001, more than 55,000 high school students were discharged without graduating, a number far larger than the 34,000 seniors who actually graduated from high school.[51] Meanwhile the number of school-age students in GED programs run by the city schools—another step on the road to dropping out for many—increased by more than 50%, from 25,500 to more than 37,000.[52]

These policy choices and outcomes were avoidable, based on the experiences of other cities and a large body of research. When Atlanta, Georgia, became one of the first cities to institute a test-based grade progression policy in 1980, increased dropout rates resulted from high failure rates and repeated retentions. The high school completion rate declined from about 70% to 61% by 1988. By 1998, the federally reported graduation rate for the city had dropped to 43%,[53] after the state set up additional test thresholds for promotion and graduation. As Gary Orfield and Carole Ashkinaze noted in their study of these reforms, "Although most of the reforms were popular, the policymakers and educators simply ignored a large body of research showing that they would not produce academic gains and would increase dropout rates. In other words, this was a policy with no probable educational benefits and large costs. The benefits were political and the costs were borne by at-risk students."[54]

The National Research Council recently summarized this research, concluding that low-performing students who are held back because of their test scores do less well academically and are far likelier to drop out than comparably achieving students who moved ahead in school[55] with grade retention increasing the odds of dropping out by as much as 250%.[56] The co-chair of the National Research Council panel, Robert Hauser, voiced profound skepticism about whether many states' or districts' high-stakes testing policies could eventually result in positive consequences for students:

It is possible to imagine an educational system in which test-based promotion standards are combined with effective diagnosis and remediation of learning problems, yet past experience suggests that American school systems may not have either the will or the means to enact such fair and effective practices. Such a system would include well-designed and carefully aligned curricular standards, performance standards, and assessments. Teachers would be well trained to meet high standards in their classrooms, and students would have ample notice of what they are expected to know and be able to do. Students with learning difficulties would be identified years in advance of high-stakes deadlines, and they and their parents and teachers would have ample opportunities to catch up before deadlines occur. Accountability for student performance would not rest solely or even primarily on individual students, but also, collectively, on educators and parents. There is no positive example of such a system in the United States, past or present, whose success is documented by credible research.[57]

Although Hauser's view may be overly bleak, his concern is supported by too many examples to dismiss. In fact, if investments in sophisticated, high-quality teaching and additional supports were made, massive grade retention would be replaced by other strategies to attend to students who are not progressing in their learning. Responding to poor performance by having students repeat a grade is a solution inherited from the century-old factory model in which students are placed back on the assembly line to have the same processes repeated if they were not successful the first time. It is not a strategy used in high-achieving countries that work continuously on the improvement of teaching. Whereas the United States has an estimated retention rate of 15 to 20% of its students annually (most of them at-risk students in central cities), on a par with countries such as Haiti and Sierra Leone, European and high-achieving Asian nations typically hold back fewer than 1% of students each year or bar grade retention entirely.[58]

Given many states' failure to make the kinds of serious investments in low-income and minority students needed to prevent failure, it is not surprising that data from the National Center for Education Statistics indicate decreases in 4-year graduation rates between 1995 and 2001 in Florida, Indiana, New York, North Carolina, and South Carolina as new high-stakes testing policies were introduced in each state[59] (see Figure 3.1). Changes in NCES graduation rate calculation methods disrupt trend lines after that date; however, state-level data show similar declines in states such as California and Massachusetts that introduced exit exams a few years later. For example, when California's exit exam was introduced in 2006, only 67% of students who had been ninth graders 4 years earlier graduated from high school, a decline from 71% the year before. As elsewhere, the declines were sharpest for African American and Latino students, whose graduation rates dropped to only 56% and 55%, respectively. The number of 12th-grade dropouts in the state increased from 14,000 in 2002 to

Figure 3.1. Graduation Rates in States Introducing New Exit Exams Between 1995 and 1998.

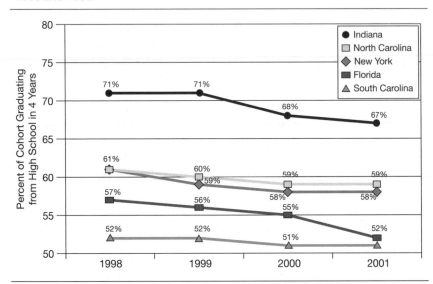

Source: National Center for Education Statistics, Common Core of Data.

24,000 in 2006, and the number of college freshmen decreased by 25,000 from 2005 to 2006, even as demands for college-educated workers increased.[60]

Overall, the number of U.S. high schools graduating less than half of their 9th-grade class in 4 years nearly doubled between 1993 and 2002, including 48% of all high schools in the nation's largest 100 districts where students of color are concentrated.[61] This has occurred as educationally focused nations are rapidly increasing their high school attendance and graduation rates, investing in stronger teaching and more thoughtful curriculum aimed at higher-order skills. These nations use their assessments to guide curriculum and inform higher education decisions, not to deny diplomas. As they have been striving for more inclusive and equitable access to secondary school and college (see Chapter 6), the United States has been moving in the opposite direction.

Punishing Schools

Although high-stakes testing was peddled by the Bush administration as a response to "the soft bigotry of low expectations," no comparable complaint was registered about the hard bigotry of egregiously poor education, which has allowed students to be victimized both by the lack of resources devoted to their learning and the denial of a diploma that would open up productive options after high school. Pedro Noguera notes that the decision to hold students back and deny them diplomas based on their test scores is "analogous to the Food and Drug Administration's setting standards for product quality by punishing individuals who consume faulty products, or the Federal Transportation Commission's setting new standards for air safety and enforcing them by punishing passengers for security violations at airports."[62] Yet students who have no control of the quality of education they receive are the ones held most accountable—and punished most severely and repeatedly—for the failures of the system in which they are trapped. That there has been little outcry is undoubtedly linked to the fact that the victims are overwhelmingly poor children of color, viewed as expendable and undeserving of serious investment.

Advocates who believe punishments should fall more heavily on adults have argued for additional strategies featuring sanctions for schools. However, these have often made matters even worse for the most vulnerable students. Noguera notes that:

> In Florida, where numerous reports have exposed severe overcrowding in schools serving the poorest children, the state has taken the bold step of placing letter grades on the front of school buildings so that all can know a failing school even before they enter. Of course, the state still allows failing schools to operate, but they pretend that by labeling such schools with a D or an F on the front door (I actually visited a school with an FF grade in Miami), they have taken tough action. In Florida and several other states, governors and state legislators have taken credit for raising standards without doing anything to improve the quality of education provided to students in schools where they know conditions are most severe.[63]

These school labeling policies, designed to humiliate schools into improvement, can actually further undermine education for their students by driving good staff away. Teachers who are well qualified and have many options have no reason to seek out or stay in environments where they will be sanctioned, threatened with firing, and held up to ridicule. Florida ranks schools based on their overall test scores—which, as elsewhere, are highly correlated with student socioeconomic status—rather than based on how much students have gained while in the schools, a fairer measure that staff could have some control over. Consequently, low-rated schools are predictably those serving the neediest students. After the policy was put in place in 1999, news reports noted that qualified teachers were leaving the schools rated D or F "in droves,"[64] to be replaced by teachers without experience and often without training. As one principal queried, "Is anybody going to want to dedicate their lives to a school that has already been labeled a failure?"

Similar results were found in a study of North Carolina's accountability system, which labels schools below a specific test score level as "low-performing." The study found that, controlling for other factors influencing teacher recruitment, the labeling system impaired the ability of low-ranked schools to recruit and retain well-qualified teachers.[65] Once labeled, such schools had higher teacher turnover, had more trouble recruiting replacements, and ended up hiring more inexperienced and underqualified teachers as a result.

To meet the need for teachers in schools like these where principals found it hard to recruit qualified staff, North Carolina created a "lateral entry" pathway to allow individuals to enter without prior preparation. A recent study found significant negative effects on achievement for North Carolina students taught by these unprepared entrants and by teachers without experience.[66]

These unhappy outcomes for students in "failing" schools occurred despite the large investments in teacher education, salaries, and professional development made under the leadership of Governor James B. Hunt throughout the 1990s, which stimulated large gains in achievement for the state system as a whole.[67] Unfortunately, the school labeling policies, which were adopted late in the decade, undermined some of these benefits for students in the highest-need schools. The researchers noted:

> Simply increasing the pressure on the personnel in low-performing schools to do better may not be the best way to improve the performance of low-performing students. Given our finding that accountability systems make it harder for schools serving low-performing students to retain quality teachers, a more systemic approach is needed to assure that low-performing students have access to effective teachers and a stable teaching environment.[68]

Indeed, the more "systemic approach" that is needed would require building the kinds of capacity found in more affluent schools with stable cadres of highly skilled teachers who are able to use standards to improve instruction. Systematic instructional improvement has proved nearly impossible when schools serving the highest-need students have poor working conditions, lack materials, have the highest turnover, and have the least knowledgeable administrators and staff. Studies in at least six states have found that, while high-capacity schools have been able to use standards to improve their practice (including some serving high-need students), low-capacity schools designated as "failing" have been unable to organize themselves to improve, instead responding to pressure by reducing the curriculum to drilling on the tests and by removing the most difficult and lowest-performing students.[69]

This phenomenon has not been limited to the United States. A study of the high-stakes accountability system launched by the Thatcher government in England found that the test-based system for ranking and labeling schools led to a dramatic increase in the exclusion rate of students, while undermining instructional quality and teachers' morale.[70] Many teachers reported that the pressures from school rankings and increased testing, combined with the dynamics of school choice and a prescriptive curriculum, helped to stigmatize low-performing students and increase dropouts. There, too, the problems of student pushout were found to be most severe in the schools with the least expert teachers. The school accountability policy that produced these outcomes has since been revised in the United Kingdom. In several other countries that are determined to avoid the same problems, test-based rankings and sanctions have been precluded by legislation.

WHEN NEW STANDARDS
MEET ONGOING INEQUALITIES

Cynically, many of the states that have enacted the most severe sanctions for students and schools have not only failed to make necessary investments in those schools serving the neediest students, but have actually opened up backdoors into teaching that have allowed tens of thousands of hard-to-fill positions to be filled by less and less prepared teachers. California's emergency permit, intern, and pre-intern teachers, Florida's and Texas's alternatively certified teachers—who can now enter with a few weeks of preparation or with none at all after taking a paper and pencil test—and North Carolina's "lateral entry" teachers are hired almost exclusively in high-poverty, high-minority schools. These teachers reduce school capacity both by their own limited skills and their higher turnover rates. In these and other cases, states have not even made a pretense of trying to improve schools' capacities to address the standards students are expected to meet.

The Texas "Miracle"

The poster child for high-stakes testing as a route to school improvement was the state of Texas, which developed a statewide testing system during the 1980s, adopted minimum competency tests for school graduation in 1987, and created the Texas public school accountability system to rate districts and schools in 1993. Large apparent gains in scores for White and minority students on the Texas Assessment of Academic Skills (TAAS) in the 1990s, while George W. Bush was governor, caused the state's reforms to be hailed as the "Texas Miracle," and led to the incorporation of many features of Texas's policy into the Bush administration's major education initiative, No Child Left Behind, in 2001.

However, a number of studies have raised questions about these apparent test score gains. Several studies in the late 1990s observed that Texas students had not made comparable gains on national standardized tests or on the state's own college entrance test over the course of that decade,[71] and the achievement gap that seemed to be closing on the state tests was actually large and widening on the National Assessment of Educational Progress.[72] These studies variously suggested that teaching to the test might have raised scores on the high-stakes test in ways that did not generalize to other tests which examine a broader set of skills; that passing scores had been lowered and the tests made easier over time to give the appearance of gains; and that many students were excluded from the state tests to prop up average scores. Other studies found increased retention rates in ninth grade and dropout rates for both middle and high school students after an exit exam was instituted in the late 1980s.[73] The effects were most pronounced for students of color, who were graduating at rates less than 50% by 1991.

High-Stakes Testing and Student Outcomes in "Brazos City." In a study conducted by Julian Vasquez Heilig and myself, these concerns were examined using a 7-year longitudinal data set of 271,000 students who attended school between 1995 and 2002 in "Brazos City," the name we use for a large urban district in Texas. The data analyses were supplemented by interviews with 160 high school students, teachers, and administrators in seven large high schools serving predominantly Latino or African American students.[74] Like most large cities in Texas, Brazos was about 50% Latino, about 30% African American, and about 20% White and Asian. More than two-thirds of students were classified as economically disadvantaged and nearly one-third as limited English proficient. The state's accountability expectations were especially challenging for all the urban districts with similar student profiles.

While our findings were specific to this single district, the study confirms many of the concerns that have been raised by other researchers, and provides more specific insights about how the process of student exclusion operated in this high-stakes testing environment. Like other researchers, we found large gains and a

Figure 3.2. Mean TAAS TLI Mathematics Scores for Brazos City Students by Group.

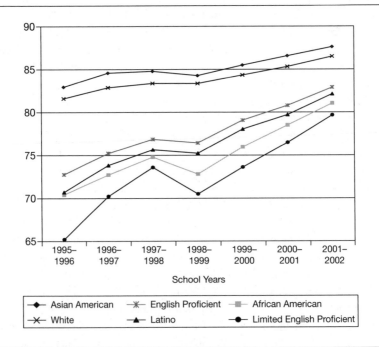

Source: Vasquez Heilig & Darling-Hammond (2008).

narrowing gap on the high-stakes TAAS tests, used for accountability rankings for schools (see Figure 3.2), but we also found that these gains did not occur in either reading or math on the low-stakes district test, the Stanford-9, which was not tied to accountability decisions about students and schools (see Figure 3.3).

This appears to be because large numbers of students were kept out of the TAAS testing pool each year. While about 95% of students took the SAT-9 each year, with no differences in participation by race, more than a quarter of students, mostly African American and Latino, failed to take the TAAS test in English. Of these, 8 to 10% took the TAAS test in Spanish, which was not used for accountability purposes, and the remainder were initially exempted as special education and limited English-proficient (LEP) students. When these exemptions were criticized and reduced in 1998, there was a temporary drop in scores, followed by a growing number of students with missing scores, climbing from 1.7% to 8.9% of the total between 1997 and 2002. This set of events was explained by a Brazos City School District (BCSD) Board member as follows:

Figure 3.3. Mean Stanford-9 Mathematics Scores for Brazos City Students by Race/Ethnicity.

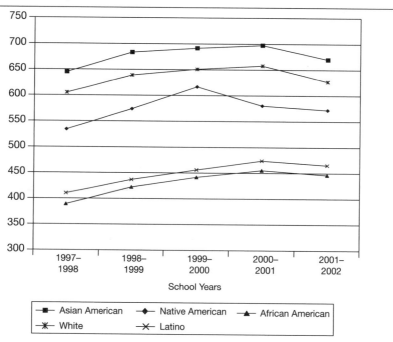

Source: Vasquez Heilig & Darling-Hammond (2008).

Figure 3.4. 1997 9th-Grade Cohort Cumulative Testing Results on the Exit TAAS, by Subject.

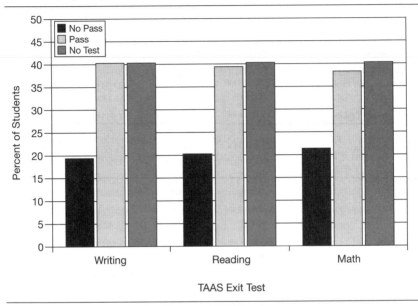

Source: Vasquez Heilig & Darling-Hammond (2008).

The waiver was set up so that if you did not pass all four core subjects at the 9th-grade level, no matter how many credits you had, you could not push forward. . . . Well, I am taking all these 10th-grade classes, except I have to wait a whole semester to take the [failed section of] Algebra I B. When I finally get that credit, I have enough credits to be a junior. I now have now 12 credits rather than my 7 credits. So I skip over taking that 10th-grade test. It's the 10th-grade test that had been used to judge the school. So I have a large group of people who are skipping over the accountability grade. . . . Here in our school, that waiver was used basically to boost the test scores. They wrote a waiver so they can circumvent the rule, so they'll know they'll have a higher percentage of students passing the test.

An administrator in another school confirmed, "The scores jumped because you put up a barrier and everybody else was still in ninth grade. . . . With that wall that you could create with the waiver, those kids never entered the accountability picture." Student groups at all of the high schools in our sample included seniors who discussed peers who had been retained in the ninth grade one or more times. Most focus groups included students who were retained in the ninth grade for 3 or 4 years. Students consistently reported that most of their peers who were retained multiple times eventually gave up and dropped out of school. This comment by a Latino student was typical:

> I have a friend that was in ninth grade for 2 years and she was 19 or 20 years old. She did not pass algebra and the school told her that if she didn't improve her grades they were going to drop her since she was older. So she . . . dropped out of school.

Many students also knew someone who had been "skipped over" the 10th-grade test and, after having been retained in the ninth grade, landed unexpectedly in the 11th or 12th grade one year, still ineligible for graduation. For example:

> This person I was telling you about . . . she was in the same year when we got here but all of a sudden she was in the 12th grade, and then she didn't know why. . . . But even though she was a senior she wouldn't be able to graduate because of [not having test results for the] TAAS.

An administrator of a school that was working against this tide explained that keeping students from taking the test was widespread and connected to high levels of dropout and pushout:

> I think that the kids are being forced out of school. I had a kid who came here from Fine Oaks High School and said, "Miss, if I come here could I ever take the [exit exam]?" And I said, "What do you mean? If you come here you must take the test." And he said, "Well, every time I think I'm going to take the test, they either say, "You don't have to come to school tomorrow, or you don't have to [take the test]" . . . we're told different things." That's when kids drop out . . . when you never give them a chance. . . . I think that what has happened at Fine Oaks is what happens at many schools. I think we've done a lot to force kids out of school.

As Figure 3.5 shows, for three cohorts of students, about half of each class did not progress from 9th to 10th grade in their second year of high school, and an additional 10% did not progress from 10th to 11th grade in their third year. Although reported dropout rates hovered just below the 6% needed to retain an "acceptable" rating in the Texas Education Association (TEA) accountability system, when we tracked individual student records, we found that, among those who entered ninth grade in 1997, only one-third of students were coded by the district as graduates within 5 years, 19% were still in school, an estimated 8% had transferred to public or private schools out of the district, and about 40% dropped out, "withdrew," or disappeared without having passed the test. More than 90% of students in these categories had not passed the exit exam.

Responding to the district's claim of an 85% graduation rate, one school administrator gave an estimate close to what our data suggested: "I would think that the graduation rate is closer to 40 to 45%, not 85%." She continued, "Ultimately what's happening is that we're letting kids down. We're using some kind of system

Figure 3.5. BCSD High School Cohort Progression (Entering Ninth Graders, 1996–1998).

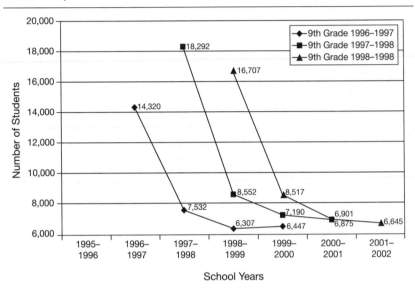

Source: Vasquez Heilig & Darling-Hammond (2008).

to disguise where they are. If you've got 600 [freshmen] in your school and 300 graduate, they're somewhere."

Accountability Pressures and Student Push Out. Brazos City placed intense pressure on administrators and teachers to meet accountability standards. In addition to the school sanctions associated with getting a less than "acceptable" rating, principals could receive stipends if scores went up or be fired if they failed to raise scores. An administrator at one high school explained, "All of us are on 'at will' contracts. So, we can be let go at the end of the year. . . . It's a lot of pressure . . . not even subtle pressure . . . just hard pressure put on you to get those scores up."

A staff member at another high school observed:

> [You] have to understand the culture of Texas. Texas is a standardized testing machine. That's the way the state is run, and that's the culture. So if a principal knows that his ninth graders are not prepared for that examination . . . he is going to put certain mechanisms in place that are going to involve students [being] held back, suspended, so on and so forth.

Still another explained.

I think each year we get a new set of regs, and we try and figure out how is the best way to use it to our advantage. . . . The game changes. . . . It's like a game that has a set of instructions. And everybody gets the same set of instructions, and everybody follows the same set of instructions. . . . If you're really savvy, and if you're really into everything, as a principal you may give your campus an advantage that another campus doesn't have.

Many staff described how schools created a range of strategies to boost 10th-grade test scores, ranging from retaining low-scoring 9th-grade students, to skipping them over 10th-grade, to encouraging them to leave school entirely. We were told about the use of zero tolerance discipline policies to rid schools of low-achieving students, expulsion for attendance problems, and students being counseled out, encouraged to enroll in GED programs, or transferred to nontraditional settings. Families were also fined by the city at the rate of $500 per day for unexcused absences over a set number, which caused many students to drop out to save their families from financial ruin—particularly those who were often absent when needed to babysit or translate for relatives visiting the doctor or conducting other business. Most of the students we talked to in high-minority schools had experienced one or more of these situations or had friends who did. Many students reported having been in ninth grade three or four times, and most described the experience of trying to get through school as an often unsuccessful struggle. For example, from a student who spent several years in ninth grade and finally gave up: "Well, that last 2 years that I was in ninth grade, there were finally classes that I passed and got credit for. But they would put me in the same classes again, so then they would catch that later in the year, when they couldn't do nothing about it, you know."

The combination of grade retention and the threat of fines for absences created a double whammy for many, like this student:

Well, I flunked ninth grade and went [back] to ninth grade again. Kept going in circles and circles, and my mom used to get tickets and tickets [to pay fines because of absences]. So, you know, it's just left for me to drop out instead of me just giving my mom nothing but tickets.

And some discovered they had been "checked out" of school involuntarily, as this one reported:

Most of the [other students] get [kicked out because of absences]. And they're not telling you that you're kicked out of school either, so if you were absent that day, they'll send somebody around to all your teachers and the teacher would just sign your paper—your checkout papers. And when you come back to school they'll tell you you're no longer enrolled in school.

Students also reported trying to enroll at schools that turned them away, and staff described schools refusing to enroll low-scoring students. As one administrator explained:

> I encountered a student just a week ago, and he is 16 years old; this is his first year in the ninth grade. His chances of graduating are slim. . . . If he does not make it to the 10th grade, he is going to be 17 years old and he is going to be a dropout. . . . No school is going to want to take him. He is going to screw up their test scores. There are no incentives [to keep him in school] unless you have a principal that is willing to work with these kids. These kids move from school to school and then dropout.

Another administrator described how schools keep their students until the enrollment count in October and then push them out: "Many schools unload their troublemakers right after the [enrollment] snapshot. They keep them until then so they can get the dollars." Students at several high schools explained that their high school was so full at the start of the year that there were not enough desks in class-rooms. However, by the time testing occurred in the spring, there were many desks available as many students were no longer attending the school.

And, we found, these strategies did work to boost school scores and ac-countability ratings. Using regression techniques to look at score changes for each school from 1997 to 2002, we found that, as student grade retention, disap-pearance, withdrawal, and dropout rates increased, schools also increased their 10th-grade reading and math grade scores. These variables explained more of the change in scores than did the combination of variables representing changes in student characteristics and school capacity (teacher certification, experience, and turnover) from year to year.

The most powerful predictor of changes in 10th-grade scores in reading and math in all of our models (with and without school fixed effects) was an increase in 9th-grade retention rates. A school could raise its TAAS Texas Learning Index (TLI) score by one point in reading by increasing 9th-grade retention by 7 percentage points and in math by increasing retention by 8 percentage points. Disappearance from school also had an effect. A one-point increase on the Reading TLI could also be achieved by an increasing student disappearance between ninth grade and tenth grade by 11 percentage points.

These variables also predicted increases or decreases in TEA accountability ratings from year to year. (TEA ratings were a function of increases in TLI scores coupled with officially reported dropout rates in relation to threshold levels.) Once again, 9th-grade retention rates strongly predicted better TEA ratings. Furthermore, as called for in the accountability system, officially reported 9th-grade dropout rates—which bore little relationship to actual school leaving rates—declined in schools whose TEA rating rose (see Table 3.2).

Table 3.2. Multinomal Logistic Regression of TEA Accountability Changes (1997–2002), Coefficients and Odds Ratios.

Model	A		B		C		D	
TEA Rating	*Same*	*Rise*	*Same*	*Rise*	*Same*	*Rise*	*Same*	*Rise*
Δ School Capacity								
Fully Certified	.083 (.054) .129	.045 (.075) 1.048	—	—	—	—	.086 (.073) 1.090	.244★ (.124) 1.277
% Novice Teacher	-.022 (.076) .774	-.043 (.106) .958	—	—	—	—	-.161 (.110) .851	-.084 (.173) .919
% Teacher Turnover	.047 (.055) 1.048	.017 (.077) 1.018	—	—	—	—	.101 (.097) 1.107	.073 (.131) 1.076
Δ 9th Student Progress								
% 9th Disappearance	—	—	-.112 (.060) .894	-.003 (.072) .997	—	—	-.061 (.079) .941	.133 (.111) 1.143
% 9th Retained	—	—	.215★★ (.071) 1.240	.294★★ (.094) 1.342	—	—	.221★ (.109) 1.248	.437★ (.156) 1.548
% 9th Withdrawal	—	—	-.149 (.077) .054	-.066 (.097) .936	—	—	-.147 (.099) .864	.044 (.147) 1.045
% 9th Dropout	—	—	-.150 (.240) .861	-.661★ (.316) .516	—	—	-.439 (.296) .645	-1.845★★ (.627) .158
Δ School Demographic								
% White	—	—	—	—	.198 (.215) 1.219	-.005 (.303) .995	.315 (.298) 1.371	.680 (.523) 1.973
% LEP	—	—	—	—	-.138 (.126) .871	-.261 (.179) .770	-.185 (.208) .831	-.164 (.310)).849
% Special Education	—	—	—	—	-.161 (.215) .851	-.638 (.337) .528	.030 (.289) 1.031	-1.203★ (.549) .300
% At-Risk	—	—	—	—	.195★★ (.068) 1.215	.040 (.085) 1.041	.189★ (.093) 1.209	-.040 (.138) .960

Note: Numbers in parentheses are standard errors. *p<.05; **p<.01.

Most staff and students we interviewed felt that practices which manipulated the student population to game the accountability system were commonplace. As one administrator put it,

BCSD . . . was billed as a [Texas miracle]. . . . And I think it's a non-miracle. It's
not a miracle to manipulate things. A miracle is saving kids actually in reality, that's
what miracles are. To go out and get these kids who were dropped out, or to get
kids who are not achieving and find ways. That's a miracle. . . . It's not to manipulate
things so that it appears [to be something it's not]. It's a façade.

It is important to note that not all school responses suggested gaming. Some
schools improved their ratings by increasing their teaching capacity, as reflected in
the percentage of fully certified teachers. Such improvements in teacher qualifications were 20% more likely in high schools with increased TEA ratings than in
schools where ratings decreased. Yet, during these years, improvements in teacher
quality occurred primarily for White students, and the racial gap in access to qualified teachers actually grew. More than one-third of African American and Latino
students were taught by uncertified teachers in each year that we studied (see Figure
3.6), and these teachers were significantly less effective than other teachers.

Indeed, this trend was true throughout Texas, where a raft of policies during
the 1990s aimed at opening up access to teaching—and keeping salary costs low—
allowed an increasing share of newly hired teachers each year to enter without

Figure 3.6. Proportion of Brazos City Students Taught by Teachers with
Standard Certification.

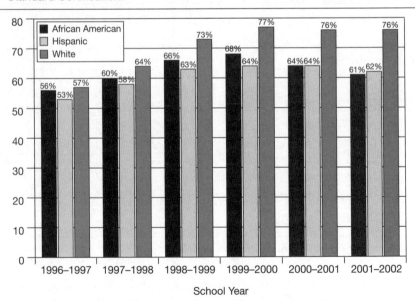

School Year

Source: Darling-Hammond et al. (2005).

having completed, or sometimes started, their preparation. Between 1996 and 2002, the proportion of new hires who were certified when they entered declined from 86% to 47%, and most of those entering without training were teaching in high-minority, low-income schools in urban districts (see Figure 3.7). About 12% of all new hires were alternatively certified (that is, teaching while completing a training program), while over 40% were teaching without even this modest safeguard. Furthermore, over these years, Texas teachers were leaving the classroom at ever mounting rates (see Figure 3.8), and the attrition rates for uncertified and alternatively certified teachers in high-poverty, high-minority schools were more than double those of fully prepared teachers in the same schools.[76]

At the end of the day, such a system of so-called "accountability" provides no incentives or capacity for schools to work with students who are challenging to teach. The accountability that students and parents desire and should be entitled to—that is, the high-quality teaching and instructional support needed to learn what the standards demand—is lacking when testing replaces investing as a lever for improvement.

Figure 3.7. Percentage of Newly Hired Texas Teachers by Certification Status (1995 through 2002).

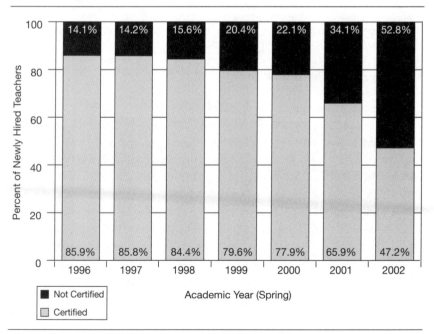

Source: Texas State Board of Education Certification Web site.
Note: "Certified teachers" indicates those teachers who held a standard certificate before December 31 of the fall semester of the academic year.

Figure 3.8. Number of Texas Public School Teachers Leaving Teaching
(1995–1996 through 2002–2003).

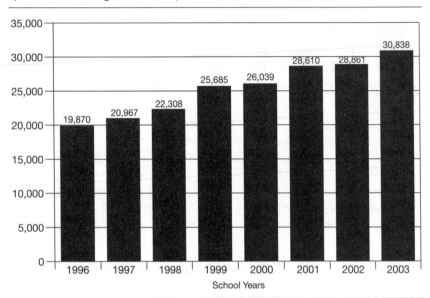

Source: Ed Fuller, Texas State Board of Education Certification.
Note: Teachers counted as quitting in a given year were employed as public school
teachers in the previous year, but not in the current year.

Massachusetts: The Untold Story

The short-circuiting of opportunities for low-income students has even occurred in generally high-achieving states like Massachusetts. Although Massachusetts
made strong improvements with school and funding reforms in the early 1990s, resource gaps were never fully closed before poor schools fell further behind with tax
cuts later in the decade. Meanwhile, school rankings were tied to student scores on
the MCAS tests beginning in the late 1990s. At the high school level, an exit exam
tied school ratings to student pass rates in the 10th grade, and took effect for high
school graduation in 2003. Students could continue to retake the test for graduation
after 10th grade, but the school's rankings, tied to rewards and sanctions, were based
on the 10th-grade scores alone. As it was phased in, greater numbers of students,
mostly African American and Latino, failed to progress from 9th to 10th grades,
where their scores would count against the school's rating (see Figure 3.9). Many of
the steepest increases in test scores occurred in schools with the highest retention
and dropout rates. A study by Anne Wheelock[77] found that, in addition to increasing
dropout rates, high schools receiving state awards for gains in 10th-grade pass rates
on the MCAS showed substantial increases in prior year 9th-grade retention rates

and in the percentage of "missing" tenth graders; that is, rising ninth graders who never arrived in 10th grade. Thus, some schools improved their scores and reaped rewards by keeping students out of the testing pool or out of school entirely.

Noguera noted in the first year the exit exam was used for graduation that

> At the high schools I work with in Boston, where in some cases half or two-thirds of the seniors will be denied a high school diploma, I hear anger and resignation among students and teachers. I speak with principals who readily admit that most of their students have not been adequately prepared to pass these exams. I also hear from anxious parents who hope desperately that at the last minute, public officials will come to their senses and reverse the policy as they recognize the folly of their actions and the devastating consequences that will befall many students.[78]

But no reprieve came. In 2003, graduation rates for the group of ninth graders who had entered high school 4 years earlier decreased for all students, but most sharply for students of color. Whereas 71% of African American students graduated on time in the class of 2002, only 59.5% graduated among those who began ninth grade with the class of 2003, a proportion that dropped further in the following year.[79] Graduation rates for Latino students went from 54% in the class of 2002 to 45% in the class of 2003.

Figure 3.9. Percentage of 9th-Grade Massachusetts Students "Lost" Between Ninth and Tenth Grades.

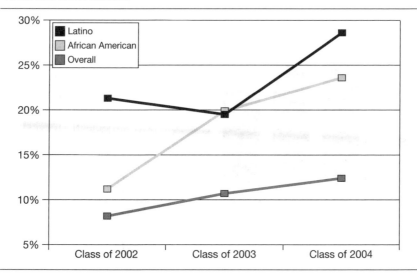

Source: Massachusetts Department of Education, Dropout Rates in Massachusetts Public Schools, 1999, 2000, 2001.

them from the testing pool or from school altogether. When a side effect of test-based accountability policies is that large numbers of students leave school earlier and with fewer skills, society acquires the burden of undereducated youth who are unable to function in the labor market and who increasingly join the welfare or criminal justice systems rather than the productive economy. Society as a whole does not benefit from school policies that raise test scores by pushing low achievers out of school to make the scores look better, or by failing to offer education that enables these students to learn.

Readers may rightly ask what the alternative is. Should students be allowed to move along from year to year failing to acquire the skills they need? Should they graduate without the minimal skills demanded by entry-level jobs in the labor market? Of course not. However, we need solutions that actually work, rather than the ones we have adopted thus far. As I illustrate in Chapter 6, the answers developed by other nations that have dramatically increased achievement focus on substantially upgrading the quality of curriculum and teaching that all children receive. There is no solution that can skirt the fact that teaching has to improve if learning is to follow.

Reform rhetoric notwithstanding, the key question for students—especially the least advantaged—is whether investments in better teaching, curriculum, and schooling will follow the press for new standards, or whether standards built upon a foundation of continued inequality in education will simply certify student failure with greater certainty and reduce access to future education and employment. A related question, a half-century after *Brown v. Board of Education*, is, what will it take to secure a constitutional right to equal educational opportunity for all the nation's children? I turn to that question in the next chapter.

CHAPTER 4

Inequality on Trial:
Does Money Make a Difference?

There is no evidence that the added resources [devoted to education in the United States over the 20th century] have improved student performance. . . .
　　　—Eric Hanushek, expert for the defense in *Williams v. California*[1]

[My ideal school] would be a classroom with enough tables, enough chairs, enough books, enough materials and a teacher who cares, not just someone who got a GED or whatever. . . . Like I said, enough supplies, enough security, and just enough everything. . . . Just because we're smaller, we are still human beings.
　　　—A high school student, testifying for plaintiffs in *Williams v. California*

High-stakes testing reforms requiring students to achieve specific standards in order to progress or graduate from school have been introduced in many states while educational experiences for students of color continue to be substantially separate and unequal. The unintended negative effects of these reforms for the most vulnerable students in the least supported schools have been deeply problematic. At the same time, an important aspect of the standards movement is that it has provided a new basis for confronting educational inequalities.

A new spate of equity litigation has been stimulated by state efforts to set standards for all students without fully ensuring opportunities to learn. These lawsuits— which may be said to constitute the next generation of efforts begun by *Brown v. Board of Education*—argue that if states require all students to meet the same educational standards, they must assume a responsibility to provide adequate resources to allow students a reasonable opportunity to achieve those standards, including a curriculum that fully reflects the standards; teachers well qualified to teach the curriculum; and the materials, texts, supplies, and equipment needed to support this teaching.

The logic is straightforward. Yet, the path to educational opportunity through the courts is torturous, both because of differing interpretations regarding what courts should take on and because our nation's comfort level with inequality often makes the current situation seem tolerable—even appropriate—to both the public and its justices. Opponents of school finance reform have argued that states have no business meddling with the unequal funding that results from local property taxation because of traditions of local control of schools. Yet, states now prescribe even more of the processes and outcomes of education than they did when the Texas Supreme Court took on the myth of local control in its 1988 decision to require reform:

> The only element of local control that remains undiminished is the power of wealthy districts to fund education at virtually any level they choose, as contrasted with property-poor districts who enjoy no such local control.... Most of the incidents in the education process are determined and controlled by state statute and/ or State Board of Education rule, including such matters as curriculum, course content, textbooks, hours of instruction, pupil–teacher ratios, training of teachers, administrators and board members, teacher testing, and review of personnel decisions and policies.[2]

Although parent and community involvement in public schools remains an important way to focus resources and decisions on local needs, and to maintain accountability to parents and students, such participation does not depend on the local production of dollars for education. In many other countries that fund schools centrally and equally, local schools have extensive flexibility to design programs and interventions and decide how funds are used. Finland, Switzerland, Canada, Australia, and even highly centralized Singapore are all places where local communities and school-based educators are actively involved in deciding what goes on in their centrally funded schools. Indeed, one could argue that a level playing field of resources might be a precondition for genuine local control of educational decisions that matter.

Another recurring argument against school finance reform is that "money doesn't make a difference." Proponents of the status quo argue that low-cost attitudinal and administrative changes contribute more to educational quality within districts than financial resources, and that no definitive correlation has been shown between money spent and educational quality. Sometimes, they point to districts like Washington, D.C., which—with constant meddling from Congress—spends far more than the national average and produces very low achievement. It is certainly true that money can be spent unwisely, and dollars spent on patronage, bloated bureaucracies, football fields, and swimming pools are less likely to translate into learning than dollars spent on sound instruction. Furthermore, the higher costs of living in many urban areas and the greater educational and noneducational needs of students who live in poverty—

for meals, health care, before- and afterschool care, and more—mean that there is not a one-to-one correspondence between dollars and the resources they buy or the net benefits they can produce. More money is needed to achieve equivalent outcomes in high-cost locations with high-need students.[3] While this complicates analyses of funding and resources, there is no logic under which it provides a justification for spending less on the education of children in poverty.

However, opponents of school finance equalization often look to the strong measured relationships between race, parent education, income, and outcomes, and argue that these are the major predictors of learning; hence, greater investments would be wasted on those who (implicitly) cannot take advantage of them. This has been a continuing refrain since 1966, when the Coleman report concluded that "schools bring little influence to bear on a child's achievement that is independent of his background and general social context."[4] Although the report pointed to many inequalities that it argued should be remedied, the statement became widely viewed as a claim that school funding does not affect school achievement. As later analyses pointed out, the high correlation between students' backgrounds and their schools' resources makes it difficult to identify the independent effects of schooling on achievement because, in the United States, race, class, and educational opportunity are so fully entangled.[5]

Although the Coleman report did not say so, the conventional wisdom became the belief that additional resources play no role in producing better-educated students. Many studies have debunked this view and have documented how specific resources—including better qualified teachers, smaller class sizes, and smaller, redesigned schools (relying on resources such as advisors, planning time for teaching teams, and support systems for students) contribute to student achievement gains.[6] Yet newspapers have often reveled in reporting the counterintuitive conclusion, as the *Wall Street Journal* put it, that "money doesn't buy better education. . . . The evidence can scarcely be clearer."[7]

These debates about whether resources make a difference for the schooling of low-income and minority students have been reprised in recent school finance cases. In *Williams v. California*, defendants argued that, despite large, documented differences in dollars, as well as in children's access to qualified teachers, textbooks, course offerings, and facilities, such resources are largely unrelated to student achievement, and that the effects of poverty—not unequal resources—drive disparities in achievement. In a sweeping indictment of educational investments over the last half-century, defense expert Eric Hanushek claimed that "there is no evidence that the added resources [devoted to education in the United States over the 20th century] have improved student performance, at least for the most recent three decades,"[8] ignoring studies finding effects of additional resources on improved student performance.

The body of research arguing that money makes no difference has been critiqued for its methodology and interpretations by other economists, statisticians, and the courts.[9] In his statement that investments have had no effect on student performance in the United States, Hanushek ignored the enormous expansion of schooling over the last half-century and more. For example, since the 1960s, the education system has added kindergarten and pre-kindergarten and expanded access to high school. As late as 1965, only 10% of 3- and 4-year-olds attended any kind of nursery school or pre-kindergarten, and three-fourths of 5- and 6-year-olds were in school. By 1998, 52% of 3- and 4-year-olds were in school, as were 96% of 5- and 6-year-olds.[10] Even more dramatic, until the 1960s, many communities did not even have high schools for Black students, Mexican American students, or American Indian students, and when they did, these were often segregated and severely underfunded. Students with disabilities were not expected to attend school, and schools did not have to serve them. By 1970, only 57% of White adults and 36% of Black adults finished high school. By 1998, the proportions had leaped to 94% and 88%, respectively.[11]

Even with the great expansion of high schools to include more low-income, minority, poor, new immigrant, and students with special education needs, average test scores continued to rise on measures such as the National Assessment of Educational Progress and on the SAT. Because of the large addition of previously excluded (and less advantaged) students to the pool of test-takers, these average scores underestimate the actual increase in knowledge acquired by high school–age students. Meanwhile, SAT scores rose steeply for students of color between 1970 and 1990, and the fact that they have continued to rise while more test-takers have been added is, arguably, a result of educational investments that dramatically extended educational opportunities in the country, boosting literacy rates and attainment all the way through college.

The evidence that increased investments have been accompanied by measurable gains does not mean that all investments have equivalent payoff. The efficiency argument has merit. Dollars can be wasted or used in counterproductive ways, and bad managerial decisions can create administrative burdens that deflect scarce resources and attention from productive teaching and learning either to less productive strategies or overmanagement of bureaucratic procedures—what Arthur Wise once called the "hyper-rationalization of education."[12] Thus, an effective system must create both a means for determining and funding adequacy and incentives to increase the likelihood of funds being wisely spent. At a minimum, states should not force schools to waste scarce resources through ill-conceived requirements.

Smart policy will be based on investments that produce strong yields in terms of children's well-being and learning. And while there will always be some uncertainties about the wisest marginal uses of dollars—and these may differ depending on the circumstances and the students—an important role of the state is to evaluate the outcomes of programs and strategies to inform the decisions of localities about where to invest most wisely. Given the enormous social costs of school failure, however, it is clear that it is *not* efficient to leave large segments of the population undereducated and unable to contribute positively to the society as a whole.

THE LEGALITY OF UNEQUAL SCHOOL FUNDING

Despite the primary state role in education—expressed in state constitutional provisions that require the provision of public education that is "free and appropriate" or "thorough and efficient" or "sound and basic," among other descriptors—courts have only gradually recognized a state obligation to fund education to any particular standard. Although concern about unequal school funding was expressed as early as the early 1900s, it was not until the mid-1960s that the legality of long-standing school finance inequities was subjected to judicial review.

The Progress of Litigation

In 1965, Arthur Wise published an article challenging the constitutionality of school finance schemes that produce radically disparate per pupil expenditures within states.[13] Arguing that such unequal spending leads to unequal educational opportunities, he suggested that this might constitute a denial by the state of equal protection under the law. A number of lawsuits were filed on these grounds, and the first major success occurred in 1973, when the New Jersey Supreme Court declared, in *Robinson v. Cahill*, that the state's school financing system was in violation of the New Jersey Constitution's Education Clause, which called for a "thorough and efficient system of free public schools" for all children between the ages of 5 and 18. In that same year, however, the U.S. Supreme Court rejected an argument in a Texas case, *San Antonio Independent School District v. Rodriguez*,[14] that education constitutes a fundamental right under the federal Constitution. This cut off further federal court challenges of educational funding inequities.

Although hopes for a sweeping indictment of school funding disparities on federal grounds were dashed by the *San Antonio* decision, state-level challenges continued in several dozen state courts during the 1970s. In 1976, in *Serrano v. Priest*, California's Supreme Court ended nearly a decade of debate by ruling that the state's system of school finance violated both the federal Constitution's 14th Amendment and California's own equal protection clause. Other victories were achieved in West Virginia and Connecticut. However, most of the challenges were unsuccessful. Civil rights lawyers Bill Taylor and Dianne Piche noted the differences in how state courts approached similar problems:

> In each case, the state court was confronted with significant fiscal disparities, but the opinions reflect that they each engaged in their own unique legal reasoning,

applying different standards, and ultimately drawing different conclusions. The indisputable impact then of the "Federalist" approach, forged by the Supreme Court
in *Rodriguez*, is that children in the poor districts of states like Connecticut and
West Virginia are guaranteed some measure of equity, while those who live in the
property-poor and urban districts of states like New York and Maryland are con-
demned to inferior educations.[15]

Ratios in funding disparities of 3 to 1 between high- and low-spending districts are common within states in which challenges have been both successful and
unsuccessful. These disparities create differences among students' educational opportunities as a function of race and socioeconomic status as well as geography. As
Taylor and Piche demonstrate:

> Inequitable systems of school finance inflict disproportionate harm on minority
> and economically disadvantaged students. On an *inter*-state basis, such students
> are concentrated in states, primarily in the South, that have the lowest capacities
> to finance public education. On an *intra*-state basis, many of the states with the
> widest disparities in educational expenditures are large industrial states. In these
> states, many minorities and economically disadvantaged students are located in
> property-poor urban districts which fare the worst in educational expenditures. In
> addition, in several states economically disadvantaged students, white and black, are
> concentrated in rural districts which suffer from fiscal inequity.[16]

Roadblocks to Equalizing Funding

In total, courts in 10 of the 31 states where suits were filed during the 1970s and
early 1980s found their state's school finance scheme to be unconstitutional.[17] This
series of state challenges was followed by a decade of little activity. One reason for this
was the dismantling of federal and state data bases that had been used to document
disparities. During the Reagan administration, some federal data collection and reporting that allowed analysis of inequalities was discontinued, and the federal funding
that had supported data collection by state departments of education was also ended.

The federal conversation was turned to educational "outcomes," which were
to be monitored and managed without regard to inputs. "Mere inputs" were dismissed as irrelevant to the real question of educational attainment. One historical
account of the argument, as it was advanced by Education Secretary William Bennett, notes:

> Bennett . . . cited countless education evaluation studies to show that twenty years
> of "dumping money" on public schools had done little to boost academic results.
> . . . Bennett's famous "wall charts" ranked states in order of per-pupil spending (as

well as test scores, poverty rates, teacher salaries, and dropout rates) to show that expenditures had little correlation with academic achievement. Bennett's critics, however, accused him of hiding behind a flurry of statistics that bore no connection to actual reforms in curriculum or instruction.[18]

Bennett pressed for greater use of tests to evaluate school performance, while seeking large cuts in the federal education budget. When criticized by both Republican and Democratic Congressmen for the size of his proposed cuts, he argued that "We are not underinvesting in education. We are inefficient."[19] Although Congress would not approve the full extent of cuts requested, the federal education budget ultimately dropped from 9.6% to 6.2% during his years in office, having dropped from 12% to 9% in the preceding years of the Reagan administration. Most of these cuts came from poor urban and rural schools. With other federal budget cuts during the Reagan years, states had to pick up greater costs not only for education, but also for health care, welfare, employment training, housing supports, and other functions. Consequently, they focused on managing their increasingly rocky economies, and raising or equalizing education funding was far from the top of the agenda.

Thus, for a time, educational opportunity was magically transported out of sight and out of mind. This sleight of hand worked to a remarkable extent. It was not until the late 1980s, when the federal Schools and Staffing Surveys were initiated, that a new data set was created allowing tracking of disparities in instructional resources—teachers, support staff, curriculum, facilities, and professional development—across states, districts, and types of schools and students. These data—and similar data sets developed on the state level—which allowed researchers to document inputs to education later allowed analyses of disparities in access to qualified teachers and other conditions for learning that informed a new wave of lawsuits.

HOW MONEY MAKES A DIFFERENCE

The argument that money makes no difference is supported by the obvious fact that not all kinds of spending improve student learning. However, recent studies have begun to demonstrate how money makes a difference. For example, based on an analysis of a data set even larger than that available to Coleman and his team of researchers, Ronald Ferguson demonstrated that expenditure levels make a difference in increasing student performance and that the strength of effects on achievement increases as funding moves closest to direct instruction of students.[20] He found that the single most important measurable cause of increased student learning was teacher expertise, measured by teacher performance on a statewide certification exam measuring academic skills and teaching knowledge, along with teacher experience, and master's degrees. The effects were so strong, and the variations in teacher expertise so great, that after controlling for socioeconomic status, the large disparities in achievement between Black and White students were almost entirely accounted for by differences in the qualifications of their teachers. Ferguson concluded, "What the evidence here suggests most strongly is that teacher quality matters and should be a major focus of efforts to upgrade the quality of schooling. Skilled teachers are the most critical of all schooling inputs."[21]

Ferguson found that, when regional cost differentials are accounted for, school district operating expenditures exert a significant positive effect on student achievement—an effect that operates primarily through the influence of funding levels on salaries that attract and retain more qualified teachers. He found that investments in teachers' salaries produce higher marginal gains in student performance than equivalent investments in other budget areas more remote from instruction.

Ferguson also found that class size, at a critical point of 18 students per teacher, was a statistically significant determinant of student outcomes, though smaller in magnitude than the teacher effect. This finding has been replicated in a number of other studies, usually below a threshold in the upper teens or lower 20s, and especially in the early grades and for lower-achieving students.[22] Most often cited is the evidence from a randomized experiment, called Tennessee STAR, which found significant gains in achievement as a result of reducing class sizes from 22 to 15 in kindergarten through third grade.[23] Although the costs of reducing class size can be large, and the effects of reducing class size are generally smaller per unit of spending than those of improving teacher quality,[24] economist Alan Krueger estimates a benefit–cost ratio of reducing class sizes of nearly 3 to 1 as a function of the earnings expectations of higher achievement.

This work suggests that the effect of funding on achievement increases as it is spent on instructionally crucial resources, such as the capacity to buy higher-quality teachers and to provide personalized class settings. These findings about the influences and relative contributions of teacher training and experience were reinforced by a review of 60 production function studies by scholars at the University of Chicago, which found that teacher education, ability, and experience, along with small schools and lower teacher–pupil ratios, are associated with increases in student achievement.[25] In their estimate of the achievement gains associated with expenditure increments on various resources, spending on teacher education was found to be the most productive investment for schools, outstripping the effect of teacher experience and reduced pupil–teacher ratios.

Reinforcing the findings on teacher investments, a study by economists Robert Strauss and Elizabeth Sawyer found that North Carolina's teachers' average scores on a teacher licensing test measuring subject-matter and teaching knowledge had a strong influence on students' average test performance. Taking into account income levels, student race, district capital assets, student plans to attend college, and pupil–teacher ratios, teacher quality had a strikingly large effect on students' failure rates on the state competency examinations: A 1% increase in teacher quality was associated with a 3% to 5% decline in the percentage of students failing the exam. The authors' conclusion was similar to Ferguson's:

> Of the inputs which are potentially policy-controllable (teacher quality, teacher numbers via the pupil–teacher ratio and capital stock), our analysis indicates quite clearly that improving the quality of teachers in the classroom will do more for students who are most educationally at risk, those prone to fail, than reducing the class size or improving the capital stock by any reasonable margin which would be available to policy makers.[26]

The Opportunity Costs of Teacher Turnover and Low Quality

Conversely, there are substantial costs associated with ineffective teachers and instability in the teaching force. The costs of poor teachers are represented not only in the costs of low achievement borne by their students, but also the costs to schools of remediation, grade retention, special education, and disciplinary problems that are often tied to school failure. Furthermore, society bears the later costs of drop-outs, incarceration, and low productivity in the workforce, currently amounting to nearly $300 billion annually, according to recent estimates.[27]

Teacher turnover also costs districts much more than they typically recognize, both for replacing teachers and remediating student achievement. The replacement costs of early departures from teaching are estimated at about $15,000 to $20,000 for each teacher who leaves. These figures include costs for separation, recruitment and hiring, and training. Adding the costs of reduced learning for students when more experienced teachers are replaced with novices drives the costs up further, with estimates ranging from $33,000 to $48,000 per teacher who leaves.[28] This is partly because education productivity declines when beginners are hired, since teacher effectiveness rises sharply after the first 2 to 3 years in the classroom.[29] As we have seen, this drop in productivity is greater when those hired are less well prepared and more likely to leave early in their careers. A study of Texas, which has higher-than-average annual attrition rates, especially for its many alternate route teachers, estimated in 2000 that teacher losses cost the state between $329 million and $2.1 billion per year, depending on the cost model used (see Figure 4.1).[30]

Failure to maintain a stable teaching force can also undo other school improvement efforts. For example, an evaluation of one urban district's effort to create a large number of new small, innovative schools found that the new school models significantly increased schools' ability to add value to student learning beyond the effects of student background. At the high school level, the districts' new schools—and specific features of the reforms, such as advisory systems, project-based learning, interdisciplinary

Figure 4.1. Three-Year Attrition Rates for Cohorts of Differently Certified
Secondary Mathematics Teachers in Texas.

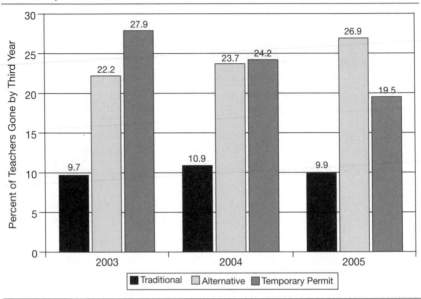

Source: Fuller (2008).

courses, and student internships—raised student achievement, controlling for student
characteristics, by 5 to 13 percentile points above those of other schools.[31] (I discuss
the benefits of these kinds of new school models further in Chapter 8).

However, the district's staffing problems, which resulted in a large and growing
share of new, alternate route teachers, exerted a much more sizable negative influence
on student achievement, overwhelming the effects of these school reforms. Controlling for student characteristics, schools with the greatest proportions of these novice
teachers lost more than 20 percentile points in achievement relative to those with
a more senior teaching force. As is usually the case, the most segregated minority
schools had the largest shares of these novice teachers. (See Figures 4.2 and 4.3).

In this underresourced district, the hiring of these novice teachers was an advance over the previous policy of balancing the budget by hiring low-cost substitute teachers rather than regular staff. However, with the struggles of learning to
teach (many of them having had little prior training), poor working conditions, and
average salaries about 20% lower than districts nearby, it was hard to keep them.
Among these beginners, more than 40% of the traditionally trained teachers and
two-thirds of those from alternate routes were gone within 4 years, contributing
to continual churn in the highest-need schools and suboptimal results in both the
schools that were staffed in this way.

Figure 4.2. Contributions to School Value-Added Productivity of School Features and Staffing Patterns.

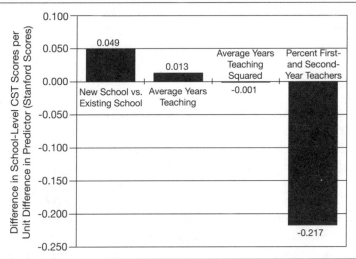

Source: Vasudeva, Darling-Hammond, Newton, & Montgomery (2009).
Note: Achievement versus expectation, holding constant prior test scores and student demographic characteristics.

Figure 4.3. Proportions of 1st- and 2nd-Year Teachers by School Population (2002–2003 to 2007–2008).

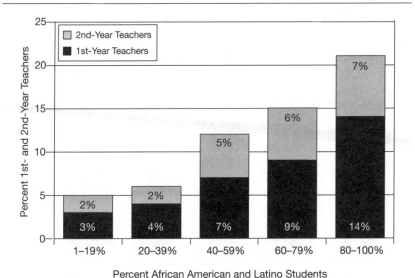

Source: Vasudeva, Darling-Hammond, Newton, & Montgomery (2009).

The most successful new school models—those that were beating the odds—had recruited and retained a more balanced teaching force led by a stable cadre of skilled, experienced teachers who carefully mentored the few beginners they hired. These schools were able to implement the new school designs effectively and to benefit over time from the extensive professional development and collaborative planning in which the teachers engaged. High-turnover schools were unable to realize the investments that had been made in the school reforms.

The Requirements for Educational Improvement

Indeed, study after study of educational reforms—whether of school design, instructional programs, curriculum, assessment, or parent involvement—has discovered that the success of the innovation depends on the capacity of teachers to carry it out, and on the capacity of organizations to implement and continually improve on the reform strategy. Implementing new practices well takes at least 3 to 5 years of steady effort: Successful change requires high-quality initial efforts, a process of learning effectively from experience—including collective analysis of data and reflection on change strategies—and the capacity to grow new knowledge and skills schoolwide.[32] Schools without an ongoing group of competent, committed teachers and a capable leader simply cannot get traction on educational improvement.

The investments needed to produce a more stable, balanced teaching force are of several kinds. As noted earlier, teachers with stronger initial preparation typically stay in teaching significantly longer, as do those who receive high-quality mentoring in their first year on the job.[33] Thus, these investments in teachers' effectiveness also have payoffs for their longevity in teaching. In addition, there is evidence that salaries and working conditions influence teacher attrition. Teachers are more likely to quit when they work in districts with noncompetitive wages,[34] especially if they work in high-demand fields such as math and science.[35] A study of California teachers found that both salaries and working conditions—ranging from large class sizes and facilities problems to multi-track, year-round schedules and poor teaching conditions—were strong predictors of high turnover.[36]

Finally, the quality of school leaders is critical to recruiting and retaining teachers, as the principal's ability to organize a productive environment, access resources, buffer the school from outside distractions, motivate adults, and support their learning is critical to teachers' satisfaction and efficacy.[37] All of these factors are amenable to policies, and, as I show in the next chapter, some states and districts have made strong gains by putting such policies in place, while others have avoided addressing these concerns and have failed to improve.

LITIGATING FOR ADEQUACY

The question should not be whether money spent on education can make a difference, but *how* strategic educational investments can influence school outcomes. This question has increasingly been considered as the standards-based reform movement has taken hold, and "adequacy" cases have been brought in more than 20 states. These have relied heavily on data about the disparities in concrete resources related to learning in ways that are needed to meet the standards. By one count, these lawsuits have succeeded in establishing the state's liability for educational investments about 70% of the time.[38]

Success, however, is often a relative concept. In many states, plaintiffs have had to return to court repeatedly over many decades, as even successful decisions do not always produce resources. Courts often have trouble fashioning useful remedies, and have little authority to ensure implementation when they do call for change. Legislatures often resist raising taxes or revising funding formulas, and may try to wait out the court, rather than acting on judicial requirements. So, even when school funding schemes are declared unconstitutional, it can take decades of ongoing litigation to get to a major reallocation of resources. Nonetheless, these cases have begun to make progress in establishing the foundations of a right to learn.

Furthermore, a growing body of evidence illustrates that when states finally act, their interventions can pay off for children. For example, a 2002 study in the *Journal of Public Economics* measured the impact on student achievement of court-ordered school finance reform targeted to underperforming lower-income districts in 12 states during the 1980s, comparing them to other states not subject to such court orders. Using SAT scores as the common measure of achievement, the study found that not only did more lower-income students take the SAT, but the greater funding "closed the gap in average SAT scores between children of highly-educated and poorly-educated parents by . . . roughly 5 percent."[39] Economists have confirmed increases in student achievement and reductions in achievement gaps in Massachusetts and New Jersey as the result of school funding investments following equity-oriented lawsuits,[40] and a study in Kansas found gains in college-going for districts aided by court-ordered spending increases.[41]

The Tortuous Process of Arguing for Equity

Despite common sense and evidence, state defendants have increasingly urged courts not to redress inadequate resources without "proof" that investments will change outcomes. In a growing number of school funding lawsuits, plaintiffs and defendants wrestle over the state's obligation to provide equivalent supports to students, including teachers who meet the state's own requirements for training.

These wrangles can go on for years, even decades. In South Carolina, for example, the descendants of African American plaintiffs who brought *Briggs v. Elliot,* one of the first cases later consolidated into *Brown v. Board of Education,* returned to court exactly 50 years later, in the same courthouse in Clarendon County, to continue to litigate the lack of educational opportunity.

The original petition that led to *Briggs,* brought by Black parents and children against the Board of Education of School District #22 in Clarendon County in November 1949 noted that the

> facilities, physical condition, sanitation and protection from the elements in . . . the only three schools which Negro pupils are permitted to attend, are inadequate and unhealthy, the buildings and schools are old and over-crowded and in a dilapidated condition . . . [with] no appropriate and necessary central heating system, running water or adequate lights, . . . and [with] an insufficient number of teachers and insufficient class room space.

Meanwhile those in the White schools were "modern, safe, sanitary, well equipped, . . . uncrowded and maintained in first class condition; [with] . . . adequate complement of teachers and adequate class room space for the students." At the close of a much longer list of complaints, the petitioners requested that the Board of Trustees "immediately stop discriminating against Negro children . . . and make available similarly situated educational advantages and facilities equal in all respects to that which is being provided to whites."[42]

Fifty years later, in 1999, after decades of failed litigation over major disparities in funding between low- and high-wealth districts, the South Carolina Supreme Court remanded a case to trial based on gross differences in resources between the same still-segregated Clarendon County schools—now serving the grandchildren of the original plaintiffs—and predominantly White and wealthier districts.[43] In 2005, when *Abbeville v. State of South Carolina* was heard, 88% of students in the plaintiff districts were minority, 86% lived in poverty, and 75% of the schools were rated by the state as "unsatisfactory" or below on the state rating system. Graduation rates ranged between only 33 and 56% across the districts.

The testimony was eerily similar to that heard in the same courthouse a half-century earlier, with plaintiffs describing crumbling and overcrowded facilities, lack of equipment, large numbers of uncertified teachers, and teacher turnover caused by salaries and benefits much lower than those in other districts. A film made about conditions in the plaintiff districts was entitled *Corridor of Shame.* The producer and director Bud Ferillo reflected on the stark conditions he saw in some of the state's oldest school buildings, such as J. V. Martin High School in Dillon School District Two. Built in 1896, it was barely heated on the morning of the first shoot when it was 18 degrees outside and nearly as cold inside. Ferillo exclaimed, "You cannot imagine how cold, bare and ill-equipped many of these rural schools are." Along with showing inadequately equipped classrooms, science labs, and media centers, the film reported recent ceiling collapses in two schools, raw sewage backing up into school hallways and closets on rainy days in two separate districts, and a cafeteria where poisonous snakes had recently crawled inside from a nearby swamp.[44]

This testimony was heard only because the state Supreme Court finally held that the education clause "requires the General Assembly to provide the opportunity for each child to receive a minimally adequate education" and defined that education to include providing students adequate and safe facilities in which they have the opportunity to acquire the skills outlined in the state standards:

1. The ability to read, write, and speak the English language, and knowledge of mathematics and physical science
2. A fundamental knowledge of economic, social, and political systems, and of history and governmental processes
3. Academic and vocational skills

The defense argued that, although the state has set academic goals for students, those goals exceed what the state is required to fund, which is only a "minimally adequate" education.[45] Interestingly, the same argument was made, ultimately unsuccessfully, by defendants in New York's *Campaign for Fiscal Equity* lawsuit, who argued that only an 8th-grade education was needed to meet the state standard for education, rather than the learning opportunities articulated in the state's own standards for issuing a high school diploma.

Demonstrating the Connection between Resources and Outcomes

One might wish that, in this day and time, a showing of such inadequacy would be sufficient to require a state remedy, but the arguments about whether money makes a difference are still hotly contested. Experts are called upon to show how sizable the effects of key school resources can be, both in relation to race and income and independently from these factors.

Interestingly, these relationships are as obvious in high-achieving but increasingly inequitable Massachusetts as they are in low-achieving and historically inequitable South Carolina. Serving as an expert witness in adequacy lawsuits in both of these states, I conducted analyses examining the effects of race, poverty, and school resources on student achievement. In both cases, plaintiff school districts—which serve many more minority and low-income students than the state as a whole—have had lower levels of overall resources, lower teachers' salaries, and lower levels of educator qualifications than other districts, as well as lower student performance. Both states have accountability systems based on the results of high-stakes testing, ranking schools based on students' scores and denying diplomas to students who do not meet cutoffs on exit exams.

Their funding histories are different, however, in ways that reflect overall achievement differences—Massachusetts students rank, on average, near the top nationally, while South Carolina's students rank near the bottom. Massachusetts made substantial progress in raising and equalizing school funding following the *Hancock v. Driscoll* decision in 1992, a suit that litigated inequalities. The school funding formula adopted in 1993 as part of the Education Reform Act stimulated substantially greater investments in needier schools through a formula that aimed to equalize funding and local effort simultaneously and added funding increments based on the proportions of low-income students and English language learners in a district.

This progressive approach helped boost educational investments and achievement as the state undertook a comprehensive reform featuring new standards and assessments demanding more intellectually ambitious teaching and learning. University of Chicago economist Jonathan Guryan examined the effects of these investments and found that increased educational funding for historically low-spending districts led to improved student achievement, especially for traditionally low-scoring students. He concluded that "increases in per-pupil spending led to significant increases in math, reading, science, and social studies test scores for 4th- and 8th-grade students."[46]

However, a decade of tax cuts ate away at these equalization efforts and converged with the national recession in 2001 to reduce state funding sharply in 2002.[47] As the state shifted more of the costs of funding schools onto localities, inequality grew, and a new lawsuit was filed.

While Massachusetts made progress and then fell backward, South Carolina never really attempted serious equalization of funding. In 1988, the South Carolina Supreme Court dismissed a lawsuit challenging the constitutionality of the state's public school funding system based on major disparities in per-pupil spending between high- and low-wealth school districts.[48] In 1993, almost half of South Carolina's 91 school districts sued the state again, challenging the finance system on grounds that it did not provide adequate education in poor districts.[49] This time, the Supreme Court upheld plaintiffs' claim, and remanded the case for a trial. It took until 2005 for the trial court to rule that the state had failed its constitutional responsibility. By 2008, 2 decades after the initial suit, no legislative action had yet occurred.[50]

In both of these very different states, however, inequalities left low-wealth districts serving low-income and minority students in very bad straits. (Recall the devastatingly poor conditions in Springfield, Massachusetts, discussed in Chapter 3.) Litigation raised the issue of whether disparities in achievement are related to students meaningful opportunities to learn, and whether the state has an obligation to ensure that students have access to the conditions that could enable them to meet the standards the state has set for progression in school and a passport to employment and college.

The analyses we conducted looked first at the effects of race and poverty on student achievement, then at the effects of key school resources, and then at the combined influences of student and school factors (see Tables 4.1 to 4.3). In both states, the data were collected at the school district level, because state funding is allocated to districts. Although the states keep somewhat different kinds of data about staffing and resources, we were able in both cases to examine the influences of teacher qualifications, teacher salaries, and student–teacher ratios (a rough proxy for class sizes) on student performance.

Table 4.1. South Carolina: Relationships Among Student Achievement, Race, and District Resources (% of Students Scoring "Below Basic" on State Tests, All Grades).

	Coefficients (T-value)			
	Model 1	*Model 2*	*Model 3*	*Model 4*
(Constant)	1.485	40.672***	49.960*	.354
	(.537)	(6.007)	(2.263)	(.021)
Poverty Index	.401***			.427***
	(5.619)			(5.107)
% Black Students	.134**			.034
	(2.706)			(.601)
% Teachers on Substandard Certificates		1.940***	1.714***	.713**
		(6.270)	(4.940)	(2.596)
% of Teachers with Advanced Degrees		−.243*	−.220	−.039
		(−2.086)	(−1.383)	(−.347)
% of Teachers with Uncompetitive Bachelor's Degrees		.059	.054	.020
		(1.149)	(.973)	(.515)
% Vacancies for More Than 9 Weeks		1.885**	1.903**	.497
		(2.988)	(2.687)	(.974)
% Out-of-State Teachers		−.173~	−.162~	.091
		(−1.900)	(−1.754)	(1.263)
% Certified Teachers with Out-of-Field Permits		−2.417***	−1.746**	−.781~
		(−5.281)	(−2.773)	(−1.725)
Student–Teacher Ratio			−.164	.040
			(−.584)	(.202)
Average Teacher Salary			.000	.000
			(−.298)	(.037)
% of Portable Classrooms			−.057	−.036
			(−1.501)	(−1.374)
R Squared	.79	.64	.65	.84

Source: Darling-Hammond (2004b).

Note: ~ $p < .10$; * $p < .05$; ** $p < .01$; *** $p < .001$.

Table 4.2. Massachusetts: Relationships Among Student Achievement, Student Demographics, and School Resources (% of Students Failing MCAS English Language Arts Test, All Grades).

	Coefficients (T-value)				
	Model 1	Model 2	Model 3	Model 4	Model 5
(Constant)	4.051***	2.446***	1.703**	18.732***	11.664***
	(13.057)	(8.971)	(3.103)	(5.529)	(4.395)
% Minority	.237***	.035			-.017
	(13.473)	(1.393)			(-.572)
% Low Income		.271***			.290
		(14.032)			(11.559)
% First Language Not English		-.014			-.022
		(-.558)			(-.954)
% of Teachers Unlicensed in Field[1]			.929***	1.100***	.272*
			(7.478)	(8.498)	(2.227)
% of Administrators not Licensed			.077*	.055~	.022
			(2.534)	(1.867)	(1.023)
% of Paraprofessionals Not Highly Qualified[2]			5.513***	4.016***	-.086
			(5.791)	(4.186)	(-.116)
Average Teacher Salary (in thousands)				-.320***	-.138**
				(-4.719)	(-3.657)
Net School Spending/ Foundation Budget[3]				-.011	-.020~
				(-.763)	(-1.826)
Student-Teacher Ratio				-.025	-.036
				(-.442)	(-.881)
R Squared	.38	.64	.39	.46	.73

Source: Darling-Hammond (2004b).

Notes: ~ $p < .10$; * $p < .05$; ** $p < .01$; *** $p < .001$.

[1] The combined portions of teachers who are not licensed at all and those who are not licensed in the field they teach.

[2] The proportion of paraprofessionals who do not meet the standards of the No Child Left Behind Act for "highly qualified" paraprofessionals.

[3] The ratio of district net school spending to the state-designated foundation budges, which is the budget level the state calculates as necessary to meet the foundation level for education, given the characteristics of students in that district.

Because research suggests that school resources such as skillful teachers and small class sizes have strong effects on student performance for historically lower-achieving students—and because the most relevant legal criterion is whether students meet the minimum standards set by the state—we focused on the effects of resources on the proportion of students failing to meet the minimum test score standards in each state. In South Carolina, this is the proportion of students scoring "below basic" on the state tests—the benchmark determining whether students will

Table 4.3. Massachusetts: Relationships Among Student Achievement, Student Demographics, and School Resources (% of Students Failing MCAS Math Test, All Grades).

	Coefficients (T-value)				
	Model 1	Model 2	Model 3	Model 4	Model 5
(Constant)	14.680***	10.868***	6.225***	40.406***	29.127***
	(21.838)	(19.964)	(4.855)	(5.247)	(5.354)
% Minority	.434***	-.062			-.050
	(11.391)	(-1.245)			(-.913)
% Low Income		.643***			.582***
		(16.665)			(12.3719)
% First Language Not English		-.005			-.028
		(-.098)			(-.699)
% of Teachers Unlicensed in Field[1]			1.502***	1.757***	.111
			(6.153)	(6.895)	(.495)
% of Math and Computer Teachers Uncertified 9–12			.168***	.115**	.032
			(4.482)	(3.071)	(1.286)
% of Administrators Not Licensed			.125*	.100	-.005
			(1.957)	(1.640)	(-.123)
% of Paraprofessionals Not Highly Qualified[2]			-.146***	.117***	.033*
			(7.439)	(6.036)	(2.411)
Average Teacher Salary (in thousands)				-.536***	-.243*
				(-3.580)	(-2.342)
Net School Spending/ Foundation Budget[3]				-6.765*	-.6.541**
				(-2.152)	(-3.116)
Student-Teacher Ratio				.061	.047
				(.548)	(.649)
R Squared	.31	.65	.50	.56	.82

Source: Darling-Hammond (2004b).

Notes: ~ $p < .10$; * $p < .05$; ** $p < .01$; *** $p < .001$.

[1] The combined portions of teachers who are not licensed at all and those who are not licensed in the field they teach.

[2] The proportion of paraprofessionals who do not meet the standards of the No Child Left Behind Act for "highly qualified" paraprofessionals.

[3] The ratio of district net school spending to the state-designated foundation budges, which is the budget level the state calculates as necessary to meet the foundation level for education, given the characteristics of students in that district.

be promoted from grade to grade and ultimately graduated from high school, and the criterion for school accountability rankings. In Massachusetts, we examined the proportion of students in a district receiving a failing score on the MCAS tests in English language arts and in mathematics, also used for school accountability ratings and, at the 10th-grade level for graduation.

The findings were remarkably similar. First, as is generally the case, student poverty levels and minority status[51] predicted much of the variation across districts in the proportions of students not meeting minimum standards on the state tests. In South Carolina, the percentage of African American students, along with the poverty index, predicted an astounding 79% of the variance in student performance. In Massachusetts, the proportion of minority students, along with the proportions of low-income and non–native English speaking students, predicted about two-thirds of the variance in the proportion of students failing the MCAS English language arts and mathematics tests.

Second, these ostensible effects of student characteristics are not solely a function of the knowledge and skills students bring to school or the conditions in which they live. School resources, as we have already described, covary significantly with pupil characteristics. When we estimated the effects on student achievement of school resources alone (without including student characteristics), these also accounted for a very large proportion of the variance in student performance. This is true despite the fact that the state data sets do not provide measures of many of the resources that might be expected to matter, such as course offerings and other measures of curriculum rigor, availability of materials and equipment, and support services, which also covary with student characteristics. The school resources we were able to include— measures of staff quality, class size, and funding—accounted for 65% of the total variance in students scoring "below basic" on the state tests in South Carolina and from 46% to 56% of the variance in students failing the MCAS in English and mathematics in Massachusetts, noticeably more than the influence of race.[52]

Most of this influence was due to teacher qualifications, which accounted for 64% of the total variance in student outcomes in South Carolina. Pupil–teacher ratios and school facilities added little (only 1%) to the explained variation. The strongest predictors of student failure were the proportion of teachers without any training or certification[53] and the proportion of vacancies open for more than 9 weeks, a measure of shortages usually associated with hiring substitutes or other less well-qualified teachers.

The proportions of teachers with advanced degrees and out-of-state training had a small positive influence on student achievement, suggesting some marginal effect of higher degrees and out-of-state training on teacher quality. When teachers trained outside the state appear more effective than those trained inside, this suggests a failure by the state to attend to the quality of teacher training programs, as well as to the quality of education in K–12 schools. (As I describe in the next chapter, some states have focused strategically on improving teachers' preparation as one of their levers for raising achievement—a particularly efficient use of state funding.)

In Massachusetts, student failure on the MCAS was significantly predicted by the proportions of uncertified teachers and administrators and underqualified paraprofessionals. These variables accounted for 50% of the variance on the math tests and 39% of the total variance in failing scores on the English test. In mathematics, a measure of the proportion of high school teachers teaching mathematics or computer science who were not certified in these fields added to the predictive power of the estimates.

Given that data to measure other dimensions of staff quality were not available in Massachusetts, it is not surprising that a measure of average teacher salary—which captures other aspects of quality—was also significant. Other resources also mattered. Both the student-teacher ratio and district spending, measured as a proportion of the state-approved foundation formula amount, which takes pupil needs into account, increased the variance explained by another 7% in English and 6% in mathematics.

When both student characteristics and these school resource measures were used to predict district performance, race and students' language status were no longer significant predictors of achievement. School resources matter strongly. In South Carolina, the combined effects of school resource variables accounted for as much of the total variance explained as did measures of race and poverty, and teachers' certification continued to exert a strongly significant influence on student achievement. In Massachusetts, teacher quality and overall spending continued to account for about 40% of the total variance in explained achievement, with the strongest predictors including average teacher salaries, the proportions of teachers unlicensed in the field they teach, and overall school spending.

The Ongoing Struggle

These analyses, like those of previous studies, make it clear that more equitable allocations of school resources could substantially reduce the failure rates of students of color and low-income students on the high-stakes measures that states have chosen to hold students and schools accountable. The issue is whether governments can be held accountable for their own performance in ensuring that all students have the conditions and resources necessary to support their right to learn.

The process continues to be a long one. In *Abbeville County School District v. South Carolina,* Judge Cooper noted that "many aspects of the system cry out for improvement," but that "this case has never been about what is *best* for the children of the State," but only to establish what would satisfy the state's obligation to provide a "minimally adequate education." The trial court denied the plaintiffs' claims for remedies regarding school facilities, qualified teachers, and support programs for struggling students, but did rule that early childhood intervention programs from prekindergarten to grade three were warranted. The matter is still in litigation on appeal.

In the *Hancock v. Driscoll* case in Massachusetts, trial court Judge Margot Botsford concurred that Massachusetts was not meeting its constitutional obligation to provide children in low-wealth school districts with an adequate education, and recent cuts in state support further reduced their ability to provide educational opportunity. The judge emphasized the importance of preschool, quality teaching, professional development for all teachers of students with disabilities, and adequate facilities, recommending that the state undertake a proper cost study to determine the extent of these needs.

On appeal, Chief Justice Margaret Marshall agreed that the "amply supported findings" of Judge Botsford reflect "serious inadequacies in public education" and "much that remains to be corrected before all children in our Commonwealth are educated." However, since the state had been making efforts at reform since an earlier school equity lawsuit in 1993, Marshall merely recommended that the legislature "rely on these findings as it continues to consider efforts to improve public education," concluding that "no one reading the . . . decision can be left with any doubt that the question is not *if* more money is needed, but how much."

UNDER WHAT CONDITIONS CAN MONEY MATTER?

In these ongoing struggles, the seemingly straightforward notion that a truly adequate investment could make a difference in school outcomes for low-income and minority students has been rejected by defenders of the status quo, who argue these students are unlikely to do better even with the resources their more affluent counterparts take for granted. Their argument takes two forms: first, that schools, especially the poor urban and rural schools that are the usual subjects of litigation, are incompetent or inefficient and would waste additional money if they received it, and second, that students are unable to benefit because they live in a "culture of poverty," experience poor parenting, or are, implicitly, though it is not usually said straightforwardly, innately inferior.

The Federal Court View

These arguments came before the U.S. Supreme Court for the first time in more than 30 years when *Flores v. Arizona* reached the Court in fall 2009. Initiated in 1992 by Miriam Flores and other parents of English language learners, the class action was brought to redress serious inadequacies in the English language learner (ELL) program in Nogales, Arizona, a small city along the Mexican border. Eight years later, a federal district court held that Arizona failed to provide school districts with the resources necessary to fulfill their obligation under the Equal Education Opportunities Act of 1974 to take "appropriate action" to overcome language barriers that impede equal participation by students.

After Arizona repeatedly failed to meet compliance deadlines, the district court threatened sanctions. The Arizona attorney general, governor, and Board of Education acknowledged that the state remained out of compliance, but the state superintendent of public instruction moved for relief from judgment, and state legislative leadership intervened to support the superintendent's motion. After an 8-day evidentiary hearing, the district court held that neither the law nor facts had changed in a manner that would change the original judgment, which remained unsatisfied. The federal Ninth Circuit Court of Appeal affirmed, and 17 years later—when children who were just born when the suit was brought were graduating from high school, if they were fortunate enough to make it through—the case reached the Supreme Court.

Experts for the state read like a who's who of conservative scholars—among them David Armor, John Chubb, Chester Finn, Eric Hanushek, Terry Moe, Frederick Hess, Paul Peterson, Michael Podgursky, and Abigail and Stephen Thernstrom—many of whom have argued against public education investments at the federal level and funding reforms for poor schools in the states. They argued that "Studies have overwhelmingly shown that court-ordered funding remedies ... are consistently ineffective," and that increased funding would encourage schools districts to "keep ELL students languishing in the program and segregated from other students to ensure that funding for ELL programming does not diminish or disappear."[54] Rather than disseminating knowledge about how funds can be used to pursue effective strategies, the state essentially argued that public officials serving low-income children would make bad decisions about spending, and thus should not be trusted with more money.

They further argued that "the dominant view of scholars [is] that educational reform should focus on student performance—the output of school systems—rather than inputs such as funding levels."[55] This opinion was rebutted in a separate amicus brief, signed by 30 current and former presidents of the American Educational Research Association and the National Academy of Education who argued that "education policy risks failure when it focuses predominantly on outcomes alone without giving sufficient attention to supports for student achievement and instructional quality. This is particularly true with regard to the education of at-risk groups such as the English Language Learners. . . . [W]ell-crafted outcome- and input-based education policies are mutually reinforcing."[56]

On June 25, 2009, in a 5–4 decision, the Court sent the Flores case[57] back to the trial court for further hearings to determine whether "changed circumstances" rendered the district court's 9-year-old order out-of-date—a move that could delay redress by several more years, or perhaps forever. Justice Samuel Alito's decision for the majority referred to "a growing consensus in education research that increased funding alone does not improve student achievement." Justice Stephen Breyer's dissent chastised the majority for including "references to the writings of [only] one side of a complex expert debate" and cited studies debunking the arguments that resources have no bearing on outcomes.

While experts and justices argue about whether educational inequities should even be acknowledged, much less corrected, the roots of inequality grow deeper and its fruit more bitter in many communities. Nonetheless when a commitment is finally made to invest thoughtfully in the education of the children who are generally left furthest behind, their ability to learn becomes obvious, with benefits to them, their communities, and our society as a whole.

Perseverance Pays Off: The Case of New Jersey

The long path to adequacy has been perhaps most torturously pursued and hard-won in the state of New Jersey, where nine court rulings over 30 years sought equalization in school funding for the urban minority districts that for decades spent far less than others serving wealthier children. The first round of the case was decided in 1973, when I was student teaching in Camden at a school more resource-poor than any I had ever before seen. It was ongoing when I worked for the Education Law Center documenting inequalities in next-door Philadelphia and wrote my dissertation on school finance in Pennsylvania, examining the New Jersey court's ruling as part of my analysis. It was relitigated several times while I went off to spend a decade as a policy analyst looking at issues of educational equity, then another as a professor in next-door New York where my students, many of whom were educators in New Jersey, discussed the extreme differences in resources encountered by those working in Newark and Paterson in contrast to those working in New Brunswick and Princeton. As the Education Law Center returned to court again and again, the state did an extended "rope-a-dope," just waiting for the lawsuits to stop. Over these years, the cities in New Jersey deteriorated nearly beyond the point of no return. Like other observers, I wondered whether the state would ever decide to take care of the Black and Brown children in its urban schools.

It took 3 decades to secure parity in funding, with a major settlement in 1998; it took until 2000 for a major investment in quality preschool to be instituted and until 2003 for an intensive instructional improvement initiative to be undertaken in the Abbott districts. By 2007, though, New Jersey had sharply increased its standing on national reading and math assessments—ranking in the top five states in all subject areas and grade levels on the NAEP and first in the nation in writing. It was also one of four states that made the most progress in closing achievement gaps between White and Black and Hispanic students over the previous 4 years in both 4th- and 8th-grade reading and math.[58] Among the top-scoring states, New Jersey served the largest share of low-income African American and Hispanic students (17% and 19% respectively), far more than other high-scorers such as Massachusetts, Vermont, Maine, and New Hampshire. Taking student demographics into account, New Jersey was the highest-achieving state in the nation by 2007.

Although there was still a long way to go to achieve parity, 4th- and 8th-grade Hispanic students scored 10 points above their peers nationwide in reading by 2007, while Black students scored 9 points above their national peers at the 4th-grade level and 5 points at the 8th-grade level.[59] In math, Hispanic students scored 7 points above their peers at both grade levels, and Black students scored 10 points above their national peers at the 4th-grade level and 5 points at the 8th-grade level.[60] The state also reduced the achievement gap for students with disabilities and for socioeconomically disadvantaged students (see Figures 4.4 and 4.5).

The Long Journey. How did this saga unfold? While the state Supreme Court first defined equalization in dollar terms in its 1973 *Robinson v. Cahill* decision, the state legislature ultimately responded with a funding scheme that preserved large inequalities in spending. It promised "thorough and efficient" education through lengthy checklists and monitoring activities that were to ensure that districts could demonstrate that they were implementing state regulations and a minimum basic skills curriculum, evaluated through state tests.[61] Paradoxically, this approach to "equity" deflected resources away from classroom instruction and toward the hiring of bureaucrats to manage elaborate planning, inspection, and reporting systems—a luxury the starving city schools could ill afford.

In 1976, New Jersey State Education commissioner Fred Burke expressed the view that has often surfaced in state resistance to equalizing funding: "Urban

Figure 4.4. New Jersey Reading Achievement Trends, 4th-Grade NAEP.

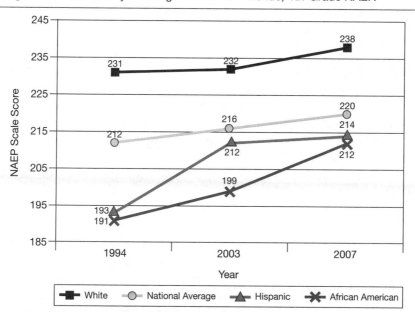

Source: National Assessment of Educational Progress, NAEP Data Trends.
Note: New Jersey was not represented in the 1998 and 2000 NAEP Assessments.

Figure 4.5. New Jersey Math Achievement Trends, 4th-Grade NAEP.

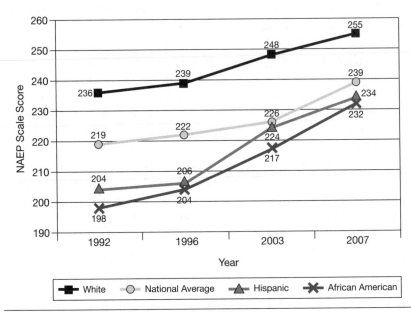

Source: National Assessment of Educational Progress, NAEP Data Trends.

children, even after years of remediation, will not be able to perform in school as well as their suburban counterparts. . . . We are just being honest."[62] These kinds of statements have appeared in many state defenses of their inequitable school finance systems to justify the status quo.

New Jersey did not appreciably close the spending or resource gap among its wealthy and poor districts until after the ninth court ruling, which was issued in 1997. Meanwhile, the status quo was well preserved. As Jean Anyon notes, "During the next two decades [after 1973] the cities, which were closely monitored by the state, did offer a basic skills curriculum to students, while the suburbs continued to offer sophisticated curriculum programs and a range of courses."[63] As plaintiffs noted in one round of litigation in the 1980s, wealthy and predominantly White Montclair offered foreign languages at the preschool level while poor and predominantly Black Paterson did not offer any until high school—and then, relatively few. And while 20% of eleventh and twelfth graders in wealthy Moorestown participated in Advanced Placement courses, none was even offered in any school in poor and predominantly Black Camden and East Orange.[64]

Along the way, inequalities in spending grew, with rich districts such as Princeton spending twice what some poor—then virtually all Black—districts had available. Responding to a second lawsuit that was brought in 1981 and finally decided in 1990, the state argued that funding should not be increased to poorer districts because it might be mismanaged and wasted and that "money is not a critical factor in the quality of education in the first place."[65] Resources such as course offerings, teacher experience and education, and class sizes or staffing ratios, the state suggested, were not reliable indicators of the quality of education. Such quality could be better evaluated by monitoring the implementation of state regulations and mandates, a massive bureaucratic activity that consumed reams of paper, but did little to ensure high-quality teaching in classrooms. The state further argued that these urban, minority students did not need the same kind or quality of education as students in wealthy suburbs: "The [basic skills] education currently offered in these poorer urban districts is tailored to the students' present need. . . . These students simply cannot now benefit from the kind of vastly superior course offerings found in the richer districts."[66]

In its 1990 decision, the Court explicitly rejected these arguments, replying that it did not believe that students in poorer districts were less capable than others, less deserving of a rich curriculum, or less able to benefit from one. Although the Court once again found the state funding system unconstitutional, it would be another decade before large infusions of funds would find their way into the by-then entirely dysfunctional urban districts after yet another major lawsuit had been brought. A tax revolt waylaid the Quality Education Act that had been passed in 1990 to remedy these inequalities, and the Court declared the system unconstitutional again in the 1994 decision with a now-familiar litany that had begun to seem like the Bill Murray movie *Groundhog Day,* in which Murray's character wakes up each day, doomed to repeat the same set of events over and over again until he can finally learn to get it right.

While New Jersey lawmakers were avoiding responsibility for paying for the education of poor, minority students, here is how the state education department described the education of students in Newark in 1994:

> Children in the Newark public schools . . . endure degrading school environments that virtually ensure academic failure. . . . [In many classrooms] there is nothing. . . . Science laboratories lack basic equipment. [Students], with rare exceptions, sit dutifully in rows, filling in the blanks in workbooks with answers to items having to do with isolated skills, or listening to a teacher deliver facts or talk about skills, divorced from meaningful context. . . . Seldom in any class observed, no matter what the grade level or subject, were students being taught how to write, how to read for understanding, how to solve problems, or how to think critically.

Physical conditions in most of the schools . . . reveal neglect. . . . Holes in floors and walls; dirty classrooms with blackboards so worn as to be unusable; filthy lavatories without toilet paper, soap or paper towels; inoperable water fountains, . . . and foul-smelling effluent running from a school into the street, speak of disregard . . . for students and teachers. . . . A virtual army of supervisors, administrators, and coordinators holds all this in place, passing various . . . forms from one layer of bureaucracy to the next, while schools go unpainted for as long as 14 years, and in classroom after classroom, whole banks of lights are without fluorescent tubes or light shields.

These conditions tell of shocking neglect. Equally shocking, however, is the lack of indignation on the part of staff. One teacher interviewed explained it this way: "After a while," she said, looking around, "You lower your expectations."[67]

Still, the state argued that money did not make a difference. In fact, the state actually decreased K–12 education funding by 3% between 1993 and 1995, while increasing the funding for prisons and other corrections budgets by 25%.[68] No doubt the money was needed to handle the swelling school-to-prison pipeline fed in large part by devastatingly poor schools in Newark, Camden, Trenton, Paterson, and Jersey City, among others. By this time, the state had also taken over three of these urban districts, appointing state administrators to run them. Ironically, after several years of state administration, with no appreciable rise in test scores, state department officials reported that they could not turn around the schools in these cities because there was not enough money to do so.[69]

First Steps Toward a Remedy. Finally, a major infusion of funding to the high-need districts, leveraged by the courts and engineered by moderate Republican governor Christine Todd Whitman, occurred in 1997. In its 1994 and 1997 *Abbott v. Burke* decisions, the New Jersey Supreme Court ordered "parity" funding—that is, state aid to bring per pupil revenues in the 28 (later 30) *Abbott* districts up to the average per-pupil expenditure in the state's 110 successful, suburban districts. The court allowed the state a phase-in period, reaching parity for the first time in the 1997–1998 school year with an allocation of $246 million in parity aid, followed by an additional $312 million in supplemental programs assistance for which districts could apply. The funds, further specified in a 1998 decision, were to be spent to implement a new state curriculum linked to the state standards, support whole school reform, ensure early childhood education for 3- and 4-year-olds and full-day kindergarten, enable class-size reduction, invest in technology, ensure adequate facilities, and support health, social services, alternative, and summer school programs to help students catch up.

Implementation issues regarding the provision of early childhood education led to yet another round of litigation that led the court in 2000 to outline the preschool requirements in more detail, including substantive educational standards, certified staff, and a maximum student-teacher ratio of 15 to 1.[70] Facilities resources were also delayed, but eventually new resources began to arrive in these educationally starved districts.

By time the new resources arrived, however, the districts had so few well-qualified staff at the school or central office levels, so much deferred maintenance, such paltry curriculum resources, and such mangled systems for everything from recruitment and hiring to purchasing and accounting that it took some time to begin to build functioning systems again. The problems of recruiting and retaining qualified staff were the most severe. There was impatience on the part of those unfamiliar with how the insides of these districts had crumbled and many in the media and the state assembly wondered why the sudden large influx of funds was not producing large, immediate gains in student achievement.

The early windup toward a solution was also somewhat slowed by the court's initial insistence that each school in the targeted districts had to choose one of the New American Schools' whole school reform models and a specific packaged reading program—in part because of the common assumption that only packaged programs and outside vendors could build capacity in these places where districts were so dysfunctional. Former state legislator Gordon MacInnes, then president of Citizens for Better Schools, noted: "By pushing [Whole School Reform] as the best path to improved literacy, the education commissioner and [New Jersey Supreme Court] were tacitly accepting the premise of the reform movement: city school districts are too corrupt, bureaucratic, or incompetent, or a mix of all three, to assume academic leadership."[71]

But MacInnes points out, this requirement created incoherence. By 2001, Newark's 75 schools had adopted 10 different models, most of which were not designed to focus on the improvement of instruction, and produced no coherent district curriculum, assessment data, or instructional supports; little professional development support; and no provisions for English language learners or special education students, other than segregation from their peers. "Districts complained of high costs, poor service, high turnover among the field staff, and inconsistent or irrelevant advice," MacInnes notes. Said one principal, "The developers have taken over."[72]

Although some of the interventions, the enhanced services (counselors, social workers, before- and afterschool programs), and the Abbott-required class-size reductions (to no more than 21 students per class in K–3) helped to some extent, most districts made only small gains in the first few years. Those that showed strong progress—Union City, West New York, and Perth Amboy—had adopted the Comer model district-wide, which created a strong student-focused culture in the schools focused on healthy development and adult collaboration, and then worked from the district level to improve instruction.

Union City, which was 96% Latino and the state's poorest district, was an ac-knowledged leader, showing the strongest gains and reaching proficiency levels for its largely low-income, English language learning students that were comparable to those for nonurban students in the state by 2006. Its strategies became the basis for the revised remedy that was put in place in 2003, which stimulated the large gains that have since occurred for urban students statewide and which demonstrate how well-spent money can make a major difference.

Elements of a Real Remedy

Analysts attribute the significant progress in New Jersey's highest-need districts after 2003 in part to two major foci that augmented the stronger resource base for instruction: the exceptionally well-managed investments in quality preschool and investments in stronger pedagogy, especially in early literacy.[73] Below, I review these strategies briefly to illustrate how a state can approach the problem of improvement at scale, when resources are available.

Investments in Quality Preschool. The 2000 *Abbott v. Burke* Supreme Court deci-sion ordered that high-quality preschool be provided to all 3- and 4-year-olds in New Jersey's 30 poorest school districts. As part of this ruling, the Court mandated that all lead teachers in these districts acquire a bachelor's degree and an early child-hood credential by September 2004—an order that many states would consider impossible to implement. In 2000, only 15% of early childhood teachers in private settings met these criteria. By 2004, approximately 90% of the Abbott districts' early childhood teaching force had a bachelor's degree and were at least provisionally certified. By 2007, 97% were fully certified and college-educated.[74]

Quality indicators based on observations of activities and interactions in pre-school classrooms increased dramatically over this time—with the number of class-rooms rated near the top of the scale doubling to 72% between 2003 and 2007, and evidence about student learning following suit. The National Institute for Early Education Research assessed more than 1,000 kindergarten students from Abbott districts in 2006 and found that those who had attended 2 years of preschool cut the "vocabulary gap" in half.[75] Districts such as Union City and West New York, which could track individual students, found that those who attended preschool performed significantly better on state tests by third grade than those who did not have pre-school, actually exceeding the state average proficiency rate on language arts tests.[76]

This impressive transformation suggests how it is possible to provide access and raise quality in a short period of time. Researchers note that these outcomes were especially associated with the investments in teacher quality. To accomplish this, New Jersey created a specialized P–3 certification with multiple preparation routes, including pre-service and in-service training with mentoring and supervision. Teachers pursuing their degrees were provided with full-tuition scholarships, tuition coupons, and loan forgiveness; a substitute teacher pool was created to give teachers time to attend school; and laptop computers were provided to provide access to distance learning opportunities.[77] The state created a statewide professional development center to help teachers get access to information and training. The state and private foundations provided grants to help build the capacity of colleges to provide early care and education courses, including on nights and weekends, and the state developed articulation agreements between 2-year and 4-year institutions so that transfers would be seamless. Finally, the state increased salaries for teachers working in Abbott pre-K classrooms, so that these better-prepared teachers would not leave the preschool sector for better-paying jobs in elementary schools.

Investments in Quality Pedagogy. In April 2003, the Court allowed New Jersey to replace the WSR mandates with an approach emphasizing instructional improvement supported by intensive professional development, following the lead of Union City. By 2005, more than 80% of districts had dropped their WSR contracts. The state created an early literacy program statewide and required it for the Abbott districts that did not have a WSR in place. New Jersey persuaded the U.S. Department of Education (USDOE) to allow its Reading First funds to be used for classroom libraries of at least 300 titles, rather than the scripted reading packages that USDOE generally endorsed. The state was permitted to include age-appropriate native language texts for English learners, which supported its bilingual instruction emphasis, also a strategy generally discouraged by the federal department at that time.[78]

New Jersey's Office of Urban Literacy supported districts in developing a comprehensive literacy curriculum, not a jumble of different packaged programs, mapped to the standards in a process involving teachers, connected to local preschool programs, and featuring significant reading of trade books and small-group instruction in the long blocks of time set aside for uninterrupted literacy work.

Extensive professional development helped administrators and teachers learn how to use frequent diagnostic assessments of student progress tied to instructional planning. Based on school needs, a wide range of professional development was made available to support reading and writing across the curriculum, special education and English language learner assistance, and extra attention for all students who fall behind—ideally provided before or after school by the regular classroom teacher who knows the students and what they need well. Administrators were expected to attend this professional development along with teachers.

The transformation of students' experiences is illustrated by this description of Orange, one of the first districts to engage in this approach. A district serving more than 70% low-income students, 83% African American and the remainder Haitian and Latino, Orange jumped from a 4th-grade reading proficiency rate of 22% in 1999 to 75% by 2007, nearly at the state average. By 2007:

A school-wide committee that includes teachers, coaches, and the school "facilitator" meets twice weekly to discuss the problems of individual students and to agree on concrete steps to be taken. Students talk freely of the books they select from the classroom library for independent reading and how they use the Internet to gather information for their research papers. What is most obvious is the shared focus on academics, the continuous use of evidence from student work, and the attention given to struggling students.[79]

The state has also launched a set of new teacher education programs specifically focused on preparing teachers for effective urban teaching in the high-need Abbott districts, operated through several state universities. These programs have created school-university partnerships to provide both intensive field experiences for teacher candidates and professional learning opportunities for veteran teachers. The department has also expanded professional development to other subject areas and grade levels, with special funding and assistance in high-need schools to model effective practices.[80] At the secondary level, these professional development initiatives are now coupled with an initiative to create personalized small learning communities that provide advisory supports (something I discuss further in Chapter 8), along with curriculum reforms to better prepare students for college and careers.

It seems clear that, in the long run, although every cent of new funding may not have been used as strategically as it might have been had the districts been rescued from disrepair earlier, money ultimately did make a difference—and, thoughtfully used, resources have created the possibility that these districts will someday provide a fully adequate, perhaps even excellent, level of education for the students they serve.

A Tale of Three States: What Happens When States Invest Strategically (or Don't)

Education is our future—it's everything. We must not settle for anything short of excellence in our schools.

—Governor James B. Hunt, North Carolina

Education has always been at the core of Connecticut's success. . . . I'm convinced that Yankee ingenuity begins in our classrooms today and grows our economy tomorrow.

—Governor M. Jodi Rell, Connecticut

[California has] become a low-spending, low-resource state, with low levels of learning . . . dilapidated buildings and inadequate textbooks, overcrowded class-rooms and unqualified teachers. . . . California (could) become a state where no one trusts its workers, a first-rank economy that has to import skilled employees, a republic with citizens unprepared for civic responsibility and susceptible to circus democracy, a once-mythic place that others shun for its high costs, poor schools, and unequal opportunity. . . . A middle-school student nails the right question: "How could a state so rich do so poorly?"

—W. Norton Grubb, Professor, University of California, Berkeley

New Jersey's story, described in the previous chapter, illustrates how smart, focused use of resources in high-need communities can make a major difference in student achievement in a relatively short period of time for students who have been furthest

behind. New Jersey's is not a lone case. Massachusetts, as we noted in the last chapter, also made strong gains with the investments that followed *Hancock v. Driscoll,* though achievement gaps started to grow again after 2003.[1] Even earlier, during the 1980s and 1990s, several states undertook purposeful systemic reforms that created the conditions for strong teaching and produced substantial achievement gains.

In this chapter, I tell the tale of two such states—Connecticut and North Carolina—that achieved strong results as a result of school funding invested where it matters most. I also tell the cautionary tale of another state—California—that invested neither adequately nor wisely, squandering the gains it could have achieved after equalizing funding (briefly) in the 1970s, and creating policies that make it harder for schools to use their limited resources effectively. Money is necessary, but money alone is not enough: Resources must be used strategically to produce strong results.

Strategic investment not only includes incentives to districts to spend their funds on things that will make a difference. It also includes forbearance from ill-considered interference that forces schools to spend resources unwisely, and it includes the construction of a strong state infrastructure to support schools with knowledge about good practice, a steady supply of well-prepared educators, useful information about performance, and assistance for ongoing improvement. These are features of governmental systems that are central to the strong performance of many high-achieving nations, though poorly developed in many U.S. states. In the next chapter, I describe strategies pursued by nations that have dramatically improved their education systems with smart, purposeful investments in the core elements of a strong public education system that allow them to operate high-quality schools at relatively moderate cost.

THE CASES OF CONNECTICUT AND NORTH CAROLINA: STRATEGIC RESOURCES USED WELL

Connecticut and North Carolina are examples of how state policymakers upgraded teachers' knowledge and skills, along with standards for students and teachers, as a means of improving student learning in states that serve large proportions of low-income and minority students.[2] Beginning in the 1980s, these two states enacted some of the nation's most ambitious efforts to improve teaching. Both of these states were extensively studied by the National Education Goals Panel when their efforts resulted in sharp increases in student performance. On the heels of their efforts, both states registered striking gains in overall student learning and narrowed achievement gaps between advantaged and disadvantaged pupils.

During the 1990s, North Carolina posted the largest student achievement gains of any state in mathematics, and it realized substantial progress in reading, becoming the first Southern state to score above the national average in 4th-grade reading and math, although it had entered the decade near the bottom of the state rankings. Of all states during the 1990s, it was also the most successful in narrowing the minority-White achievement gap.[3] In 2007, it remained the top-scoring Southern state in mathematics, ranking on a par with states such as Idaho and Maine, which had many fewer poor and minority students.

Similarly, in Connecticut, fourth graders ranked first in the nation in reading and math on the NAEP by 1998, despite increasing numbers of low-income, minority, and new immigrant students in the state's public schools during that time.[4] More eighth graders in Connecticut were proficient in reading and writing than in any other state, and, in the world, only top-ranked Singapore outscored Connecticut students in science. The achievement gap between White and minority students decreased, and the more than 25% of Connecticut's students who were Black or Hispanic substantially outperformed their counterparts nationally[5] (see Figures 5.1 and 5.2).

In 2007, among the states that ranked in the top five in reading, writing, and mathematics on the NAEP, Connecticut and New Jersey were the only two that had African American and Latino students comprising more than 30% of their public school populations (see Table 5.1 and Figure 5.3).

Figure 5.1. Trends in 4th-Grade Reading Achievement, NAEP (1992–1998).

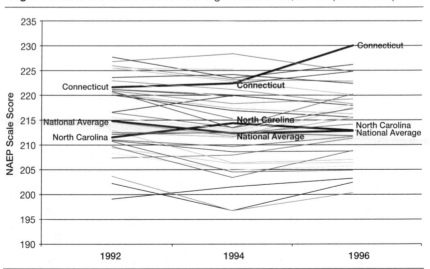

Source: National Assessment of Educational Progress State Data Trends.

Figure 5.2. Trends in 4th-Grade Math Achievement, NAEP (1992–2000).

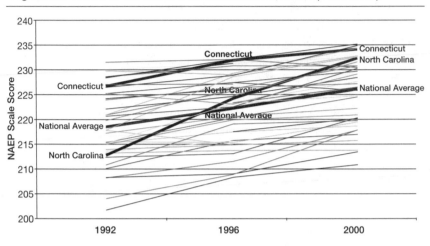

Source: National Assessment of Educational Progress, State Data Trends.

Figure 5.3. Student Demographics in States Scoring in the Top Decile in Reading, Writing, or Mathematics on the 2007 National Assessment of Educational Progress.

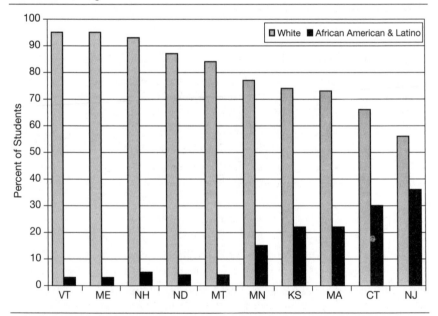

Source: National Assessment of Educational Progress, State Profiles (2008).

Table 5.1. State Rankings on the National Assessment of Educational Progress, 2007 (Percentage of Students Scoring "Proficient" or Above).

Rank	Reading		Writing	Math	
	4th	*8th*	*8th*	*4th*	*8th*
1	MA (49)	MA(43)	NJ (56)	MA(58)	MA(51)
2	NJ (43)	VT (42)	CT (53)	KS (51)	MN(43)
3	NH (42)	MT (39)	MA (45)	NH (51)	KS (41)
4	CT (41)	NJ (39)	VT (40)	NJ (51)	ND(41)
5	VT (41)	CT (38)	ME (39)	MN(50)	VT (41)
		MN(38)	NH (39)		

Source: National Assessment Educational Progress (2007a; 2007b).

Connecticut's reforms followed the 1977 *Horton v. Meskill* decision,[6] in which the Connecticut Supreme Court became one of the first of the state high courts, along with California's and New Jersey's, to invalidate a state education finance system because its reliance on local property taxes generated greatly unequal spending. Later reforms were prodded by the filing of the *Sheff v. O'Neill*[7] lawsuit in 1989, challenging racially segregated schools. North Carolina reforms occurred as a committed education governor, James B. Hunt, serving a total of 16 years over the course of 2 decades, pledged to lift what was initially a low-achieving state to much higher levels of education.

Both of these states raised standards for teacher education and licensing, while also raising and equalizing teacher salaries and creating subsidies for preparing teachers who would work in high-need fields and high-need locations. North Carolina required all of the state's public teacher education institutions to become nationally accredited, leveraging improvements as they met more rigorous standards. Connecticut increased standards for state accreditation of teacher education. Both states funded professional development school initiatives for improving teacher training; both instituted mentoring for beginning teachers; and both created an infrastructure for ongoing intensive professional development.

Each of these states instituted new learning standards for both students and teachers, and created assessments to evaluate progress. Connecticut created performance assessments that engaged students in writing extensively and solving open-ended problems. North Carolina created new assessments emulating the National Assessment of Educational Progress, to upgrade the expectations for critical thinking and problem solving. Most notably, both held to the course of these reforms over a sustained period—more than 15 years in each case. In what follows I describe how these two states pursued these similar reforms in different ways, appropriate to the distinctive political cultures of a Northern state with a strong tradition of local control and a Southern state with a tradition of stronger state management.

Connecticut: Developing a Teaching Profession

Strategic Investments in Teaching. In explaining Connecticut's strong achievement gains, the National Educational Goals Panel[8] cited the state's teacher policies as a critical element. Following the recommendations of a blue-ribbon commission appointed by the governor, the 1986 Education Enhancement Act pursued a theory of action that professionalizing teaching would improve student learning. At that time, there were severe shortages of teachers in the state's cities, and large numbers of teachers were hired without preparation. There were also concerns across the state about teachers' content knowledge and their training for teaching. The bill coupled major increases in teacher salaries with higher standards for teacher education and licensing, and substantial investments in beginning teacher mentoring and professional development.

An initial investment of $300 million—the result of a state surplus—was used to boost minimum beginning teacher salaries in an equalizing fashion that made it possible for low-wealth districts to compete in the market for qualified teachers. As a local control state, Connecticut did not require districts to meet the minimum salary level, but provided substantial salary aid to districts that used the funds to do so. Funds were allocated based on the number of fully certified teachers, creating incentives for districts to recruit those who had met the new high certification standards, and for individuals to meet these standards. Salary schedules remained locally bargained, and the new minimum created a floor on which the rest of the schedule was raised. Between 1986 and 1991, the average teacher's salary increased by more than 50%, from $29,437 in 1986 to $47,823 in 1991. The equalizing nature of the state aid made it possible for urban districts to compete for qualified teachers.

With these incentives, emergency credentials were eliminated. To ensure an adequate supply of qualified teachers, the state offered incentives including scholarships and forgivable loans to attract high-ability teacher candidates, especially teachers of color and those in high-demand fields, and encouraged well-qualified teachers from other states to come to Connecticut by creating license reciprocity. These initiatives quickly eliminated teacher shortages, even in the cities, and created surpluses of teachers within 3 years of its passage.[9] This allowed districts to be highly selective in their hiring and demanding in their expectations for teacher expertise. By 1990, nearly a third of the state's newly hired teachers had graduated from colleges rated "very selective" or better in the Barron's Index of College Majors, and 75% had undergraduate grade point averages of "B" or better.[10]

This alone would not have been enough to raise teaching quality, however. The state also raised teacher education and licensing standards by requiring a major in the discipline to be taught plus extensive knowledge of teaching and learning—including knowledge about literacy development and the teaching of special needs students. Candidates were required to pass tests of subject matter and knowledge of teaching to receive a license, after which they received support from trained mentor teachers and completed a sophisticated assessment program using state-trained assessors for determining who could continue in teaching after the initial year.

These assessments evolved into portfolio assessments modeled on those of the National Board for Professional Teaching Standards, which assess teachers' abilities by examining teachers' plans, videotapes of their teaching, evidence of student learning, and teachers' analyses of their practice.

Together, these activities have had far-reaching effects. Most Connecticut teachers and principals—and many teacher educators—have participated in the new teacher assessment system as candidates, mentors, or assessors trained to score the portfolios. Teacher preparation was organized around the development of evidence connected to the standards. Because the assessments focus on the development of teacher competence, are tightly tied to student standards, and lead to sophisticated analysis of practice, the assessment system serves as a focal point for improving teaching and learning.

As part of ongoing teacher education reforms, the state agency supported the creation of professional development schools linked to local universities and more than 100 school-university partnerships. It funded a set of Institutes for Teaching and Learning and developed courses on teacher and student standards that could be applied toward the master's degree, which is required for a continuing license. Intensive professional development programs in the teaching of reading and writing were launched, along with 4-week summer institutes in mathematics, science, and technology for elementary, middle, and high school teachers.[11]

In 2000, the state launched an Early Reading Success initiative to train a cadre of literacy experts in the use of diagnostic assessments and individualized instruction. The initially trained teachers, librarians, and principals continued to meet monthly to update their skills, receiving followup support from regional service centers. The training expanded over time to encompass all educators in priority high-need schools. A state Blueprint for Reading was developed to guide pre-service teacher preparation as well as in-service training and school curriculum.[12]

Investments in School Leadership. Connecticut also developed standards for school leaders and used them to guide all aspects of state education leadership policy, including accreditation of preparation programs, licensing of administrators, continuing professional development requirements, and administrator evaluation. These standards are much more focused on instructional leadership than programs in many other states; principals are required to study learning and pedagogy, curriculum development, supervision and evaluation of teachers, and the teaching of exceptional children. The state works closely with universities and districts to advance instructional reforms consistent with standards.

In 2001, the state created the Connecticut Administrator Test (CAT), an innovative performance assessment that poses challenging, authentic problems for potential principals based on the standards. The CAT consists of four modules lasting 6 hours. Two modules require the candidate as an instructional supervisor to make recommendations for supporting a teacher in response to the teacher's lesson plan, videotaped lesson, and samples of student work. The other two modules ask the candidate to describe a school improvement process or respond to a particular schoolwide problem based on school and community profiles and data about student learning. Candidates must pass this rigorous test in order to be licensed to practice, and state accreditation for universities depends, in part, on how well its candidates do on the test. If 80% or more do not pass, the university must redesign its program.

Furthermore, because the assessment is evaluated by experienced Connecticut administrators and university faculty, who are trained for scoring, it provides a powerful professional development opportunity for these other Connecticut professionals and a shared sense of standards of practice throughout the state. In line with the expectations of the assessment, Connecticut principals reported, in a recent national survey, that they were more likely to be engaged in problem-based learning in their preparation programs than those in other states and more likely to work with parents and staff on solving schoolwide problems.[13]

Building on its rigorous initial licensing assessment, the state developed school leader evaluation and professional development guidelines in 2002, which are the basis for targeting specific instructional leadership skills to be included in each principal's professional development plan. Given these strategies it is not surprising that Connecticut principals reported in a national survey that they felt better prepared than others nationally to evaluate teachers and provide instructional feedback, develop curriculum and instruction to support learning, and develop professional development for teachers.[14]

Development of Student Standards and Assessments. In addition to the state's major investments in teaching and leadership, the Goals Panel analysis of Connecticut's gains also pointed to the thoughtful use of student standards and assessments. In 1987, following the teaching reforms, student learning standards were adopted in one of the earliest efforts to link student expectations to teacher education standards and expectations for teaching. In 1993–1994, the student standards were updated to emphasize higher-order thinking skills and performance abilities, and new assessments were developed; these include constructed response and performance assessments that measure reading and writing authentically and reflect more challenging learning goals than the previous tests. Students write extensively, conduct scientific investigations, and solve complex multistep problems while explaining the reasoning for their answers. In line with professional testing standards, the law precludes the use of these assessments as the basis for promotion or graduation of students. Instead, they are used primarily for ongoing improvements of curriculum and teaching.

The Goals Panel report noted the benefits of the state's low-stakes testing approach, which reports and analyzes data in ways that help teachers and school leaders deeply understand the standards and students' progress. The State Department of Education supports the diagnostic use of test results by giving districts computerized data sets that allow analyses at the district, school, teacher, and individual pupil level to guide school improvement. The department also assists districts in analyzing the data so they can identify needs and areas for concentrated work.

Improvements in Urban Districts. This approach to assessment enabled districts to clarify their teaching priorities and helped galvanize district efforts to make major revisions in curriculum and instruction. The state provided targeted resources to the neediest districts, including funding for professional development for teachers and administrators, preschool and all-day kindergarten for students, and smaller pupil–teacher ratios, among other supports. Among the 10 Connecticut districts that made the greatest progress in reading between 1990 and 1998, three—New Britain, Norwalk, and Middletown—were urban school systems in the group identified as the state's "neediest" districts based on the percentage of students eligible for free lunch programs and their state test scores (see Figure 5.4).

Figure 5.4. Gains in Connecticut Mastery Test Scores, 1993–1998.

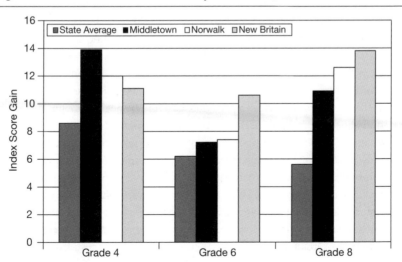

Source: Baron (1999).

Among the policies that contributed to this success were those that enabled districts to hire and retain highly qualified teachers who had been prepared to teach a wide range of learners and that provided state-trained mentors for all novice teachers, thus increasing the knowledge and skills of veteran teachers along with beginners involved with the program.[15]

In addition, district administrators and teachers described how helpful they found the state- and locally supported professional development around the teaching of reading. Consistent with the student standards and the state assessments, professional development funds were orchestrated to improve teachers' knowledge of how to teach reading through a balanced approach to whole language and skill-based instruction, how to address reading difficulties through specific intervention strategies, and how to diagnose and treat specific learning disabilities. Most of the districts had developed cadres of teacher trainers or coaches who were experts in literacy development and who were available to work with colleagues in the schools, offering demonstration teaching as well as classroom coaching. A number used state grants to sponsor intensive summer literacy workshops focused on the teaching of at-risk readers.

The approaches to reading instruction used in improving districts relied on the enhanced teacher knowledge spurred by Connecticut's teacher education reforms and reflected in the state's teaching assessments: systematic teaching of reading and spelling skills (including linguistics training); use of authentic reading materials—children's literature, periodicals, and trade books—along with daily writing and discussion of ideas; ongoing assessment of students' reading proficiency through strategies such as running records, miscue analyses, and analysis of reading, writing, and speaking samples; and intervention strategies for students with reading delays, such as Reading Recovery, which was used in 9 of the 10 sharply improving districts and was widely used across the state.[16] Ironically, Reading Recovery is one of several programs that were made ineligible for federal funds just a few years later as a result of the problematic management of the Reading First program.

District administrators also noted the importance of the system's coherence, which allowed them to pursue these sophisticated strategies for teaching and learning. In addition to their work on teacher development, they described how they had realigned district curriculum and instruction to the student learning standards and assessments, and how they had used the rich information about student performance made available by the state department of education as the basis for school problem solving and teachers' individual growth plans, which are part of the state-required teacher evaluation system. They also credited the fact that the state assessments measured reading and writing in authentic ways, the preparation and professional development programs were supportive of the same approaches, and beginning teachers were coming to them better prepared to teach to these standards, while veterans also had many opportunities to develop.

Summary. Improved achievement in Connecticut can be traced to a well-developed statewide infrastructure designed to encourage high-quality teaching by

- Developing thoughtful, subject-specific standards for both students and teachers that also emphasized inquiry and applications of skills through the use of performance assessments
- Raising and equalizing salaries, while simultaneously raising standards for preparing, entering, and remaining in teaching
- Providing intensive support and assessment of prospective and beginning teachers and school leaders
- Requiring and supporting continued high-quality professional development for teachers and administrators

These factors helped establish a foundation of professional expertise that enabled educators to improve instruction when they analyzed student achievement results, and set out to develop school improvement plans. In the absence of deep professional knowledge, these often become frustrating and fruitless activities that lead to little productive change.

North Carolina: Pursuing a Higher Standard

Investments in Teaching. North Carolina's reforms were launched with omnibus legislation in 1983, toward the end of Governor James B. Hunt's first two-term stint in office, as part of his strong commitment to lift North Carolina up from the status of a low-spending, low-achieving state, like others in the Southeast at that time. The Elementary and Secondary School Reform Act, which enhanced school funding, also upgraded curriculum expectations for students; increased licensure and preparation standards for teaching and school administration; upgraded standards for schools of education; created expectations for more professional staffing and evaluation of personnel, while lowering class sizes and increasing instructional time; established the principle of salary differentiation by teachers' education and performance, as well as seniority; authorized a new scholarship program to recruit talented individuals into teaching; and expanded professional development. This bill laid the groundwork for a series of initiatives throughout the 1980s, which were expanded further in the 1990s.

With a deep respect for teaching, Governor Hunt was the son of the school teacher, and had himself trained to teach, receiving a B.S. in agricultural education before, as he jokingly likes to say, he decided teaching was too challenging, and he went on to law school. He also attributes his later interest in standards for teaching in part to his student teaching experience, which he has observed did not have clearly stated expectations for what a good teacher was supposed to know and be able to do.[17] Hunt later served as the founding chair of the National

Board for Professional Teaching Standards, launched in 1987 as the first national effort to set professional standards for teaching and to assess teachers' capacity in the classroom.

As a policymaker, Hunt was determined to ensure that teachers would have the opportunity to become competent and effective, that the profession would be able to attract and retain talented teachers, and that all students would have access to strong teaching. Thus, across his two long terms in office (from 1977 to 1985 and from 1993 to 2001), North Carolina continually worked on the improvement of teaching.

Following the omnibus act in 1983, the state increased licensing requirements for teachers and principals, requiring tests of subject-matter and teaching knowledge, as well as stronger training. It also required all publicly funded schools of education to become professionally accredited by the National Council for the Accreditation of Teacher Education (NCATE), which caused many colleges to have to improve their curriculum and increase their investments in preparing teachers in order to stay in business.

The state also launched teacher development initiatives such as the Mathematics and Science Education Network (NC-MSEN), created in 1984 and still operating today, which operates a variety of programs to improve the quality of mathematics and science teaching and learning. Through 10 centers located on campuses of the University of North Carolina and one center located at the North Carolina School of Science and Mathematics, NC-MSEN trains teacher leaders and coaches as well as offering annual institutes. In addition, the NC-MSEN Pre-College Program supports enrichment for middle and high school students to increase the pool of students who graduate from North Carolina's high schools prepared to pursue careers that require mathematics and science. The state's strong achievement gains in mathematics are often attributed to these initiatives. Professional development initiatives were also undertaken across other subject areas, including instructional support for reading, the National Writing Project, and supports for using technology.

To ensure that good candidates could be recruited and could afford to enter teaching, the state launched an aggressive fellowship program to recruit hundreds of able high school students into teacher preparation each year by entirely subsidizing their college education. The highly selective North Carolina Teaching Fellows program—launched in 1986 and still in operation today—pays all college costs, including an enhanced and fully funded teacher education program, in return for several years of teaching. The program enhances the teaching pool by bringing a disproportionate number of males, minorities, and math and science teachers into the profession. After 7 years, retention rates in teaching for these recruits have exceeded 75%, with many of the other alumni holding positions as principals or central office leaders.[18]

To keep teachers in the profession, North Carolina also launched one of the nation's first beginning teacher mentoring programs in the 1980s, offering support to new teachers and financial incentives for mentor teachers. This program was expanded during the 1990s. A 1998 report by the National Education Goals Panel applauded North Carolina for having made large gains in mentoring beginning teachers as well as the greatest student achievement gains of any state.[19] These efforts were supplemented by professional development academies and a North Carolina Center for the Advancement of Teaching, which offers additional help to novice teachers for learning to teach the state curriculum. To make teaching a more attractive profession and to recruit individuals who could meet the new, higher standards, North Carolina boosted salaries in the mid-1980s and again in the 1990s.

In another major round of reform during his second stint as governor, Hunt passed the 1997 Educational Excellence Act. This followed his service as chair of the National Commission on Teaching and America's Future, which outlined a set of reforms to improve recruitment, preparation, retention, and career development for teachers. The 1997 law was primarily aimed at further efforts to upgrade the quality of teacher preparation and teaching quality, pouring hundreds of millions of dollars into a new set of reforms. The act created a professional standards board for teaching and required that all colleges of education create professional development school partnerships as the sites for yearlong student teaching practicums. It also funded a more intensive beginning teacher mentoring program, further upgraded licensing standards, created pay incentives for teachers who pursue master's degrees and Board certification, and authorized funds to raise teacher salaries to the national average, a goal once viewed as dauntingly far off, but ultimately achieved.

With a statewide minimum salary schedule, North Carolina was able to make sweeping changes within the schedule, and was the first state to add an increase of 12% to the base salary of all teachers who were able to achieve the distinction of National Board certification—a groundbreaking initiative to establish performance pay based on teachers' competence in the classroom.

Board certification is awarded to veteran teachers based on a structured portfolio of evidence about practice—including videotapes illustrating specific practices, student work samples, and teacher commentaries that provide analyses of teaching intentions, rationales, and outcomes—as well as tests of content and pedagogical knowledge in the area of the certification. In addition to the fact that teachers' performance on this measure has been found in most studies to predict their effectiveness in supporting learning gains for students,[20] teachers often find it one of the most powerful professional learning experiences they have ever had.[21] North Carolina introduced the most wide-ranging set of incentives in the nation for teachers to pursue National Board certification and at the time of this writing boasted more Board-certified teachers than any other state.

A recent North Carolina study found that student achievement gains in the state were significantly greater for students whose teachers were National Board certified, as well as for those whose teachers had the strong academic and teaching preparation and lengthier experience in teaching the state's policies have tried to leverage.[22]

Investments in School Leadership. In its second wave of reforms, North Carolina also launched one of the nation's most ambitious programs to improve school leadership training. The state's Principal Fellows Program (PFP) was launched in 1993 to attract outstanding aspiring principals. With annual scholarship loans of $20,000 for each of 2 years, the program underwrites preparation in eight state universities, including full-time internships during the second year with expert principals in participating school districts. In exchange, each Principal Fellow pledges at least 4 years of service as a principal or assistant principal in the state's schools. This program has supplied the state with 800 highly trained principals, and half of all current candidates for the masters' in school administration. Most principals in North Carolina have now had the advantage of an internship under the wing of a veteran principal as part of their training—a practice that is still relatively rare across the United States.[23]

In addition, to ensure a stable source of learning opportunities for school leaders, North Carolina created the Principals' Executive Program (PEP), funded by the state legislature and located at UNC–Chapel Hill. PEP has been offering continuing education for principals in North Carolina for more than 20 years through residency programs as well as topical courses, seminars, and conferences. In a recent national study of leadership development, North Carolina's principals rated the helpfulness of the university courses and research opportunities they experience as extraordinarily helpful and significantly more highly than their peers nationally.[24]

Early Learning Investments. These extensive investments in teaching and school leadership occurred alongside general K–12 spending increases that lowered pupil–teacher ratios and sizable investments in early childhood education, including the Smart Start program, an award-winning early childhood initiative launched in 1993. Smart Start is a public–private initiative that provides early education funding to all of the state's 100 counties to improve childcare quality and accessibility, as well as access to health services and family support. Evaluations have found that the program has contributed significantly to preschool quality and to children's outcomes on skills and abilities associated with readiness to succeed in school.[25]

Standards and Assessments. In the early 1990s, new curriculum standards were also introduced and accompanied by an extensive program of professional development for teachers statewide. In 1995, the state launched a statewide assessment system linked to the curriculum standards and, shortly thereafter, substantially aligned to the NAEP tests. The standards and assessments have provided a focus for the state's instructional efforts and for its professional development investments. As in

Connecticut, the state department established a division to work with low-performing schools and assistance programs to support improvement.

A study of high-minority, low-income schools in North Carolina that were rapidly closing the achievement gap found that key factors included collegial leadership by principals who provide instructional focus and extensive professional development supports, especially in writing; regular diagnostic assessments to focus improvement efforts, with data analyzed for different grade levels and groups of students at the school level; use of technology resources in teaching core academic skills; and one-on-one tutoring, as well as small-group work in classrooms.[26]

Summary and Postscript. A combination of substantial investments in early learning and K–12 education—coupled with raised standards for students, teachers, and school leaders and supports for professional learning—helped improve student achievement in North Carolina and reduced the achievement gap over 2 decades from 1983 through about 2003. Since then, state equalization funding and professional development investments have flagged, and some policies have tugged in the opposite direction, including the introduction of "lateral entry" teachers without preparation for teaching. As a result, student achievement on the National Assessment of Educational Progress has declined in both absolute and relative terms. Although state performance remains above the national average in mathematics (though lower than it once was), it has fallen below in reading and writing.[27]

After 1997, the state implemented a new accountability system tying a set of rewards and sanctions to school scores on the state tests; these sanctions were further reinforced by NCLB requirements after 2002. This certainly has even more closely focused school attention on the tests, which has had both positive and negative consequences. As attention has turned to greater testing and accountability, without companion investments, inequality has grown. Studies have found that the state accountability program's strategy of sanctioning low-performing schools—most of which serve low-income and minority students in communities that have fewer resources—has made it even more difficult for these schools to attract and retain qualified teachers,[28] and that the associated recruitment of untrained teachers into hard-to-staff schools, through the state's lateral entry route, negatively affects student achievement.[29]

These concerns have caused renewed attention to school funding disparities. In 2004, the North Carolina Supreme Court found that the state's funding method does not comply with the constitutional mandate "of ensuring that all children of the state be provided with the opportunity for a sound basic education." The court stated that:

> An equal opportunity to obtain a sound basic education requires that each child be afforded the opportunity to attend a public school which has the following educational resources, at a minimum: First, that every classroom be staffed with a compe-

tent, certified, well-trained teacher who is teaching the standard course of study by implementing effective educational methods that provide differentiated, individualized instruction, assessment and remediation to the students in that classroom. Second, that every school be led by a well-trained competent Principal with the leadership skills and the ability to hire and retain competent, certified and well-trained teachers who can implement an effective and cost-effective instructional program that meets the needs of at-risk children so that they can have the equal opportunity to obtain a sound basic education by achieving grade level or above academic performance. Third, that every school be provided, in the most cost-effective manner, the resources necessary to support the effective instructional program within that school so that the educational needs of all children, including at-risk children, to have the equal opportunity to obtain a sound basic education, can be met.[30]

In response to the court's order that these needs be addressed by the legislature, the state's 2006–2007 budget included a nearly 10% increase in K–12 education spending, with more money for low-wealth districts, a salary increase for teachers and administrators, and statewide expansion of a pilot program for disadvantaged students. An additional $17.9 million in lottery proceeds were also earmarked to expand the More at Four pre-kindergarten program.[31] Clearly, progress requires steady effort and investment, and renewed efforts to build capacity in the state's high-need schools will be required to maintain and amplify the substantial progress that was made over the last 2 decades.

THE CASE OF CALIFORNIA:
WHERE MISMANAGEMENT MEETS AGGRESSIVE NEGLECT

As we have seen, funding litigation has occasioned serious equity-oriented investments in some states' schools: among others, Connecticut following *Horton* and *Scheff*; Massachusetts in the wake of *Hancock*; New Jersey after 30 years of litigation from *Robinson* to *Abbott*; New York in the *Campaign for Fiscal Equity* case, decided in 2006; and North Carolina in the recent 2004 *Hoke County* litigation.

Not all litigation aimed at school equity has resulted either in investments or in positive reform, however. California represents backward progress—the steady downward slide of a state that was thought to be "equalized" after the landmark *Serrano v. Priest* decision in 1975. Shortly after *Serrano*, in 1979, voters passed Proposition 13 limiting property taxes, and over the next 2 decades, state spending slipped markedly, while local resources became more unequal.[32] The state's 25-year roller-coaster slide in funding took it from "first to worst," as a recent documentary about the state's education system was entitled.[33] Only a few dozen wealthy districts excluded from the *Serrano* equalization reform (the so-called "basic aid" districts), which are able to raise nearly all of their own resources from their large local property tax bases, have been able to keep up with school needs as state funding declined.

Not only did the state disinvest in public education, but it adopted policies that exacerbated inefficiencies and reduced educational effectiveness. Although California's image is as a high-technology, future-oriented, culturally diverse state, it is, by any measure, rapidly throwing away its assets by underfunding and mismanaging its schools.

California is a case of extraordinarily short-sighted state decision making that illustrates how policies can create both inequality and inefficiency at the same time, preventing schools from making good use of the limited resources they have available, and—while issuing a boatload of top-down mandates—ignoring much of the necessary state role for developing a system of schools. I describe California's situation as a cautionary tale that should be understood by those seeking remedies for past and current inadequacies, so that hard-won advances actually translate into better education for students.

The Steady Slide Downward

In the 20 years following Proposition 13, while California has become a "majority minority" state and funding for schools shrank, inequality in educational opportunities and outcomes increased. By 2000, California ranked first in the nation in the number of pupils it served, but 38th in expenditures per student (48th when adjusted for cost of living), 48th in K–12 expenditures as a share of personal income, and 50th in the ratio of students per teacher, despite the class-size reductions made during the late 1990s.[34] As the 21st century dawned, California employed a greater number of underqualified teachers[35] than any other state in the country, and it ranked in the bottom 10% of states in class size, staff/pupil ratio, library quality, and most other school resources.[36] Not surprisingly, California earned a grade of "F" for "resource adequacy" on *Education Week*'s state report card.

By 2006, the spending ratio between the highest-spending and lowest-spending school districts was more than 3 to 1 (from just over $6,000 per pupil to as much as $20,000 per pupil).[37] Such differentials might be justified if the highest-spending districts were in urban areas with higher costs of living and greater pupil needs. However, this was far from the case. Most of the state's cities spent below the state average, and wealthier districts spent much more. When *Serrano* sought to equalize funding, it drew a comparison between high-rolling Beverly Hills and low-spending Baldwin Park, which served a predominantly Black population a few miles away. The remedy was meant to put the two districts on a par, but 25 years later, wealthy Beverly Hills was spending 40% more per pupil than low-income Baldwin Park and Compton, both low-income, segregated minority communities in Los Angeles that spent well under the state average.[38] At the northern end of the state, San Francisco—with its high cost of living, high rates of poverty, and large proportions of English learners—spent about $6,400 per student, also less than the state average, while nearby Sausalito Elementary District in Marin County—where tourists throng and yacht clubs flourish—spent more than twice as much, at $16,600.

This inequitable system of school funding leads to unequal salaries for teachers and great disparities in access to qualified teachers. In 2000, salaries for comparably educated and experienced teachers varied by an extraordinarily large ratio of almost 2 to 1, and the disparity grew larger rather than smaller when adjusted for local labor market differences—reaching a 3 to 1 ratio.[39] Adjusted for cost-of-living differences, beginning salaries in all-minority Alum Rock School District, near San Jose, were only half the state average in 2001, while those in Vallecito Union district, over 85% White, were 60% more than the state average. Not surprisingly, Alum Rock hired nearly half of its teachers without training, while Vallecito's educators were all fully prepared and highly qualified—one of the key elements of the district's mission statement. Cities such as Oakland and San Francisco offer nearly $10,000 less for a beginning teacher than wealthy suburbs such as Los Altos and San Mateo, and the disparities grow to as much as $30,000 a year for a teacher at the top of the scale. Furthermore, teachers in these urban districts often need to spend more of their own money for books and supplies, and they must contend with larger class sizes and fewer support services for themselves and for their students.

The primary result of these disparities is that low-paying districts often have shortages of teachers. An analysis of hiring practices and salaries in California counties showed that the number of teachers on emergency permits and waivers could be predicted by wage differences between high-need districts and their neighbors.[40] By 2001, there were 50,000 individuals teaching on such substandard credentials, and, while 40% of the state's schools had no unqualified teachers, nearly one-fourth had more than 20% of their teachers teaching without full credentials.[41] These latter schools enrolled more than 1.7 million children, mostly African American and Latino, who frequently were taught by short-term, underprepared instructors throughout their entire school careers.[42]

The Results of Inadequate and Unequal Funding

Given these conditions, it should not be surprising that, once among the highest-spending and highest-achieving states in the nation, California sank to the bottom of the state rankings on the National Assessment of Educational Progress by the year 2000 and has remained there, ranking in the bottom five states on virtually every measure, below even those Southern states that once were known for their paltry investments in education before a set of education governors took over during the

1990s. Indeed, South Carolina was spending considerably more on the education of its poor and minority children than California was at the time of their respective lawsuits. Columnist Peter Schrag wrote a book on the "Mississippication" of California as a metaphor for the state's lack of investment in public schools, drawing a parallel to the very poor and consistently low-achieving state of Mississippi.[43]

Although an influx of immigrants affected student performance, several studies confirmed that—even after adjusting for demographics such as language background, race/ethnicity, poverty, and parent education—California students lost more ground and came to perform considerably worse than comparable students in other states on national tests.[44] A report by Policy Analysis for California Education (PACE) in 2000 noted: "Over the past six years, the relationship (between socio-economic measures and achievement scores) has strengthened, not diminished."[45] As Figure 5.5 shows, a nearly perfect relationship emerged between school poverty and the proportion of teachers on emergency credentials—both of which were perfectly and negatively related to schools' achievement scores on the state Academic Performance Index.

As a consequence of these trends, plus the addition of an exit exam for graduation from high school, by 2006 only 56% of African American students and 55% of Latino students were graduating with a diploma within 4 years of entering high

Figure 5.5. The Relationship Between California Elementary School API Scores, Student Socioeconomic Status, and Teacher Qualifications, 2000.

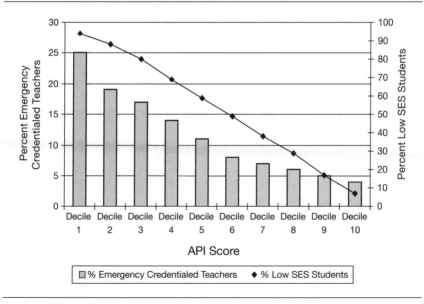

Source: Darling-Hammond (2003a).

school, and only 12 to 14% were graduating having met the requirements to attend a state university.[46] These proportions were even lower in most urban districts.

An increasing share of young African American and Latino men were populating the state's growing prison system, rather than its higher education system. During the 1990s, as 50,000 new African American inmates were added to the California state prison system, African American enrollment in higher education declined: For every 57 who were added to the state corrections system, one was lost from higher education. In addition, three Latino males were added to the prison population for every one added to the 4-year public university system.[47] These inmates, most of them high school dropouts, cost over $46,000 each to incarcerate,[48] while the state would not spend even a quarter of that amount each year to give them a high-quality K–12 education. With declines in real spending on public universities and sharp increases in prison enrollments and costs, by 2008, the state was spending as much on corrections as on public higher education.[49]

As the White population shrinks to a third of the state total by 2025, and Latinos grow to about half, California is on track to have a less well-educated citizenry in the future than it has today, even while labor force demands for highly educated workers increase. Researchers from the Public Policy Institute of California note that "one of the most threatening trends is the potential mismatch between the education requirements of the new economy and the amount of education its future population is likely to have."[50]

Clearly, the state's high-tech economy cannot flourish in this context, and yet, as another state budget crisis emerged in 2009, schools and colleges took more than $6 billion in cuts, while prison budgets were protected—exacerbating the vicious cycle that, unstopped, will fill the prisons ever further and drain the state's coffers as young people are placed on the school-to-prison pipeline rather than a college-to-well-paying-jobs pathway.

What Children Experience

Growing segregation has supported these conditions. By 2004, California was one of the five most segregated states for African American students and one of the three most segregated for Latino students, with 87% of African American students and 90% of Latino students attending predominantly "minority" schools. Nearly half of California's Latino students and more than one-third of African American students attended schools that were more than 90% students of color. A picture of life in these schools was painted by many descriptions filed as evidence in the *Williams v. California* lawsuit brought by low-income students of color in 2002. Here is just one:

> All of the 800 children attending Urban Elementary School #4 qualify for free or reduced lunch. Sixty-two percent are English learners, 65% are Latino, and 33 per-

cent are African-American. The facility consists of one main building and dozens of portables, separated by narrow alley-like walkways. Both students and strangers, some being chased by police, hide in these alleys during the school day. . . . Disrepair is everywhere. Graffiti covers many of the windows of the portable classrooms, as well as the exterior walls of the school buildings. The very few bathrooms for students or faculty frequently lack toilet paper, soap, and/or paper towels. The water fountains do not always work. The classrooms often have cockroaches. Although a large playing field surrounds two sides of the school, the school provides no play equipment. During recess, students must entertain themselves or use materials provided by individual teachers. One teacher observed, "They usually run around and fight."

Most UE#4 teachers are inexperienced, only 10 percent hold full credentials; several are recent arrivals from Spain. Teacher absences are frequent and the turnover rates are very high. In 2000–2001, for example, 12 of the school's 38 teachers left. UE#4's high teacher absenteeism and tardiness rates are particularly troublesome because the school has difficulty finding enough substitutes. Often, the administrators split absent teachers' students up among other teachers. Last year, for example, one teacher had extra students for 56 out of 180 instructional days. When these students arrive, typically with no materials, teachers must modify their instructional plans. When substitutes can be found, their quality is "hit and miss," with teachers often finding their rooms damaged and their students having done no work upon their return.

UE#4 provides students few textbooks and instructional materials, and students who are English Language Learners or struggling readers are particularly hard hit. Although teachers have class sets of relatively new reading books and math workbooks (but no math textbooks) for use in class, the school prohibits teachers from sending these materials home with students. The school does not provide teachers with science, social studies, or English Language Development textbooks, or with any dictionaries, thesauruses, reference books, or writing paper. To provide students picture books in both English and Spanish, math manipulative, art supplies, and photocopies, teachers must spend their own money, with some spending as much as $1000 per year. UE#4's one copier was broken until Christmas, so teachers had to make copies at their own expense. In part because of the lack of appropriate learning materials, some teachers do not regularly teach social studies or science. One lamented, "If I want to teach them, I have to provide all the resources, and I'm strapped financially."[51]

Students encounter the same kind of conditions in their middle school of more than 2,000 students, designed to serve 400 fewer than currently attend. They study science in classrooms without running water, lab tables, or equipment; math without manipulatives, graph paper, or calculators (even though the state standards require middle school students to do graphing and use calculators); English without dictionaries or novels; and social studies without maps. When they get to the local high school, their classes are equally ill-equipped, and they continue to encounter underprepared teachers and substitutes. There, most do not get the courses in chemistry or physics needed to qualify for college, since the turnover of science teachers and the lack of lab space conspire to prevent these classes from being offered.[52]

As Michelle Fine's study of student reactions to these conditions found, students in these settings know they were not getting the kind of education that more advantaged students are getting, as they describe trying to learn without books, chairs to sit in during overcrowded classes, math and science classes (because, as they are told, there "aren't enough" classes for all students to take them), or the opportunity to study the material on the tests they encounter each year. These students come to "believe that schools want them *not* to succeed, so that the students will leave and classes will become smaller, with no adult responsibility for the loss of student bodies. . . . [and] that the government, Californians at large, the public education system, and some of their teachers so fundamentally undervalue them that they wish their disappearance."[53] Fine also found that where substandard school conditions reflect racial and socioeconomic disparities, the stigmatizing impact on students of color also diminishes student self-esteem, attachment to school, and performance. She concluded:

> In educational contexts such as those represented in the plaintiff class, permeated by low expectations, high rates of teacher turnover, environmental stress, and a sense of buildings that are out of control, youth develop, over time, what is called *academic learned helplessness*: a site-specific belief that trying doesn't matter and that they are unable to effect change in their schools. Some complain that lack of access to books or instructional materials hinders their abilities to learn and master academic materials. Others cite the frequent loss of educators and lack of continuity that interrupts academic progress. The often-remarked-upon substitute who doesn't know his/her content area comes to be a symbol that the system is neglecting the education of poor and working-class youth and youth of color. Relations with faculty, and the structural environment, become disrupted and stressful. These elements bode ill for academic performance.[54]

As one young woman explained in response to the question, "What would your [ideal] school look like?"

> It would be a classroom with enough tables, enough chairs, enough books, enough materials and a teacher who cares . . . not just somebody that got a GED or whatever, got their diploma and is going to sit there and talk to us in any kind of way. They [the teachers] wouldn't want that for them[selves]. They wouldn't want the principal coming inside the classroom and going like, "Shut up. You're going to listen to what I've got to say right here," and that's the same way that they treat us. . . . I would have a teacher that understands where kids are coming from, especially living in the area that we do and . . . that cares. Like I said, enough supplies, enough security, and just enough everything. . . . We are the same, just because we're smaller and don't know as much as they know, we are the same human beings.

Rebutting the Evidence

The *Williams* case was brought to achieve a more minimal objective than full parity: It sought merely the basic resources needed for districts to implement the state standards adopted during the 1990s. California had incorporated these standards into tests used to allocate rewards and sanctions to schools and to determine grade promotion and graduation for students, used them to select state-approved textbooks, and incorporated them into licensing standards for teachers. However, it did not ensure that schools had the resources to implement the standards, purchase the necessary materials, or hire qualified teachers prepared to teach the standards.

Despite a mountain of evidence about the dramatic shortcomings of many such schools, the state argued vehemently in *Williams* that it had no responsibility to address these conditions. The state used every argument under the sun to avoid responsibility, arguing on the one hand that it "agrees with Plaintiffs' central argument that every student deserves qualified teachers, adequate instructional materials, and clean and decent facilities that are conducive to learning,"[55] and, on the other hand, that these resources do not make a difference for student achievement, and therefore, are not required.

The state's experts even tried denying that any problems existed: One testified, ostrich-style, that "California has a system of school finance that is highly equalized," and suggested, without reference to the actual data, that "if all districts are spending roughly the same amount, then variations in the specific allocations of resources must balance out."[56] The state also tried arguing that governmental action would violate local control of education—despite its top-down control of testing, curriculum, and textbook choices—and that, conversely, California's test-based accountability system was, in and of itself, sufficient to ensure educational equity.

The plaintiffs presented an extensive body of research demonstrating the relationship of student achievement to the availability of textbooks and high-quality materials, instructional time (since many poor schools had reduced the length of the school day and school year), reasonable class sizes, and adequate facilities.[57] They also presented a number of California studies that found that differences in teacher quality are significantly related to student achievement in both mathematics and reading, before and after controlling for students' demographic characteristics.[58] For example, a study of student achievement across more than 7,000 California schools by the Public Policy Institute of California found that teacher qualification variables were the strongest predictors of student achievement, after controlling for the effects of socioeconomic status. The report noted:

> Among the school resource measures, the level of teacher experience and a related measure—the percentage of teachers without a full credential—are the variables most strongly related to student achievement. Teachers' level of education, measured by the

percentage of teachers with a master's degree or higher, in some cases is positively and significantly related to test scores but not nearly as uniformly as the measures of teacher experience. Similarly, a higher percentage of teachers with only a bachelor's degree within a given grade is negatively related to student achievement.[59]

Nonetheless, the state argued that none of the remedies requested by the plaintiff schoolchildren make a difference in student learning, even when their collective absence in highly segregated schools constitutes conditions that Gloria Ladson-Billings has characterized as "aggressive neglect."[60]

With respect to the large disparities in teachers' qualifications, experts for the defense sought to limit the analysis to a small set of disadvantaged schools to show that teachers' qualifications make less difference for student learning than plaintiffs had shown. Yet, when their data were re-analyzed, the findings illustrated even more vividly how access to qualified and experienced teachers influences students' learning. The percentage of fully certified teachers strongly predicted school achievement both for the state as a whole and for highest-need schools (those with the most low-income and minority students and the fewest certified teachers). This was true even though restricting the range in this way underestimates the influence of resource variables, because socioeconomic status and resources are codetermined (see Table 5.2).

Furthermore, in this group of high-need schools, changes in the proportion of fully certified qualified teachers over a period of several years were the strongest predictor of changes in school achievement levels, explaining more of the difference in achievement gains than changes in the percentages of minority and low-income students combined.[61] This suggests that student achievement responds positively to policies that bring more qualified teachers into high-need schools—and, conversely, that it declines when such teachers leave schools (see Table 5.3).

Where Neglect and Mismanagement Meet

The case for inadequate resources could probably be made more clearly in California's high-minority schools than anywhere else in the country, with most of these schools in urban areas funded below the state average, despite their higher costs-of-living and greater pupil needs, in a state where the average spending, adjusted for cost of living, was ranked 48th in the nation at the time of the lawsuit. The defense was willing to agree with the plaintiffs that dollars alone are not the only issue, and that management of resources matters. Given the state's concern for raising achievement, and its scarce public resources, constrained by tax caps, one would think that there would be strong efforts to ensure that limited funds were spent in the fashion most likely to support learning. Yet, the state engaged for more than a decade in short-sighted policies, dysfunctional decisions, and poor management that made matters considerably worse for these schools and the children they served.

Table 5.2. Predictors of School Level Achievement (API scores) in California, Coefficient (t-value).

	Sample 1: Schools in top quartile of low-income and minority students and bottom quartile of % fully certified teachers (*n* = 818)	*Sample 2:* All CA Schools (*n* = 7203)
% Minority Students	-2.457★★★ (-3.33)	-.417★★★ (-9.55)
% Fully Certified Teachers	0.758★★★ (4.73)	1.085★★★ (18.18)
% Free or Reduced-Price Lunch	0.596★ (2.05)	-1.360★★★ (-31.99)
% English Learners	-0.066 (-0.47)	.647★★★ (10.19)
Student Mobility Rate	-0.691★★★ (-4.15)	-.819★★★ (-15.38)
% Parents with Less Than a High School Education	-1.484★★★ (-10.41)	-2.138★★★ (-30.14)
Plaintiff School	-9.248 (-0.56)	-35.127★★ (-3.31)
Constant	-14352.8★★★ (-3.94)	-17230.99★★★ (-14.77)
R squared	.19	.66

Note: * p <. 05; ** p < .01; ***p < .001.

Table 5.3. Influences of Changes in Teacher Qualifications and Changes in Student Demographics on Changes in School Level Achievement (API scores) from 1999 to 2002, Coefficient (t-value).

	Sample 1: Schools in top quartile of low-income and minority students and bottom quartile of % fully certified teachers (*n* = 739)
Change in % Minority Students	-1.310 (-1.66)
Change in % Fully Certified Teachers	1.151★★★ (7.87)
Change in % Free or Reduced-Price Lunch	.202 (1.09)
Change in % English Learners	-1.128★★★ (-5.63)
Change in % Parents with Less Than a High School Education	.026★★★ (3.50)
Plaintiff School	-22.979 (-1.73)
Change in Student Mobility Rate	-.432★★ (-3.20)
Constant	242.728★★ (3.10)
R squared	.15

Note: * p <. 05; ** p < .01; ***p < .001; **** p < .0001.

Myopic Teaching Policies. In 1970, California became the only state in the nation to eliminate undergraduate teacher education, moving all preparation to the post-baccalaureate level and limiting training to no more than one year. This cut off a major supply source for teachers, which was not revived as shortages set in during the 1990s. It also meant that California's teacher training institutions were unable to offer the depth of training of those in Connecticut, North Carolina, and other states that were raising their expectations for teacher knowledge and skill. The state had no licensing reciprocity with other states and was unable to expeditiously hire thousands of qualified out-of-state teachers who wanted to teach in the state, even as the Commission on Teacher Credentialing was using blanket approvals to allow districts to hire individuals on emergency permits by the thousands. Rather than funding colleges to expand production or providing incentives for preparing teachers to teach in high-need fields and in high-need schools, the state's major response to shortages was to reduce standards for teachers, bringing in tens of thousands through emergency permits, a move that created expensive turnover and workforce instability, while depressing student achievement.

In the late 1990s, Governor Gray Davis finally instituted some productive teacher recruitment policies that began to transform opportunities in high-need schools—forgivable loans and scholarships to train teachers for these schools,[62] subsidies to hard-to-staff schools to recruit and retain qualified teachers and to improve working conditions,[63] state recruitment centers to assist districts in finding and hiring qualified applicants—and these noticeably reduced teacher shortages.[64] However, Davis's successor, Arnold Schwarzenegger, eliminated nearly all of these initiatives during frequent rounds of budget cuts.[65] A number of strong programs for teacher and leadership development were also reduced or ended—including the state Subject Matter Projects offering professional development for teachers and the California School Leadership Academy, supporting principal learning and school turnarounds that had been models for programs in other states across the country. The legislature periodically invented new initiatives that were poorly implemented, because they had to be started from scratch with little lead time, and nearly always short-lived in the yo-yo process that state policy engendered under fragmented governance, chaotic executive leadership, and legislative term limits.

Poorly Implemented Class Size Reduction. All of these problems were exacerbated by the state's poorly planned and hurriedly implemented class-size reduction reform in 1996. By then, California had the largest class sizes in the nation, often topping 30 students in elementary grades and 40 in high schools, as compared to the norm of about 20 nationwide. When a budget surplus appeared briefly, the state spent nearly all of it on class-size reduction for grades K–3, allocating funds on the basis of a rigid class-size ratio of 20 to 1 just before school opened, leaving schools without sufficient classroom space or teachers to make smaller classes work.

Low-income schools—many of them already overcrowded—had to hold classes in auditoriums, gymnasiums, closets, and other nonclassroom spaces. Meanwhile, the policy precipitated a rapid migration of credentialed teachers away from schools in low-income communities to those in more affluent areas with better salaries and working conditions, leaving poorer schools to hire untrained teachers on emergency permits. This exacerbated disparities in teacher qualifications across schools and further increased the achievement gap. For example, the percentage of underprepared teachers teaching in schools where 40% or more of students were English learners increased from 3.7% to 23.9% after the implementation of class-size reduction.[66] Thus, the neediest students did not experience the achievement gains that might have accompanied smaller classes[67] had they been introduced carefully along with the necessary incentives to ensure an adequate supply of qualified teachers.

Failure to Enforce the State's Own Policies. State agencies made it ever easier for districts to allocate untrained teachers and administrators to schools serving low-income students by authorizing emergency permits even when districts had been found to bypass applications from qualified personnel in order to hire less expensive substitutes, emergency hires, and interns.[68] Furthermore, when helpful and thorough reviews of local operational problems were completed by the state's Fiscal Crisis and Management Assistance Team (FCMAT), along with detailed recommendations for improvements in dysfunctional hiring systems, FCMAT had no authority to require change and there was no follow up from agencies that could have done so.

Similarly, when the state was asked to investigate problems with the unavailability of mandated resources, such as textbooks, its actions often reinforced rather than ameliorated inequities. For example, the California state auditor conducted a study in 2002 in response to the legislature's concern about disparities between high- and low-performing schools in the quantity and quality of textbooks available to students in Los Angeles. The audit found both shortages and disparities in the supply and quality of textbooks, especially in predominantly Latino schools. However, the report minimized the effects of these disparities, suggesting that textbook shortages were less important to achievement than factors such as socioeconomic status, English proficiency, and parents' level of education.[69]

Overly Prescriptive Curriculum Mandates. These policies undermining the quality of instruction were exacerbated by heavy-handed state mandates constraining instructional decision making at the local level. In highly politicized battles over state standards, the State Board created wide pendulum swings in instructional direction with a set of viciously fought curriculum wars pitting "back to the basics" advocates against "critical thinking" proponents in each of the subject areas. By the late 1990s, the Board revised all of the subject-matter standards initially developed in the early 1990s to focus more squarely on skills such as decoding and factual recall to reduce what was seen as an overemphasis on reasoning, analysis, and inquiry in the curriculum. The resulting state standards guide the construction of state tests and the state's adoption of specific textbooks for local use—a prescriptive practice in which few states engage.

Although there was some détente in the final standards seeking balance between the "basics" and "thinking" camps, the textbook adoption decisions have precluded access to some highly effective reading, math, and science programs widely used in higher-achieving states and required instead the use of textbooks about which there remains considerable discord among researchers and practitioners.[70] The states' decisions have also precluded state funding of books and curriculum materials other than textbooks, which are especially needed for students to exercise their skills in authentic ways that go beyond answering the questions at the end of the chapter. Indeed, while New Jersey was investing in extensive classroom libraries for students in poor communities so that they could learn to read books, California teachers in many low-income districts were forced to eliminate or hide their books when their classrooms were inspected, since books were not part of the scripted reading curriculum.

Ironically, in addition to the widely publicized reading and math wars, the state that is home to Silicon Valley sought, over the last decade, to eliminate investigation from the science curriculum. After much arm wrestling, the Board reluctantly agreed that up to 25% of science instructional time could be spent in hands-on investigation, but continued to insist on the use of state-approved textbooks, rather than curriculum materials developed by organizations such as the National Science Foundation that are widely used for inquiry-based science instruction across the country and around the world.[71] In 2004, after 7 years of noninquiry science and the prospect of an even more restricted curriculum ahead, CEOs of major high-tech firms, leading scientists from Stanford and the University of California system, and college presidents finally wrote collectively to the State Board, arguing that:

> U.S. businesses and industry seek from today's high school graduates a high capacity for abstract, conceptual thinking, and the ability to apply that capacity to complex real-world problems. The [Board's] Criteria . . . greatly restrict access to nationally produced, widely acclaimed instructional materials for grades K–8 that promote these skills and habits of mind. While acquisition of knowledge is essential, it is well known that students do not easily acquire scientific knowledge without, at the same time, learning to understand the facts by engaging in active experimentation. . . . Thus, the [Board's] Criteria are counterproductive to the hope of expanding California's economy, and they will severely limit the opportunities for California's children to learn science and scientific methods.[72]

This finally changed the rhetoric of the standards, but has not yet, as of this writing, affected the local adoption of materials suitable for 21st-century science.

When poorly informed top-down mandates preclude schools from using the best available materials and engaging in the best available practices, state control can reduce rather than enhancing school effectiveness, and resources can be wasted.

In 2007, while California students had made some gains in mathematics, 4th- and 8th-grade students still ranked 47th and 45th, respectively, among the 50 states on the National Assessment of Educational Progress.[73] In reading, California fourth graders ranked 48th in 2007, and eighth graders ranked 49th, having slipped even further behind their national peers over the prior decade.[74] And California students ranked 49th in both 4th- and 8th-grade science, surpassing only Mississippi.[75]

Incoherent Funding and Management. These problems are all symptoms of a fragmented and incoherent approach to education policymaking that grew up willy-nilly as the state rapidly evolved from one favoring local control to one managed through state-directed mandates issued by a variety of agencies uncoordinated with—and frequently at odds with—one another. These include an elected state superintendent often contending with the governor but reporting to a State Board appointed by the governor, plus a Secretary of Education position created by the governor. Add to this an independent Teacher Credentialing Commission, a separate facilities financing agency, another separate auditing agency, an activist legislature operating under term limits, and a referendum process not fully controlled by anyone, and the recipe for chaotic policy making could scarcely be more perfect.

Meanwhile, the state resorted primarily to a fragmented and disequalizing array of categorical grants after Proposition 13. This dizzying array of grants—which became smaller in size and ever more specific in their uses—deflected state and local attention away from developing well-functioning, efficient school systems to the bureaucratic requirements of administering hundreds of small, disconnected programs, many of which did not allow districts to underwrite the major areas where they needed to make investments. Rather than giving poor districts unrestricted funds that could be used to raise teacher salaries, improve working conditions, or fix crumbling buildings, the state gave them (or allowed them to apply for) dozens of smaller grants—often late in the planning cycle and for purposes that were not always renewed from year to year—for things such as half a counselor, or a few instruments for a music program they could not fully fund, or a small-scale, nonrecurring professional development effort. Furthermore, with separate spending and reporting requirements for each grant, precious resources were deflected from instruction to administration.

By 2002, nearly half of the funds coming to the poorest districts were in the form of such categorical grants—causing former State Board president Michael Kirst to bemoan the state's unhealthy "hardening of the categoricals." When another budget surplus appeared briefly in 2006, the governor spent all of the education funds on a bevy of small, one-time categorical grants for unfunded areas such as art, music, and physical education that the Department of Education could not even administer in time for the start of the school year and schools could not use to build sustained programs. A year later, most of these programs disappeared and the same governor cut a set of long-standing programs supporting teacher and school leader recruitment and training from the budget, many of which had been effective in reducing the state's labor market problems.

Finally, even though the theory of standards-based reform was to allocate resources, set clear goals, and allow localities to figure out how best to meet them, the state became more focused on mandates for school practice as its contribution to school funding dwindled, and as legislators increasingly distrusted the capacity of schools they had decapacitated. As Jeannie Oakes commented in summarizing the plaintiffs' expert reports in the *Williams* case:

> For more than three decades, the State failed to incorporate its increased State involvement and pressure for reform into a plan with clear lines of State responsibility or support for implementing and overseeing the new State policies and programs. . . . As each of these State entities became more focused on improving the quality of the State's schools, each became more engaged in specifying the details of school organization, curriculum, teaching, instructional materials, testing and assessment, special programs, and more. The result was a proliferation of uncoordinated policies layered onto the existing system, exacerbating the fragmentation and incoherence of the State's education policy system. . . . Efforts in the 1990s to develop more systemic reform policies that could ensure both quality and opportunity were derailed by the state's lack of an adequate state governance and finance system, by the state's increasingly single-minded focus on test scores, and by its adoption of a wrong-headed view of "local flexibility."[76]

That view was the same one the Texas court decried—that localities, and the state, should be "free" from expectations about equalizing resources, even while they were increasingly told how to manage their limited funds.

California was not always incapable of managing its affairs. The state had a well-functioning, well-resourced department of education and teacher credentialing commission in the 1980s, and it had launched one of the nation's earliest and most ambitious standards-based reforms with strong capacity-building elements, which were largely dismantled by the mid-1990s with changing politics and dwindling resources. Indeed, as in many other states, the capacity of the state department of education declined with both the withdrawal of federal—and later state—funds and with the decline in the interest and willingness of the state executive to examine the availability of resources to students.

As one marker of executive branch unwillingness to take responsibility for school capacity, Governor Gray Davis vetoed a measure in 1999, passed overwhelmingly by the state legislature, which would have required the public reporting of students' opportunities to learn—including their access to qualified teachers, high-quality curriculum, and other learning conditions. In his veto message, Governor Davis declared that the state had done enough to invest and equalize resources and that

> the appropriate role for the state is to hold districts accountable for their results. . . . [T]he Public Schools Accountability Act of 1999 . . . provides for a system of accountability which ranks schools by the results of their efforts, and provides financial rewards and sanctions for their performance. The High School Exit Examination will also help the state hold school districts accountable for the opportunity they provide their students to learn."[77]

With a penstroke, the question of opportunity was dismissed, as it was to be on future occasions when Governor Arnold Schwarzenegger vetoed similar bills. Thus, severe inequalities in resources continue to this day, and the *Williams* lawsuit, which was temporarily settled in 2004, will be brought again, as conditions have improved little in subsequent years. Perhaps deliberately, as Oakes notes:

> California's system cannot prevent, detect, and correct the inadequacies and disparities in the State's schools because it has not been designed to do so. The large gaps in the system make it impossible for the State to know where unequal conditions exist, how they affect students' performance, and how these conditions could be remedied. The current test-based approach may have provided State policymakers with a politically attractive alternative to one that would ensure adequate and equal conditions for all students. Perhaps not surprisingly, the communities that stand to lose most in this shift toward test-based accountability—low income communities of color—are precisely the communities that lack the political power to shape State policies.[78]

THE MORAL OF THE STORIES

What California illustrates is not only the lack of adequate and equitable funding for schools, but the lack of a state system for supporting good education. Despite ongoing hand-wringing about the persistence of the achievement gap, we know the critical components of schools that make a difference in achievement for students who are typically left behind. These include high-quality teachers and teaching, especially teachers' abilities to teach content to diverse students in ways that effectively support the learning process;[79] access to intellectually rigorous and relevant curriculum;[80] and personalized schools that allow students to be well known and well supported, and that forge positive connections to their communities and families.[81] Such organizations, in turn, require skillful leaders who can build good practices working within a reasonably steady and sympathetic policy environment.

Of course, these features of good schools cannot exist unless they are supported by adequate resources that assure competitive wages and strong training for teachers, supportive teaching and learning conditions, and the materials needed for learning—up-to-date curriculum materials, computers, libraries, science labs, and more. Such conditions also require policies that support an infrastructure for universally strong education. In each of these areas, innovative educators in schools and districts across the country have shown what can be done. Innovation is not in short supply in American education. More rare are the *systems* that proactively construct the conditions under which high-quality teaching and schooling can be widely available.

A critical point is that greater resources to schools will produce student success only if schools can use them to access teachers and leaders who are well prepared and who then work within productive school organizations. Local schools and districts cannot, by themselves, produce an infrastructure for training effective teachers and principals at a societal scale, nor can they manage the overall supply and distribution of educators. Pioneering school leaders can develop innovative organizations, engaging curriculum for students, and useful assessments, but most cannot easily withstand short-sighted governmental policies that stand in the way of good practice and require outmoded or inefficient approaches.

States have an important role to play beyond guiding the flow of money from taxpayers to schools—one that is vital in creating productive conditions for education. In addition to avoiding ill-informed intrusions, this role is to create well-functioning structures and policies that foster the development of high-quality curriculum, assessments, and school designs, and the production of knowledgeable and skilled teachers and leaders. The tales of Connecticut and North Carolina (and that of New Jersey in the previous chapter)—all states that serve large numbers of low-income and minority students—provide insights about how states can increase educational quality and reduce inequality when governments assume this role. The tale of California shows how, when governments do not assume a supportive leadership role, scarce resources for education are wasted, and both children and society are harmed.

All of these cases demonstrate how fragile progress toward equality is in the United States, as plaintiffs in each of these states have been back to court over and over again, relitigating children's right to quality education. Meanwhile, many other nations have simply gotten about the business of building strong, equitable systems of public education that are preparing all of their children well for the world they will inherit. I turn to their stories in the next chapter.

CHAPTER 6

Steady Work:
How Countries Build Strong
Teaching and Learning Systems

The aim [of Finnish education policy] is a coherent policy geared to educational equity and a high level of education among the population as a whole. The principle of lifelong learning entails that everyone has sufficient learning skills and opportunities to develop their knowledge and skills in different learning environments throughout their lifespan.

—Finland Ministry of Education, 2009[1]

Two distinctive features of Korean education are worth noting: the egalitarian ideal and the zeal for education. . . . Since the modern school was introduced in Korea, the government has been keen to ensure equal opportunity for all—regardless of gender, religion, geographic location or socioeconomic class. Second, Korean society has traditionally placed a high value on education. . . . The zeal for education was reinforced by the recent past, in which Japanese colonialism and the Korean War convinced Koreans to invest more in people than in physical capital.

—Gwang-Jo Kim, 2002[2]

Innovation is no longer simply encouraged; it has to become an imperative of all professional endeavour in business, government and education. . . . A new mindset and new strategies are needed to foster innovation, and all organizations, especially schools, will have to respond to the imperatives of innovation at work around us. Schools are knowledge organizations. . . . They must therefore serve as catalysts for learning and discovery, and the wellsprings of the knowledge society.

—Teo Chee Hean, Minister of Education, Singapore[3]

It is exhausting even to recount the struggles for equitable funding in American schools, much less to be engaged in the struggles, year after year, or—more debilitating—to be a parent or student who is subject day-by-day, week-by-week to the aggressive neglect often fostered in dysfunctional, underresourced schools.

One wonders what we might accomplish as a nation if we could finally set aside what appears to be our de facto commitment to inequality, so profoundly at odds with our rhetoric of equity, and put the millions of dollars spent continually arguing and litigating into building a high-quality education system for all children. To imagine how that might be done, one can look at nations that started with very little and purposefully built highly productive and equitable systems, sometimes almost from scratch, in the space of only 2 to 3 decades.

In this chapter, I briefly describe how three very different nations—Finland, South Korea, and Singapore—built strong educational systems, nearly from the ground up. None of these nations was educationally successful in the 1970s, when the United States was the unquestioned education leader in the world. All created productive teaching and learning systems by expanding access while investing purposefully in ambitious educational goals using strategic approaches to build teaching capacity.

I use the term *teaching and learning system* advisedly to describe a set of elements that, when well designed and connected, reliably support all students in their learning. These elements ensure that students routinely encounter well-prepared teachers who work in concert around a thoughtful, high-quality curriculum, supported by appropriate materials and assessments. Furthermore, these elements of the system are designed to help students, teachers, leaders, and the system as a whole continue to learn and improve.

Although none of these countries lacks problems and challenges, each has created a much more consistently high-quality education system for all of its students than has the United States. And while no system from afar can be transported wholesale into another context, there is much to learn from the experiences of those who have addressed problems we encounter. A sage person once noted that, although it is useful to learn from one's own mistakes and experiences, it is even wiser to learn from those of others. These stories are offered with that goal in mind. In later chapters, I describe how key elements can be incorporated in culturally appropriate ways to build a teaching and learning system in the United States.

THE FINNISH SUCCESS STORY

Finland has been a poster child for school improvement since it rapidly climbed to the top of the international rankings after it emerged from the Soviet Union's shadow. Once poorly ranked educationally, with a turgid bureaucratic system that produced low-quality education and large inequalities, it now ranks first among all the OECD nations on the PISA assessments in mathematics, science, and reading. The country also boasts a highly equitable distribution of achievement,[4] even for its growing share of immigrant students.

High and Equitable Education Achievement and Attainment

In a recent analysis of educational reform policies in Finland, Pasi Sahlberg describes how, since the 1970s, Finland changed its traditional education system "into a model of a modern, publicly financed education system with widespread equity, good quality, large participation—all of this at reasonable cost."[5] In addition to the gains in measured achievement, there have been huge gains in educational attainment at the upper secondary and college levels. More than 99% of students now successfully complete compulsory basic education, and about 90% complete upper secondary school.[6] Two-thirds of these graduates enroll in universities or professionally oriented polytechnic schools. And over 50% of the Finnish adult population participates in adult-education programs. Ninety-eight percent of the costs of education at all levels are covered by government, rather than by private sources.[7]

Although there was a sizable achievement gap among students in the 1970s, strongly correlated to socioeconomic status, this gap has been progressively reduced as a result of curriculum reforms starting in the 1980s—and it has continued to grow smaller and smaller in the 2000, 2003, and 2006 PISA assessments. By 2006, Finland's between-school variance on the PISA science scale was only 5%, whereas the average between-school variance in other OECD nations was about 33%.[8] Large between-school variation is generally related to social inequality, including both the differences in achievement across neighborhoods differentiated by wealth and the extent to which schools are funded and organized to reduce or expand inequalities.

Not only is there little variation in achievement across Finnish schools, but the overall variation in achievement among Finnish students is also smaller than that of nearly all the other OECD countries. This is true despite the fact that immigration from nations with lower levels of education has increased sharply in recent years, and there is more linguistic and cultural diversity for schools to contend with. One recent analysis notes:

> Over the past 15 years Finnish people as well as institutions have had to adjust to new policies and practices. In education, the emergence of new cultural and linguistic minorities has created challenges to basic values of education, curricula, and also to teachers in Finnish schools having increased social and ethnic diversities. In some urban schools, total immigrant children or those whose mother tongue is not Finnish approach close to 50%.[9]

Although most immigrants still come from places such as Sweden, the most rapidly growing newcomer groups since 1990 have been from Afghanistan, Bosnia, India, Iran, Iraq, Serbia, Somalia, Turkey, Thailand, and Vietnam.[10] Among them, new immigrants speak more than 60 languages. Yet, achievement has been climbing in Finland *and* growing more equitable, even as it has been declining in some other OECD nations (see Figure 6.1).

Meanwhile, Finland's economy was transformed from a rustic agrarian society as late as the 1950s—when it was thought to be about 40 years behind its neighbor, Sweden—to a knowledge-based economy ranked the most competitive in the world by the World Economic Forum in 4 out of 5 years from 2001 to 2005.[11] Its recovery from a major banking crisis and near-economic collapse in the early 1990s was accomplished by the emergence of new knowledge-based industries supported by a very high level of human capital, widespread use of global information and communication technologies (an arena in which Finland is now ranked as one of the top in the world), and education and research institutions redesigned to foster innovation.[12]

Strategies for Reform

Because of these trends, many people have turned to Finland for clues to educational transformation. As one analyst notes:

> Most visitors to Finland discover elegant school buildings filled with calm children and highly educated teachers. They also recognize the large autonomy that schools enjoy; little interference by the central education administration in schools' everyday lives, systematic methods to address problems in the lives of students, and targeted professional help for those in need.[13]

Figure 6.1. Performance Over Time on PISA Mathematics Tests Across Selected OECD Countries.

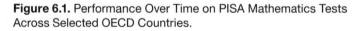

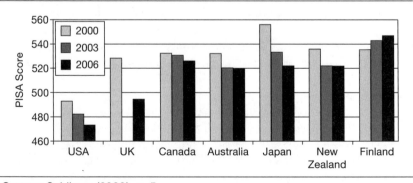

Source: Sahlberg (2009), p. 5.

However, less visible forces account for the more tangible evidence visitors may see. Leaders in Finland attribute these gains to their intensive investments in teacher education—all teachers receive 2 to 3 years of high-quality graduate-level preparation completely at state expense—plus a major overhaul of the curriculum and assessment system designed to ensure access to a "thinking curriculum" for all students. A recent analysis of the Finnish system summarized its core principles as follows:

- Resources for those who need them most
- High standards and supports for special needs
- Qualified teachers
- Evaluation of education
- Balancing decentralization and centralization.[14]

The process of change has been almost the reverse of the policy progression in the United States. Over the past 40 years, Finland has shifted from a highly central-ized system emphasizing external testing to a more localized system in which highly trained teachers design curriculum around very lean national standards. Except for sample assessments and voluntary college matriculation exams created by high school and college faculty, all assessments are school-based, designed by teachers to evalu-ate higher-order thinking and performance skills. This new system is implemented through equitable funding and extensive preparation for all teachers. The logic of the system is that investments in the capacity of local teachers and schools to meet the needs of all students, coupled with thoughtful guidance about goals, can unleash the benefits of local creativity in the cause of common, equitable outcomes.

Meanwhile, the United States has been imposing more external testing—often used in ways that exacerbate differential access to curriculum—while creating more inequitable conditions in local schools. As resources for children and schools in the form of both overall funding and the presence of trained, experienced teachers have become more disparate, poor schools have less capacity to meet the outcomes that are, ostensibly, sought. Finnish policy analyst Sahlberg notes the differences in the path Finland has taken:

> The [No Child Left Behind] legislation, according to many teachers and schol-ars, has led to fragmentation in instruction, further interventions uncoordinated with the basic classroom teaching, and more poorly-trained tutors working with students and teachers. As a consequence, schools have experienced too many in-structional directions for any student, with an increase of unethical behaviors and a loss of continuity in instruction and systematic school improvement (Grubb, 2007; Nichols & Berliner, 2007; Valli & Buese, 2007). The difference between this and the Finnish approach is notable: The Finns have worked systematically over 35 years to make sure that competent professionals who can craft the best learning conditions

for all students are in all schools, rather than thinking that standardized instruction and related testing can be brought in at the last minute to improve student learning and turn around failing schools.[15]

Sahlberg identifies a set of reforms, popular in many countries, that Finland has *not* adopted, including standardization of curriculum enforced by frequent external tests; narrowing of the curriculum to basic skills in reading and mathematics; reduced use of innovative teaching strategies; adoption of educational ideas from external sources, rather than development of local internal capacity for innovation and problem solving; and adoption of high-stakes accountability policies, featuring rewards and sanctions for students, teachers, and schools. By contrast, he suggests:

> Finnish education policies are a result of four decades of systematic, mostly intentional development that has created a culture of diversity, trust, and respect within Finnish society, in general, and within its education system, in particular. . . . Education sector development has been grounded on equal opportunities for all, equitable distribution of resources rather than competition, intensive early interventions for prevention, and building gradual trust among education practitioners, especially teachers.[16]

Equity in opportunity to learn is supported in many ways, in addition to basic funding. Finnish schools are generally small (fewer than 300 pupils) with relatively small class sizes (in the 20s), and are uniformly well equipped. The notion of caring for students educationally and personally is a central principle in the schools. All students receive a free meal daily, as well as free health care, transportation, learning materials, and counseling in their schools, so that the foundations for learning are in place.[17] Beyond that, access to quality curriculum and teachers has become a central aspect of Finnish educational policy.

Improving Curriculum Content and Access. Beginning in the 1970s, Finland launched reforms to equalize educational opportunity by, first, eliminating the practice of separating students into very different tracks based on their test scores along with the examinations previously used to enforce it. This occurred in two stages between 1972 and 1982, and a common curriculum was developed throughout the entire system through the end of high school. These changes were intended to equalize educational outcomes and provide more open access to higher education.[18] During this time, social supports for children and families were also enacted, including health and dental care, special education services, and transportation to schools.

By the late 1970s, investment in teachers was an additional focus. Teacher education was improved and extended. Policymakers decided that if they invested in very skillful teachers, they could allow local schools more autonomy to make decisions about what and how to teach—a reaction against the oppressive, centralized system they sought to overhaul.

This bet seems to have paid off. By the mid-1990s, the country had ended the highly regulated system of curriculum management (reflected in older curriculum guides that had exceeded 700 pages of prescriptions). The current national core curriculum is a much leaner document—featuring fewer than 10 pages of guidance for all of mathematics, for example—which guides teachers in collectively developing local curriculum and assessments. The focus of 1990s curriculum reforms was on science, technology, and innovation, leading to an emphasis on teaching students how to think creatively and manage their own learning. As Sahlberg notes:

> Rapid emergence of innovation-driven businesses in the mid-1990s introduced creative problem-solving and innovative cross-curricular projects and teaching methods to schools. Some leading Finnish companies, such as Nokia, reminded education policy-makers of the importance of keeping teaching and learning creative and open to new ideas, rather than fixing them to predetermined standards and accountability through national testing.[19]

Indeed, there are no external standardized tests used to rank students or schools in Finland, and most teacher feedback to students is in narrative form, emphasizing descriptions of their learning progress and areas for growth.[20] Like the National Assessment of Educational Progress in the United States, Finland uses a centrally developed assessment given to samples of students at the end of the 2nd and 9th grades to inform curriculum and school investments. The focus of these open-ended assessments is to provide information to support learning and problem solving, rather than to allocate sanctions and punishments.

Finland maintains one exam prior to attending university: the matriculation exam, organized and evaluated by a Matriculation Exam Board appointed by the Finnish Ministry of Education. This board taps faculty in the relevant subject areas to develop the tests. Although not required for graduation from high school, it is a common practice for students to take this set of four open-ended exams, emphasizing problem solving, analysis, and writing.[21] Most universities use the scores as part of their admissions decisions. The exams are given in the candidate's mother tongue (Finnish, Swedish, or Saami) plus at least three subjects of the candidate's choosing from a list that includes the second national language, a foreign language, mathematics, and one of a general battery of tests in sciences and the humanities. The exams include extensive written work, as well as oral and listening components. Because the tasks posed are complex and require extended responses, each exam features only 6 to 10 items. Teachers use official guidelines to grade the matriculation exams locally, and samples of the grades are re-examined by professional raters hired by the Matriculation Exam Board.[22] Although it is counterintuitive to those accustomed to external testing as a means of accountability, Finland's use of school-based, student-centered, open-ended tasks embedded in the curriculum is often touted as an important reason for the nation's success on the international exams.[23]

The national core curriculum provides teachers with recommended assessment criteria for specific grades in each subject and in the overall final assessment of student progress each year.[24] Local schools and teachers then use those guidelines to craft a more detailed curriculum and set of learning outcomes, along with approaches to assessing benchmarks in the curriculum.[25] According to the Finnish National Board of Education (June 2008), the main purpose of assessing students is to guide and encourage students' own reflection and self-assessment. Consequently, ongoing feedback from the teacher is very important. Teachers give students formative and summative reports through both verbal and narrative feedback.

Inquiry is a major focus of learning in Finland, and assessment is used to cultivate students' active learning skills by asking open-ended questions and helping students address these problems. In a Finnish classroom, it is rare to see a teacher standing at the front of a classroom lecturing students for 50 minutes. Instead, students are likely to be conducting science investigations; measuring, building, or calculating answers to design problems; and reading and writing for a variety of audiences and purposes. In many classrooms, students determine their own weekly targets with their teachers in specific subject areas and choose the tasks they will work on at their own pace. Students are likely to be rotating through workshops or gathering information, asking questions of their teacher, and working with other students in small groups.[26] They may be completing independent or group projects in science or social studies or writing articles for their own magazine. The cultivation of independence and active learning allows students to develop metacognitive skills that help them to frame, tackle, and solve problems; evaluate and improve their own work; and guide their learning processes in productive ways.[27]

An orientation to well-grounded experimentation, reflection, and improvement as a dynamic cycle for individual and organizational learning characterizes what students are asked to do in their inquiry-based lessons, what teachers are asked to do in their professional problem solving and curriculum development, and what schools are asked to do in their drive for continual progress. Sahlberg notes: "A typical feature of teaching and learning in Finland is encouraging teachers and students to try new ideas and methods, learn about and through innovations, and cultivate creativity in schools, while respecting schools' pedagogic legacies."[28]

Improving Teaching. Greater investments in teacher education began in the 1970s with expectations that teachers would move from 3-year normal school programs to 4- to 5-year programs of study. During the 1990s, the country overhauled preparation once again to focus more on teaching diverse learners higher-order skills such as problem solving and critical thinking in research-based master's degree programs. Westbury and colleagues[29] suggest that preparing teachers for a research-based profession has been the central idea of teacher education development in Finland.

Prospective teachers are competitively selected from the pool of college graduates—only 15% of those who apply are admitted[30]—and receive a 3-year graduate-level teacher preparation program, entirely free of charge and with a living stipend. Unlike the United States, where teachers either go into debt to prepare for a profession that will pay them poorly or they enter with little or no training, Finland, like some other Scandinavian countries, made the decision to invest in a uniformly well-prepared teaching force by recruiting top candidates and paying them to go to school. Slots in teacher training programs are highly coveted, and shortages are virtually unheard of.

Teachers' preparation includes both extensive coursework on how to teach— with a strong emphasis on using research based on state-of-the-art practice—and at least a full year of clinical experience in a school associated with the university. These model schools are intended to develop and model innovative practices, as well as to foster research on learning and teaching. Teachers are trained in research methods so that they can "contribute to an increase of the problem solving capacity of the education system."[31]

Within these model schools, student teachers participate in problem solving groups, a common feature in Finnish schools. The problem-solving groups engage in a cycle of planning, action, and reflection/evaluation that is reinforced throughout the teacher education and is, in fact, a model for what teachers will plan for their own students, who are expected to use similar kinds of research and inquiry in their own studies. Indeed, the entire system is intended to improve through continual reflection, evaluation, and problem solving, at the level of the classroom, school, municipality, and nation.

Teachers learn how to create challenging curriculum and how to develop and evaluate local performance assessments that engage students in research and inquiry on a regular basis. Teacher training emphasizes learning how to teach students who learn in different ways, including those with special needs. It includes a strong emphasis on "multiculturality" and the "prevention of learning difficulties and exclusion," as well as on the understanding of learning, thoughtful assessment, and curriculum development.[32] The egalitarian Finns reasoned that if teachers learn to help students who struggle, they will be able to teach all students more effectively and, indeed, leave no child behind.

Most teachers now hold master's degrees in both their content and in education, and they are well prepared to teach diverse learners—including those with special needs—for deep understanding. They are also well prepared to use formative performance assessments on a regular basis to inform their teaching so it meets students' needs.[33] Teachers are well trained both in research methods and in pedagogical practice. Consequently, they are sophisticated diagnosticians, and they work together collegially to design instruction that meets the demands of the subject matter as well as the needs of their students.

In Finland, like other high-achieving nations, schools provide time for regular collaboration among teachers on issues of instruction. Teachers in Finnish schools meet at least one afternoon each week to jointly plan and develop curriculum, and schools in the same municipality are encouraged to work together to share materials. Time is also provided for professional development within the teachers' work week.[34] As is true in many other European and Asian nations, nearly half of teachers' school time is used to hone practice through school-based curriculum work, collective planning, and cooperation with parents, which allows schools and families to work more closely together on behalf of students.[35] The result is that

> Finnish teachers are conscious, critical consumers of professional development and in-service training services. Just as the professional level of the teaching cadre has increased over the past two decades, so has the quality of teacher professional development support. Most compulsory, traditional in-service training has disappeared. In its place are school- or municipality-based longer term programs and professional development opportunities. Continuous upgrading of teachers' pedagogical professionalism has become a right rather than an obligation. This shift in teachers' learning conditions and styles often reflects ways that classroom learning is arranged for pupils. As a consequence of strengthened professionalism in schools, it has become understood that teachers and schools are responsible for their own work and also solve most problems rather than shift them elsewhere. Today the Finnish teaching profession is on a par with other professional workers; teachers can diagnose problems in their classrooms and schools, apply evidence-based and often alternative solutions to them and evaluate and analyze the impact of implemented procedures.[36]

The focus on instruction and the development of professional practice in Finland's approach to organizing the education system has led, according to all reports, to an increased prevalence of effective teaching methods in schools. Furthermore, efforts to enable schools to learn from each other have led to "lateral capacity building"[37] across schools; that is, the widespread adoption of effective practices and experimentation with innovative approaches across the system, "encouraging teachers and schools to continue to expand their repertoires of teaching methods and individualizing teaching to meet the needs of all students."[38]

A Finnish official noted this key lesson learned from the reforms that allowed Finland to climb from an inequitable, mediocre education system to the very top of the international rankings:

Empowerment of the teaching profession produces good results. Professional teachers should have space for innovation, because they should try to find new ways to improve learning. Teachers should not be seen as technicians whose work is to implement strictly dictated syllabi, but rather as professionals who know how to improve learning for all. Teachers are ranked highest in importance, because educational systems work through them.[39]

KOREA'S CLIMB TO EXTRAORDINARY EDUCATIONAL ATTAINMENT

Investment in teachers has also been an important linchpin of South Korea's stunning climb from an uneducated population to one of the top-ranked nations in the world educationally. "Don't even step on the shadow of a teacher," states a Korean proverb, reflective of the deep respect for knowledge and teaching that is part of its Confucian heritage. From a nation with a largely illiterate population and almost no school buildings in 1953,[40] South Korea (hereafter referred to as Korea) emerged on the PISA assessments in 2003 as first ranked in problem solving, second in reading, third in math, and fourth in science. Furthermore, although Koreans worry about inequalities in their system, the impact of socioeconomic background on student performance is below the OECD average, as is the variance in achievement across schools.[41]

Access to education has expanded at an unbelievably fast pace. In 1945, Korea was liberated from Japanese occupation, but the Korean War followed almost immediately thereafter, destroying more than 80% of school buildings between 1950 and 1953.[42] Despite these difficulties, the new nation was strongly committed to education. As soon as the war ended, the government sought to put in place the plans conceptualized in 1948 by the Korean Education Committee. The Education Committee articulated the ideal of an educated person—"*Hong Ik In Gan*," which literally means a person devoted to the welfare of people—and called for easy access to an education relevant to the needs of a growing nation and compatible with education systems elsewhere, "accommodating the worldwide trends of educational practice."[43]

Korea attained universal primary education in the 1950s, but it restricted access to middle and high schools based on examinations. In reaction to what was called "exam hell," which educators felt required too much emphasis on rote memorization and cramming, the entrance examination to middle school was abolished in 1968 and the examination for entry to high school was abolished in 1974, as part of a "high school equalization policy."[44] Access to secondary school education was opened up to the more than 90% of students who could pass a basic qualifications standard, and students were randomly assigned to geographic clusters of high schools—including private schools paid for by government subsidies. "Exam hell" then moved to high schools as students competed for entrance to college, so in

1980, the government greatly expanded admission to college while prohibiting separate university entrance exams and private tutoring, leaving only a national Scholastic Achievement Test (SAT), like the one used in the United States, as a measure for providing college entrance information.

This rapid democratization of access to education has rapidly transformed the education level of the Korean population over a 30-year period. Whereas in 1970, only 20% of Korean young people attended high school, by 2005, over 90% were graduates. In 2006, school transition rates were 99.9% from elementary to junior high school, 99.7% from junior high to senior high, and 82.1% from senior high to college—much higher than the United States[45] (see Figure 6.2). About two-thirds of Korean students attend academic high schools, and about one-third attend vocational high schools. Even the college-going rate of Korean vocational high school students (69%, as compared to 88% from academic high schools)[46] exceeds the college-going rate in the United States, where only about 70 to 75% graduate from high school and only 60% of these go on to college—less than half of the age cohort. Ultimately, only about a third of young people complete a college degree in the United States, less than half the current rate of college completion in Korea.

Figure 6.2. Expansion of Korean School Enrollments, 1970–2006.

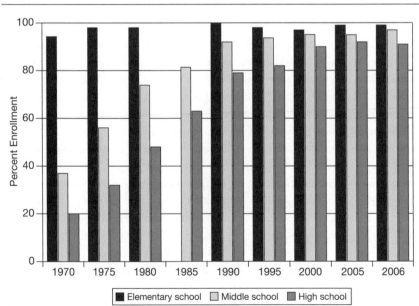

Source: Korean Educational Development Institute (2008).

Korean policymakers and educators agreed that the rapid increase in access to education emphasized quantity over quality, and there has been considerable effort to improve instruction and reduce class sizes, especially since 1990. Whereas class sizes averaged about 60 students per class in 1970, they were reduced to just over 30 students per class by 2005.[47] The rapid expansion of access and the steady reduction of class size have provoked a continuing demand for teachers, which has been dealt with by comprehensive teacher recruitment and retention policies described below. Rather than lower standards for teachers to expand supply, as has occurred in California and many other U.S. states (see Chapters 4 and 5), Korea has expanded the teaching force while raising standards for certification and preparation, using purposeful incentives and supports.

In March 1985, just as the United States was responding to the 1983 *Nation at Risk* report, a Korean Commission for Educational Reform also proposed a set of innovations for the purpose of "Cultivating Koreans to Lead the 21st-Century." These included expanding education investments, upgrading school facilities, securing high-quality teachers, improving curriculum and teaching methods, promoting science education, improving the college entrance system and college education, and establishing a lifelong education system.[48] Unlike the United States, which has started, stopped, and often ignored its reform ideas, these measures have been pursued on a continuous basis, and many have been substantially accomplished.

Curriculum

The development of and refinement of curriculum has been a formal process in Korea in a cycle of revisions that occurs every 5 to 10 years. Historians of Korean education note that curriculum thinking in the 1950s and 1960s was strongly influenced by the child-centered ideas of John Dewey, with whom prominent Korean educators had studied, and that later refinements were influenced by Jerome Bruner's ideas about the importance of discovery and inquiry in the disciplines.[49] These notions are reflected in a curriculum that blends concerns for the development of the whole child—aesthetically, spiritually, morally, and physically, as well as intellectually—with concerns for the thoughtful teaching of the disciplines.

Implementing the Curriculum. The ministry describes the goals of Korean education as including:

- The balanced development of mind and body and the development of a mature sense of self-identity
- The abilities to recognize and solve problems in daily life; to engage in logical, critical and creative thinking; and to express their own feelings and ideas

- Attitudes for appreciating tradition and culture in a way appropriate for the global setting
- Developing knowledge and skills for engaging in the diverse world of work, fostering love for neighbors and country as well as awareness as global citizens[0]

Interestingly, while U.S. schools have been reducing the time they spend teaching subjects other than reading and math, the Korean curriculum devotes the large majority of time to a liberal arts curriculum that devotes significant time at every grade level to social studies, science, physical education, music, fine arts, moral education, foreign language (English), practical arts, and a range of extracurricular activities and electives.[51] All of these subjects are to be integrated into three broad areas: disciplined life, intelligent life, and pleasant life (see Table 6.1).

National standards guide these courses, but curriculum frameworks are developed at the regional level, and actual curriculum materials and lessons are developed at the school level by teachers. Textbooks are written, commissioned, or approved by the government, but parents and teachers at the school level play a strong role in textbook selection.

Table 6.1. Korean School Curriculum (Number of Hours Annually).

Subjects	Grade 1	2	3	4	5	6	7	8	9	10	11	12
			Elementary School				Middle School			High School		
Korean Language	Korean Language 210	328	238	204	204	204	170	136	136	136		
Moral Education	Mathematics		34	34	34	34	68	68	34	34	Korean History 68	
Social Studies	120	136	102	102	102	102	102	102	136	170		
Mathematics	Disciplined Life		136	136	136	136	136	136	102	136		
Science	60	68	102	102	102	102	102	136	136	102		
Practical Arts	Intelligent Life		·	·	68	68	Technology Home Economics 68	102	102	102	Elective Courses	
Physical Education	90	102	102	102	102	102	102	102	68	68		
Music	Pleasant Life		68	68	68	68	68	34	34	34		
Fine Arts	180	204	68	68	68	68	34	34	68	34		
Foreign Languages (English)	We are the first graders 80	·	34	34	68	68	102	102	136	136		
Optional Activities	60	68	68	68	68	68	136	136	136	204		
Extracurricular Activities	30	34	34	68	68	68	68	68	68	68	8 units	
Grand Total	830	850	986	986	1,088	1,088	1,156	1,156	1,156	1,224	144 units	

Source: Korean Institute for Curriculum and Evaluation (2008).

Curriculum quality is monitored through systematic curriculum evaluation procedures that result in regular refinements. Inspectors from the regional and local educational authorities regularly visit individual schools to examine curriculum plans and teaching. National research institutes such as the Korea Institute of Curriculum and Evaluation (KICE) often conduct research related to curriculum implementation and instruction. The Ministry of Education has also piloted methods for school self-evaluation of curriculum implementation, resembling the strategies used in nations like Finland. There is now no individual-level external testing of students before the end of high school, but there is a sample test, like the NAEP in the United States, which tests 1% of students at grades 6 and 9, and 3% of students in grade 10 as the basis for curriculum evaluation in Korean, math, science, social studies, and English. Performance-based items are designed to be at least 30% of the total.

Evaluations of student performance are teacher-designed and administered within the school. In addition to paper-and-pencil tests, school-based student assessments have begun to include performance assessments, such as laboratory experiments in science. The ministry has encouraged the use of more essay examinations and performance tests as part of its efforts, since the mid-1990s, to increase attention to critical thinking and problem-solving skills.

Current Reforms. Korea took very seriously the framework for education put forth in UNESCO's widely disseminated Delors (1996) Report, and its notion that education should develop the richness and diversity of talent for every human being. The education system has sought to develop the report's four pillars of learning: learning to know, learning to do, learning to be, and learning to live together. Published goals for education include, along with knowledge and applied skills, emotional skills and qualities, creative/aesthetic sensibilities, spiritual well-being, and self-knowledge, as well as attitudes that support tolerance, peace, and respect for others. Korea's holistic view of the purposes of education and the associated breadth of the school curriculum is, ironically, much more comprehensive than that found in many American schools today, especially those serving less affluent students.

Still, Koreans worry about the narrowing of the curriculum that they attribute to the nation's college entrance examination. One observer notes: "College entrance examinations are a national obsession."[52] The exams influence the high school curriculum and inspire extensive out-of-school cram courses. To reduce this influence, universities are currently prohibited from using their own paper-and-pencil tests, high school classification (academic or vocational), or parent donations as a basis for admitting students. In an effort to further deemphasize the effects of the SAT, which Korean officials view as distorting the rest of the curriculum and "relying far too much on memorization and recall of fragmented knowledge,"[53] colleges are encouraged to place greater importance on high school evaluations and students' performance in various fields, including essays they submit, rather than the national SAT scores.

Despite these admonitions, the competition around college admissions has given rise to an extensive private tutoring industry in Korea that is bemoaned in virtually every government report over the last decade. To offset the advantages that more affluent students receive from private tutoring, the Korean government now provides free academic afterschool programs, as well as lessons on television and the Internet and special scholarship programs for students from low-income families.[54]

Since 1997, the Ministry of Education has been moving assertively to replace what has been characterized as an overcrowded curriculum focused on content coverage with one focused on deeper understanding of concepts in ways that foster higher-order thinking and problem-solving skills. The ministry describes the seventh National Curriculum as designed to address the needs of a global knowledge-based economy, developing students' abilities to think originally, to create new knowledge, and to communicate that knowledge effectively to others.[55] Infusion of technology is an additional goal. Every Korean school had high-speed Internet connections in classrooms by 2002, and ICT usage must be incorporated into at least 10% of every subject.[56]

Current curriculum reforms are aimed at reducing the total number of instructional hours, along with the amount of subject-matter content students need to cover each year, minimizing redundancies and increasing opportunities for in-depth study, the proportion of optional activities in school that encourage students' self-directed learning, students' independent study skills, and other creative activities. Professor Chong Jae Lee, former director of the Korean Educational Development Institute, notes that current reforms aim to better develop core competencies such as higher-order thinking, self-control, responsibility, independence, creativity, self-directed learning capabilities, and social capital development.[57]

Although Korean students attend school for 220 days a year, the total number of instructional hours annually—which ranges from 553 in the primary school to 1,020 in the high school—is generally less than the 900 to 1,080 common in the United States. It is difficult to draw a direct correlation from these seat time requirements to learning outcomes, as Korean students engage in significant out-of-school studying, yet both the United States and Korea require substantially more time than the number of instructional hours in high-achieving nations such as Finland and Japan (see Table 6.2). Indeed, as of this writing, Korea was in a transitional period from the 6-day school week to a 5-day school week, to be in place by 2010.[58] This reflects the ministry's view that education will be enhanced through qualitative differences in the kind and quality of learning required of students rather than by the quantity of contact hours alone.

Table 6.2. Number of Total Instructional Hours per Year.

	Primary School					Middle School				High School		
	1	2	3	4	5	6	7	8	9	10	11	12
Korea Current	553	567	657	657	725	725	867	867	867	1020	1020	1020
Korea Draft	531	544	612	612	680	380	816	816	816	963	963	963
China	769	798	855	855	855	855	965	965	965	1140	1110	1080
Japan	587	630	683	709	709	709	817	817	817	719	719	719
Finland	542	542	656	656	684	684	855	855	855	713	713	713

Source: Korean Institute for Curriculum and Evaluation (2008).

Teaching

Efforts to improve the quality of learning have rested equally on changes in the curriculum and investments in teachers. Teachers are highly qualified in Korea: 100% of them have completed teacher education and a set of written and performance tests to attain certification. Korea's strong showing on the international mathematics assessments has been attributed to the fact that more than 95% of all Korean secondary school math teachers have a degree in mathematics or mathematics education as well as teaching certification, as compared to only about 70% of U.S. math teachers.

Both elementary and secondary candidates typically complete a 4-year undergraduate teacher education program, although graduate programs for preparing teachers have also begun to appear. Eleven public universities and two private universities produce teachers. Regardless of the institution or program, a standard program of studies in content and pedagogy is required. This program focuses on subject matter, general and content-specific teaching methods, child development and learning, the study of curriculum and assessment, uses of technology in education, and how to teach special populations, such as students with exceptional needs. To be employed, candidates must complete this preparation and take a certification examination testing their knowledge of subject-matter content, general pedagogy, and content-specific pedagogy. This two-part examination not only includes short-answer and essay questions, as well as some multiple-choice responses, but it also includes interviews and performance elements, including a classroom demonstration and a computer proficiency assessment for secondary teachers.

Teachers are much respected in Korea, ranking with priests in a recent opinion poll as the most trusted members of society. The Confucian saying "King, teacher, and parents are equal" reflects this regard. So do teachers' attractive salaries, which rank right behind those of Korean doctors and above those of engineers, and which yield purchasing power within the local economy nearly 250% higher than those of

U.S. teachers.[59] Salaries are on a unitary scale nationwide, determined by seniority, academic credentials, and position.

After completing preparation, teachers receive a lifetime certificate, which adds to the desirability of the career; however, competition for jobs is extremely intense, especially in the cities, with only one in 20 applicants receiving a job in Seoul in 2008, for example. Once hired, teachers are automatically tenured until they reach retirement. Analysts Kang and Hong note that this is an attractive feature in South Korea, "where lifetime service and employment are respected and valued."[60]

The Korean Educational Development Institute notes that there is a huge oversupply of teacher candidates for secondary schools—with about five times as many available candidates as positions. A small, temporary need for elementary teachers has occurred because of the abrupt reduction of the teacher retirement age combined with an aggressive class-size reduction policy, but policy steps are under way to rectify this quickly by recruiting more prospective teachers into the elementary grades.

Working conditions are also viewed as highly desirable. In South Korea—much like Japan and Singapore—only about 35% of teachers' working time is spent teaching pupils, less than half the ratio in the United States, where instruction comprises about 80% of teachers' time, and virtually all planning and grading occurs after school. The Korean system allows teachers to attend to grading, administrative work, meeting with parents and students, and shared planning and professional learning within the work day where they have access to colleagues. Teachers work in a shared office space during out-of-class time since the students stay in a fixed classroom while the teachers rotate to teach them different subjects. The shared office space facilitates the sharing of instructional resources and ideas among teachers, which is especially helpful for new teachers.[61]

Beginning teachers are also supported with a 6-month induction program that is managed by the principal, vice principal, and advisor teachers, who provide classroom guidance and supervision. In-service development courses are offered and fully paid for by the ministry and by local offices of education. After their fourth year of teaching, South Korean teachers are required to take 90 hours of professional development courses every 3 years. Also, after 3 years of teaching, teachers are eligible to enroll in a 5-week (180-hour) professional development program approved by the government to obtain an advanced certificate, which provides an increase in salary and eligibility for promotion to vice principal and principal.

Professional learning opportunities are increasingly available online as well as at the school site. As part of its major investments to become one of the world's largest telecommunications centers, for example, Korea established Edunet, an online teaching-learning center that acts as a clearinghouse for information pertaining to learning. As of 2003, 80% of all teachers participated in the service. The ministry is currently creating a Digital Library Support System for Edunet.[62]

A wide range of incentives is available for engaging in professional learning and for serving in areas where there are staffing needs. Typically, excellent veteran teachers aim for the principalship. Promotion is based on length of service, performance, and research achievements. Those who serve in high-need areas also earn bonus points toward promotion. Other incentives for equitable distribution of teachers include smaller class sizes, less in-class teaching time, stipends in addition to salary, and opportunities to choose later teaching appointments for those who initially take assignments in rural areas or low-socioeconomic urban schools.[63] The end result is a highly qualified, experienced, and stable teaching force in all schools, providing a foundation for strong student learning.

HOW SINGAPORE BECAME A "LEARNING NATION"

The themes of support for expert teaching, expansion of access, and a press to prepare students for innovation and inquiry are also found in Singapore's education system, which has been a source of intense interest for policy analysts since its students took first place in the Trends in International Mathematics and Science Study (TIMSS) assessments in mathematics and science in 1995, 1999, and 2003. These rankings are based on strong achievement for all of the country's students, including the Malay and Tamil minorities, who have been rapidly closing what was once a yawning achievement gap.[64] About 90% of Singapore's students scored above the international median on the TIMSS tests. This accomplishment is even more remarkable given that fewer than half of Singapore's students routinely speak English, the language of the test, at home. Most speak one of the other official national languages of the country—Mandarin, Malay, or Tamil—and some speak one of several dozen other languages or dialects.

Because of the nation's bilingual language policy, adopted in 1966, all instruction is in English, but all students must also maintain one or more other languages through supplementary teaching of the students' "mother tongue," represented by one of the other three national languages.[65] Some students, who do not speak one of these languages at home, may study other Chinese or Indian dialects that are their actual home languages in school or in classes offered by community-based organizations. Thus, Singapore has established itself not only as a center of mathematics, science, and technology, but as a nation with fluency in the current and emerging world and regional languages for business and trade.

Intensive investment and reform over a period of 30 years have completely transformed the Singaporean education system, managing to broaden access and increase equality while orchestrating a system that includes a complex system of independent, "autonomous," and public schools, some of them inherited from the colonial era when ethnic groups and churches started schools, all of which are now part of the national system and receive government subsidies. These schools are intentionally diverse in many ways, as local schools are urged to innovate and distinguish themselves from one another, but purposefully common in instructional expectations and supports. The ministry has set up or encouraged specialized schools in areas such as arts, sports, mathematics, and science, in order to cater to students' different interests and talents. All schools must maintain the country's bilingualism policy and incorporate national education into the curriculum, so that they nurture "a Singaporean spirit and character."[66] For those who are interested in what is currently called a "portfolio" approach to creating and operating diverse school types while maintaining quality and a large measure of equity, Singapore offers some tantalizing insights.

Since the prime minister introduced the "thinking schools, learning nation" initiative in 1997, Singapore's explicit focus in its reforms of curriculum, assessment, and teaching has been to develop a creative and critical thinking culture within schools, by explicitly teaching and assessing these skills for students—and by creating an inquiry culture among teachers as well, who are supported to conduct action research on their teaching and to continually revise their teaching strategies in response to what they learn. This initiative was married to a commitment to integrating technology into all aspects of education—a mission nearly fully accomplished a decade later—and dramatically opening up college and university admissions. I return to all of these issues later, after describing some of the journey Singapore took to get where it is today.

Reform Strategies

Singapore had few natural resources other than its strategic trading location when it emerged from British colonial rule and was founded as an independent republic in 1965. At that time, with no compulsory education and relatively few people entering and staying in school through high school, a highly tracked elite system produced only a tiny number of high school or college graduates and few skilled workers. Today, by contrast, about half of young people complete college in Singapore or abroad—about 50% more than in the United States—and nearly all of the remainder receive a postsecondary technical or vocational degree that prepares them for work, which is increasingly likely to be in a high-tech field in one of the many multinational corporations settling in Singapore.

Over the intervening years, the education system has changed radically, with the government frequently referring to Singapore's population as its only natural resource and its education system as the primary resource developer. The goal of the education system is described as developing the talents of each individual so that each can contribute to society and to the ongoing struggle to make Singapore productive and competitive in the international marketplace, something it has substantially achieved with a booming economy today.[67]

The first wave of reforms launched in 1979—15 years after colonial rule—expanded vocational education so as to reduce the dropout rate and to see that students left school with marketable skills, and created a set of junior colleges to extend academic study for 2 years beyond grade 10, when secondary schools end in the Singaporean system. (The basic structure is a 6-year primary school and a 4-year secondary school.) By 1987, about 10% of secondary students attended special vocational schools; the remainder attended academic high schools. Fifteen junior colleges operating by late 1989 enrolled the "most promising" 25% of their age cohort and were equipped with computers, laboratories, and well-stocked libraries. Although some represented the elite private schools of the colonial period, others founded in the 1980s were located in the centers of the public housing estates where most low-income residents live.

A decade later, the government set a goal of increasing education spending from 4% to 6% of the gross domestic product (GDP), to match the levels of Japan and the United States. (In 2009, with a growing GDP, education consumes about 5%.) Expanded investments during the 1990s improved school conditions and curriculum, and allowed greater access to the private schools established in the colonial era that were previously inaccessible to lower-income students. Regardless of the school, primary education is now free to all, and the government offers funding for tuition, textbooks, and uniforms to those in any school—including independent or autonomous schools—who cannot pay for them. More affluent families also pay more for post-secondary education. Officials view this public/private partnership as lassoing the resources of the wealthy in support of education while lassoing the resources of government to be sure that the best opportunities created in any sector are accessible to all students without financial barriers.

Higher education is also heavily subsidized so that tuitions are low, and need-based aid is available to make up any difference between what families can afford and the costs of a program to which students have been admitted. The indigenous Malays, who represent about 15% of the population, receive free education all the way through university.

Higher education is now available to virtually all Singaporeans. Based on their interests, the manpower needs determined by the government, and the results of their grades, O-level exams, and other accomplishments, students pursue one of three pathways after 10th grade when secondary school ends: About 25% attend junior college for 2 years, followed by university, which leads to professional paths such as teaching, science, engineering, medicine, law, and the civil service; about 60% attend a polytechnic college for 3 years, after which about half go on to the university while the others go into jobs in technical and engineering fields; and the remainder—about 15%—

attend an Institute of Technical Education for 2 years, and some then continue on to college or university. Polytechnics and technical institutes are well-resourced, state-of-the-art facilities linked to contemporary labor market demands, offering strong routes to occupational mobility. Virtually everyone finishes one of these pathways. Students are also encouraged and frequently supported to attend college overseas. To address growing demand, a fourth major university is currently being built in Singapore in partnership with the Massachusetts Institute of Technology (MIT).

Singapore is different from Finland and South Korea—two largely homogenous societies, each with one dominant language (Finnish and Korean, respectively)—in that it is multiethnic and multilingual, and has worked to overcome a colonial past in which schooling was an instrument of division and inequality. Analysts suggest that one of the great triumphs of post-colonial education policy in Singapore was its successful use of the school to create greater equity and social cohesion among disparate groups, including minorities who had been poorly educated, while strengthening civil loyalties. The schools have undertaken a deliberate effort, through curriculum and school ritual, to strengthen acceptance of and appreciation for differences and to level the playing field for all members of society.[68]

A history of Singapore notes how the combination of an egalitarian ethos with a goal of integrating diverse ethnic groups is joined with a meritocratic, competitive culture in a unique blend that has created these unusually strong educational outcomes:

> More clearly than any other social institution, the school system expressed the distinctive vision of Singapore's leadership, with its stress on merit, competition, technology, and international standards, and its rejection of special privileges for any group. Singaporeans of all ethnic groups and classes came together in the schools, and the education system affected almost every family in significant and profound ways. Most of the domestic political issues of the country, such as the relations between ethnic groups, the competition for elite status, the plans for the future security of the nation and its people, and the distribution of scarce resources were reflected in the schools and in education policy. . . . It was in the schools, more than in any other institution, that the abstract values of multiracialism and of Singaporean identity were given concrete form.[69]

From Rote Learning to "Thinking Schools"

Historically, the schools have operated a modified British-style system in which secondary students took the same examinations as their counterparts in Britain. The GCE (General Certificate of Education) O-level examinations are based on common course syllabi that outline what is to be taught; they require short and long open-ended responses and essays across a wide range of content areas from which students choose the ones in which they want to be examined. Although the results are used to guide college admissions, and are not used to determine graduation from high school, they exert substantial influence on the high school curriculum. To reduce this influence, the ministry has begun to open up admissions at all levels of the system to a wider range of indicators of student ability and talent beyond test scores.[70] As described below, recent reforms are changing the curriculum and assessment system to make it more keenly focused on creativity and independent problem solving.

Although Singaporean schools, like those in many other Asian nations, have had a reputation for being rote-oriented—and the nation has been explicitly seeking to reduce instruction that calls for memorization and recall—this is not an entirely accurate characterization of traditional instruction. As researcher Harold Stevenson noted from his research nearly 2 decades ago, Asian systems that have been stereotyped in this way have actually tended to cover content at a more in-depth level, use more manipulatives and hands-on supports for learning, engage in more collaborative learning activities, and require applications of knowledge to more complex problems than is often true in the United States—especially in those underresourced American districts where worksheets accomplished through unaided seat work assigned by harried, underprepared teachers dominate instruction.[71]

As in Japan and Hong Kong, China, math students frequently work in pairs or small groups on problems contextualized in real-world situations, come to the board to explain their answers, and question one another about their findings and conjectures, creating a strong mathematical discourse that supports understanding. Students often derive formulas after they have deeply understood a mathematical concept and create their own word problems to test their own and their classmates' understanding further, gradually coming to "own" the knowledge for themselves.[72]

Transforming the Curriculum. Nonetheless, there has been a substantial effort to transform the curriculum since the "thinking schools, learning nation" initiative was launched in 1997. As Ng Pak Tee from Singapore's National Institute of Education explains "Syllabi, examinations and university admission criteria were changed to encourage thinking out of the box and risk-taking. Students are now more engaged in project work and higher order thinking questions to encourage creativity, independent, and inter-dependent learning."[73]

This initiative was accompanied by a plan for infusing technology in every school and for cultivating "Innovation and Enterprise" throughout the system in order to develop intellectual curiosity and a spirit of collective initiative. The amount of content covered by national syllabi was cut by 10 to 30% in 1998 to allow for more project work and independent learning.[74] This impulse was further reinforced by Prime Minister Lee Hsien Loong's speech during the 2004 National Day Rally in which he urged, "We have got to teach less to our students so that they will learn more."[75]

The paradoxical encouragement to "teach less, learn more," now a widely used slogan in Singapore, is intended to replace the goal of covering a large quantity of material in the curriculum with a goal of enhancing teaching quality within a curriculum that allows more depth of study and allows more "white space" for teacher and student initiative. Then Minister of Education Tharman Shanmugaratnam explained, while answering questions in the Parliament, that the goal is "to give students themselves the room to exercise initiative and to shape their own learning. The students have to become engaged learners—interested and proactive agents in the learning process."[76] He urged a shift of priorities, with

> less dependence on rote learning, repetitive tests and a "one size fits all" type of instruction, and more on engaged learning, discovery through experiences, differentiated teaching, the learning of life-long skills, and the building of character through innovative and effective teaching approaches and strategies, [as well as] holistic learning so that students can go beyond narrowly defined academic excellence to develop the attributes, mindsets, character and values for future success.[77]

Nice reform rhetoric, one might say, but what about the reality? When visiting schools in Singapore, I was struck by how much of this vision has been actualized through the highly connected work of the ministry; its major partner for professional preparation, the National Institute for Education, and the school sites. At every school, an emphasis on holistic education to develop well-rounded human beings was apparent. Explicit efforts to develop students cognitively, aesthetically, spiritually, morally, and socially were obvious throughout the curriculum. In addition to project work visible in nearly every classroom, children were extensively involved in music, arts, calligraphy, physical education, sports, and an amazing variety of clubs and self-initiated activities aimed at building creativity and entrepreneurship.

Innovation in Action. Entering Ngee Ann Secondary School, for example, which is located in the center of the Tampines housing estate (one of many publicly subsidized housing areas), there is a grand piano frequently used by students and a beautiful exhibit of professional-quality student art in the outdoors for all to view. The school's strong emphasis on students becoming self-initiating and innovative is expressed in many ways: Among other things, students are given seed money to start their own small businesses, and the funds they make go back into the school. They prepare a concept proposal and a business plan. Those that are selected can use the small stalls lining one walkway to sell their wares, which may include everything from creating and selling baked goods to designing and selling computer or video games. The businesses are licensed; if they violate regulations, they can be closed down for a week, as in real life, so students learn how the world operates.

Principal Chua Chor Huat notes, "We try to build values and leadership in everything we do." In addition to sponsoring a student leadership group, all cocurricular activities, from the *Green Movement* to the debate and robotics clubs, also have student leaders. The drama club had just participated in a competition debuting a play the students wrote called "Internet Addiction," a sign of the technology-intensive lives of the students.

The innovation theme is apparent throughout the school. In physical education, the students are engaged in creating "Innovative Games." They work in groups to invent a game, and then they teach it to the other students. In "Design and Technology"—a course required for seventh and eighth graders that can be continued through exam level work at ninth and tenth grades—students design and execute a range of products. A design folio explores a theme assigned by the exam board and a wide range of design and technology issues associated with it. It includes a design for a new product with options and alternatives explored, drawings to scale, rationales for design decisions, and finally, a constructed artifact—an outdoor barbecue, a cell phone holder, or whatever meets the design challenge expectations.

Science classes also support inquiry and invention. For example, a set of students from one biology class undertook a project to create an insect repellent that is 100% natural, safe, environmentally friendly, convenient, and effective. They discovered that common spices such as cinnamon, cloves, and star anise have insect repellant properties and extracted oils to create an effective product in paper, liquid, and solid form. They were among the finalists in one of the many competitions that seem to be common in every domain of life and learning in Singapore.

Technology infusion and collaborative learning are other goals visible throughout the school. In a science class, students worked in pairs using their laptop computers to draw a concept map of the three states of matter and the properties of each. Those who were ready moved on to map the features of kinetic particle theory (KPT) while the teacher circulated to ask questions and assist. He was planning to review the work that evening to identify misconceptions and understandings as the basis for planning the next day's work.

Another class of much younger students shared an inquiry they had conducted to find out, using a tachometer, what shapes of blades produce the most revolutions per minute. Their "action research," presented by PowerPoint, featured careful questions and controls, and students were able to answer additional questions about how to go further in their investigation to sort out whether weight or shape was the key variable. They also explored applications to wind power for a greener approach to energy. Their teacher explained that, "Action research is concerned with changing situations, not just interpreting them. . . . The aim is not only to make students learn why the world works in a certain way, but rather what they can do to improve it."

Addressing the explicit effort to change the culture of right answers that has dominated in the past, the teacher also emphasized that her goal was to teach students to be comfortable in asking good questions: "Creativity and innovation may surface when there may be no clear answers, and students have to be OK working with unanswered questions."

Redesigning Assessment. As part of this quest, Singapore has been moving toward more open-ended assessments that require critical thinking and reasoning. The high school tests are accompanied by school-based tasks, such as research projects and experiments designed and conducted by students. The science test includes laboratory investigations. These school-based components, which are designed by teachers to specifications, count for up to 20% of the examination grade. Selected projects are submitted to the university as part of the application as well.

Integrated program schools have exempted students from the "O" level examinations to reduce test-based influences on the curriculum; particularly high-achieving students may move directly to junior college without taking these tests. The goal is to "free up more time for students to experience a broader and integrated curriculum that will engage them in critical and creative thinking."[78]

Meanwhile, a new "A" level curriculum and examination system was introduced in 2006 in the junior colleges that offer grades 11 and 12. Designed by the Ministry of Education, the Singapore Examinations and Assessment Board, and the University of Cambridge Local Examinations Syndicate, the new exams are meant to encourage multidisciplinary learning by including courses such as "Knowledge and Inquiry" and by requiring that students "select and draw together knowledge and skills they have learned from across different subject areas, and apply them to tackle new and unfamiliar areas or problems."[79] To reassure nervous parents, a brochure from the Examination Board lists quotes from prestigious universities in the United Kingdom and the United States about the new exams. For example, from Yale University (quoted along with Harvard, Princeton, and the London School of Economics): "Yale welcomes the new curricular design . . . which encourages the acquisition of life skills and values, a broad knowledge base and multi-disciplinary perspective. . . . These changes show promise of helping to create a generation of students better prepared for life and for useful service to their country and the world.[80]

In the curriculum and assessment guidelines that accompany the national standards, teachers are encouraged to engage in continual assessment in the classroom, using a variety of assessment modes, such as classroom observations, oral communication, written assignments and tests, and practical and investigative tasks. The ministry has developed a number of curriculum and assessment supports for teachers. For example, SAIL (Strategies for Active and Independent Learning) aims to support more learner-centered project work in classrooms, and provides assessment rubrics to clarify learning expectations. All schools have received training for using these tools. The ministry's 2004 Assessment Guides for both primary and lower secondary mathematics contain resources, tools, and ideas to help teachers incorporate strategies such as mathematical investigations, journal writing, classroom observation, self-assessment and portfolio assessment into the classroom. Emphasis is placed on the assessment of problem solving and on metacognition, the self-regulation of learning that will enable students to internalize standards and become independent learners.[81]

In a useful demonstration of how the strong emphasis on professional learning enables Singapore's efforts at reform, the Institute of Education has held a variety of workshops to support learning about the new assessments and integrated the new strategies into teacher development programs. Mathematics teacher associations have organized conferences on assessments. A group of the secondary school mathematics department heads produced a book for other teachers on journal writing in the mathematics classroom, which has been widely used, and other teachers have produced materials and exemplars of assessments that are frequently shared.[82] Change is a collective enterprise energetically pursued with strong supports and a sense of shared mission.

Investments in Teaching and School Leadership

This new curriculum emphasis is intently reinforced in teachers' pre-service and in-service training. When I visited Singapore's National Institute of Education (NIE)—the nation's only teacher training institution—nearly everyone I spoke to described how they were working to develop teachers' abilities to teach a curriculum focused on critical thinking, inquiry, and collaboration, in part by engaging teachers in inquiry themselves.

Teacher education is a serious investment throughout the career. To get the best teachers, students from the top one-third of each graduating high school class are recruited into a fully paid 4-year undergraduate teacher education program (or, if they enter later, a 1- to 2-year graduate program) and immediately put on the ministry's payroll. When they enter teaching, they earn as much or more than beginning engineers, accountants, lawyers, and doctors who are in the civil service,[83] which eliminates concerns for shortages. During the course of preparation, there is a focus on learning to use problem-based and inquiry learning, on developing collaboration, and on addressing a range of learning styles in the classroom.

Teacher education programs were overhauled in 2001 to increase teachers' pedagogical knowledge and skills, on top of their content preparation, which includes, even for elementary teachers, a deep mastery of one content area plus preparation for the four major subjects they must teach (English language, mathematics, science, and social studies). The joint location of content and pedagogy specialists in the same department helped strengthen these ties. Practicum training was expanded and located in a new "school partnership" model that engages schools more proactively in supporting trainees. Growing efforts have been made to engage candidates in the kind of inquiry and reflection in which they are expected to engage their students in the schools, so that they can teach for independent learning, integrated project work, and innovation.[84]

Candidates learn to teach in the same way they will be asked to teach. Every student has a laptop, and the entire campus is wireless. The library spaces are consciously arranged with round tables and groups of three to four chairs so that students will have places to share knowledge and collaborate. A comfortable area with sofa and chair arrangements is designed for group work among teachers and principals. The grouping areas are soundproofed with an overhead circular cone, so that several groups can work together in the same room. They have access to full technology supports (e.g., DVD, video and computer hookup, and a plasma screen for projecting their work as they do it. The wall is a white board for recording ideas).

Candidates have practicum opportunities in classrooms with teachers deemed good models of these practices during each of their 4 years of study, and the institute has been creative in thinking about how to help teachers envision new modes of practice even beyond those they might see in their student teaching. For example, a "Classroom of the Future" has been constructed at NIE to give educators a vision of what learning will be like in the 21st century. It includes handheld computers used in a range of places: a coffee bar where students meet around round tables and work on educational video games; a library where students communicate electronically with students in other countries working on solving a problem together (e.g., identifying a virus that is spreading; collecting data; running tests; accessing information via the Internet); a subway car where students are tracking their friends; at home, where interactive technology connects families and friends in communication; and finally in a classroom which, again, features round tables surrounded by chairs where students are engaged in more inquiry and problem solving. These settings are used as the site for learning new teaching strategies.

After initial preparation, as in other highly ranked countries, novices are not left to sink or swim. Expert teachers, trained by the National Institute as mentors, are given released time to help beginners learn their craft. During this structured mentoring year, beginning teachers also attend courses in classroom management, counseling, reflective practices, and assessment offered by the National Institute and the ministry.

Thereafter, the government pays for 100 hours of professional development each year for all teachers in addition to the 20 hours a week they have to work with other teachers and visit one another's classrooms to study teaching. Currently, teachers are being trained to undertake action research projects in the classroom so that they can examine teaching and learning problems, and find solutions that can be disseminated to others.

Among Singapore's many investments in teacher professional learning is the Teacher's Network, so named in 1998 by the Ministry of Education as part of the "Thinking Schools" initiative. The mission of the Teacher's Network is to serve as a catalyst and support for teacher-initiated development through sharing, collaboration, and reflection. The Teacher's Network includes learning circles, teacher-led workshops, conferences, and a well-being program, as well as a website and publications series for sharing knowledge.[85]

In a Teacher's Network learning circle, four to 10 teachers and a facilitator collaboratively identify and solve common problems chosen by the participating teachers using discussions and action research. The learning circles generally meet for eight 2-hour sessions over a period of 4 to 12 months. Supported by the national university, Teacher's Network professional development officers run an initial whole-school training program on the key processes of reflection, dialogue, and action research, and a more extended program to train teachers as learning circle facilitators and mentor facilitators in the field. A major part of the facilitator's role is to encourage the teachers to act as colearners and critical friends so that they feel safe to take the risks of sharing their assumptions and personal theories, experimenting with new ideas and practices, and sharing their successes and problems. Discussing problems and possible solutions in learning circles fosters a sense of collegiality among teachers and encourages teachers to be reflective practitioners. Learning circles allow teachers to feel that they are producing knowledge, not just disseminating received knowledge.

Teacher-led workshops provide teachers with an opportunity to present their ideas and work with their colleagues in a collegial atmosphere where everyone, including the presenter, is a colearner and critical friend. Each workshop is jointly planned with a Teacher's Network professional development officer to ensure that everyone will be a colearner in the workshop. The presenters first prepare an outline of their workshop, then the professional development officer helps the presenters surface their tacit knowledge and assumptions and trains them in facilitation so that they do not present as an expert with all the answers, but share and discuss the challenges they face in the classroom. The process is time consuming, but almost all teacher presenters find that it leads to them grow professionally.[86]

In Singapore, master teachers are appointed to lead the coaching and development of the teachers in each school.[87] And teachers continue to advance throughout the career. With help from the government, Singapore teachers can pursue three separate career ladders that help them become curriculum specialists, mentors for other teachers, or school principals. These opportunities bring recognition, extra compensation, and new challenges that keep teaching exciting.

Leadership development is also taken very seriously. All principals and department heads are fully trained at government expense before they take on their posts. There is also an extensive executive development program for current leaders. Leaders are identified, cultivated, and recruited from among teachers who demonstrate promise. Each year, teachers are evaluated on their leadership skills as well as their teaching skills in a multifaceted, competency-based process, and the ministry keeps tabs on up-and-coming potential leaders, reviewing evaluations and checking in regularly with principals about which faculty members are ready for additional challenges and learning opportunities. When potential pricipals are identified, they are given opportunities to take on new responsibilities and to engage in various kinds of training. The most able are recruited into principal preparation programs and the most able among these are appointed to school leadership positions.

Leadership training integrates university-based coursework with school-based apprenticeship, focusing on how to develop instruction and, increasingly, how to manage schools as inquiry-based learning organizations. Singapore's talent development system is tightly integrated around the country's goals for educational reform, creating an additional engine for steady educational progress.

EDUCATIONAL LEAP FROG:
THE COMMON PRACTICES OF STEEPLY IMPROVING COUNTRIES

Although Finland, Korea, and Singapore are very different from one another culturally and historically, all three have made startling improvements in their education systems over the last 30 years. Their investments have catapulted them from the bottom to the top of international rankings in student achievement and attainment, graduating more than 90% of their young people from high school and sending large majorities through college as well, far more than in the much wealthier United States. Their strategies also have much in common. All three have:

- *Funded schools adequately and equitably* and added incentives for teaching in high-need schools. All three nations have built their education systems on a strong egalitarian ethos, explicitly confronting and addressing potential sources of inequality. While Finland has an almost entirely public system, Korea and Singapore have gradually brought their private schools (starting during colonial times by missionaries and elites) under the public umbrella, contributing to their costs and paying tuition and fees for any students who cannot afford them, thus working to equalize access for students to all parts of the system.
- *Eliminated examination systems* that had previously tracked students for middle schools and restricted access to high school. Finland and Korea now have no external examinations before the voluntary matriculation exams for college. In addition to the "O" level matriculation examinations, students in Singapore take examinations at the end of primary school (grade 6), which are used to calculate value-added contributions to their learning that are part of the information system about secondary schools. These examinations require extensive written responses and problem solving, and include curriculum-embedded projects and papers that are graded by teachers.
- *Revised national standards and curriculum* to focus learning goals on higher-order thinking, inquiry, and innovation, as well as the integration of technology

throughout the curriculum. Teachers develop school-based performance assessments to evaluate student learning, which include research projects, science investigations, and technology applications. Students are increasingly expected to learn to reflect on, evaluate, and manage their own learning.

- *Developed national teaching policies* that built strong teacher education programs that recruit able students and completely subsidize their extensive training programs, paying them a stipend as they learn to teach well. Salaries are equitable across schools and competitive with other careers, generally comparable to those of engineers and other key professionals. Teachers are viewed as professionally prepared and are well respected, and working conditions are supportive, including substantial participation in decision making about curriculum, instruction, assessment, and professional development.

- *Supported ongoing teacher learning* by ensuring mentoring for beginning teachers and providing 15 to 25 hours a week for veteran teachers to plan collaboratively and engage in analyses of student learning, lesson study, action research, and observations of one another's classrooms that help them continually improve their practice. All three nations expect teachers to engage in research on practice and create incentives for them to do so, and fund extensive ongoing professional development opportunities in collaboration with universities and other schools.

- *Pursued consistent, long-term reforms,* setting goals for expanding, equalizing, and improving the education system and steadily implementing these goals, making thoughtful investments in a quality educator workforce and in school curriculum and teaching resources that built the underpinnings for success. This has been made possible in part by the fact that these systems are managed by professional ministries of education, which are substantially buffered from shifting political winds. Frequent evaluations of schools and the system as a whole have helped guide reforms.

All three nations have undertaken these elements in a systematic fashion, rather than pouring energy into a potpourri of innovations and then changing course every few years, as has often been the case in many communities in the United States, especially in large cities. And while these three small nations—each comparable in size to a mid-sized U.S. state—have conducted this work from a national level, similar strategies have been employed at the state or provincial level in high-scoring Australia, New Zealand, and Canada, and provinces such as Hong Kong and Macao in China, also with positive outcomes. (I discuss some of these efforts in later chapters.) They demonstrate how it is possible to build a system in which students are routinely taught by well-prepared teachers who work together to create a thoughtful, high-quality curriculum, supported by appropriate materials and assessments that enable ongoing learning for students, teachers, and schools alike.

CHAPTER 7

Doing What Matters Most: Developing Competent Teaching

The experience of [high-performing] school systems suggests that three things matter most: 1) getting the right people to become teachers; 2) developing them into effective instructors and; 3) ensuring that the system is able to deliver the best possible instruction for every child.

—Michael Barber and Mona Mourshed[1]

As equality of opportunity comes to rest more squarely on the need for quality instruction, issues of how to enhance the professional competence of educators become more important. To ensure equal opportunity in today's context means enhancing, not limiting, the professional nature of teaching, and for that task state policy as it has been conceived in the past is hardly the best instrument . . . We need new ways of conceiving the state role and the strategies at the state's disposal.

—Richard Elmore and Susan Fuhrman[2]

Nations that have steeply improved their students' achievement, such as Finland, Korea, Singapore, and others, attribute much of their success to their focused investments in teacher preparation and development. Creating an infrastructure that can routinely recruit and prepare teachers effectively and can support successful teaching at scale is the arena in which the United States has lagged the most. Although there are some great teachers in every community, and some strong professional preparation and development programs sprinkled across the country, the landscape of supports for quality teaching looks like Swiss cheese. In some states, the holes are smaller, and in others they are gaping, but in no case is there a fully developed system of instructional support even remotely comparable to that in high-achieving nations. And of course, as we have seen, the system is weakest in communities where students' needs are greatest.

Some have argued that the answer to weak teaching in the United States is to eliminate "barriers" to teaching, such as teacher education and certification requirements, allow anyone into the classroom who wants to teach, and fire those who prove not to be effective.[3] Often, this idea is accompanied by arguments for performance incentives, including merit pay, tied to student test scores. Although the interest in teacher effectiveness is important and overdue, this approach does not offer a strategy to ensure that teachers will have opportunities to gain the knowledge and skills they need in order to be effective, or that all schools will have the resources to entice and hire the best teachers. Nor does it protect the students—almost always those in low-income, high-minority schools—who will be the victims of unprepared novices in the years until these teachers have proved their mettle, demonstrated their incompetence, or left the field.

A prescription focused on easy access and easy firing ignores the question of how to develop widespread teaching competence and ensure a strong supply of highly able teachers for all schools. Without such a supply, principals will be unable to hire strong teachers even if they are free to hire whomever they please, and, evidence shows, they are unlikely to fire weak teachers, because they feel they won't be able to replace them. Even if they do, there is little guarantee that the quality of teaching will improve. Although there are good reasons to argue for stronger evaluation practices for removing incompetent teachers and for recognizing excellent ones (issues I treat later in this chapter), a theory that the major problems with teaching can be solved by carrots and sticks alone leaves the development of teaching competence to chance.

No high-achieving country approaches teaching in this way. These nations realize that, without a comprehensive framework for developing strong teaching, new resources in the system are less effective than they otherwise would be: Reforms are poorly implemented where faculty and leaders lack the capacity to put them into action; districts and schools are often unable to develop and maintain comprehensive training opportunities at scale, and scarce professional development dollars are wasted where teachers turn over regularly. Furthermore, when a profession's knowledge is not organized and made available to the practitioners who need it most, advances in the state of both knowledge and practice are slowed.

Although researchers have extensive and growing knowledge about how people learn and how to teach them effectively,[4] such knowledge is useless for improving practice unless it gets into the hands and minds of teachers and administrators who need to use it. The American university system has provided incentives for publishing articles in research journals not read by practitioners, and has only occasionally developed strong professional preparation programs that use this research and train practitioners to use it—which is the route by which knowledge would actually travel to the field.

Although it is common to hear at professional conferences that "we know how to create effective schools and classrooms," the "we who know" about what has proven effective does not include the broad swath of educators in the trenches. This conversation encompasses a small subset of practitioners who have gained access to strong training and other elites—pundits, consultants, and researchers—who talk mostly to one another. The American tradition of under-investing in preparation creates relatively little shared knowledge or skill within and across individual schools, except in extraordinary districts and in those states like Connecticut that have tackled a system-wide set of investments around shared standards and learning while eliminating the practice of emergency teacher hiring (see Chapter 5).

If teachers, principals, superintendents, and other professionals do not share up-to-date knowledge about effective practices, the field runs around in circles: Curriculum and teaching practices are inconsistent, many poor decisions are made, and the efforts of those who are successful are continually undermined and counteracted by the activities of those who are uninformed and unskilled. The American educational landscape is littered with examples of successful programs and schools that were later undone by newly arrived superintendents and school boards marching to a less-well-informed drummer. Equally common are successful initiatives that were not sustained when the teachers and principals who made them succeed moved on to be replaced by others with less skill.

Good teachers create little oases for themselves, while others who are less well prepared adopt approaches that are ineffective or even sometimes harmful. Some seek knowledge that is not readily available to them; others batten down the hatches and eventually become impermeable to better ideas. Schools are vulnerable to vendors selling educational snake oils when educators and school boards lack sufficient shared knowledge of learning, curriculum, instruction, and research to make sound decisions about programs and materials. Students experience an instructional hodge-podge caused by the failure of the system to provide the knowledge and tools needed by the educators who serve them.

These counterproductive conditions will continue until teaching becomes a profession like medicine, architecture, accounting, engineering, or law, in which every practitioner has the opportunity and the expectation to master the knowledge and skills needed for effective practice, and makes the moral commitment to use this knowledge in the best decisions of their clients. Teaching is today where medicine was in 1910, when Abraham Flexner conducted the famous study of medical education that eventually led to its overhaul. At that time, doctors could be prepared in a 3-week training program in which they memorized lists of symptoms and corresponding "cures" or, at the other extreme, in a graduate program of medicine at Johns Hopkins University that included extensive coursework in the sciences of medicine along with clinical training in the newly invented teaching hospital.

In his introduction to the Flexner Report, Henry Pritchett, president of the Carnegie Foundation for the Advancement of Teaching, noted that, although there was a growing science of medicine, most doctors did not get access to this knowledge because of the great unevenness in medical training. He observed that "very seldom, under existing conditions, does a patient receive the best aid which it is possible to give him in the present state of medicine, . . . [because] a vast army of men is admitted to the practice of medicine who are untrained in sciences fundamental to the profession and quite without a sufficient experience with disease."[5] Similarly, few students—especially in the neediest schools—receive the quality of education it is possible to deliver today, in substantial part because so many of their teachers have not had the opportunity to learn what is known about how to teach them effectively.

In 1910, there were many who felt that medicine could best be learned by following another doctor around in a buggy, learning to apply leeches to reduce fevers, and selling tonics that purported to cure everything from baldness to cancer. Flexner's identification of universities that were successful in conveying new knowledge about the causes and treatment of disease and in creating strong clinical training for medical practice was the stimulus for the reform of medical education. Despite resistance from weaker training sites, the enterprise was transformed over the subsequent 2 decades through the efforts of state, and later national, accrediting and licensing bodies that ensured doctors would get the best training the field had to offer.

Creating a strong profession in education is not a task that can be tackled school by school or district by district. And creating uniformly strong schools cannot be accomplished without a strong profession. Ultimately, a well-designed state and national infrastructure that ensures that schools have access to well-prepared teachers and knowledge about best practices is absolutely essential. Not incidentally, such an infrastructure will support much better education at lower cost in many more schools because it will reduce the gross and recurring inefficiencies that come from the high-turnover, Swiss cheese system we are currently operating. In this chapter, I describe the kind of supports that can help produce strong teaching on a wide scale, especially for students who would be least likely to experience it otherwise.

A GLOBAL CONTRAST

As we have seen, system-wide supports for recruiting, preparing, and supporting a strong, equitably distributed teaching force have been developed and sustained over time in only a few states. With sparse and fragmented governmental support, teachers in the United States typically enter the profession:

- With dramatically different levels of knowledge and skill—with those least prepared teaching the most educationally vulnerable children

- At sharply disparate salaries—with teachers in the poorest communities earning the least
- Working under radically different teaching conditions—with those in the most affluent communities benefiting from small class sizes and a cornucopia of books and other materials, up-to-date computers and equipment, specialists, and supports, while those in the poorest communities teach classes 50% larger without class sets of books, computers, or other supplies
- With little mentoring, on-the-job coaching, or embedded professional learning opportunities available in most communities

Meanwhile, around the world, there is growing recognition that expert teachers and leaders are the key resource for improving student learning, and the highest-achieving nations make substantial investments in teacher quality.[6] These countries see no advantage to be gained in constructing a fundamentally unequal system in which a large share of the teaching force is poorly prepared, assigned to the neediest students, and left unsupported. In top-ranked nations, supports for teaching have taken the form of

- *Universal high-quality teacher education,* typically 3 to 4 years in duration, completely at government expense, featuring extensive clinical training as well as coursework
- *Mentoring for all beginners* from expert teachers, coupled with a reduced teaching load and shared planning time
- *Ongoing professional learning,* embedded in 15 to 25 hours a week of planning and collaboration time at school, plus an additional 2 to 4 weeks of professional learning time annually to attend institutes and seminars, visit other schools and classrooms, conduct action research and lesson study, and participate in school retreats
- *Leadership development* that engages expert teachers in developing curriculum and assessment, mentoring and coaching others, and leading professional development, as well as pathways that recruit strong teachers into programs that prepare them as school principals who are instructional leaders
- *Equitable, competitive salaries,* sometimes with additional stipends for hard-to-staff locations, which are comparable with those of other professions

Strong Beginnings

All of the highest-achieving nations have overhauled teacher education to ensure stronger programs across the enterprise, and to ensure that able candidates can afford to become well prepared as they enter the profession. For example, teacher candidates in Finland, Sweden, Norway, and the Netherlands now receive 2 to 3 years of graduate-level preparation for teaching, completely at government expense, *plus* a living stipend. Typically, this includes at least a full year of training in a school connected to the university, like the model schools in Finland (see Chapter 6), which resemble professional development school partnerships created by some U.S. programs. Programs also include extensive coursework in content-specific pedagogy and a thesis researching an educational problem in the schools.

This is also the practice in Asian nations like Singapore and South Korea, and in jurisdictions such as Hong Kong and Chinese Taipei, where most teachers prepare in 4-year undergraduate programs, although graduate programs are growing more common. Unlike the United States, where teachers either go into debt to prepare for a profession that will pay them poorly or enter with little or no training, these countries invest in a uniformly well-prepared teaching force by overhauling preparation, recruiting top candidates, and paying them to go to school. Slots in teaching programs are highly coveted in these nations, and shortages are extremely rare.

Once teachers are hired, resources are targeted to schools to support mentoring for novices. In a model like that found in a number of Asian nations, the New Zealand Ministry of Education funds 20% release time for new teachers and 10% release time for second-year teachers to observe other teachers, attend professional development activities, work on curriculum, and attend courses.[7] Mentor teachers also have time set aside to observe and meet with beginning teachers. In places like Singapore, mentor teachers receive special training and certification and additional compensation in the salary schedule to work with both novice and veteran teachers.[8]

Countries such as England, France, Israel, Norway, Singapore, and Switzerland also require formal training for mentor teachers.[9] Norwegian principals assign an experienced, highly qualified mentor to each new teacher, and the teacher education institution then trains the mentor and supports in-school guidance.[10] Through its National Literacy and Numeracy Strategies, England trains coaches for new teachers about both effective pedagogies for students and techniques to enable teachers to employ them.[11] In some Swiss states, the new teachers in each district meet in reflective practice groups twice a month with an experienced teacher who is trained to facilitate discussions of common problems and practices.[12]

Support for Collaboration and Inquiry

There is also a continuous effort to improve the practice of both teaching and teacher development. For example, the many articles that have been written about the "secret" to Finland's success point to its dramatic overhaul of teacher education and teaching since the early 1990s. This was part of a series of reforms grounded in ongoing evaluations of its teaching systems—ranging from preparation programs to school and classroom practices, with teachers centrally involved in the process. The government invests substantial funding in both teacher education programs and in research on teaching and teacher education, in order to improve them regularly.[13]

All new Finnish teachers complete a master's thesis that involves them in research on practice. Programs aim to develop "highly developed problem solving capacity" that derives from teachers' deep understanding of the principles of learning and allows them to create "powerful learning environments" that continually improve as they learn to engage in a "cycle of self-responsible planning, action and reflection/evaluation."[14] Leaders are drawn from among these highly skilled and reflective teachers, and receive additional support to thinking organizationally about improvement. The entire teaching and schooling system is also continually evaluated as part of the reflective cycle. This is a key element of what Sahlberg calls "intelligent accountability" in a context where external student testing is rare, but analysis of practice and student learning is pervasive.[15]

These practices are widespread. For example, OECD reports that more than 85% of schools in Belgium, Denmark, Finland, Hungary, Ireland, Norway, Sweden, and Switzerland provide time for professional development in teachers' work day or week.[16] This time is frequently focused on the kind of action research that catalyzes change in teaching practice.[17] In Denmark, Finland, Italy, and Norway, teachers participate in collaborative research on topics related to education both in their pre-service preparation and in their ongoing work on the job.[18] Similarly, England, Hungary, Ontario (Canada), and Singapore have created opportunities for teachers to engage in school-focused research and development. Teachers have time and support to study and evaluate their own teaching strategies and school programs and to share their findings with their colleagues within the school, and through conferences and publications.[19]

Inquiry about practice is also pervasive in Asian nations, made possible by the extensive time that teachers have to work with colleagues on developing lessons, participating in research and study groups, observing one another's classrooms, and engaging in seminars and visits to other schools. Lesson study is a popular approach, which involves teachers in jointly crafting a lesson, observing while a colleague teaches it, then studying student responses and learning evidence to refine the lesson further. When engaged in lesson study, groups of teachers observe one another's classrooms and work together to refine individual lessons, expediting the spread of best practices throughout the school.[20]

In Japan, for example, *kenkyuu jugyou* (research lessons) are a key part of the learning culture. Every teacher periodically prepares a best possible lesson that demonstrates strategies to achieve a specific goal (e.g., students becoming active problem solvers or students learning more from one another) in collaboration with other colleagues. A group of teachers observes while the lesson is taught; teachers record the lesson in a number of ways, including videotapes, audiotapes, and narrative and/or checklist observations that focus on areas of interest to the instructing teacher (e.g., how many student volunteered their own ideas). Afterward, the teachers, and sometimes outside educators, discuss the lesson's strengths and weaknesses, ask questions, and make suggestions to improve the lesson. In some cases, the revised lesson is given by another teacher only a few days later and observed and discussed again.[21]

The research lessons allow teachers to refine teaching strategies, consult with other teachers and get colleagues' observations about their classroom practice, reflect on their own practice, learn new content and approaches, and build a culture that emphasizes continuous improvement and collaboration. Some teachers also give public research lessons, which expedite the spread of best practices across schools; allows principals, district personnel, and policymakers to see how teachers are grappling with new subject matter and goals; and gives recognition to excellent teachers.[22]

These lessons, which become the joint property of the teaching community, have been compared to "polished stones" because they have been worked on so carefully. In their study of mathematics teaching and learning in Japan, Taiwan, and the United States, Jim Stigler and Harold Stevenson noted that "Asian class lessons are so well crafted [because] there is a very systematic effort to pass on the accumulated wisdom of teaching practice to each new generation of teachers and to keep perfecting that practice by providing teachers the opportunities to continually learn from each other."[23]

Use of Time for Improving Teaching

Whereas teachers in high-achieving nations spend 40 to 60% of their time preparing and learning to teach well, most U.S. teachers have no time to work with colleagues during the school day. They typically receive only about 3 to 5 hours weekly in which to plan by themselves, and they get a few "hit-and-run" workshops after school, with little opportunity to share knowledge or improve their practice. A far greater percentage of U.S. teachers' work time is spent teaching than in most countries—about 80%, as compared to 60% on average for secondary teachers in the 31 OECD countries. U.S. teachers have more net teaching time—nearly 1,100 hours per year—than any other OECD country, far greater than the OECD average of 800 hours per year for primary schools and 660 hours per year for upper secondary schools[24] (see Figure 7.1). The amount of teaching time in countries such as Korea and Japan is even lower at the secondary level, giving teachers more time and opportunity to develop sophisticated practice (see Figure 7.2).

Systems for Formal Professional Development

In addition to supporting ongoing work to improve practice within schools, many high-achieving nations, such as Singapore and Sweden, fund and require as much as 100 hours of professional development time for each teacher annually. A

Figure 7.1. Number of Hours Teachers Spend in Instruction Annually.

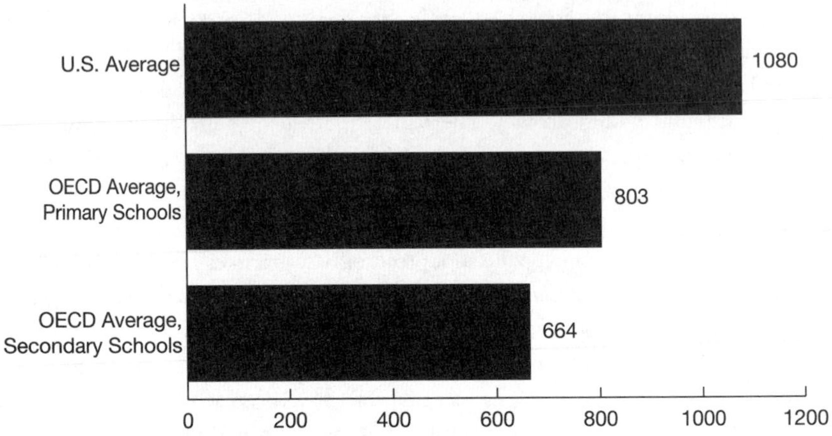

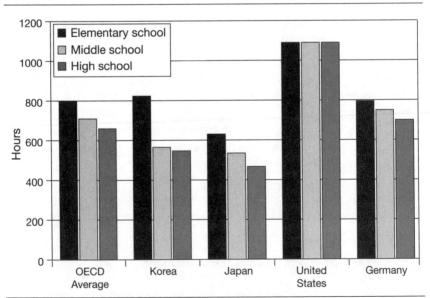

Source: OECD, Education at a Glance (2007).

Figure 7.2. Annual Teaching Time, by Country (in Hours).

Source: Korean Educational Development Institute (2006).

number of countries have organized very intensive, systematic professional development that disseminates successful practices in much more effective ways than publishing articles in research journals that practitioners don't read, or describing ideas in bulleted lists to hand out on professional development days.

England, for example, instituted a national training program in "best-practice" teaching strategies, which led to increases in the percentage of students meeting the target standards in literacy from 63% to 75% in just 3 years.[25] The training program is part of the National Literacy Strategy and National Numeracy Strategy, which provide resources to support implementation of the national curriculum frameworks. These include packets of high-quality teaching materials, resource documents, and videos depicting successful practices. A "cascade" model of training—similar to a trainer of the trainers approach—is structured around these resources to help teachers learn and use productive practices.

The National Literacy and National Numeracy Centers provide leadership and training for teacher training institutions and consultants, who train school heads, lead math teachers and expert literacy teachers, who in turn support and train other teachers.[26] As more teachers become familiar with the strategies, expertise is increasingly located at the local level, with consultants and lead teachers providing support for other teachers.[27] In 2004, England began a new component of the Strategies designed to allow schools and local education agencies to learn best practices from each other by funding and supporting 1,500 networks of six schools each to engage in collaborative inquiry and knowledge-sharing together.[28]

Similarly, since 2000, the Australian government has been sponsoring the Quality Teacher Programme, a large-scale multi-tiered program to update teachers' skills in priority areas and enhance the status of teaching in both government and non-government schools. Teaching Australia (formerly the National Institute for Quality Teaching and School Leadership) facilitates the development and implementation of nationally agreed-upon teaching standards, conducts research and communicates research findings, and facilitates and coordinates professional development courses. A set of National Projects is designed to identify and promote best practice, support the development and dissemination of professional learning resources in priority areas, and develop professional networks for teachers and school leaders nationwide. The State and Territory Projects fund a wide variety of professional learning activities for teachers and school leaders that are tailored to local needs. These projects include school-based action research, conferences, workshops, online and digital media resources, and training of trainers, school project leaders, and team leaders.[29]

Western Australia's highly successful Getting It Right (GIR) Strategy provides primary schools with specialist teaching personnel, professional development, and support to improve literacy and numeracy outcomes of high needs students, with a focus on

Aboriginal and other at-risk students.[30] Each school selects a highly regarded teacher with interest and expertise in numeracy or literacy to be a Specialist Teacher (ST), who is then trained through a series of seven 3-day intensive workshops over the course of their initial 2-year appointment. The Specialist Teachers work "shoulder to shoulder" with teachers in their schools, for about half a day each week for each teacher. The Specialist Teachers monitor and record student learning, help teachers analyze student learning, model teaching strategies, plan learning activities to meet the identified needs of students, assist with the implementation of these activities, and provide access to a range of resources, sharing expertise and encouraging teachers to be reflective about their practice.[31] Evaluations show that this has greatly enhanced teachers' knowledge about how students learn reading, writing, and mathematics, their teachers' teaching and assessment skills, and their ability to use data to identify and diagnose students' learning needs and to plan explicit teaching approaches to address these needs.[32]

U.S. Teachers' Learning Opportunities

Although intensive, focused professional development of this kind is sometimes available in the United States (see the descriptions of the literacy initiatives in New Jersey and Connecticut in Chapters 4 and 5, for example), national data show that it is still rare. Although most teachers participate in some kind of professional development each year, very few have the chance to study any aspect of teaching for more than a day or two. And fewer than half are involved in any kind of mentoring, coaching, or collaborative research.[33] Even though mentoring programs for beginning teachers are becoming more common, only about half of novices receive mentoring from a teacher in their teaching field or have common planning time with other teachers.[34]

Short workshops of the sort generally found to trigger little change in practice are the most common learning opportunity for U.S. teachers. In 2004, for example, mathematics teachers averaged only 8 hours of professional development on how to teach mathematics and 5 hours on the "in-depth study" of topics in the subject area. Fewer than 10% experienced more than 24 hours of professional development on mathematics content or pedagogy during the year. Sixty percent of teachers received some professional development in reading instruction, but only 20% worked on these issues for 2 days or more. Fewer than one-third of U.S. teachers received even 8 hours of professional development on strategies for teaching students with disabilities or English language learners, despite the strong desire that teachers voice for more learning opportunities in these areas.[35]

Most of this professional development does not meet the threshold needed to produce strong effects on teaching practice or student learning. A summary of experimental research found that short-term professional development experiences of 14 hours or less appear to have no effect on teachers' effectiveness, while a variety of well-designed content-specific learning opportunities averaging about 49 hours over a 6- to 12-month period of time were associated with sizable gains: students of participating teachers gained about 21 percentile points more than other students on the achievement tests used to evaluate student learning.[36]

Similarly, research suggests that both teachers' effectiveness and their retention in the profession are affected by their initial preparation, but our nonsystem also provides radically different access to such high-quality preparation for individuals entering the profession. Evidence suggests, for example, that some preparation programs are much more effective than others, based on graduates' feelings of preparedness, supervisors' ratings of graduates' effectiveness, and measures of their contributions to student learning gains.[37] In a New York City study that evaluated the contributions to value-added student achievement of beginning elementary teachers from different programs, for example, several pre-service programs had much stronger outcomes than any of the other traditional or alternative routes[38] (see Figure 7.3, which shows that value-added achievement gains of students taught by each program's graduates). The researchers examined the features of these programs, and found that, in addition to strong faculty, they had:

Figure 7.3. Teacher Education Program Effects on Student Learning Gains in Mathematics (x-axis) and English Language Arts (y-axis).

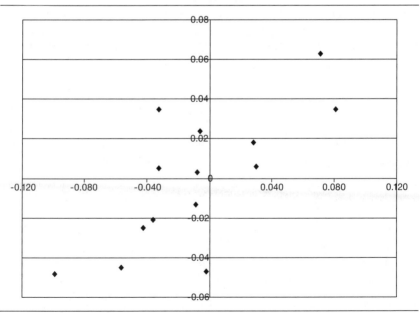

Source: Boyd, Grossman, Lankford, Loeb, & Wycoff (2009).
Note: Institutions with 40 or more 1st-year teachers with value-added estimates of student achivement gains, 2000–2001 through 2005–2006.

- More coursework in content areas (e.g., math and reading) and in how to teach that content
- Carefully selected and supervised student teaching experiences, well matched to the contexts in which candidates will later teach
- A focus on helping candidates learn specific practices and tools that they apply in student teaching tightly connected with their coursework
- Opportunities to study and evaluate the local district curriculum
- A capstone project—typically a portfolio of work done in classrooms with students—which examines the quality of their practice

Other studies of highly effective teacher education programs reinforce these same features and identify related elements, such as coursework and clinical work that are interwoven and pointed at a common conception of good teaching; emphasis on understanding curriculum, learning, and assessment, as well as methods of teaching; and use of case methods, action research, and performance assessments to develop skills for reflecting on teaching in relation to learning.[39]

The issue in the United States is not that we don't know what to do to improve teaching and learning. It is that, beyond a few states, we have not organized ourselves to do it systematically. And because of the severe inequalities in funding and capacity between wealthy and poor school districts, the places where schools recruit the least-prepared teachers to begin with are those that also have the fewest resources to support learning once teachers are in the classroom. Thus, as in most things, the rich get richer and the poor get poorer when it comes to both students' and teachers' opportunities to learn.

BUILDING AN INFRASTRUCTURE FOR QUALITY TEACHING

Ultimately, if the United States is to be able to build a productive, competitive educational system, we will need a national teacher supply policy[40] that can take account of the fact that teacher markets are no longer local and that national policies are needed to get well-prepared teachers to the places where they are needed. We also need a national teacher development policy that includes a rethinking of the teaching career so that teachers can become highly effective, have strong reasons to stay in the career, and use their skills where they are needed most—both in communities serving the most underserved students and in capacities where they can affect school reform more broadly. A systemic approach that builds a strong teaching profession and recruits and retains teachers where they are most needed must:

1. *Overhaul teacher preparation,* so that teachers can meet 21st-century learning needs and develop sophisticated skills

2. *Fix teacher recruitment and retention* so as to get well-qualified teachers to every classroom and keep the best of them there, thus building a stable, effective teaching force
3. *Develop, recognize, and share teacher knowledge and skill* to create widespread expertise that can improve schools

There is a strong argument for a federal role in this arena. Individual innovative programs at the local level will not by themselves solve the problems we face. Federal strategies have precedents in the field of medicine as well as teaching. Since 1944, Washington has subsidized medical training to meet the needs of underserved populations, to fill shortages in particular fields, and to build teaching hospitals and training programs in high-need areas. This consistent commitment has contributed significantly to America's world-renowned system of medical training and care. A similar approach to supporting teaching in the 1960s and early 1970s—when teachers prepared on National Defense and Education scholarships and engaged in new Master of Arts in Teaching (MAT) programs and Urban Teacher Corps initiatives—eliminated teacher shortages by the 1970s, before support for these programs was ended in 1981. In this chapter, I describe the kind of preparation teachers need, as well as the kind of performance assessments that can focus and improve practice. In Chapter 9, I outline the policies needed to ensure that high-quality learning opportunities are available to all teachers, and well-prepared teachers are available in every school.

Preparing Teachers to Succeed with All Students

Clearly, if students are expected to achieve 21st-century learning standards, we can expect no less from their teachers and from other educators. Yet teachers' access to knowledge about effective teaching is much more haphazard in the United States than in any other industrialized country. Preparation programs range from excellent to extremely weak, and state regulatory systems are very uneven from state to state. Furthermore, teachers need to know a lot more to teach today's diverse students to more challenging learning standards than ever before—including how to teach much more ambitious disciplinary content and cross-disciplinary skills and how to teach special needs learners, English language learners, and others who require specialized forms of teaching.

The Current Problem. Although we have many well-prepared and supported teachers, especially in forward-looking states and in affluent districts, in other states, tens of thousands of teachers are underprepared and undersupported, especially in schools serving low-income students of color. As a consequence of these policy problems, research on teaching in urban schools suggests that teachers' limited skills and limiting beliefs about their students lead to a steady diet of low-level material coupled with unstimulating, rote-oriented teaching.[41] Many teachers hold particularly low expectations of African American and Latino students, treat them more harshly than other students, discourage their achievement, and punish them disproportionately.[42]

While these issues are often chalked up to racism, they are substantially a function of the underpreparation of teachers who enter without training or from weak programs. Teachers who enter teaching without adequate preparation often wind up resenting and stereotyping students whom they do not understand, especially when these teachers' lack of skills render them less successful. Even decent people who want to do good work can be sabotaged by their lack of knowledge and skill.

The transmission of these expectations occurs in part when new teachers are socialized by undereducated teachers already on the job. For example, Chandra Johnson,[43] a newly prepared teacher from Teachers College, Columbia University, was finishing her year of student teaching at a school in New York City's largely Dominican Washington Heights neighborhood. She described how two first-year teachers, in an effort to be helpful, took her aside to offer advice. The two had entered the classroom through a program that offered only a few weeks of summer training, and both of them had struggled throughout the year. They wanted to share with this novice what they had learned on the job. "The first thing you need to understand," the two told her, "is that you really have to yell at these students. It's the only thing they understand." Their struggles continuing, neither of the two returned for a second year of teaching.

Chandra did not take this unsolicited advice—as she had already seen that the positive strategies she brought with her were much more successful with her students—but she decided not to work in this school, where the culture would undermine her goals to offer a different kind of experience for students. Thus, dysfunctional schools become even more so, as more thoughtful teachers avoid working with colleagues who are marginally competent. In fact, studies show that one of the greatest incentives in teachers' choices of schools is the opportunity to work with other skillful and committed colleagues, and to be in environments where they can be efficacious.[44] As I describe in the next chapter, such schools can be and have been built in low-income communities and can attract skillful teachers. But strategies for solving these problems cannot rely, as has often been the case, on sending individual new teachers into problematic environments where they are carrying the lone torch.

Although people who enter teaching with poor preparation do learn from their experience, they do not always learn the right things. With little knowledge to inform their decisions, teachers can draw the wrong inferences about why things went wrong and what to do about it. Jennifer Winters, an underprepared recruit who also entered teaching with just 6 weeks of training, described how she found herself experiencing the same tendency to blame her students before she left teaching after her first year to enter the teacher preparation program at UC–Berkeley:

> I found myself having problems with cross-cultural teaching issues—blaming my kids because the class was crazy and out of control, blaming the parents as though they didn't care about their kids. It was frustrating to me to get caught up in that. . . . Even after only ¾ of a semester in my teacher education program at Berkeley I have learned so much that would have helped me then.

An analyst who followed a group of underprepared beginning teachers through their first year described the pathway from initial teaching failure to a rote oriented curriculum, coupled with heavy-handed attempts at discipline based on denying students recess and other "privileges":

> That is how it begins . . . or how it begins to end. You come to your first class and they eat you up and you vow that it will not happen again. And you learn what you have to learn to make sure it doesn't. You learn the value of workbooks because even if they're numbingly dull they keep the kids busy, and if the kids are busy they are not making trouble for you.[45]

The practice of lowering standards for entry rather than ensuring teachers have access to the knowledge they need to be effective is often excused by the argument that teaching is learned on the job anyway, and formal teacher education contributes little. Yet research has found that strong teacher education results in teachers' significantly greater use of strategies that produce higher-order learning and that respond to students' experiences, needs, and learning approaches.[46]

Among other things, knowing how to plan and manage a classroom allows teachers to focus on the kind of complex teaching that is needed to develop higher order skills. Since the novel tasks required for complex problem solving are more difficult to manage than the routine tasks associated with "drill and kill," lack of classroom management ability can lead teachers to "dumb down" the curriculum in order to control student work more easily.[47] This often leads to a kind of worksheet-based teaching that does not add up to real learning. Eric Cooper and John Sherk describe how such instruction focused on the discrete "skill" bits featured on multiple-choice tests impedes students' progress toward literacy:

> When hundreds of these worksheets, each of which presents a small, low-level skill related to reading, have been completed, children are said to have completed the "mastery" skills program. Often, these children still cannot read very well, if one defines reading as the ability to discern connected prose for comprehension. . . . [Furthermore], worksheets are devised in such a way, teachers are told,

that the material teaches itself. As a result, the amount of oral communication between pupil and teacher and between pupil and pupil is drastically reduced. . . . [Yet] if children are to learn language, a part of which is reading, they must interact and communicate. They must have some opportunity to hear words being spoken, to pose questions, to conjecture, and to hypothesize.[48]

These authors' discussion of what teachers should be able to do to support children's literacy development maps onto what is known about the knowledge base for effective instruction. As reading expert Dorothy Strickland notes, to teach early literacy, teachers must be able to accommodate a variety of cognitive styles and learning rates, with activities that broaden rather than reducing the range of ways students are invited to learn and respond. Teachers are more effective when they have learned to construct active learning opportunities that involve students in using oral and written language in many different ways; when they build on students' prior knowledge and experience; and when they stimulate students' higher-order thought processes, including their capacities to hypothesize, predict, evaluate, integrate, synthesize, and express ideas.[49] In order to do this, they must learn curriculum and teaching strategies based on what experts know about language development, child development, and learning, so they can support children where they are and take them where they need to go.[50]

What Good Preparation Can Accomplish. Contrary to much conventional wisdom, it *is* possible to prepare teachers systematically and effectively for this kind of teaching, including in high-need communities. In contrast to the unfortunate experiences of the underprepared recruits we heard from earlier, consider these comments from two young teachers in the tough urban district of Oakland, California, who attended strong teacher education programs:

> I arrived at my first teaching job 5 years ago, mid-year. . . . The 1st-grade classroom in which I found myself had some two dozen ancient and tattered books, an incomplete curriculum, and an incomplete collection of outdated content standards. Such a placement is the norm for a beginning teacher in my district. I was prepared for this placement, and later came to thrive in my profession, because of the preparation I received in my credential program. The concrete things Mills College gave me were indispensable to me my first year as they are now: the practice I received developing appropriate curricula; exposure to a wide range of learning theories; training in working with non–English speaking students and children labeled "at-risk." . . . It is the big things, though, that continue to sustain me as a professional and give me the courage to remain and grow: My understanding of the importance of learning from and continually asking questions about my own practice, the value I recognize in cultivating collegial relationships, and the development of a belief in my moral responsibility to my children and to the institution

of public education. . . . I attribute this wholly to the training, education, and support provided to me by Mills.

—A graduate of the teacher education program at Mills College in Oakland

I'm miles ahead of other first-year teachers. There are five other first year teachers here this year. I am more confident. I had a plan for where I was trying to go. The others spent more time filling days. . . . I knew what I was doing and why—from the beginning.

—A graduate of the University of California, Berkeley's
Developmental Teacher Education (DTE) Program

This second recruit was observed as part of a study of seven powerful teacher education programs I conducted with colleagues.[51] These programs—undergraduate and graduate, large and small, found in public and private universities—were selected from among dozens nominated across the country because they provided evidence that they prepare new teachers to work extraordinarily well with diverse learners from their first days on the job, creating the kinds of classrooms that engage students in learning complex skills effectively. As researcher Jon Snyder describes:[52]

Maria Gregg teaches in a portable classroom at Wilson Elementary School in an urban California district. Wilson's 850 students, most of them language minority, are the largest population of Title I–eligible students in the district. Maria's room, a smaller than usual portable with a low ceiling and very loud air fans, has one kidney shaped teacher table and 6 rectangular student tables with 6 chairs at each. Maria has 32 first graders (14 girls and 18 boys) and no teacher's aide. Twenty-five are children of color, including recent immigrants from Southeast Asia, African-American students and Latino students.

Despite the small size of the room, Maria fosters an active learning environment with her active group of students. She has plastered the walls from floor to ceiling with student work—math graphs, group experience stories, a student collage from *Bringing the Rain to Kapiti Plain*. The ceiling provides another layer of learning. Hanging down so that adults have to duck when walking through the room are student-constructed science mobiles and a variety of "What We Know and What We Want to Know" charts. In one corner, a reading area is set up with books and a carpet.

On a February noon with the Bay Area fog beginning to lift, Maria eats lunch with two other first grade teachers in a classroom within the main building, discussing the afternoon's science activity. The other two teachers, while not enamored with the pre-packaged activity, have decided to use the materials pretty much as directed. The DTE graduate describes the activity she will use instead—a "sink or float" activity that teaches the same concepts as the pre-packaged lesson and uses the same materials but provides active engagement for the students. Unlike the pre-packaged lesson, Maria's re-design engages students in both the recording of data and in the generation and testing of hypotheses based on the data. The other teachers laugh and ask if she "woke up with this one." "No," she responds, "It was in the shower this time." On the way back to the classroom, she explains that the packaged curriculum, like many others, dumbs down the content and "leaves out the kids entirely." In order to introduce higher order skills and strategies that can engage her students, Maria explains how she has replaced the language arts program; tweaked the math program, and created a new science curriculum.

Once in the classroom, she groups the students in mixed language and gender cohorts and introduces the science activity she has designed. The room is full of materials needed for the lesson. There are cups in large tote trays, 2 trays filled with salt water; 2 with regular tap water; small totes full of small plastic bears, different kinds of tiles, quarters, rocks, and paper clips. The activity is to experiment with how many objects it takes to sink the cup in the different types of water.

The 30 students conduct experiments, record on yellow stickies how many objects it takes to sink the cup, and then place the yellow stickies on a large piece of chart paper Maria has labeled in two columns, salt water and tap water. Before starting the activity she reads the labels and asks students to read the labels. She has the students point out interesting language and spelling features. Two children excitedly point out, "That's the same weird spelling we saw this morning," referring to an earlier activity that introduced the vocabulary they were to use later. While organizing the groups Maria gives directions for students to go to their assigned table and sit on their hands. She points out that they will be unable to put their hands in the water if they are sitting on them. This is one of many "management techniques" she uses to assure students the opportunity to engage in the work.

Once into the science activity, management appears invisible. There is, of course, some splashing and throwing things into the water, but yellow stickies start to show up on the class chart and the students regulate themselves. Soon Maria brings the class together to discuss the recorded information. Students generate their own hypotheses and then, with teacher encouragement, match their hypotheses with the data. When the language becomes more abstract, she asks students to come to the front of the room and demonstrate their idea with the materials all had used. In California, this is one component of what is called "specially designed academic instruction in English" (SDAIE), a pedagogical strategy to make content accessible to English language learners. Other SDAIE components visible in Maria's teaching include her skillful use of cooperative groups that enable peer teaching; alternative assessments such as performance tests, projects, portfolios and journals; the development of products and research projects; extensive use of visuals such as slides, posters, videotapes, and real-world artifacts like classroom aquariums and terrariums; integration of first language, culture, and community members into class activities; and well-developed scaffolding techniques.

Instead of the impoverished learning so common in urban classrooms—where students are either completing mountains of worksheets or ignoring the teacher—

all of Maria's students were learning complex concepts in ways expected of much older students in much more affluent school settings. Furthermore, Maria created a climate in which each of her students was respected and enabled to participate actively and effectively. She avoided needing to chastise students by anticipating what normal busy children are likely to do and having a plan to keep them focused, well behaved, and engaged in learning. Her careful planning allowed students to succeed at a complex task without punishment, discouragement, conflict, or failure.

In our study of other extraordinary programs we studied nationwide,[53] we saw beginning teachers like Maria teaching in Boston, Charlottesville (Virginia), Milwaukee, New York City, Portland (Maine), and San Antonio—well prepared to teach all students from their first days in the classroom and exhibiting leadership early in their careers. Like Maria, they had a deep understanding of how children learn and how to structure tasks so that students could successfully undertake challenging intellectual work. They knew how to develop lessons that would add up to a curriculum that could achieve central academic goals, and they knew how to use assessments that would give them diagnostic information about each child so they could target students' individual needs. They built well-functioning learning communities among the students and a sense of responsibility for each other's welfare.

Maria's teaching illustrates what scholars have found regarding effective teachers of students of color: that such teachers, whatever their own racial/ethnic background, develop classrooms that create a sense of community and team, featuring cooperative learning strategies and inclusive participation. They use an active, direct approach to teaching: demonstrating, modeling, discussing, organizing engaging tasks, giving feedback, reviewing, and emphasizing higher-order skills. They teach skills explicitly and thoroughly by having students apply what they are learning to real projects and problems, rather than relying on rote methods. They are able to form and maintain connections with their students, inviting children to share who they are and what they know in a variety of ways. As they develop curriculum, they also draw on cultural referents—texts, examples, and models of people and practices—that connect to students' experiences and identities, honor their families and communities, and provide a message of inclusion to all students.[54]

What Successful Teacher Education Programs Do. All of the programs we studied develop new teachers who can teach with the assurance and skill of more experienced, very thoughtful veterans.[55] The programs do this by creating a tightly coherent set of learning experiences, grounded in a strong, research-based vision of good teaching, represented both in coursework and clinical placements where candidates can see good teaching modeled and enacted.

Like teacher education programs in Finland, these programs focus on developing teaching strategies and skills that can be successful with a wide range of learners, for without such skills, beliefs that "all children can learn" soon devolve into little more than rhetoric. They engage candidates in intensive study of learning, child development, curriculum, assessment, cultural contexts, and subject-specific teaching methods. This study is connected to at least a full year of student teaching and practicum experiences in carefully selected placements with expert teachers who model excellent teaching in diverse urban classrooms. Candidates' experiences in these classrooms are linked to guided discussions and readings that help them interpret what they are seeing, learning, and doing as they gradually take on more responsibility for teaching.

Like the internships and residencies doctors experience, such apprenticeships with great teachers are critical for learning to teach effectively, especially where students have a wide range of needs that require sophisticated skills from their teachers. In this way, prospective teachers can grow roots on a more complex form of practice that will allow them to teach diagnostically, rather than from scripts or by merely plowing through the text, insensitive to student learning. They learn to adapt their lessons based on ongoing assessment of students' needs, and they acquire a wide repertoire of practices, which they can apply judiciously based on what is needed for different students and different goals in different circumstances.

This is critically important because teaching cannot be learned from books or even from being mentored periodically. Teachers must see expert practices modeled and must practice them with help. However, such experiences are rare for urban teachers in the United States, since some traditional and most alternative programs fail to provide the opportunity to learn under the direct supervision of expert teachers working in schools that serve high-need students well. Student teaching is often conducted in classrooms that do not model expert practice, or it is in classrooms that do not serve high-need students—and what is learned does not generalize to other schools. In alternative programs, it is often reduced to a few weeks or omitted entirely. This fundamental problem has to be tackled and solved if we are to prepare an adequate supply of teachers who will enter urban or poor rural classrooms competent to work effectively with the neediest students and confident enough to stay in teaching in these areas.

It is not just the availability of classroom experience that enables teachers to apply what they are learning. The experience must be well guided, allowing teachers to learn to use specific *tools* in the classroom, such as assessments, specific reading strategies, writers workshop techniques, mathematics manipulatives, and others. Teachers need to know how to use and augment curriculum materials and assessment strategies; they need techniques for organizing productive group work and planning well-structured projects and inquiries; and they need opportunities to *practice* with these tools in specific subject areas with real students. This is how teachers learn to connect theory to practice in a well-grounded fashion and to develop the adaptive expertise they will need to address new problems in the specific classrooms they later encounter.[56]

Candidates also learn to become skilled teachers by analyzing student work and learning, teachers' plans and assignments, videotapes of teachers and students in action, and cases of teaching and learning, which—as they do in law and medicine—help teachers draw connections between generalized principles and specific events.[57] In these powerful programs, candidates developed case studies on individual students—including English language learners, special education students, and others—and on specific aspects of teaching, curriculum, families and communities by observing, interviewing, examining students' approaches to learning, and analyzing these data.

In all of these ways, successful programs support teaching that is content-rich as well as culturally and individually responsive, providing teachers with concrete tools for learning about students' lives and contexts—tapping what Luis Moll calls the "funds of knowledge" that exist in their homes and communities[58]—and turning that information into resources that can be tapped for learning. This includes learning to work with parents as partners who can provide insights about their children's interests and needs, and who can work collaboratively on supporting learning at home. Thus, successful programs help teachers structure the interaction between students and subject matter that must be intertwined, like the double helix of a DNA chain, if learning is to occur.

The Importance of Developing "Teaching Schools." Finally, all of the exemplary programs we studied had developed strong relationships with local schools—some of which were formal professional development schools (PDS) that partnered closely with the university. Some colleges even helped to start new schools that were models of practice. For example, Bank Street College, a large, internationally renowned teacher education institution, maintains strong connections with many public schools in New York City, partnering with at least a dozen new and older innovative schools, some of them populated almost entirely by graduates of the College's teaching and leadership programs. These schools serve racially, ethnically, linguistically, and economically diverse student populations and are committed to experiential and project-based learning. Similar relationships have been developed by Trinity University with schools in San Antonio, the University of Southern Maine with schools in Portland and surrounding communities, and Alverno College with schools in Milwaukee, as well as many other universities across the country.

Since settings that offer excellent education to low-income students of color simply do not exist in large numbers, they must be created if practice is to change on a wide scale. Simply seeking to acquaint candidates with diversity by placing them in schools serving low-income students or students of color that suffer from the typical shortcomings many such schools face can actually "work to strengthen pre-service teachers' stereotypes of children, rather than stimulate their examination, and ultimately compromise teachers' effectiveness in the classroom."[59] For this reason, a growing number of universities—including Clark University, Stanford University, the University of Chicago, the University of Pennsylvania, and others—have actually created new urban schools and developed partnerships that support and help transform existing schools to demonstrate state-of-the-art practices and to serve as training grounds for teachers.

These kinds of relationships, which simultaneously transform schools and teacher preparation, are critical to long-term reform, because it is impossible to teach people how to teach powerfully by asking them to imagine what they have never seen or to suggest they "do the opposite" of what they have observed in the classroom. It is impossible to prepare teachers for schools as they should be if teachers are constrained to learn in settings that typify the problems of schools as they have been—where isolated teachers exhibit idiosyncratic practice that is rarely diagnostic and infrequently illustrates strategies that can teach a wide range of learners well. No amount of coursework can, by itself, counteract the powerful experiential lessons that shape what teachers actually do.

In highly developed professional development school partnerships, faculty from the school and university work together to teach children and prospective teachers, developing curriculum, improving instruction, and undertaking school reforms. As in a teaching hospital in the medical profession, the entire school becomes a site for learning and feedback for all of the adults, as well as the students.[60] Many such schools actively pursue an equity agenda, confronting the inheritances of tracking, poor teaching, inadequate curriculum, and unresponsive systems.[61] In these schools, student teachers or interns are encouraged to participate in all aspects of school functioning, ranging from special education and support services for students to parent meetings, home visits, and community outreach to faculty discussions and projects aimed at ongoing improvement. This kind of participation helps prospective teachers understand the broader context for learning and begin to develop the skills needed for effective participation in collegial work around school improvement throughout their careers.

Studies of highly developed PDSs have found that new teachers who graduate from such programs feel better prepared to teach and are more highly rated by employers, supervisors, and researchers than other new teachers. Veteran teachers working in such schools describe changes in their own practice as a result of the professional development, action research, and mentoring that are part of the PDS. Studies have documented gains in student performance tied to curriculum and teaching interventions resulting from PDS initiatives.[62] Creative centers for continuous professional learning is essential for turning around schools that serve the students most often left behind because their teachers are left behind.

Teacher Residency Models. Building on these successful approaches, several cities—including Chicago, Boston, and Denver—have developed Urban Teacher Residencies to recruit and retain strong teachers in their districts. As high-quality alternative routes, these programs carefully screen and recruit talented college graduates who are interested in a long-term career in urban teaching, offering them a yearlong paid residency under the tutelage of master teachers. During the year, while they learn to teach *in the classroom* of an expert teacher, recruits take carefully constructed coursework from partner universities who work closely with the residency sponsor to connect the courses to the clinical experience. Rather than trying to learn through a sink-or-swim model without ever seeing good teaching, these recruits watch experts in action and are tutored into accomplished practice. They receive a salary or a stipend during this year and a master's degree and credential at the end of the year. They continue to receive mentoring in the next 2 years. In return, they pledge to teach for at least 4 years in the city's schools.

In the Chicago program, after candidates take 8 weeks of initial summer coursework that launches a tightly constructed yearlong curriculum taught by faculty at National-Louis University and the University of Illinois at Chicago, recruits undertake their residency with a master teacher at one of six Teaching Academy schools run by the Academy for Urban School Leadership (AUSL) as part of the Chicago school system. These schools, which serve low-income students of color, are themselves an important part of the innovation, as they are designed to exemplify best practices in urban schooling and are staffed by highly effective, experienced Chicago public school teachers, who are paid an additional 20% of their salary to serve as mentor teachers and leaders. Such schools are designed as sites that can provide state-of-the-art education for both children and professionals-in-training.

Recruits become independent teachers in the following year, having learned to meet the needs of their students by studying effective practices at the elbow of a successful urban teacher while studying relevant theory and research. They continue to receive mentoring for 2 years after they have become full-time teachers. Their master's degree is underwritten by a loan that is forgiven as they teach. In return, they are expected to teach for at least 5 years in the district, the point at which most teachers commit to the profession. The Chicago program has even begun to take on failing schools and restaff them with master teachers and graduates of the residency program. These turnaround schools have shown sizable achievement gains, upgrading the quality of education for the system as a whole.

The residency models exert high standards both at entry and for graduation, selecting high-ability candidates with needed characteristics and skills and graduating them into teaching positions when they have demonstrated they are ready to teach effectively. In Boston's residency program, for example, 53% of entrants are candidates of color and 59% of the middle and high school recruits have backgrounds in math or science. Experience shows that the vast majority of these recruits stay on, teaching successfully in high-need schools. Data on both Chicago's and Boston's programs show retention rates in teaching of more than 90% for the first four cohorts of graduates.[63] Programs like these can solve several problems simultaneously—creating a pipeline of committed teachers who are well prepared to teach in high-need schools, while creating demonstration sites that serve as models for urban teaching and teacher education.

Beginning Teacher Mentoring. The mentoring component of the residency approach is not to be overlooked, both for developing teachers' competence and reducing attrition. Other high-achieving countries invest heavily in structured induction for beginning teachers: "They fund schools to provide released time for expert mentors, reduced loads for new teachers, and other learning opportunities, such as seminars, visits to other teachers' classrooms, and joint planning time."

With 30% of new teachers leaving within 5 years (and more in urban areas), the revolving door cannot be slowed until beginning teachers are better supported. Beginners stay in teaching at much higher rates when they have had strong initial preparation and when they have a mentor in the same subject area and/or grade level, common planning time with teachers in the same subject, and regularly scheduled collaboration with other teachers.[64] Their practice is enhanced further when their mentors also receive formal training and have release time to provide one-to-one observation and coaching in the classroom, demonstrating effective methods and helping them solve immediate problems of practice.[65]

Evaluating Effective Teaching

Developing good teaching on a wide scale requires not only opportunities for teacher learning but also a shared conception of what effective teachers do, and assessment tools that reflect and develop that kind of practice. One currently prominent proposal is to use value-added student achievement test scores from state or district standardized tests as a key measure of teachers' effectiveness. The value-added concept is important, as it reflects a logical desire to acknowledge teachers' contributions to students' progress, taking into account where students begin. Furthermore, as suggested by the studies I have cited in this chapter, value-added methods (VAM) are proving valuable for research on the effectiveness of groups of teachers who have had distinctive preparation or professional development experiences, demonstrating whether, on average, their students learn more than those of teachers without these experiences.

However, technical and educational challenges make it more difficult to draw strong inferences about *individual* teacher effectiveness from value-added measures by themselves, especially for high-stakes purposes such as personnel decisions. In addition to the fact that testing systems in most states and districts do not allow for value-added estimates of achievement for students in most grades and subject areas, teachers' ratings of effectiveness are not highly stable across different tests, classes, and years, and are influenced by the characteristics of their students as well as the school context in which they teach.[66] Summarizing the results of many studies, including a recent research review by the RAND Corporation, Henry Braun of the Educational Testing Service concluded:

> VAM results should not serve as the sole or principal basis for making consequential decisions about teachers. There are many pitfalls to making causal attributions of teacher effectiveness on the basis of the kinds of data available from typical school districts. We still lack sufficient understanding of how seriously the different technical problems threaten the validity of such interpretations.[67]

Thus, while value-added models are useful for looking at the outcomes of groups of teachers, and they may provide one measure of teacher effectiveness among several (as described further below), they are problematic as the sole or primary measure for making evaluation decisions for individual teachers.

Fortunately, in recent years, performance-based assessments of teaching have been designed that not only detect aspects of teaching that are significantly related to teachers' effectiveness, but also help develop more effective teaching. These include *teacher performance assessments* like those used for National Board Certification and for beginning teacher licensure in states such as Connecticut and California, as well as *standards-based teacher evaluation systems* used in some local districts. These include evidence of teacher practices associated with effectiveness, and, often, evidence about contributions to student learning as well.

These assessments have high leverage as policy tools, as they can help shape who enters and remains in teaching, as well as who should be recognized as expert for purposes of compensation and selection as potential mentors and coaches for other teachers. Furthermore, participation in these assessments has been found to support learning both for teachers who are being evaluated and educators who are trained to serve as assessors, thus growing greater competence in the teaching force and focusing the efforts of educators on common practices.

Standard-setting for licensing, certification, and accreditation represents "professional policy," used as an alternative to governmental prescriptions for practice in fields where knowledge is always growing and its appropriate application is contingent on many different factors. Professional standards hold members of a profession accountable for developing shared expertise and applying it appropriately, rather than imposing standardized procedures that would fail to meet clients' different needs.[68] As Richard Elmore and Susan Fuhrman note:

As equality of opportunity comes to rest more squarely on the need for quality instruction, issues of how to enhance the professional competence of educators become more important. To ensure equal opportunity in today's context means enhancing, not limiting, the professional nature of teaching, and for that task state policy as it has been conceived in the past is hardly the best instrument.... We need new ways of conceiving the state role and the strategies at the state's disposal.[69]

Teacher Performance Assessments. A standards-based approach to assessing teachers was initially developed through the work of the National Board for Professional Teaching Standards, launched in 1987 and comprised of expert teachers and other members of the public. The Board developed standards for accomplished teaching in each major subject area and then developed an assessment of accomplished teaching that assembles evidence of teachers' practice and performance in a portfolio that includes videotapes of teaching, accompanied by commentary, lesson plans, and evidence of student learning. These pieces of evidence are scored reliably by trained raters who are expert in the same teaching field, using rubrics that define critical dimensions of teaching as the basis of the evaluation. Designed to identify experienced accomplished teachers, a number of states and districts use National Board Certification as the basis for salary bonuses or other forms of teacher recognition, such as selection as a mentor or lead teacher. California offers a $20,000 bonus, paid over 4 years, to Board-certified teachers who teach in high-need schools, which has helped to distribute these accomplished teachers more fairly to students who need them.

A number of recent studies have found that the National Board Certification assessment process identifies teachers who are more effective in raising student achievement than others who have not achieved certification.[70] Equally important, many studies have found that teachers' participation in the National Board process supports their professional learning and stimulates changes in their practice. Teachers note that the process of analyzing their own and their students' work in light of standards enhances their abilities to assess student learning and to evaluate the effects of their own actions, while causing them to adopt new practices that are called for in the standards and assessments.[71] Teachers report significant improvements in their performance in each area assessed—planning, designing, and delivering instruction; managing the classroom; diagnosing and evaluating student learning; using subject-matter knowledge; and participating in a learning community—and studies have documented that these changes do indeed occur.[72]

These standards, along with the performance assessments that have been developed to evaluate them, greatly raise the expectations for teachers. They incorporate deep understanding of content and how to teach it, a strong appreciation for the role of culture and context in child development and learning, and an insistence on ongoing assessment and adaptation of teaching to promote learning for all students. By examining teaching in the light of learning, these new standards put considerations of effectiveness at the center of practice—a shift from the behaviorist approach that has viewed teaching as the implementation of set routines, whether or not they actually produce success.

Because of this, National Board participants often say that they have learned more about teaching from their participation in the assessments than they have learned from any other previous professional development experience.[73] David Haynes's statement is typical of many:

> Completing the portfolio for the Early Adolescence/Generalist Certification was, quite simply, the single most powerful professional development experience of my career. Never before have I thought so deeply about what I do with children, and why I do it. I looked critically at my practice, judging it against a set of high and rigorous standards. Often in daily work, I found myself rethinking my goals, correcting my course, moving in new directions. I am not the same teacher as I was before the assessment, and my experience seems to be typical.[74]

Following on the work of the National Board, a consortium of more than 30 states (the Interstate New Teacher Assessment and Support Consortium, or IN-TASC), working under the auspices of the Council of Chief State School Officers, created standards for beginning teacher licensing. Most states have now adopted these into their licensing systems, and the National Council for Accreditation of Teacher Education (NCATE) incorporated the standards into a new performance-based approach for accrediting teacher education programs.

In the study of exemplary teacher education programs reported earlier, my colleagues and I witnessed the importance of these standards in shaping practice, as they were translated into courses, performance tasks, and assessment tools used to guide prospective teachers in developing much stronger teaching skills for a much wider range of students than was previously expected.[75] We also saw how the new performance-based accreditation standards drove important changes in colleges, creating greater coherence, changes in courses and clinical work, and greater resources for supervising and supporting teachers-in-training.

In a few pioneering states, performance assessments for new teachers, using these INTASC standards and modeled on the National Board assessments, are being used in teacher education as a basis for the initial licensing recommendation (as in California), or in the teacher induction period, as a basis for moving from a probationary to a professional license (as in Connecticut).

These performance-based assessments of teaching ability have also proved to be critically important in driving more effective training and practice. Despite a proliferation of teaching tests over the last 2 decades—candidates must often pass three or more tests to be licensed in a given state—most are multiple-choice tests of basic skills or subject-matter knowledge that do not measure much of what candidates learn in teacher education and do not provide any evidence of whether they can actually teach.

In contrast, these assessments require teachers to document their plans and teaching for a unit of instruction, videotape and critique lessons, and collect and evaluate evidence of student learning. Like the National Board assessments, beginning teachers' ratings on the Connecticut assessment, used to grant a professional license around the third year of teaching, have been found to significantly predict their students' value-added achievement gains on state tests.[76]

When combined with mentoring, such assessments also help teachers improve their practice. Connecticut requires districts who hire beginning teachers to provide them with mentors who are also trained in the state teaching standards and assessment system. Studies in Connecticut have reported that teacher education and induction programs have improved because of the feedback from the assessment; beginning teachers and mentors also feel the assessment has helped them improve their practice as they become clearer about what good teaching is and how to develop it. Thus, the program enhances teacher effectiveness as it guides preparation and mentoring. A beginning teacher who participated in the assessment described the power of the process, which requires planning and teaching a unit, and reflecting daily on the day's lesson to consider how it met the needs of each student and what should be changed in the next day's plans. He noted:

> Although I was the reflective type anyway, it made me go a step further. I would have to say, okay, this is how I'm going to do it differently. It made more of an impact on my teaching and was more beneficial to me than just one lesson in which you state what you're going to do. . . . The process makes you reflect on your teaching. And I think that's necessary to become an effective teacher.[77]

The same learning effects are recorded in research on the very similar Performance Assessment for California Teachers (PACT) assessment used in California teacher education programs. Launched by the University of California campuses with Stanford University, Mills College, San Jose State University, and San Diego State University, and now used by 32 universities, the assessment requires student teachers or interns to plan and teach a week-long unit of instruction mapped to the state standards; to reflect daily on the lesson they've just taught and revise plans for the next day; to analyze and provide commentaries of videotapes of themselves teaching; to collect and analyze evidence of student learning; to reflect on what worked, what didn't and why; and to project what they would do differently in a future set of lessons. Candidates must show in their plans how they take into account students' prior knowledge and experiences, including adaptations for English language learners and for students with special needs. Analyses of student outcomes are part of the evaluation of teaching.

Faculty, supervisors, mentors, and cooperating teachers score these portfolios using standardized rubrics after training, with an audit procedure to calibrate standards. Faculties use the PACT results to revise their curriculum. Both novice teachers and scorers describe how their experiences improve their practice. For example:

> For me the most valuable thing was the sequencing of the lessons, teaching the lesson, and evaluating what the kids were getting, what the kids weren't getting, and having that be reflected in my next lesson . . . the "teach-assess-teach-assess-teach-assess" process. And so you're constantly changing—you may have a plan or a framework that you have together, but knowing that that's flexible and that it has to be flexible, based on what the children learn that day.
>
> —Prospective teacher

> This [scoring] experience . . . has forced me to revisit the question of what really *matters* in the assessment of teachers, which—in turn—means revisiting the question of what really *matters* in the *preparation* of teachers.
>
> —Teacher education faculty member

> [The scoring process] forces you to be clear about "good teaching;" what it looks like, sounds like. It enables you to look at your own practice critically, with new eyes.
>
> —Cooperating teacher

> As an induction program coordinator, I have a much clearer picture of what credential holders will bring to us and of what they'll be required to do. We can build on this.
>
> —Induction program coordinator[78]

In addition to selecting teachers who can, indeed, teach well, these kinds of assessments help teachers learn to teach more effectively, improve the quality of preparation programs, and create standards and norms that are widely shared across the profession, so that good teaching is no longer a magical occurrence.

Standards-Based Evaluations of Teaching. Similarly, some districts use standards-based evaluations of teachers to assess teachers and to help them improve their practice. Like the performance assessments described above, these systems for observing teachers' classroom practice are based on professional teaching standards grounded in research on teaching and learning, and they predict teachers' effectiveness in promoting student learning growth.[79] They use systematic observation tools to examine teaching along a number of dimensions, such as classroom management, teaching of content, and student assessment.

Such evaluation systems have been used to evaluate beginning teachers for continuation and tenure and to identify struggling teachers for additional assistance and potential dismissal. The most long-standing successful systems are Peer Assistance and Review Programs that use highly expert mentor teachers with released time to conduct evaluations and provide assistance to both new and experienced teachers who need it. A due-process and review system involves a panel of both teachers and administrators in making recommendations about personnel decisions based on the evidence presented to them from the mentor teacher and principal evaluations. Studies of the systems in Rochester, New York; Cincinnati, Columbus, and Toledo, Ohio; and Seattle, Washington found they provide successful coaching and a much higher bar for tenure and continuation in the profession.[80]

In these systems, beginning teachers have been found to stay in teaching at higher rates because of the mentoring they receive, and the ones who leave (generally under 5%) are those the district has chosen not to continue rather than those who quit in frustration. Among veteran teachers identified for assistance and review (usually 1–3% of the teaching force), about half improve sufficiently with intensive mentoring to be removed from intervention status and about half leave by choice or by district action. Because teacher associations have been closely involved in designing and administering these programs in collaboration with the district, the union does not bring grievances when a teacher is discontinued.

In Rochester and Cincinnati, which have developed career ladders, the accomplished teachers identified through more advanced evaluations of practice serve as mentors for these beginning teachers, among other leadership roles. These evaluations depend both on standards-based assessments of teaching—through local evaluations and/or National Board Certification—and, in Rochester's case, evidence of student learning assembled by the teacher in a portfolio.

Other systems also include standards-based measures as part of teacher evaluation systems, including those used in career ladder programs. For example, the Teacher Advancement Program (TAP) offers one well-developed example of a highly structured teacher evaluation system that is based on the standards of the National Board and INTASC and the assessment rubrics developed in Connecticut and Rochester, New York, among others.[81] In the TAP system of "instructionally focused accountability," each teacher is evaluated four to six times a year by master/mentor teachers or principals who are trained and certified as evaluators using a system that examines designing and planning instruction, the learning environment, classroom instruction, and teacher responsibilities. Evaluator training is a rigorous 4-day process, and trainers must be certified based on their ability to evaluate teaching accurately and reliably. Teachers also study the rubric and its implications for teaching and learning, look at and evaluate videotaped teaching episodes using the rubric, and engage in practice evaluations. After each observation, the evaluator and teacher meet to discuss the findings and to make a plan for ongoing growth.

Like other well-developed career ladder systems, TAP provides ongoing professional development, mentoring, and classroom support to help teachers meet these standards. In addition, TAP reorganizes the school to provide regular time for collaborative planning and learning. Teachers in TAP schools report that these opportunities, along with the intensive professional development offered, are substantially responsible for improvements in their practice and the gains in student achievement that have occurred in many TAP schools.[82] Data from this extensive teacher evaluation and development system are combined with evidence about schoolwide and individual teacher student achievement gains in making judgments about teachers' appointment to specific roles in the career ladder.

Interestingly, a recent evaluation found that 70% of teachers in TAP schools felt highly supportive of the level of collegiality the program had engendered, 60% were very pleased with the professional development, and 57% were strongly supportive of the standards-based evaluation system. These were more important to teacher support than the multiple career paths offered by the program (strongly supported by about 31% of teachers) and the performance-based compensation (strongly supported by only 18% of teachers).[83] This confirms many other studies showing that teachers appreciate well-designed support and evaluation that help them improve their practice—and are motivated more by these factors than by pay. This is not entirely a surprise, since individuals who choose to enter teaching do so primarily because of their desire to help children and not because of their desire to make large sums of money. (If that were their motivation, they would have chosen another occupation!) The altruistic and egalitarian ethos of the profession leads to a strong emphasis on collaboration, collegiality, and continual learning, which are important parts of a successful career development system.

Several successful career ladder plans use similar evaluation processes and rubrics as part of their systems. The Denver Procomp system, which uses a standards-based evaluation protocol as one of its components, describes its system as including well-developed rubrics articulating different levels of teacher performance; interrater reliability; a fall-to-spring evaluation cycle; and both peer and self-evaluation components.[84] In the Procomp system, in addition to observations of practice, teachers set two goals annually in collaboration with the principal, and document student progress toward these goals using district-, school-, or teacher-made assessments to show growth.

Arizona's career ladder program—which encourages local districts to design their own systems—requires evidence from both standards-based evaluations of practice and student assessments that illuminate teachers' effectiveness. One study of the Arizona career ladder programs found that, over time, participating teachers demonstrated an increased ability to create locally developed assessment tools to assess student learning gains in their classrooms; to develop and evaluate pre- and posttests; to define measurable outcomes in "hard-to-quantify areas" such as art, music, and physical education; and to monitor student learning growth. They also showed a greater awareness of the importance of sound curriculum development, more alignment of curriculum with district objectives, and increased focus on higher-quality content, skills, and instructional strategies.[85] Thus, the development and use of standards-based evaluations of practice combined with student learning evidence developed by teachers seem to be associated with improvements in practice.

Evaluations that help teachers understand and develop professional standards of practice enable them to become more effective during their initial training and later in their careers. Furthermore, teachers and administrators involved in assessing other teachers using standards-based tools also improve their own understanding of teaching, thus spreading good practice and increasing coherence.

These results led one analyst to conclude that tying teachers' advancement and compensation to their knowledge and skills and using evaluation systems that help develop those skills may ultimately produce more positive change in practice than evaluating teachers based directly on student test scores.[86] Certainly, knowing what teachers are doing that is leading to improvements in student learning is more valuable than merely watching scores go up or down without clues as to the practices that are associated with these changes. When individual teachers, collegial groups of teachers, and schooling systems examine how practices are related to student learning, they can develop strategies to improve teaching throughout the profession as a whole.

Enabling Teachers to Continue to Improve

A strong system of teacher learning must provide not only a solid foundation of knowledge for entering the profession but also ongoing opportunities for learning throughout the career. Over the last 2 decades, a new paradigm for professional development has emerged from research based on approaches that have been shown to impact teachers' practices and student outcomes. Unlike the typically ineffective one-shot workshops that proliferate, effective professional development is sustained, ongoing, content-focused, and embedded in professional learning communities where teachers work over time on problems of practice with other teachers in their subject area or school.[87] Furthermore, it focuses on "concrete tasks of teaching, assessment, observation and reflection,"[88] looking at how students learn specific content in particular contexts, rather than emphasizing abstract discussions of teaching. Equally important, it focuses on student learning, helping teachers to analyze the skills and understandings students are expected to acquire and what they are in fact learning.[89]

The Design of Effective Professional Learning Opportunities. Research has found that teachers are more likely to try classroom practices that have been modeled for them in authentic settings. And teachers judge professional development to be most valuable when it provides opportunities to do "hands-on" work that builds their knowledge of academic content and how to teach it to their students, and when it takes into account the local context (including the specifics of local school resources, curriculum guidelines, accountability systems, and so on).[90] Equally important, professional development that leads teachers to define precisely which concepts and skills they want students to learn, and to identify the content that is most likely to give students trouble, has been found to improve teacher practice and student outcomes.[91] To this end, it is often useful for teachers to be put in the position of studying the very material that they intend to teach to their own students, as they do in the very successful National Writing Project and in some other effective professional development programs.

What does this kind of professional development look like? One well-known study focused on elementary science teachers who participated in a 100-hour summer institute, during which they actively engaged in a standard science "learning cycle" that involved exploring a phenomenon, coming up with a theory that explained what had occurred, and applying it to new contexts. After going through this process, teachers went on to develop their own units and teach them to one another before taking them into their classrooms. Later, the researchers tested randomly selected students in those classrooms and found that they scored significantly higher in their scientific reasoning ability than did a control group of students taught by teachers who had not had this experience.[92]

Similarly, David Cohen and Heather Hill distinguished successful from less successful approaches to professional development in their study of California's decade-long effort to reform the teaching of mathematics.[93] The new curriculum required elementary teachers and students to understand complex concepts of mathematics, not simply computational algorithms. Of the many professional development opportunities that were offered to support this reform, only two contributed to changes in teachers' practices and increases in student achievement.

The first of the two successful approaches was organized around new curriculum units developed to teach these new standards. An ongoing set of workshops engaged teachers in using the mathematics strategies students were expected to learn and then on developing strategies for teaching the units well. Teachers taught the units and returned to debrief their experiences with other teachers and to problem solve next steps, while preparing to teach subsequent units. Over time, these teachers reported more reform-oriented practices in their classrooms, and their schools showed larger gains in achievement.

The second effective approach involved teachers evaluating student work on assessments directly linked to the reform curriculum. While assessing student work, which revealed students' problem-solving strategies and reasoning, teachers examined conceptual roadblocks students faced on the assessments and became knowledgeable about how to anticipate these misunderstandings and address them in their classrooms. Student achievement was ultimately higher for these teachers as well.

In another study of mathematics teachers, researchers found large gains in conceptual understanding for students whose teachers had focused on looking at student work and learning through the Integrated Mathematics Assessment (IMA) program. These teachers attended a 5-day summer institute and then met 13 times, once every 2 weeks, throughout the year. During the workshops, teachers looked at samples of student work or videotapes of problem solving; learned to assess student motivation, interests, goals, and beliefs about abilities; and developed specific teaching methods, including how to lead whole-class discussions, assess student works with rubrics, and use portfolios. They discussed their practice and solved problems collaboratively. Ultimately, they developed and piloted assessment tools of their own and publicly shared their work. This propelled extensive changes in practice that led to significant student learning gains. Meanwhile, researchers found no gains for students whose teachers received traditional workshops, or who participated in a professional community without a strong focus on curriculum content and student learning.[94]

Many studies have found it useful for groups of teachers to analyze and discuss student performance data and samples of students' course work (science projects, essays, math tests, and so on), in order to identify students' most common errors and misunderstandings, reach common understanding of what it means for students to master a given concept or skill, and find out which instructional strategies are or are not working, and for whom.[95] Notably, studies of high-achieving or steeply improving schools have found that student gains were associated with teachers' regular practice of consulting multiple sources of information on student performance, including student work samples and observations of their classroom performances, as well as test scores, and using those data to inform discussions about ways to improve instruction.[96]

Contexts for Effective Professional Learning. Professional development is also more effective when it is a coherent part of the school's overall efforts, rather than the traditional "flavor of the month" workshop.[97] Teachers are unlikely to apply what they have learned if it is at odds with other expectations in their school. Curriculum, assessment, and professional learning opportunities need to be seamlessly integrated to avoid disjunctures between what teachers learn in professional development and what they are required to do in their classrooms and schools.

When schools create shared time and productive working relationships within and across academic departments or grade levels, the benefits include greater consistency in instruction, more willingness to share practices and try new ways of teaching, and more success in solving problems of practice.[98] For example, a comprehensive 5-year study of 1,500 schools undergoing major reforms found that achievement increased significantly in math, science, history, and reading in schools where teachers formed active professional learning communities. Student absenteeism and dropout rates were also reduced. Particular aspects of teachers' professional communities—including a shared sense of intellectual purpose and a sense of collective responsibility for student learning—were associated with a narrowing of achievement gaps in math and science among low- and middle-income students.[99] A number of large-scale studies have identified specific ways in which professional community-building can deepen teachers' knowledge, build their skills, and improve instruction.[100]

Perhaps the simplest way to break down professional isolation—but one that rarely occurs in most schools—is for teachers to observe one another's teaching and to provide constructive feedback. In an evaluation of 12 schools implementing Critical Friends Groups—in which teachers observe and give feedback to colleagues using a common set of protocols—researchers found that teachers began to focus more on their students' learning, rather than merely covering the material. Teachers in these schools also reported having more opportunities to learn and a greater desire to continuously develop more effective practices than teachers who did not participate.[101]

Researchers have found that teachers tend to form more productive professional communities in smaller schools, schools that invest more in teaching (that is, where more staff members are classroom teachers and fewer are assigned to specialist and administrative jobs), schools where teachers are more involved in educational decision making, and, especially, schools that schedule regular blocks of time for teachers to meet and plan curriculum together,[102] much as they do in other nations. In the next chapter, I describe how these kinds of schools have been organized in cities around the country, with strong benefits for students.

A Comprehensive Approach. Some urban districts have demonstrated how it is possible to create a systemic approach that radically improves the quality of urban teaching. A new and comprehensive paradigm for improving instruction was created in New York City's Community School District #2, an extremely diverse, multilingual district of 22,000 students, of whom large numbers were immigrants (speaking, collectively, more than 100 languages), more than 70% were students of color, and most were from low-income families.[103] During the decade-long tenure of Superintendent Tony Alvarado, from 1987 to 1997, district achievement rose steeply in reading and mathematics, scoring above New York State norms as well as New York City averages, even while the population of the district grew more diverse. This strong performance continued for another decade under the leadership of Alvarado's deputy, Elaine Fink, followed by Shelly Harwayne, who had been a successful principal in the district.

In the late 1990s, Alvarado and Fink moved to San Diego—another city serving largely low-income students of color, most of them immigrants from Central and South America—and replicated substantial aspects of the reform between

1998 and 2004, with strong positive results for student achievement there as well.[104] Meanwhile, several other districts (for example, New York's Community Districts #3, #10, and #15 and later structures, such as Region 1, which combined districts) adopted similar strategies, and many of the practices spread to districts like Boston, which—under the skillful leadership of superintendent Tom Payzant, who also undertook major reforms of instruction—showed substantial improvements in teaching quality and student achievement as well.[105]

Based on the belief that student learning will increase as the knowledge of educators grows, these districts made the careful selection and intensive development of teachers and leaders the central focus of management and the core strategy for school improvement.[106] Rather than treating professional development as just a set of disparate workshops, these districts made professional development the most important focus of all district efforts, its most prominent budgetary commitment, and a key part of every leader's and every teacher's job.

For example, after consolidating categorical funds and focusing them on a coherent program of professional learning, District #2 moved most of its central office personnel positions back to school sites to focus on the improvement of practice. In both New York and San Diego, Alvarado aggressively recruited instructionally knowledgeable teachers and principals from the strongest preparation programs, and created new program pipelines with colleges where they were needed. He also created pointed expectations and opportunities for teacher and principal professional development around the deepening of instructional practice—first in literacy and then in mathematics—and replaced underskilled principals and teachers who were unable or unwilling to develop their practice through retirements, "counseling out," or personnel actions. Both principals and teachers were expected to learn about best practices in teaching literacy and mathematics, and school leaders were held accountable for their own and their colleagues' increasing skill, for the quality of instructional practice in their buildings, for recruiting well-prepared new teachers, and for moving ineffective teachers out of the district.

Staff development was designed to provide continuous support embedded in a coherent instructional system focused on the practical details of what it means to teach effectively. Intensive summer institutes focused on core teaching strategies in literacy and mathematics were combined with on-site coaching to help teachers apply what they learned. The district provided time for teachers and principals to visit and observe one another, develop study groups, participate in peer networks, and pair up for work together on particular problems of practice. Innovative strategies such as the "professional development laboratory," created with New York University, allowed visiting teachers to spend 3 weeks in the classrooms of expert resident teachers who were engaged in practices they want to learn, while other expert teachers (often highly skilled retired veterans) substituted in their home classrooms, teaching students those same practices. The goal of all of this activity was the development of shared expertise—which is the essential foundation of a profession. As Elmore and Burney explain:

> Shared expertise takes a number of forms in District 2. District staff regularly visit principals and teachers in schools and classrooms, both as part of a formal evaluation process and as part of an informal process of observation and advice. Within schools, principals and teachers routinely engage in grade-level and cross-grade conferences on curriculum and teaching. Across schools, principals and teachers regularly visit other schools and classrooms. At the district level, staff development consultants regularly work with teachers in their classrooms. Teachers regularly work with teachers in other schools for extended periods of supervised practice. Teams of principals and teachers regularly work on districtwide curriculum and staff development issues. Principals regularly meet in each others' schools and observe practice in those schools. Principals and teachers regularly visit schools and classrooms within and outside the district. And principals regularly work in pairs on common issues of instructional improvement in their schools. The underlying idea behind all these forms of interaction is that shared expertise is more likely to produce change than individuals working in isolation.[107]

In order to enable shared expertise within the schools, Alvarado bought time for teachers to get out of their classrooms to observe other teachers and have shared planning and learning time. To rethink the design of schooling, he also created a number of new "option" schools and encouraged the redesign of other schools. These schools developed grouping practices that often kept teachers and students together for more than one year, schedules that allowed collaborative planning and professional development for teachers within the school day, and more coherent, intellectually challenging curriculum supported by ongoing diagnostic and performance assessments of student learning. School redesign was joined with professional development in a conscious strategy to improve both teachers' expertise and schools' ability to support in-depth teaching and learning.

In addition to the highly focused strategies the district used to improve the quality of teaching practice system-wide, there were targeted efforts for students who did not initially succeed. Reading Recovery training for an ever-widening circle of teachers created the first foundations of the teacher development initiative. This effort was used to improve teachers' knowledge about how to teach reading to their entire classrooms of students, in addition to providing one-on-one tutoring to students with special reading needs. Like the literacy strategies describe in New Jersey and Connecticut (Chapters 4 and 5), classroom teaching focused on integrated approaches to the teaching of reading and writing that engaged students in significant reading and discussion of leveled books supported by extensive writing about books and ideas. Teachers learned to target their instruction by assessing individual students' reading skills and strategies using tools such as running records, miscue analyses, and analyses of student work samples. As district staff, consultants, and principals learned how to change teaching practice through the literacy initiative, drawing on local university supports like Teachers College's Writing Institute and the Lehman College Literacy Institute as well as district expertise, Alvarado began a parallel effort in mathematics using a similar model that drew in part on mathematics coaches trained at Bank Street's School of Education.

Beyond the use of Reading Recovery strategies, which were extremely successful with struggling readers and reduced unnecessary assignments to special education, the district invested in teacher training to teach English language learners and students with disabilities, replacing the common practice of assigning special education students to untrained paraprofessionals with a strategy of hiring highly trained special educators who worked with students but also shared their expertise with other teachers, so that "regular" education teachers, too, became more expert. Rather than retaining large numbers of students in grade when they were behind, Alvarado focused intensive services on students with lagging achievement and assigned students with the lowest scores to the most expert teachers. This stands in contrast to the usual practice of assigning the least experienced and well-trained teachers to these students.

Professional development for principals was as important as for teachers. The view that principals must know instruction well if they are to act as effective instructional leaders produced a tightly woven web of learning opportunities and support for principals in both New York and San Diego on Alvarado's watch. In the much larger district of San Diego, the city's 175 principals were divided into seven "learning communities," each of which was led by an "instructional leader" (IL), replacing the traditional area superintendents whose role had been administrative rather than instructional in nature. Each IL was a former principal who had demonstrated high levels of understanding and skill as an instructional leader. These leaders organized monthly principal conferences on issues of instruction and ongoing networks of support; visited classrooms with principals, helping them learn how to look at teaching through instructional "walkthroughs" of each classroom followed by debriefings about the practice of each individual teacher; set up professional development sessions attended by principals and their teachers; and put in place resources—ranging from mentor principals and consultants to individualized professional development plans—to solve instructional problems. In a sense, the ILs become the principals' principals, and the district's principal development programs became a critical pipeline for transforming the nature of the principalship and reinforcing the district's focus on instruction (see Figure 7.4).

As one principal explained, her IL supported her in learning about literacy and mathematics teaching and how to implement new instructional strategies:

The opportunity to have that more knowledgeable other [is invaluable], so that principals have that person they can ask for support . . . navigating the system and taking action for you at the central office level. . . . It's absolutely about solving instructional problems and helping me always see what's the next level that we can bring teacher practice to in schools?[108]

These examples show how districts can mobilize resources to support sustained improvement in teaching practice and substantial improvements in student learning. When combined with serious state efforts to develop strong preparation programs, systems of mentoring, and focused performance assessments for guiding professional learning, it is possible to create classrooms in which all educators have the opportunity to become expert and all children have the opportunity to be well taught. In the next two chapters, I describe the steps needed to create school organizations and state systems that can support powerful learning for both students and their teachers.

Figure 7.4. A Web of Opportunities for Principal Learning.

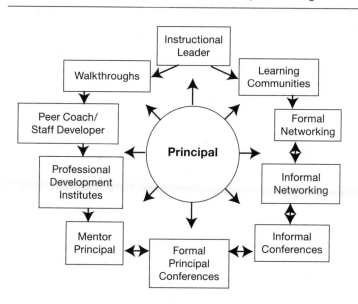

Source: Darling-Hammond, Meyerson, LaPointe, & Orr (in press).

Organizing for Success:
From Inequality to Quality

School should not be mass production. It needs to be loving and close. That is what kids need. You need love to learn.

> —A student at Vanguard High School in New York City[1]

Small size means I can do a literature seminar with the bottom 20% of kids in the city. Kids who didn't read are reading books like *Jane Eyre* to write their essays. We can work with them during lunch. You find out who can't read, type, etc. These are the kids who would sit in the back of the room, be in the bathroom, and would deliberately get lost. I know dedicated teachers in big schools who teach 150 kids. They can't do this.

> —A teacher at Vanguard High School in New York City

As we have seen, it is possible to develop more expert teachers on a wide scale, as many nations and some states and districts have done. But skillful teachers are only part of the puzzle. For teachers to be highly effective, they need to work in schools that are organized for success—schools that enable them to know and reach their students, teach to worthwhile learning goals, use productive tools and materials, and continually improve their practice.

In addition to ensuring that teachers have the knowledge and skills they need to teach a wide range of students, a growing number of urban schools have abandoned the factory-model assumptions of a century ago and have redesigned school structures to support more intensive learning for both students and teachers, with much stronger results. Many of these schools, serving low-income students of color and new immigrants, have demonstrated that they can graduate more than 80%

of their students, most of whom would have failed to graduate from traditional schools, and can send more than 80% to college.[2]

These include several hundred new model high schools in New York City that are graduating students at twice the rate of the factory-model warehouses they replaced,[3] and a range of successful new public schools in cities such as Chicago, Oakland, Los Angeles, and San Diego that launched new schools initiatives in the 1990s. Some, like the New Tech High and High Tech High networks of schools launched in California, have organized their work around a project-based, technology-supported curriculum. Others, like the network of International High Schools started in New York City, use what they call an activity-based curriculum designed for English language learners to launch new immigrants on successful paths to college. Career academies around the country have teamed up with local industries to create a hands-on curriculum that prepares students for college and careers. Early College high schools, partnered with universities, are enabling students to take college courses while they are still in high school.

Community school models, like those operated by the Children's Aid Society in Chicago, New York, Portland, and elsewhere, combine high-quality K–12 schooling with vital services such as health care, preschool, and before- and afterschool care. The Harlem Children's Zone, launched by Geoffrey Canada, takes this idea to scale in a community-wide initiative. Other elementary models, supported by organizations ranging from the Comer School Development Program to the Basic Schools Program and the Core Knowledge Foundation, have helped to create more coherent curriculum and more effective support systems to enhance student learning.

Demonstrating the folly of the recurring curriculum wars, in which polarized advocates have battled over content versus skills and basics versus deep understanding, these schools illustrate how knowledge and skills can be taught well together. They are living proof that strong disciplinary (and interdisciplinary) learning is not at odds with the development of so-called 21st-century skills, such as problem solving, critical and creative thinking, the capacity for independent learning, reflection, and communication. Indeed, as Diane Ravitch has appropriately noted, aside from the uses of new technologies, most of these skills have been central to the definition of a well-educated person for centuries, although they are in higher demand in today's economy.[4]

So, for example, at a Core Knowledge School in Brooklyn, New York, developed around the ideas of E. D. Hirsch, students engage in project-based learning and performance assessments as they study a coherent sequential curriculum that treats English, history and geography, mathematics and science, the art of many civilizations, visual arts, and music. Both organized acquisition of central ideas and opportunities to develop thinking and performance skills are emphasized. As Ravitch described when visiting the school's annual Core Knowledge Fair:

The day's festivities began with the sixth-grade chorus singing Beethoven's "Ode to Joy," followed by Duke Ellington's classic "Take the A Train." . . . Two radiant sixth-grade children declaimed Maya Angelou's poem "On the Pulse of Morning," which she wrote for President Clinton's inauguration. A first-grade group of twenty played violins, bowing out *Twinkle, Twinkle, Little Star* by Mozart. Fifth graders reenacted the writing of the Declaration of Independence and hailed its significance in today's world; another group from the same grade declaimed on the historical injustices that had violated the spirit of Mr. Jefferson's great document. Third graders dramatized the tragedy of Julius Caesar, betrayed by his friends and the Roman mob. . . . The walls of the school overflow with student projects about ancient Greece, ancient Rome, American history, the principles of science, and African American achievements.[5]

Similarly, in the many successful urban schools I have seen and studied, students generally follow a common core curriculum that prepares them for college and for the kind of work they will need to do in a world where thinking and invention matter, and they are challenged to meet high standards embodied in graduation requirements requiring scientific investigations, historical and social science research papers, mathematical problems and models, essays and literary critiques, and oral defenses of their work—the kind of work these same students in most schools would be presumed unable to attempt, much less master.

Some of these are among the more successful charter schools that have been released from state and district regulatory constraints. Most are district-run schools created by innovative teachers and leaders who began to develop new designs as long ago as the 1970s and who mentored new school models into existence in the intervening years. Their strategies have often included creating smaller schools as well as advisory structures, "looping" that keeps groups of students with their teachers for 2 or more years, cooperative, project-based learning, and teaching teams that ensure that students are well known and teachers have opportunities to work together. Many of the successful urban high schools teach a college preparatory curriculum supported by performance assessments that enable students to apply their knowledge and that provide rich information for improving teaching and learning. And they ensure that targeted supports and services are available for students when they are needed. These schools also invariably create many opportunities for developing shared knowledge and commitments among teachers, administrators, parents, and community members.[6]

In this chapter, I discuss how successful urban schools serving low-income students have created conditions for high-quality student and teacher learning by redesigning the school organization, curriculum, instruction, and assessments so that they enable high standards with high supports.

THE NEED FOR MAJOR REDESIGN

Today's expectation that schools will enable *all* students, rather than just a small minority, to learn challenging skills to high levels creates an entirely new mission for schools. Instead of merely "covering the curriculum" or "getting through the book," this new mission requires that schools substantially enrich the intellectual opportunities they offer while meeting the diverse needs of students who bring with them varying talents, interests, learning styles, cultures, predispositions, language backgrounds, family situations, and beliefs about themselves and about what school means for them. This demands not only more skillful teaching, but contexts in which students can be well known, in which they experience a coherent curriculum that lets them learn essential concepts in ways that develop strong thinking skills.

Major changes in school organizations and the systems in which they sit are needed to accomplish this. Unfortunately, the bureaucratic school created at the turn of the 20th century was not organized to meet these needs for intellectual development or for individual responsiveness. Most of today's schools were designed when the goal of education was not to educate all students well but to batch process a great many efficiently, selecting and supporting only a few for "thinking work." Strategies for sorting and tracking students were developed to ration the scarce resources of expert teachers and rich curriculum, and to justify the standardization of teaching tasks and procedures.

Teaching work was designed to be routine, with little need for professional skill and judgment, and no built-in structures for developing these abilities. Instead of investing directly in teachers' knowledge, a bureaucracy was constructed to prescribe, manage, and control the work of teachers, deflecting funds from the classroom to a long hierarchy of managers and a bevy of personnel outside the classroom. Texts and tests were designed to support and monitor the transmission of facts and basic skills, with little demand for complex applications. Indeed, the rote learning needed for early-20th-century objectives still predominates in many of today's schools—especially those that serve the children of the poor—reinforced by top-down prescriptions for teaching practice, scripted curriculum packages, standardized tests that focus on low-cognitive-level skills, and continuing underinvestment in teacher knowledge.

A business world maxim holds that "every organization is perfectly structured to get the results that it gets." A corollary is that substantially different results require organizational redesign, not just incentives for staff to try harder within traditional constraints. This lesson was learned by U.S. businesses that saved themselves from extinction in the 1980s by realizing that they needed to restructure from the old bureaucratic, assembly line model to new quality management systems emphasizing problem-solving teams rather than prescriptive hierarchies. In education, however, most initiatives have focused on trying to make the educational system inherited from the early 1900s perform more efficiently, rather than fundamentally rethinking how schools are designed, how systems operate, how teaching and learning are pursued, and what goals for schooling are sought. As David Kearns, the CEO who helped restructure the Xerox Corporation, explained:

> Lockstep, myopic management is still the norm in American education today, just as it was in American business. . . . Our entire way of thinking needs to be replaced. Today's high-tech firm is lean: It has stripped away middle management. It is decentralized, relying on the know-how and professionalism of workers close to the problem. It is innovative in the deployment of personnel, no longer relying on limiting job classifications. It spends heavily on employee education and training. It invests heavily in research.[7]

The effort to create learning organizations in both the business and education sectors has sought to replace the bureaucratic forms of organization dominant throughout the 20th century with new organizational designs that are less rigid and more adaptive, more able to accommodate diversity, and more capable of continuous invention. Efforts to invent 21st-century organizations tend to

- Use incentives and structures that motivate through collaboration rather than coercion
- Build strong relationships and norms rather than relying solely on rules for governing behavior
- Encourage quality by structuring work around whole products or services rather than disconnected piecework (in the case of schools, organizing teams that can take responsibility for children's overall success, not just for stamping them with a lesson and moving them along the assembly line)
- Create information-rich environments that support widespread learning and self-assessment among workers, rather than relying primarily on hierarchical supervision of work routines

Such organizations aim to stimulate greater thoughtfulness and creativity, rather than focusing largely on enforcing compliance with predetermined procedures.[8] Their success, then, depends on the creation of new opportunities for teacher and school learning, new modes of accountability, and new kinds of incentives for continual improvement and problem solving.

Just as businesses that have survived major economic changes have had to restructure their work to obtain significantly better results, schools that have achieved much greater levels of success have restructured staffing patterns, reconceptualized the use of time, reallocated funds, and redesigned curriculum, teaching, and assessment. These changes have been made not only to afford more time for teacher learning and collaboration, but also to create settings in which teachers can work much more productively with students toward more ambitious learning goals.

The kinds of changes needed are not a mystery. A number of studies have found that, all else being equal, schools have higher levels of achievement when they create smaller, more personalized units in which teachers plan and work together around shared groups of students and common curriculum.[9] In addition to many case studies of successful schools, research on 820 high schools in the National Education Longitudinal Study (NELS) found that schools that had restructured to personalize education and develop collaborative learning structures produced significantly higher achievement gains that were also more equitably distributed.[10] The schools' practices included

- Creating small units within schools
- Keeping students together over multiple years
- Forming teaching teams that share students and plan together
- Ensuring common planning time for teachers
- Involving staff in schoolwide problem solving
- Involving parents in their children's education
- Fostering cooperative learning

Researchers have discovered that in such "communitarian" schools, students are better known, and faculty develop a more collective perspective about the purposes and strategies for their work.[11]

Intellectual content also matters. For example, a study of more than 2,000 students in 23 restructured schools found higher achievement on intellectually challenging tasks for students who experienced what the researchers termed *authentic pedagogy*—that is, instruction, curriculum, and assessment that requires students to apply their learning in real-world contexts, consider alternatives, use knowledge as disciplinary experts do (for example, engage in scientific inquiry, historical research, literary analysis, or the writing process), and communicate effectively to audiences beyond the individual teacher.[12] The NELS study noted above also found that students in schools with high levels of *authentic instruction*—instruction focused on active learning calling for higher-order thinking, extended writing, and products that resemble how knowledge is used in the world outside of school—experienced greater achievement gains.[13]

What do these kinds of schools look like and what do they do to create better outcomes for students, especially in high-need communities? In the next section, I describe the common strategies of many such schools, focusing especially on urban secondary schools, because they are, in general, the most unsuccessful part of our educational system and the most toxic for low-income and minority students. The historic mission of high schools to select and sort, rather than support and develop, coupled with the inappropriateness of large warehouse settings for students who most need care and connections, leads to enormous temptations to allow or even encourage struggling students to drop out. To overcome these conditions, successful schools have had to return to first principles in designing settings that are more productively focused on teaching and learning.

DESIGNING SCHOOLS FOR TEACHING AND LEARNING

Eduardo Rodriguez had struggled in school all his life. As a special education student, he had managed to progress through to high school reading at only a 5th-grade level, and for a considerable time could not spell his last name. When he was in 10th grade, he attended a chaotic school that was unable to meet his needs: "He wasn't learning, he wasn't reading," his mother explained, adding that he was constantly teased and often drawn into the many fights that occurred. The last straw came when Eduardo was almost stabbed while trying to defend a student who was about to be attacked. His mother decided to pull him out of school that day. She felt at that time that "either they would have killed him in school, or he would have been in prison. They just did not expect anything of him."

Mrs. Rodriguez tried to enroll Eduardo in private school, but he could not pass the entrance requirements. When she found out about New Tech High School in Sacramento and went to visit in 2004, she was impressed with how courteous and articulate the students were. She enrolled her son at New Tech even though it was a 45-minute drive from her home. Mrs. Rodriguez warned the principal and the counselor that her son was unlikely to ask for help or talk to the teachers. However, Eduardo soon developed close relationships with his teachers and his counselor, whom he calls on a regular basis, including during holiday breaks. His mother reports that his reading level has risen six grade levels and is now nearly on par with his current grade level, that he creates products and writes enthusiastically, and has developed close friendships with other students. She voices her astonishment at the change:

> I'm so used to all the years since he was 5 years old, when nothing was expected of him. Here, he's a different person. . . . I never thought that would be possible. I would pay for my son to come here; it's amazing what he's learned. It is expected of him to perform. It's not, "We'll see if you can do it," but, "You can do it and you're going to do it." So he thinks like that now.[14]

At New Tech High School, Eduardo and his classmates use technology to complete complex projects in all of their classes, modeling the expectations of employees in a high-tech economy. Every classroom has a computer for each student, used in the course of each collaborative project, which represents a real-world problem drawing on skills in many domains. In a combined math and physics class, for example, small groups of students are working on the aftermath of a car crash. Students representing each driver and the driver's lawyers have to figure out what happened to cause the cars to crash, which driver was at fault, and how to prepare a defense of their client. Like other projects, this one calls upon their knowledge of physics and mathematics as they evaluate the physical crash and estimate the damage, as well as their skills in analysis, written and oral expression, personal presentation, collaboration, planning, and follow-through.

As a result of regular engagement with these kinds of projects, New Tech students stand out in their self-confidence and their ability to articulate the purpose of their work and its relevance. In addition, in 2007, when we studied the school, state data showed a graduation rate of 96%,[15] with 100% of the predominantly minority, low-income students going on to 2- or 4-year college—more than twice the rate of the state as a whole.[16] Students prepared for this during high school by completing, in addition to their high school courses, at least 12 college credits at the local community college and 40 community service hours, which helped build their independence and sense of responsibility.

In a study I conducted with colleagues at Stanford University and the Justice Matters Institute, New Tech High was one of five California high schools we examined in 2007 that graduated more than 85% of their primarily low-income students of color and sent 80 to 100% of their graduates to college. Two of these were new small schools recently started within school districts: Stanley E. Jordan Construction Tech Academy, a small school in what had become a complex of small schools within the former Kearney High School building in San Diego, and June Jordan School for Equity in San Francisco. Two were independent charters: Animo Leadership High School in Inglewood (Los Angeles) and Leadership High School in San Francisco. New Tech High was started as a dependent charter—part of the Sacramento district, staffed by regular district teachers belonging to the teachers union—but allowed autonomy in budget, curriculum, and hiring.

Despite their different governance arrangements, student populations, and locations, the schools have many design features in common, as I describe below. And, indeed, these schools are genealogical descendents of schools in other parts of the country that were launched more than a decade earlier, whose designs have since been emulated many times over. Colleagues and I identified very similar features in a set of distinctive new high schools, started in the 1990s in New York City, that also sent 80 to 100% of their predominantly low-income minority and recent immigrant students to college, having graduated them from high school at rates significantly above city averages.[17]

Several hundred new model schools have been created under the terms of six separate chancellors since Chancellor Joe Fernandez issued his first Request for

Proposals to innovators wanting to start new schools in 1989. Indeed, New York City's efforts to rethink schools on a large scale signal the invention of 21st-century school designs in a city that was the prototypic home of the factory model nearly a century ago. These successful school designs later seeded initiatives in Chicago, Milwaukee, Philadelphia, San Diego, Boston, and other major cities.

Launched by teachers and principals who had ideas about how schools could better support high-quality teaching and learning, often working in collaboration with community based organizations, most of these schools are part of regular school districts, not charters or private schools. Many built on the early successes of models like Central Park East Elementary and Secondary Schools, started by school innovator Deborah Meier, who designed not only a set of schools that she created and ran personally, but also 50 schools she helped others launch as part of the New York City Annenberg challenge and dozens more in a later Pilot Schools effort in Boston. These early schools, along with many others, including the Urban Academy, launched by Ann Cook and Herb Mack as a second-chance high school for students who had dropped out of other schools, and the International High School, created for new immigrant students by Eric Nadelstern, were protected from district regulations and political swings by the Alternative Schools Superintendency, a special division created inside the New York City schools during the early 1980s to tend and nurture nontraditional schools.

These "older" schools, which mentored a large group of 50 new schools in the early 1990s, providing both the designs and lead staff for many of them, had established track records of succeeding with students who typically would have failed in traditional New York high schools, regularly graduating 90% of their students and sending 90% or more to college.[18] The first of these birthing projects was the Coalition Campus Schools project, which closed down two of the city's more troubled large high schools—Julia Richman High School in Manhattan and James Monroe High School in the Bronx, each serving about 3,000 students—by not admitting new students while hot-housing new schools at other sites. Later, some of the new schools moved into the original buildings with other small schools and social service agencies, while others occupied nearby sites serving students from the original catchment area.

In 1992, the city had 20 such neighborhood high schools, most of which exhibited high rates of academic failure. In that year, Julia Richman had a 4-year graduation rate of 36.9%, and Monroe graduated only 26.9%.[19] By 1998, when my colleagues and I studied the set of new small schools created to serve the students at Julia Richman, their 4-year graduation rates for a comparable population of students had climbed to 73%, and their college-going rate for these graduates was 91%, well above city averages despite the fact that they served a significantly larger number of low-income, minority, and limited English proficient students, special education students receiving resource room services, and students overage for their grade than the city as a whole. Continuing to support students who needed more time, the schools posted a 6-year graduation rate of 85% by 2000.[20]

The Coalition Campus schools project not only started a set of new schools; it also transformed the Julia Richman campus—once a violent, graffiti-ridden building patrolled by police and vandalized daily—into a safe, vibrant community school complex. The new Julia Richman Education Complex (JREC) now includes four high schools, including two of the Coalition Campus Schools (Vanguard and Manhattan International High Schools) and one of the parent schools (the Urban Academy), as well as a performing arts program (Talent Unlimited), a special education program serving autistic junior high school students, and the Ella Baker Elementary School. Also part of JREC are a day care coupled with a Teen Parenting Center, a health center offered by a neighborhood teaching hospital, and a professional development institute that collaborates with universities and the teachers union to provide seminars for teachers across the city. The other schools started by the project are housed in nearby buildings, collectively serving the student population that formerly attended Julia Richman.

This multigenerational approach brings adolescents into daily contact with children and babies, giving them opportunities to set a good example for the young ones, which they feel responsible for living up to. The high schools involve their students in reading to, tutoring, and taking care of the elementary and nursery school students as part of their community service and internships. While individual schools occupy their own floors of the building, schools share an auditorium, art and dance studios, a cafeteria, and the gymnasium where a joint set of JREC sports teams play. The airy, bustling building experiences almost no graffiti or vandalism; it houses a community, rather than a compound.

All but two of the so-called Coalition Campus schools adapted their designs from the model of Central Park East Secondary School (CPESS), a high school of 450 students founded by Deborah Meier in East Harlem in 1985. Teachers in most of the new schools—Vanguard, Landmark, Manhattan Village, and Coalition School for Social Change—decided to work in interdisciplinary grade level teams responsible for groups of 40 to 80 students to whom they teach a college preparatory, core curriculum framed by a set of "habits of mind." The schools require students to weigh evidence, address multiple perspectives, make connections, speculate on alternatives, and assess the value of the ideas they have studied. In some of the schools, teachers "loop" with their students for 2 years. Class periods are generally 70 minutes or more in length, enabling intensive study and research. In the 11th and 12th grades, the schools developed variations on the portfolios developed at CPESS and the Urban Academy that engage students in performance assessments in each core subject area as a basis for graduation.

Another school—Manhattan International—was designed to serve new immigrant students and followed the model of its mentor school, International High School, which was started in 1985 in Queens, New York. With a population of

100% limited English proficient students, International's collaborative, activity-based instruction—now used in all International high schools in New York and California—supports students in learning English while they are engaged in academic study. Students who speak different native languages are placed in collaborative teams to complete teacher-developed performance tasks that require them to use English to communicate. Seventy-minute periods provide time for intensive project work that is evaluated through performance assessments and exhibitions. Teams of teachers in the core disciplines jointly plan for shared groups of about 75 students to whom they teach a thematic, interdisciplinary curriculum all day long. Teachers problem solve around the curriculum and the needs of their students constantly. A counselor is also attached to each of these student groups to support everything from personal needs to college counseling. In some of the schools, the teams stay with a group of students for 2 years to promote accountability and student success.

And the schools are successful. Accepting only recent immigrant students who score in the bottom quartile on the English language proficiency test, in 2005, the Internationals network—then eight schools serving students speaking more than 100 different native languages in New York City—graduated 89% of the cohort of students who began in 1998 over the 7-year period tracked by New York City. This compared to only 31% for the same cohort of English language learners citywide. Of these, all were English proficient and 92% were college-bound by the time they graduated.[21]

The Julia Richman approach has since been the model used to replace most of the neighborhood "zoned" high schools in New York, with support from the Gates and Carnegie foundations, among many others, and leverage from subsequent chancellors. By 2009, there were more than 300 new small schools in New York City, begun over the previous 2 decades, and many dozens in other cities. Studies in Boston, Chicago, Philadelphia, and elsewhere have found similar design features for the most successful school models, especially in graduating low-income students of color and sending them to college.[22] These features, shared by elementary and secondary schools alike, include

1. Small size for the school or learning communities within the school
2. Structures that allow for personalization and strong relationships
3. Intellectually challenging and relevant instruction
4. Performance-based assessment
5. Highly competent teachers who collaborate in planning and problem solving

I discuss these features below, illustrating how they operate with examples from the five New York City high schools and five urban California high schools described earlier.[23]

Small School Units

In all of these schools, which typically serve from about 300 to 450 students (although several may be located within a larger building), teachers, students, and parents emphasize the importance of small size to the schools' success. Their comments focus on safety and being known, not surprising since one of the first indicators to improve when small urban schools are created is a sharp increase in safety and decrease in incidence rates when the adults know all of the students in the school well.[24] As a Landmark student commented,

> There is less violence compared to bigger schools. Everyone here knows one another. . . . Bigger schools are louder and crazier. No one will bother you here.

A Vanguard humanities teacher described "the family feeling," arguing:

> You are just not going to fall through the cracks here. You are an important individual. For the first time, [students] are seen as important individuals in the school system. I compare this with my experience in large schools with 35 students in a class, where kids regularly fall through the cracks.

And a parent at New Tech High observed:

> There's a lot more opportunity for the kids to be seen, be heard, and be noticed to participate in just about any thing they want.

These experiences underscore evidence accumulated over several decades that suggests that, overall, smaller high schools are associated with greater safety, more positive student attitudes about school, higher levels of student participation and attendance, much lower dropout rates, and—depending on other design features described below—higher achievement.[25] Studies have found that a range of sizes may allow for these benefits, depending on the context and student population. However, schools above about 1,200 students in size are invariably found to be less effective for students, and those in the range of about 300 to 500 appear to be most effective for the lowest-income and traditionally lowest-achieving students. This is especially true when these schools are designed to offer close attachments to caring adults, a common curriculum, and personalized supports for learning.[26]

In analyses of school- and district-level achievement, small schools have been found to reduce the influence of poverty on school and district performance, "disrupting the usual negative relationship between socioeconomic status and student achievement."[27] One study found, for example, that the relationship between smaller school size and achievement is significant when at least 30% of students are low-income and grows ever stronger as the poverty rate increases.[28] At grade nine, the effect of a standard deviation increase in size (about 260 students) in the poorest communities was associated with a loss of just over 0.5 standard deviations in achievement, or about half a year of learning, while there was no effect in the wealthiest communities, where students may need fewer highly personalized supports to succeed.

These findings are particularly noteworthy given that so many failing urban schools still serve 2,000 or more students in organizations that spend enormous amounts of energy and dollars creating a prison-like environment focused on control rather than instruction. Metal detectors, security guards, truant officers, and scores of administrative staff are funded to manage students who are scheduled to see seven or eight different teachers a day (each of whom may see as many as 200 students a day) in 50-minute blocks of time where relationships are nearly impossible to forge. Even in suburban areas, violence such as the shootings at Columbine High School, where two students shot 15 others one day in 1999, and the many other middle and high school shootings that have occurred since then, are generally the result of students being poorly known and isolated from staff and peers, often in large, impersonal school settings.[29]

However, small size alone does not create better education; it merely creates conditions that can, if well used, foster greater attachment and more positive behavior. Any influence of school size on student achievement depends as well on other features of the environment that shape what students have the opportunity to learn—the quality of curriculum and teaching, as well as academic supports.[30]

Structures for Personalization

A key feature in these successful schools—perhaps most striking in contrast to the traditional urban high school—is their degree of personalization. The schools' efforts to ensure that students are well known include the construction of small learning communities; continuous, long-term relationships between adults and students; advisory systems that systematically organize counseling, academic supports, and family connections; and small class sizes and reduced pupil loads for teachers that allow them to care effectively for students.

Advisory Systems. In these high-performing schools, teachers have an advisory group of 15 to 25 students who meet with them several times a week and, in most cases, stay with them for 2 to 4 years. The advisor works closely with the student, the family, and with other teachers to ensure that the academic and personal supports needed for success are available. Advisors meet with parents or family members several times a year to review student work, call home if students are absent or have difficulties—and to celebrate successes—and are available to parents who need to discuss family and student problems and needs. As one teacher noted, "We look out after our advisees in all of their classes. Our conversations are informal, but it gets them back in the groove if they have fallen out."

Students do not have to fall through the cracks to get needed assistance. Support is proactive and built into the central organization of the school. For example, Landmark's advisory groups, which place 13 students with one adult for ongoing academic and personal support, meet five times per week. This teacher's explanation of how advisories work is typical: "We have daily conversations and know how they are doing. We contact parents. The advisor takes major responsibility. We may call in [the principal], but it doesn't get passed to the office to take care of kids' performance. It stays with us."

A community organizer who works closely with the staff at June Jordan School for Equity in San Francisco voiced the same commitment: "When kids are slipping, there's this expectation that teachers grab hold of them and will not let go." This expectation has been well-tested. June Jordan was launched when a group of teachers and parents joined with community organizers to convince the school district to open a small school for low-income students of color who were failing at high rates. Located on the southeast side of San Francisco near the highest-poverty neighborhoods, the school provided the local community with its first college-going option, as the city's college prep–oriented high schools are on the other side of the city where affluent residents reside.

Most students, such as James Williams, enter the school many grade levels behind in their basic skills and with personal experience of the neighborhood's high levels of crime and homicide. The advisory system was critical to James's eventual success at June Jordan. Growing up in poverty and moving from one low-income neighborhood to the next, James faced the kind of challenges that lead many young Black men in similar circumstances to drop out of school. His mother was out of work for several years due to health challenges, and struggled to raise a family on her own, often leaving her son to care for his younger sister. James notes that, although he was raised "around drug use and alcoholism, I never got into gang violence or street life. I always knew that I wanted to go to college."

Although James's mother wanted him to attend a "nice high school and go to college," he could not get into any of the college prep high schools in San Francisco, so she enrolled him at June Jordan when it was initially founded. The school combines a college preparatory curriculum organized around social justice issues with highly personalized instruction and a strong advisory system. James notes that all of these supports were important to his success: "All throughout June Jordan I had close relationships with all my advisors. It made me give my trust to people more; there were so many people there to help me and make sure that I do well." With two other young children to care for, his mother could not easily attend parent conferences, so June Jordan teachers went to her home to meet with her, ensuring that a strong family connection would be built. James's advisor provided emotional, academic, and financial support to help him get through a rough patch when his family faced a number of hardships.

As a result of the school's constant support, as well as its emphasis on extensive writing and inquiry, James decided to attend the University of California at Santa Cruz, where he is now considering a major in literature or writing. When he first arrived at college, James reflected on how well he was prepared for this next chapter in his life:

> Today we had orientation about our core classes; they were telling us that we have just 10 weeks to do all these essays. I feel like I am very confident in writing. I enjoy it. June Jordan got me ready for a four-year college. They helped us become independent. We had a lot of help, and people had our backs at June Jordan, but they also made sure that we were able to take care of ourselves when we needed to.

James was not alone in this success. Among his colleagues in June Jordan's first graduating class in 2007, 95% were admitted to college, with 73% of them going to 4-year colleges at the University of California and California State campuses, as well as private colleges such as Clark Atlanta, Dartmouth, Smith, and Yale Universities.

As suggested by research on communal school models,[31] we found that strong relationships between and among students and faculty were central to participants' views of what enabled them to succeed. Students often compared their school to a family and linked their achievement to their caring relationships with teachers. As the Vanguard student quoted at the chapter opening said,

> School should not be mass production. It needs to be loving and close. That is what kids need. You need love to learn.

Another, who was eligible for the most restrictive special education setting, said about his experience at Vanguard,

> I was bad all the way back from elementary and junior high school. I would have got lost in the system. I would not have made it. I would have dropped out. I needed someone to be there to show they care about me for me to be motivated.

The principal at Animo-Inglewood described how the family relationship motivates students:

> We build a really close family relationship between students, their families, and the staff in the school. Students work hard not to let the family down.

A senior at San Diego's Construction Tech Academy put it this way.

> You're with [teachers] for much longer and you get to interact with your teachers
> a whole lot more and get to know them. . . . When you're learning from a friend,
> not just from some random person, it's a lot easier to learn.

Reduced Pupil Loads. In order to personalize instruction, these schools have redesigned staffing and scheduling to include more classroom-based staff teaching in
longer blocks of time, thus enabling smaller class sizes and reduced pupil loads for
teachers—typically as low as 40 or 50 for humanities teachers teaching English and
history/social studies together—or as high as 80 to 100 for single-subject teachers.
This is about half the pupil load of teachers in most urban schools, where teachers
are likely to see 150 to 200 students each day. The reorganization of schedules allows teachers to teach fewer students for longer blocks of time (70 to 120 minutes),
often in interdisciplinary configurations, which immediately reduces pupil load significantly. Students generally take fewer courses at a time, generally four rather than
six or seven. The more streamlined set of offerings stands in contrast to the "shopping mall high school" approach[32] that has offered a dizzying array of courses and
sections, rather than a focused, core curriculum.

The schools' allocation of resources to core instructional functions creates
structures that allow teachers to care effectively for their students.[33] By knowing
students well, teachers are more able tailor instruction to students' strengths, needs,
experiences, and developing interests. Both students and teachers describe how
these structures enable teachers to support intellectually challenging work and to
sustain a press for higher standards of performance. As a 22-year veteran of large
schools who moved to Vanguard explained:

> Small size mean I can do a literature seminar with the bottom 20% of kids in the
> city. Kids who didn't read are reading books like *Jane Eyre* to write their essay. We
> can work with them during lunch. You find out who can't read, type, etc. These are
> the kids who would sit in the back of the room, be in the bathroom, and would
> deliberately get lost. I know dedicated teachers in big schools who teach 150 kids.
> they can't do this.

A student at Manhattan Village Academy reinforced this point:

> This school will get the worst student to do the work. Teachers are not like this at
> other high schools where they have [too many] kids. Troubled kids need attention
> and they can get it here. Kids can see other kids like them working.

An unanticipated benefit is that students can focus more effectively when they are
taking a smaller number of classes. As a student at Landmark commented:

> I really like that it's only four classes that we take; in the old school you had to
> study a little on each subject and keep eight subjects in your head at once.

In this context, teachers can be committed to students' learning, not just to cranking through the assembly line each day. A student at Coalition School for Social Change (CSSC) expressed the sentiments of others when he said, "Because the school is small, teachers have more time to help us. They don't go crazy and we get to learn better." Another student at the same school observed, "The teachers here care for you and your work. They know your potential and keep pushing you to do your best." A student at Manhattan International explained, "If we have personal problems like depression we can talk to the teachers. . . . The teachers know us really well because we always work together, one on one." A Manhattan Village Academy student explained, "I was pregnant last year. The teachers were really behind me. I am still in school and I'm doing well in my classes. The teachers push you here. They want you to graduate."

Intellectually Challenging and Relevant Instruction

The structures described above help schools care more effectively for students. Equally important is how the schools facilitate intellectual development. Each of the schools has designed an ambitious, coherent instructional program that enables students to overcome barriers to access that are often associated with race, poverty, language, or initially low academic skill. In order to fill large skill gaps for students who have been previously underserved by the school system, schools must meet students where they are and enable them to make large strides.

Each school has addressed this by establishing high expectations, offering a common, untracked, college preparatory curriculum with a comprehensive set of academic supports, ensuring explicit teaching of intellectual and research skills in the context of rigorous coursework. The schools' efforts are consistent with research finding that schools offering a more common curriculum with a narrower range of academic courses tend to produce higher levels of achievement for all students, and greater equity in course-taking, graduation, and college-going.[34] This coursework includes both career-oriented and college preparatory learning, with a strong focus on applying knowledge in real-world settings through projects, community service, and internships.

Challenging and Engaging Curriculum. The schools' programs focus on preparing students for the demands of college. Teachers have worked out a coherent curriculum that teaches the core disciplinary concepts, sometimes in interdisciplinary ways, through carefully constructed and sequenced instructional units that add up across the grade levels. Most assignments require the production of analytic work— research papers and projects, demonstrations and discussions of problems, experiments and data collection organized to answer open-ended questions. Worksheets and fill-in-the-blank tasks are rare. Extensive reading and writing are expected in all academic courses. Many classes require large end-of-course projects that include extensive written documentation, often presented and defended orally.

Manhattan Village Academy's director, Mary Butz, described how reading, writing, and data collection skills are taught explicitly in the context of major projects:

> We demand a lot of work. In the 9th grade, students work on an autobiography that emphasizes writing skills. In the 10th grade there is an inter-cultural project where we teach them research skills. They must use three sources, respond to specific questions, and make comparisons.

As part of this work, students are taught research conventions such as compiling a bibliography, using multiple forms of documentation, and formats for report writing.

Teachers provide opportunities for ongoing revision of work in response to feedback from peers and outside experts as well as themselves, using a mastery approach to learning along with culturally relevant pedagogies to connect to students' needs and experiences. According to teachers and students, revision is a way of life. Faculty voice the belief that students learn by tackling substantial tasks and getting feedback against standards that guide their efforts to improve. Their beliefs are borne out by a large body of research showing very substantial gains in achievement for students who experience formative assessment and feedback with continuous opportunities to revise and improve their work.[35]

A 27-year veteran history teacher who had been at Vanguard for 5 years explained how this instruction is supported by the schools' flexible scheduling and small pupil loads:

> I can use in-depth approaches and assign college level research projects. For 2 months, each morning, we teach students research skills and essay skills so that they can do a minimum 20-page research paper in history. I give them internal motivation to come up against the challenge. They choose the topic. We develop their topic together. This gets them into the different sides of the topic. They are stimulated and internally motivated because it is something they want to learn. I take them to the Donnell Library. . . . They browse through different books, take notes, and order their thoughts in an outline. . . . Then, the kids have to listen to their teachers and peers criticizing their work. Then they have to rewrite. They have to cite references, show evidence, and prove their thesis.

The projects often combine library research with contemporary investigations in the community and studies of literature or the arts. A humanities teacher at CSSC described how a recent project made curricular connections among history, fiction, and contemporary life:

Last year we did a study of Latin America with a focus on the Dominican Republic. We read Julia Alvarez's *In the Time of the Butterflies* to look at the extremes the dictatorship went to. We then went up to Washington Heights and interviewed senior citizens who had lived through this period. These interviews were powerful learning experiences for our students.

Although there are efforts to link the curriculum to students' own lives and interests, this does not limit the students' studies only to their immediate concerns. The assignments often blend classical studies with multicultural content. In our sampling of student portfolios, we found that students had studied works by Allende, Brecht, Ibsen, Chekhov, de Maupassant, Marquez, Arthur Miller, Toni Morrison, Poe, Sanchez, Shakespeare, R. L. Stevenson, Tolkien, and Richard Wright, among others. In social studies, students studied topics such as the U.S. Constitution, immigration, political prisoners, and Supreme Court cases. Some of the schools used curriculum such as the American Social History Project, which examines history from multiple perspectives. In science, students studied biology, chemistry, and physics as well as aerospace and the environment. The arts are both taught separately and integrated into other subject areas.

All of the schools also prepare students for higher education by making arrangements for students to enroll in courses at local colleges. These experiences enable students to learn about college demands first-hand. One student's account of his experience in a modern American history course at a college in the CUNY system reflects many others we heard:

At first I was ready to quit because I felt I was not ready for it. But when I talked to my teachers, they gave me advice on study habits—how to manage time better, especially for doing homework for both my school and the college courses. I spent more time reading the books. If I didn't understand, teachers here would explain the material. They gave me other books. I took the mid-term and did O.K. It gave me insight on what college would really be like.

Explicit Teaching of Academic Skills. A key element of instruction in these schools is careful scaffolding for the learning of complex skills. In contrast to many high school curricula, which assume that students have already mastered skills of reading, writing, and research, the schools construct a curriculum that explicitly teaches students how to study, how to approach academic tasks, what criteria will be applied, and how to evaluate their own and others' work.

Sylvia Rabiner, founding principal of Landmark High School, described how skills instruction is built into Landmark's curriculum from the first day the students enter:

When students enter Landmark in the 9th grade, they are immediately taught how a library works. They are taught how to do a research paper. They are introduced to the habits of mind and rubrics that will be used to assess their work as they progress from grade to grade and ultimately, their graduation portfolios. They are taught how to do exhibitions so that by the time they defend their portfolios, they have had several years experience in oral presentations.

All of the schools offer structured supports for the teaching of reading and writing, either as part of courses in the 9th and 10th grades or as special classes for students who need support.

Flexible Supports. Access to challenging curriculum does not automatically translate into student success. The schools have sought to marry high standards with a variety of supports to help students negotiate the demands. As a group, the schools provide students—including those who enter high school below grade level, who are new English learners, or who are special education students—with integrated in-class and beyond-class supports. Almost all of the schools make time available before or after school so that students can obtain help. Some have peer tutoring programs and/or Saturday programs.

Because everyone is working together to help students meet standards, students typically perceive these additional learning opportunities as privileges, rather than punishments. For example, at New Tech, where Saturday school is one source of support, a parent explained:

> [Saturday school] was not punitive; it's help. [For] kids who aren't turning in assignments or kids who need to improve on their assignments, it's like a second chance. [My son] came a couple of times. The last time was because the semester was ending, and he knew that he had to do better on something. He didn't have to come; he said, "I need to go to Saturday school so I can do some assignment." It was the last Saturday before Christmas, and he chose to come because he knew he needed to improve.

Many schools provide additional skills classes focused on closing gaps in reading, math, or English language development alongside the untracked college preparatory classes in which all students are enrolled. English language learners and special education students are included in regular classes, often with additional classes or resource room supports to help them complete the same assignments other students receive.

Animo-Inglewood provides a good example of how a set of comprehensive supports can operate. The school's high expectations were modeled by the instructional leadership provided by founding principal, Cristina de Jesus, who went on to lead professional development at Green Dot, the parent charter management organization that started Animo, and her successor, Annette Gonzalez. Both women are highly accomplished, National Board Certified teachers. Gonzalez, who came from the more affluent Santa Monica/Malibu school district, was determined to hold the same expectations and provide the same resources for her Animo students in Inglewood as she did for her former students in Santa Monica. She explained to them: "We have these really high expectations for you; we believe you're going to go to college; we know that you can do it. We're going to push you hard, hard, hard to get there, but we're going to support you every step of the way."

Struggling students are required to attend an afterschool support class taught by their teachers, and teachers talk with parents to help determine effective strategies for supporting each student. Other supports for student learning include office hours held by teachers; Homework Café, a free afterschool tutoring program staffed by local college students; and curriculum skills courses in SAT preparation and skill building.

The coupling of expectations with support is reflected in the way that Animo addresses algebra, among other gateway courses. All 9th-grade students are enrolled in an algebra course, regardless of placement scores or previous coursework. To ensure that all students can succeed, incoming ninth graders are required to partici-pate in a 5-week summer bridge program designed to build basic math skills and introduce higher-order math concepts. The lead math teacher in the Green Dot Network, who also serves as Animo's math department chair, was assigned to teach 9th-grade algebra. Algebra, like other classes, is taught on a block A/B schedule with 95-minute periods that allow teachers to teach concepts deeply and provide opportunities for student exploration of ideas. If students struggle when they are enrolled in algebra, they also take a curriculum skills math class, which meets three times a week and is taught by the same teacher.

As a consequence of these strategies, the proportion of Animo students scoring proficient on the state standards test in Algebra I in 2007, when we studied the school, far outstripped that for the state as a whole, and African American and Latino students at Animo were proficient at triple the rate of their peers elsewhere in the state.

Multiple Strategies for Active Learning. Psychologist Robert Glaser has argued that schools must shift from a selective mode—"characterized by minimal variation in the conditions for learning" in which "a narrow range of instructional options and a limited number of ways to succeed are available"—to an adaptive mode in which "the educational environment can provide for a range of opportunities for success. Modes of teaching are adjusted to individuals' backgrounds, talents, interests, and the nature of past performance."[36]

In all of these schools, teachers consciously use multiple instructional strategies to give students different entry points to the material under study. They engage in direct instruction through occasional class lectures and regular discussions as well as guided inquiry, small-group work, and coaching of independent research, proj-

ects, and experiments. Most classes involve students in a variety of learning strategies to tackle long-term projects as well as short-term tasks. At Vanguard a student
remarked, "Teachers work around the differences in how kids learn to help you
complete your projects." As another student put it, "You get to create 3D models,
do research, and exhibitions. You do projects. You come up with your own topics
and problems. You create the questions and answer them. You write theme, plot, and
character essays. You do visuals. [The teachers] don't want it to be boring for you."

Well-managed small-group work is common. Although the group work we
observed allowed students to take an active role in their own learning, the work
was usually highly structured through activity guides that provided guidance for
the tasks and deliberate teacher coaching that anticipated student needs. Teachers
know the content they want students to master, have carefully selected texts and
other materials, and have clear goals for student learning of both subject matter and
specific skills. One of CSSC's humanities teachers described how the use of group
work drawing on different learning and performance modes is structured to promote growing independence:

> We want students to do independent work and work in cooperative groups. We
> get them started and they work independently. Teachers circulate among the
> groups.... For example, in a recent project, students self-selected into groups, did
> research, close reading, individual writing assignments, and presentations. Each
> presenting group had to teach the class what they learned.

Real-World Connections. Curricula often incorporate real-life applications,
which helps to sustain student interest and involvement in difficult tasks. A teacher
at CSSC explained how a science class simulates the work done by environmental
consulting firms:

> They identify a problem, make a plan for how to study it, do field work, and write
> up conclusions. Another class did a project with Central Park rangers, who are short-
> staffed, and identified tree samples for them. This is real-world, meaningful work.

A teacher at Manhattan Village Academy described how teachers link academic
content to the students' lives:

> We try to relate historical issues to the present day and have them form an opinion.
> We connected Fourth Amendment rights to locker searches when a book bag was
> stolen. We discuss individual responsibility and what you want the government to take
> over. We discuss and debate to get them to develop their thoughts a step further.

Community Service and Internships. All of the schools place students in external
learning experiences such as internships and community service activities that

occur during the regular school day and are accompanied by seminars that help students process what they are learning about the world of work. Linked to students' interests, these may include placements in hospitals, medical research labs, nonprofit organizations, social service agencies, businesses, and schools. The experiences are part of the core program for all students, not a separate track. They are intended to help adolescents assume responsibility, learn how to engage the world outside of home and school, gain an understanding of how different kinds of organizations operate, and explore their interests.

Students reported that, even when they found they did not like the work or setting they had chosen, or when they experienced conflicts on the job, their internships made them feel more capable, responsible, and confident about solving problems and succeeding in the world beyond school. Many said the commitments they developed in these settings spurred them on in school and motivated them to persevere. As a 12th-grade student at San Diego's Construction Tech Academy (CTA) put it: "It makes it easier to come to school. . . . We learn from textbooks, and we go on to apply them to real-life projects that we're working on in class, and then you see how the textbook work is relevant."

While most of the schools use internships as part of their curriculum, Construction Tech Academy takes this concept further than most. The guiding vision behind the school is the desire to create authentic curriculum through "real-world immersion." CTA stakeholders believe that a focus on how knowledge is used in the world of work adds relevance to the curriculum, which in turn leads to increased student attendance, engagement, and retention, especially for those who often disconnect from school. CTA's focus on the construction trades—including architecture, construction, and engineering—prepares students for college, the destination for over 80%, and skilled trades, which the remaining students enter through apprenticeships after high school.

The school strives to emulate authentic work settings by having students work in heterogeneous teams on complex projects that require diverse skills and abilities. Professionals from the engineering, architecture, and construction fields collaborate with students on projects and review student work. All students take both a college preparatory sequence and a full complement of vocational courses. Teachers act as coaches to support student-based inquiry, projects, and collaborative group work, as well as provide one-on-one assistance.

The concept of "real-world" at CTA is grounded in two central assumptions. The first is that "expertise" is something that comes from a combination of study and "hands-on" application, rather than from books alone. As principal Glenn Hillegas explained: "Advanced Placement has a really high rigor to it, but a really low application. To me, the best education is when you take something of high rigor and you apply it. When kids *apply* knowledge, they gain a deeper understanding."

The second assumption is that students need to learn how to direct their own learning and to work in heterogeneous teams, because that is how work in the "real world" happens. The best teachers at CTA act as coaches and guides, helping to support student-based inquiry with one-on-one assistance. The school also creates individual learning plans for each student, and sends home bimonthly reports tracking student's academic progress on "paydays."

"Real-world" applications occur as industry professionals come into the classroom to provide support to students and teachers as they work on projects and help review and evaluate project work once it is complete. For example, in ninth grade, students go to nearby Legoland when it is closed so they can see the "inner workings" of an amusement park and take an engineering tour. They then form small groups led by student foremen to design their own amusement parks, including two-dimensional plot plans and scale models of their parks. Students present their plans to industry professionals and receive a critique on their work.

Real-world application also occurs through the job shadows and internships that occur in the 11th and 12th grades. In their senior portfolios, seniors are required to prepare a resume, fill out an application for college, prepare a budget for college expenses, and interview a professional in a field of their interest. CTA also supports a range of field trips to help students think about the kinds of practical trade-offs that professionals make when designing or constructing buildings. For example, when students from the Architecture, Construction, and Engineering (ACE) afterschool club expressed interest in designing an airport for their spring project, a field trip was arranged so that they could go "behind the scenes" at San Diego airport to understand how airports really work. In the words of the principal, "rigor and relevance are driven into the school from the outside. It's a different level of work for the kids."

Performance-Based Assessment

All of the schools engage students in completing complex projects and investigations of various kinds, and most of them require the completion of portfolios for graduation, which include high-quality work illustrating disciplinary inquiry in each of the major subject areas. These pieces of work are often exhibited before a jury of teachers, parents, students, and reviewers from outside the school. A sense of press is supported by these assessment systems, which set public expectations for performance. As a teacher at June Jordan explains:

> We have our portfolio system, which is really effective in making sure that all kids get pushed. There are requirements in order for them to graduate from the school. . . . If they don't get a passing score, they have to re-present. It's a really good way to make sure that students aren't just getting by.

A San Diego district official who attended the exhibitions at Construction Tech noted:

> Having industry [members] involved in the exhibition of student work has raised the rigor way beyond what these teachers could have done on their own. I believe that authenticity, having to stand up in front of a group of professionals and defend your work, is so important. I remember the very first exhibition when a student wasn't prepared, and he admitted it, and the committee said, "Well, son, what is it going to take next time?" He was held accountable for why he didn't complete that work. He had to dig deep into his own heart to figure out why he didn't complete that work on time. That student became a very successful student here at Construction Tech, and he has graduated and moved on.

Students understand that this process deepens their learning. A student at Leadership High in San Francisco put it this way:

> At other high schools, it's just "you passed." Kids can't tell what they got out of high school. Students here know what they've learned.

All of the New York schools we studied require students to complete a common set of seven or more performance tasks for graduation as part of their overall portfolio. These are mapped to each disciplinary area and involve research papers, including a social science investigation and a scientific experiment, a literary critique, an arts product or analysis, a mathematical model or project, and an analysis of one of the student's internship experiences. Often, students will have completed an autobiography and a graduation plan that looks ahead to their futures. Traditional tests are also sometimes included in the portfolio. The schools' portfolios vary in content and structure. However, all of the assessment systems include:

1. Written and constructed or performed products requiring in-depth study
2. Oral presentation by the candidate before a committee of teachers and a peer who assess the quality of the work and pose questions to test for understanding
3. Rubrics embodying the standards against which students' performances are judged
4. Rating scales to assess students' products and oral presentations

In order to graduate, each student's committee must pass on his or her entire set of portfolios. The rigor of the process and the varying levels of skills with which students enter mean that, in all of the schools, some students take more than 4 years to graduate. The schools' content and performance standards are mapped to New York State's curriculum standards and enabled the schools to receive a state waiver from the Regents examinations for all areas except English language arts.

The portfolios are not only evaluation instruments; they are also learning experiences that engage students in what Fred Newmann and colleagues call "authentic achievement."[37] The tasks require students to organize information, engage in disciplined inquiry and analysis, communicate orally and in writing, problem solve, and make a cogent presentation before an audience. Students frequently remarked on how the portfolio experience deepened their understanding. These comments were common:

> You get to do most of the thinking when you work with your portfolio. You have to explain in detail how to do something or why something is important, so that someone who doesn't know it can understand it.

> When you take a test, you don't feel like you need to know it after it is done. The portfolio sticks in your brain better.

> You have to manage your time before, after, and during school to do the portfolio.

And as a new English language learner, noted:

> The portfolio makes you develop your writing. It makes more sense for us to have to do an oral presentation, to answer oral questions about our work to see how we learned English.

Our research team watched students defending their portfolios before committees of teachers and peers. The exhibitions we observed reflected a range from work that was rated as marginal, which students then revised, to work evaluated as distinguished. Even when the work was less developed and required multiple revisions, the schools enabled all of their students to produce these kinds of research papers and multipart projects, and in the process, to expand their skills and their ability to organize and persist at a complex undertaking.

At Vanguard, a special education student could not be distinguished from a regular education student as he presented his history portfolio on the role of Japan during World War II, displaying knowledge of the geography of the region and of the politics of Japanese imperialism. At Landmark, a student deconstructed his development as a writer and reader over the course of his 4 years at the school by referencing specific papers he wrote over the 4 years. Using a set of overheads with quotes and diagrams, he graphically compared and contrasted his current knowledge to his former ignorance, which the audience could see as his earlier and later papers were placed in parallel alignment. He made a similar presentation on the changes in his capacity to analyze literature and in his literary preferences. Without interruption, the student made a clear, tightly constructed argument on his development as a reader and writer for 40 minutes.

In all cases, the committees questioned the presenters, scored the presentations according to a common rubric and presented their evaluations to the students. The conversations about the work probed the students' reasoning, asked for evidence supporting key ideas, and referenced the schools' habits of mind (e.g., drawing connections to other ideas, using evidence, understanding perspectives, presenting clearly and with appropriate use of conventions). The process was personally supportive, but often substantively critical. Some students found that either their paper or their presentation did not yet meet the portfolio standard, and they would have to revise and re-present. Some met the minimal standard but decided to revise in order to improve the quality of their work and to obtain a higher rating. Others met the standard and were satisfied with their work, going on to work on other portfolios.

All of the students felt a deep sense of accomplishment from the experience, and, having repeated it several times before graduation, a growing sense of confidence. In follow-ups of graduates, students pointed to these research papers and presentations as a key reason they believe they have been able to succeed in college. Unlike many of their peers, who have learned passively from textbooks, they feel comfortable defining and pursuing questions, using the library and the laboratory, framing and defending their ideas orally and in writing, and managing their time to accomplish substantial tasks that require planning and perseverance.

Professional Learning and Collaboration

These schools succeed in part because of their ability to recruit and develop very strong faculties and leaders, using many of the strategies for teacher learning that are common in schools abroad but rare in the United States.

In New York City, many of the schools we studied are connected to pre-service and in-service programs run by local universities that prepare teachers for progressive teaching practices, such as Bank Street College, City College, New York University, the New School, and Columbia University's Teachers College. A similar relationship exists for June Jordan with San Francisco State and with Stanford University, which supplies teachers for many small or redesigned district-run and charter schools in the Bay Area. The schools host student teachers and engage in collaborative learning through these networks. While new schools must fight the battle of potential burnout, their well-developed pipelines, collegial environments, and close relationships with students mean that most of the schools have many more applicants than they can hire, even though the districts generally have difficulty filling all of their vacancies.

The schools are able to recruit teachers who are committed to their approaches. During the 1990s, the new schools in New York City were able to negotiate changes in the collective bargaining agreement to allow them to choose their own faculty through a peer review process that allows existing staff to evaluate teaching and collaboration skills. Among the California schools, charters have the ability to select their own staff, and the district-run schools have been able to negotiate autonomy for selecting all or most of their teachers.

Collaborative Professional Learning. Many researchers have identified the collaboration associated with a professional community of teachers as a key element of successful schools.[38] Over multiple studies, Fred Newmann and colleagues found that professional community is one of three common features of schools achieving high levels of student learning.[39] (The others are a shared focus on high-quality student learning and authentic pedagogy, discussed earlier.) Their research and that of others suggests that smaller schools providing more collegial professional environments for teachers generate greater collective responsibility for school improvement and student learning.[40]

The successful schools we studied work continually to improve the quality of their instruction by making it the consistent focus of their professional learning time. Part of this commitment includes allocating considerable time for teachers to collaborate, design curriculum and instruction, and learn from one another. The schools organize extensive summer learning opportunities and retreats to look at student learning evidence and to plan and organize instruction, advisory practices, and student supports. Although faculty members participate in external professional development, most professional development is internal. Overall, the schools allocate 7 to 15 days to shared professional learning time throughout the year.

The schools encourage teachers to learn about and from their colleagues' practice, organizing substantial time during the week—usually 5 to 10 hours in addition to the teachers' individual planning time—for teachers to plan and problem solve together around students and subject matter. With teachers operating in grade-level teams that meet regularly, the schools create structures for examining student progress, as well as for creating a more coherent curriculum and allowing teachers to learn from one another. Planning within departments also occurs regularly, and teachers develop curriculum and assessments in order to ensure that students will be prepared to meet the common schoolwide outcomes that have been established. Teachers use these collaborative opportunities to examine students' progress, figure out how to adjust their instruction, and socialize new staff into the schools' approaches. Noting the power of these approaches, at New Tech High, a Sacramento district official observed admiringly: "It's all about co-planning, co-teaching and analyzing, and having time out of the regular teaching day to do these analyses."

Manhattan International principal William Ling explained how collaboration within teacher teams strengthens accountability:

> Everyone holds each other accountable for meeting the [school] goals. The clusters work together on the year's goals. They plan together, discuss kids together, they observe each other, and they support each other's development.

Similarly, principal Sylvia Rabiner noted that at Landmark:

> (T)eachers share what they are doing in a formal way in team meetings. They plan together and share what they have done. There is whole school sharing and there are summer institutes where we have more time to reflect. There is more coherence than in big schools where teachers work alone.

At June Jordan, teachers participate in a professional learning retreat before school starts, and in professional learning meetings twice a month. Teachers also meet weekly, by subject matter and grade level, during common planning times to collaborate on planning curriculum and unit projects and discuss student needs. Whether in a professional development session, staff meeting, or team planning session, teachers are asked to reflect on their practice and experience in the classroom. According to one teacher:

> It's easy to grab onto someone's best practices. We've developed a culture for that. . . . The practice of common planning time really lends itself to being able to serve students better and think about ways to support them.

These structural supports for teacher learning are augmented by mentoring and coaching systems for new and veteran teachers, focused inquiry about problems of practice that occurs in staff meetings, and the learning about student thinking, standards, and curriculum that occurs when teachers collectively evaluate student portfolios, projects, and exhibitions.

School-Based Inquiry. Essential to each of the schools' success in maintaining a coherent instructional focus that is based on its students' needs and its school vision is each school's ability to shape its own professional learning time. Most schools examine student work and other data each summer to set the focus for the coming year. Most also structure deliberate inquiries into areas of the curriculum, school organization, or instruction that seem to need attention. As a counselor at Leadership High explained:

Leadership High School has a particularly well developed model for professional learning. Everything is very intentional here. At other places I've worked, it is like, "Let's try this. Let's try that." Here, we look at the research; we look at the data and figure it out. There are reasons for everything.

The Leadership model uses a value-driven approach focused on equity to guide professional learning that is informed by data. An extensive data-based inquiry process is supplemented by regular weekly planning meetings. Department coaches (DCs) are strong, equity-minded teachers given an extra prep period to serve as the first line of support for teachers, providing coaching and one-on-one support for teachers as well as leading the inquiry process. In addition to meeting monthly with the principal, the DCs meet weekly with one another to discuss the best ways to coach, as well as how to use inquiry to build teachers' capacity for deep reflection on their practice. The DCs have 7 release days throughout the year to examine achievement data (e.g., grades, test scores, graduation assessments) and student experience data (e.g., suspension rates, attendance, measures of student satisfaction) as the basis for guiding staff-wide inquiries and professional development. According to the principal:

Throughout all these days, particular attention is paid to surfacing patterns of achievement and failure so that we can more equitably serve all our students and narrow the predictable achievement gaps that persist in our school.

The schoolwide focus determined through the inquiry process is presented to staff during their 6-day professional development retreat at the end of the summer. Based on their work in the retreat, the staff develops a central question that they all focus on for the year. As an extension of the focus, each staff member applies the focus in his or her own individual work, creating an individual goal that directs personal, professional, and collaborative objectives. All staff participate, including security staff and counselors. As principal Elizabeth Rood explained, "We are trying to build a coaching culture and an action-research culture at the school and are constantly doing inquiry and constantly being reflective."

The yearly focus is carried through the 3 days a semester when staff meets all day for professional learning. In addition, these times are used to focus on individual students and continue the data-based inquiry process. For example, early in the year, the staff dedicated half a day to talk about a set of specific students, taking 45 minutes for each student and using a protocol to identify the supports that are and are not working for the student.

In their weekly professional learning meetings, attendees follow a protocol in which staff take rotating roles as facilitator, time keeper, and so on, so that all teachers get comfortable in various leadership roles. The meetings also rotate through each teacher's classroom so that every teacher can see the kind of work that is going on across the school. The principal describes this professional learning time as "intentional. . . . (T)his is not a staff meeting [or] loosey goosey collaboration time. . . . It is important time, it is sacred time for us as a staff." Topics have included reciprocal teaching, scaffolding, student discourse, and cultural competence. All the discussions address issues of equity. For example, as staff met to discuss parent conferences, they discussed parents' potential discomfort at school because of their own or their children's previous negative experiences in school. Teachers planned how to make parent conferences constructive, given any tensions, anxiety, or concerns that parents might have.

Where there is serious school-led professional development, learning is often a vehicle for shared leadership. All the schools engage teachers in a range of leadership roles and in democratic decision making. Shared governance also often involves students, parents, community members, and even industry leaders, supporting widespread commitment to the vision and mission of the school. Everyone—students, staff, and parents alike—works harder when that buy-in has been achieved. These schools illustrate how designs that foster intentional student, teacher, and family supports result in successes with many young people who would fall through the cracks elsewhere.

CREATING SYSTEMS OF SUCCESSFUL SCHOOLS

Designing schools that serve low-income students of color well is not impossible. Since the groundbreaking research of Ron Edmonds more than 3 decades ago,[41] many studies have documented the practices of unusually effective schools and have uncovered similar features of those that succeed with students who are historically underserved.[42] However, to create such schools on a much wider scale, a new policy environment must be constructed that routinely encourages such schools to be developed and sustained.

Supporting Successful Innovation

Creating new schools and innovations is a great American pastime. Waves of reform producing productive new school designs occurred at the turn of the 20th century when John Dewey, Ella Flagg Young, Lucy Sprague Mitchell, and others were working in Chicago, New York, and other Northern cities, and African American educators such as Anna Julia Cooper, Lucy Laney, and Mary McLeod Bethune were creating schools in the South. A wave of new school designs swept the country in the 1930s and 1940s when the Progressive Education Association helped redesign and study 30 "experimental" high schools that were found, in the famous Eight-Year Study, to perform substantially better than traditional schools in developing high-achieving, intellectually adventurous, socially responsible young people able to succeed in college and in life.[43] Urban school reform movements occurred in the 1960s and 1970s—producing schools such as the Parkway Program in Philadelphia and Central Park East Elementary in New York, for example; and in the 1990s when the impulse for innovation returned once again with the kinds of schools I've described in this chapter.

Despite more successful and more equitable outcomes than most traditional schools, few of these innovative schools were sustained over time. Any educator who has been in the field for any period of time has participated in what former Seattle teacher union leader, Roger Erskine, has dubbed "random acts of innovation"[44] that have come and gone, regardless of their success. Generally, this is because, like bank voles and wolf spiders, urban districts often eat their young. Changes in superintendents and school boards create swings in policies, including efforts to standardize instruction, go "back to the basics," and bring innovators to heel. Even when they achieve better outcomes, distinctive school models confront long-standing traditions, standard operating procedures, and expectations, including, sometimes, the expectation that the students who have traditionally failed should continue to do so, so that the traditionally advantaged can continue in their position of privilege. Indeed, Anna Julia Cooper's progressive M Street School in segregated Washington, D.C., which offered a "thinking curriculum" to Black students and outperformed two of the three White high schools in the city, was attacked for both of these reasons in the early 20th century.[45]

Sometimes, successful schools and programs fade because special foundation or government money has dried up, and the district does not have the foresight or wherewithal to preserve what is working. Other times, the challenges of replenishing the capable, dynamic teachers and leaders who have created a successful school prove too great to sustain the model. Historian Lawrence Cremin argued that the successes of progressive education reforms did not spread widely because such practice required "infinitely skilled teachers," who were never prepared in sufficient numbers to sustain these more complex forms of teaching and schooling.[46]

New York City's unusual renaissance was facilitated by the creation of an innovation silo in the form of the Alternative Schools Superintendency—which buffered schools from many regulations and forged new solutions to old bureaucratic problems, and by a rich array of professional resources in support of reforms—including expert practitioners who created networks of learning and support, a large set of public and private universities offering expertise and intellectual resources, philanthropists and researchers who provided additional professional and political support to these efforts. The United Federation of Teachers (UFT) ran its own Teachers Center, and many of the teachers active in this professional development were involved in the new schools initiatives. Over time, the UFT incorporated many supports for reform-oriented schools into its contracts—first through waivers and later through changes in collective bargaining agreements—and, in some cases, became part of the protection for further reforms. Even when frequent changes in leadership might have led to abandonment of the new schools initiative, these forces kept the reform momentum going.

In most places, however, the lack of investment in professional education that would allow teachers and school leaders to acquire the knowledge they need to undertake sophisticated practices has proved to be an ongoing problem. Another recurring problem is the lack of policy development that could encourage the growth of such schools rather than keeping them as exceptions, on waiver, and at the margins. As Paul Hill has argued:

> Today's public school system tolerates new ideas only on a small scale and it does so largely to reduce pressures for broader change. The current system is intended to advance individual, community, and national goals, but is, in fact, engineered for stability. That is normally a good thing. We want schools to open on time, teachers to count on having jobs from one day to the next, and parents to feel secure knowing that their children will have a place to go to school. Stability alone, however, is the wrong goal in a complex, fast-changing, modern economy. Students—disadvantaged students, in particular—need schools that are focused on providing them with the skills they will need to succeed in today's society, schools that are flexible enough to try a variety of teaching methods until they succeed in reaching these goals.[47]

In the current environment, some, including Hill, suggest that charters, contract schools, or performance schools that are essentially licensed by school boards to provide a particular model or approach may provide a way to spark innovation and protect it from the vicissitudes of district politics and changes of course. This strategy has the potential virtue of enabling continuity of educational direction and philosophy within schools—where, arguably, coherence is most important—and holding schools accountable for results, rather than for bureaucratic compliance.

Certainly, some important new school models have been launched through charters. In California, where the state has used chartering as a major lever for innovation, three of the five high schools we studied—Animo, Leadership, and New Tech—were charters. This allowed them to outline a specific approach to education and hold onto it, without being buffeted by changing district views or intruded upon by curriculum, testing, and management mandates. Although collective bargaining agreements from the industrial era often create cumbersome constraints in many districts, new approaches to bargaining have also begun to emerge, and two of these three charters employ unionized teachers.

Many other successful new small school models have been started and expanded through special arrangements for autonomy from district regulations or through charter organizations: Some, like Envision Schools, Asia Society, High Tech High, Uncommon Schools, and others, have introduced substantially new educational approaches, including performance assessments, exhibitions of learning, curriculum focused on global understandings, advisory systems, and more. Odds are that, within many districts, without formal protection, their adventurousness would have been quashed by some school board or superintendent's insistence on introducing a new standardized curriculum or testing system, or pressuring the schools to grow in size and revert to factory-model designs, or requiring the hiring of teachers or leaders who are not prepared for or bought into the model. (Both district practices of centralized assignment and collective bargaining agreements that require seniority transfers can be culpable in this problem.) Even when there are good intentions to support innovation, local districts are subject to a geological dig of laws, regulations, precedents, and standard operating procedures that can be enormously difficult to untangle before they strangle change efforts.

For these reasons and others, Hill suggests an entirely new role for school districts as managers of a portfolio of relatively autonomous schools, rather than as school operators:

> Today, boards oversee a central bureaucracy which owns and operates all the schools in a given district. It is time to retire this "command-and-control" system and replace it with a new model: portfolio management. In this new system, school boards would manage a diverse array of schools, some run by the school district and others by independent organizations, each designed to meet the different needs of students. Like investors with diversified portfolios of stocks and bonds, school boards would closely manage their community's portfolio of educational service offerings, divesting less productive schools and adding more promising ones. If existing schools do not serve students well, boards would experiment with promising new approaches to find ones that work.

This notion of a portfolio of schools—also advocated by the Gates Foundation—has many potential virtues to recommend it. Certainly, choice is better than coercion in the management of education. Students and families could find better fits with their interests and philosophies, and make a greater commitment to schools they have chosen. Choice could make schools more accountable and attentive to student needs. Schools that create successful designs should benefit from more autonomy to refine and maintain their good work. If a portfolio strategy works well it should "ensure a supply of quality school options that reflects a community's needs, interests, and assets ...and [ensure] that every student has access to high-quality schools that prepare them for further learning, work, and citizenship."[48] A portfolio structure is essentially what has emerged in New York City within the regular district structure (now divided into sets of school zones and networks) and, on a smaller scale, in Boston, which has launched a set of Pilot Schools—alternatives that provide a variety of educational options sharing the features described earlier in this chapter, which are succeeding at rates far above those of many other schools serving similar students.[49]

However, neither choice nor charters alone is a panacea. And not all innovations are useful ones. Although some public schools of choice have been successful, others have made little difference. For example, a recent evaluation of Chicago's Renaissance 2010 initiative—which replaced a group of low-performing schools with charters and other autonomous schools of choice run by entrepreneurs and the district—found that the achievement of students in the new schools was no different from that of a matched comparison group of students in the old schools they had left, and both groups continued to be very low-performing.[50]

Results for charters nationally have also been mixed. Reviews of the evidence have found positive impacts in some places and insignificant or negative impacts in others.[51]

A study of 16 states, covering 70% of all charter schools, found that only 17% of charters produced academic gains that were significantly better than traditional public schools serving demographically similar students, while 37 percent performed worse than their traditional public school counterparts, and 46% showed no difference from district-run public schools. [52] The fact that outcomes differ across states suggests that different approaches to regulation and funding may be important. For example, in Ohio, where an unregulated market strategy created a huge range of for-profit and nonprofit providers with few public safeguards, charter school students were found to achieve at consistently lower levels than their demographically similar public school counterparts. Studies have also found lower average performance for charter students in the poorly regulated charter sectors in Washington, D.C., and Arizona, where charters can be granted for 15 years and fewer safeguards for students are required.[53]

A recent study of Minneapolis charters found that, despite individual successes, on average, they produce significantly lower achievement relative to district public schools serving similar students.[54] Indeed, the only significant positive effect on achievement was for those students who were part of an inter-district choice plan that allowed them to leave the district to attend suburban public schools. On the other hand, in Wisconsin, where laws authorize few providers (outside of Milwaukee, where different rules hold) and require more academic and financial oversight, as well as explicit attention to innovation, students were found to perform slightly better than their demographically matched peers in most areas.[55]

In the longest-standing portfolio approach, launched in Milwaukee in the late 1980s with vouchers and, later, a wide range of charters and other schools of choice, studies have found few improvements in any sector over more than 15 years. Studies of the voucher program have produced conflicting results, ranging from no effects on achievement for students receiving vouchers to small positive effects on achievement in one subject area.[56] And the traditional system has performed poorly, overall, appearing to improve little as a result of competition, with short-lived upturns in scores generally balanced by downturns. By 2006, only 39% of Milwaukee tenth graders in the public school system scored proficient in reading, as compared to 74% in the state as a whole, and only 29% of Milwaukee tenth graders scored proficient in math, as compared to 70% of Wisconsin tenth graders.[57]

The most substantial improvements in achievement occurred between 2006 and 2009, when Milwaukee superintendent Bill Andrekopoulos launched an initiative to build instructional capacity across the district, with a set of teaching standards outlining exemplary practices, a new professional evaluation system, and professional development supported by coaching for both teachers and principals.[58]

Interestingly, his journey mirrors that of Superintendent Tony Alvarado, who first initiated a choice plan in New York City District #4, which produced some extraordinary schools, including Debbie Meier's first school in East Harlem at Central Park East Elementary. However, Alvarado decided that the "let a thousand flowers bloom" approach often resulted in only a few flowers blooming, so it needed to be supplemented with a district-wide capacity-building approach to enable strong instruction in all schools, which led to his more systemic approach to reform when he moved in District #2. (See Chapter 7.)

Finally, the pressures under recent accountability regimes to get test scores up have led to growing concerns that some new schools—charters and otherwise—have sought to exclude those students who are the most challenging to teach, either by structuring admissions so that low-achieving students and those with special education or other needs are unlikely to be admitted, or by creating conditions under which such students are encouraged to leave. Studies of new schools created in New York City after 2000, for example, have found that these schools, unlike the earlier pioneers, enrolled more academically able students and fewer English language learners or students with disabilities than the large comprehensive schools they replaced. This enabled them to show better outcomes.[59]

Thus, it is not the governance mechanism or the degree of autonomy alone that determines whether schools will succeed. In places where new school models and redesigned schools have done well without ignoring or pushing out struggling students, attention has been paid both to sparking new educational possibilities and building schools' capacities for good instruction, to removing unnecessary constraints and creating appropriate safeguards for students.

Sustaining Change

The goal, ultimately, is not just to support a vanguard group of unique schools, but to enable all schools to adopt practices that will be more successful for all of their students. For this to happen, districts must find ways to foster innovation and responsiveness without compromising equity, access, and the public purpose of schools to prepare citizens who can live, work, and contribute to a common democratic society. This will require redesigning districts as well as schools, rethinking regulations and collective bargaining, while building capacity and allocating resources in smarter and more equitable ways.

Redesigning Districts. For successful schools to become the norm, districts must move beyond the pursuit of an array of ad hoc initiatives managed by exception to fundamental changes in district operations and policy. Throughout the 20th century, most urban districts adopted increasingly bureaucratic approaches to managing schools. They created extensive rules to manage every aspect of school life—from curriculum, instruction, and testing to hiring, purchasing, and facilities—along with complex, departmentalized structures to manage these rules and procedures. Siloed bureaucrats have had the mission of administering procedures that often get in the way of practitioners' instructional efforts, rather than managing quality by being accountable for figuring out ways to support success. To create a new paradigm, the role of the district must shift

- From enforcing procedures to building school capacity
- From managing compliance to managing improvement
- From rewarding staff for following orders and "doing things right" to rewarding staff for getting results by "doing the right things"
- From rationing educational opportunities to expanding successful programs
- From ignoring (and compounding) failure in schools serving the least powerful to reallocating resources to ensure their success

To a large extent, these changes represent a switch from bureaucratic accountability—that is, hierarchical systems that pass down decisions and hold employees accountable for following the rules, whether or not they are effective—to professional accountability—that is, knowledge-based systems that help build capacity in schools for doing the work well, and hold people accountable for using professional practices that enable student success.

In a new paradigm, the design of the district office should also evolve from a set of silos that rarely interact with one another to a team structure that can integrate efforts across areas such as personnel, professional development, curriculum and instruction, and evaluation, with the goal of creating greater capacity in a more integrated fashion. These supports should include

- Recruiting a pool of well-prepared teachers and leaders from which schools can choose—and building pipelines to facilitate their training and availability
- Organizing access to high-quality, sustained professional development and resources, including skilled instructional mentors and coaches that schools can call upon and that can be deployed to diagnose problems and support improvements in schools that are struggling
- Ensuring that high-quality instructional resources—curriculum materials, books, computers, and texts—are available
- Providing services, such as purchasing and facilities maintenance, to school consumers in effective and efficient ways—if schools choose to acquire them from the district

If they incorporate choice, districts will need to ensure that all schools are worth choosing and that all students have access to good schools. This means they must continuously evaluate how schools are doing, seeking to learn from successful schools and to support improvements in struggling schools by ensuring that these schools secure strong leadership and excellent teachers, and are supported in adopting successful program strategies. Districts will need to become learning organizations themselves—developing their capacity to investigate and learn from innovations in order to leverage productive strategies, and developing their capacity to support successful change. Where good schools and programs are oversubscribed, districts will have to learn how to spread good models rather than rationing them, and where schools are failing, they will need to learn how to diagnose, address problems, and invest resources to improve them. These capacities are needed in all systems, whether or not they adopt choice strategies.

If education is to serve the public good, it is critical to guard against the emergence of a privatized system in which schools are separated by their ability to choose their students, rather than by the ability of students and families to choose their schools. For choice to work, districts must also not only provide information and transportation to parents; they must also manage parents' and schools' choices so that schools recruit and admit students without regard to race, class, or prior academic achievement, both to preserve the possibilities for integrated, common schools and to ensure that some schools do not become enclaves of privilege while others remain dumping grounds. Managed choice arrangements in cities such as Cambridge, Massachusetts, and (in some eras) New York City have created strategies for doing this, allowing parents to state several preferences and requiring schools to admit a diverse student body from all parts of the achievement range. However, these districts have also learned that such strategies require constant vigilance and are not by themselves enough to guarantee access to quality schools for all students. In particular, without the right support and incentives, many schools will seek to recruit the most advantaged students and deflect or push out the least advantaged ones. These incentives, as I discuss below, have to do with the level of capacity to serve students well, with resources, and with accountability measures.

Building Professional Capacity. As I outlined in Chapter 7, building professional capacity ultimately requires investments in effective preparation, hiring, mentoring, evaluation, and professional development for school leaders, as well as teachers and other staff. In addition, systems need to develop strategies for sharing good practice across schools, ranging from research that is widely disseminated to the establishment of networks of schools, teachers, and principals that develop and share practice with one another, to the creation of strategies such as school quality reviews that allow educators to examine one another's practice and get feedback that can help them grow.

Growing successful new schools or improving existing ones is not likely to be accomplished merely by a replication strategy in which external agents seek to transplant programs or designs from one school into another. Replication efforts have an inglorious history, largely because they quickly run up against differences in staff knowledge and capacity, resources, and contexts of receiving schools. Unless they are accompanied by intensive, long-term professional development support, schools can rarely attend to the nuances and implications of new strategies in ways that would permit strong implementation over the long run. When the purportedly effective techniques don't work immediately, especially for students who are challenging to teach, staff will tend to revert to old approaches and/or focus on reaching those who are easiest to teach given what teachers already know how to do and have the resources to support.

Another approach was used to achieve the surprisingly consistent and sophisticated practices we found across the Coalition Campus Schools we studied, which allowed them to be successful with normally low-achieving students. Following what might be called a birthing and parenting strategy, many of the new school "launchers" had been teachers in the older, successful schools. They were mentored by expert veteran principals and teachers while belonging to a set of networks that facilitated ongoing sharing of practice and supported problem solving.

Networking strategies have increasingly been found to be powerful for sharing practitioner knowledge. Teacher-to-teacher networks such as the National Writing Project help teachers develop effective pedagogical practices; principal networks have become critically important within many districts seeking to support stronger instructional leadership and create opportunities for shared problem solving; and, in both the United States and abroad (see Chapters 6 and 7), school networks are enabling educators to share departmental and schoolwide practices through collective professional development, observational visits, and pooling of intellectual resources.

Managing and Allocating Resources. For schools to succeed with all students, they also must be adequately resourced to do so. As we have seen, disparities in funding between states, districts, and schools often leave those working with the neediest students with the fewest resources. States can begin to change this by costing out what would be required to provide an adequate education to graduate all students, having met the state standards, and then allocating resources equitably to each student on a per pupil basis adjusted for regional cost-of-living differentials and pupil needs. The weighted student formula approach, advocated by many school finance reformers and adopted in some cities to equalize within-district funding, is intended to provide an added increment for students with disabilities, new English language learners, and low-income students, determined by estimating the costs of educating these students to the state's standards. Schools serving large concentrations of high-need students would receive additional funds to provide the services that so many of their students require.

Schools and districts also need the flexibility to spend their funds in optimal ways. Among the distinctive features of successful, redesigned schools is the fact that they use the resources of people and time very differently from traditional systems in order to provide more intense relationships between adults and students and to ensure collaborative planning and learning time for teachers, as schools in other nations do. As described earlier, the United States spends much less of its educational budget on classroom instruction and on teachers—just over 50%, as compared to 70 to 80% in other countries.[60] This weakens instruction.

In part, this is because the United States spends more on several layers of bureaucracy between the state and the school, made necessary in part by the dizzying array of federal and state categorical programs schools are expected to manage because they are not trusted to make good decisions about resources. These categorical programs themselves create inefficiencies in spending—requiring administrative attention and audit trails, as well as fragmenting programs and efforts in schools in ways that undermine educational outcomes. Often, these programs and other regulations prescribe staffing patterns and other uses of resources that reduce focus and effectiveness.

In addition, the United States spends more of its personnel budget on a variety of administrative staff and instructional aides rather than on teachers directly, implementing the outdated model that added a variety of pull-out programs and peripheral services to make up for the failures of a factory-model system, rather than investing in the instructional core of expert teachers given time to work productively with students whom they know well. Thus, whereas full-time teachers engaged in instruction comprise about 70 to 80% of education employees in most Asian and European nations, they are only about half of education employees in the United States.[61] In 2003, for example, whereas only 51% of school district employees in the United States were classroom teachers, the proportion of full-time classroom teachers in Japanese schools was 89% of all educational staff. The proportion is 72% of all employees, if one also includes the large number of doctors, dentists, and pharmacists who are based in Japanese schools (see Figure 8.1).[62] Indeed, Japanese schools had, proportionately, as many doctors as there were instructional aides in U.S. schools, but only one-third the proportion of administrative staff.

Successful, redesigned schools often invest more of their resources in classroom teachers and organize teachers in teams that share students over longer periods of time, to create more sharing of knowledge, as well as to focus on accountability for student needs and success. They consolidate their resources to offer a strong, common core curriculum and key supports, resisting the temptation to diffuse their energies or spend on peripherals at the expense of the central goals of the school. The implications for staffing patterns, resource allocations, and the uses of teachers' and students' time are even more distinctive for schools that engage students in extended internships outside the school, as the Met and its network of schools do; for schools that are engaging students in a range of college courses while they are in high school; and for schools that are embracing technology-based approaches to project work as the New Tech network of schools does.

Figure 8.1. U.S. and Japanese School Staffing Patterns, 2003.

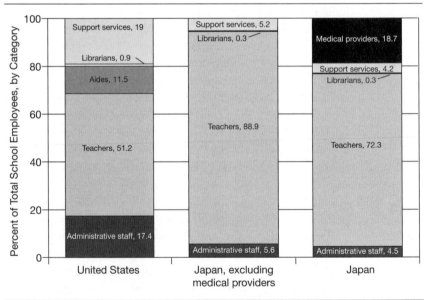

Source: Japanese Ministry of Education (2005) and National Center for Education Statistics (2005).

States and districts will need to encourage more thoughtful and inventive uses of resources by resisting the temptation to prescribe old factory-model requirements for staffing and uses of time and funds, and by providing supports for school leaders to learn how to design organizations that use resources in ways that are likely to produce the desired outcomes.

Deregulating Strategically. As I have suggested, a challenge in scaling up more effective school designs is that the century-old model of school organization that has shaped most schools is now reinforced by layers of regulations that often do not produce the most effective forms of education. Most state regulatory frameworks for schools have not yet shifted to accommodate or encourage the design choices made by new school models.

Where innovations are made possible by relief from regulations, they cannot spread unless the same regulatory relief is applied to other parts of the system. Few states have examined ways to deregulate public schools strategically in ways that would permit greater focus and success while preserving core public values. In recent years, as charters and other relatively autonomous schools have been created to permit flexibility in one part of the system, heavy-handed regulation has often increased in the remainder of the system.

The Boston Pilot Schools and the New York City alternative schools are proof that large public organizations can create organizational firewalls that allow space for successful innovation. But to do so, they must always be conscious of the impact of their policies on school-level practice, and they must, over time, allow innovators to help change the rules as well as avoid them. Regulations protecting access and providing equitable allocations of resources should provide the foundation of a redesigned system, while professional standards and investments in professional capacity that allow educators to be trusted should replace efforts to micromanage teaching and the design of schools.

Changing Contracts. Over time, many of the features of the factory model have been incorporated into collective bargaining agreements by both unions and school boards. Among the most problematic aspects for school reforms are constraints on how time and work are structured and procedures for faculty hiring and assignment that have assumed, in the assembly-line era, that teachers are interchangeable parts.

The success of schools committed to a set of educational principles depends on their ability to hire faculty who believe in those principles and have the capacity to enact them. Thus, centralized assignments of teachers can be a problem, whether in the initial hiring of teachers or due to seniority transfers that give teachers rights to transfer into schools where their skills and philosophy may not fit. Some districts have begun to change these traditions by taking on the responsibility to build a strong pool of well-prepared personnel from which schools can then recruit, and by placing teachers who want to transfer schools into this pool when openings are available, with rights to an early interview but not to placement in a specific school.

In New York, for example, the new school development process triggered important system reforms, including in the key area of selecting teachers. With the cooperation of the Board of Education, the United Federation of Teachers (UFT) and the CCS Project negotiated a process for selecting staff in which a committee of teachers reviews resumes, interviews prospective candidates—and often observes them teaching or planning collaboratively—and selects those most qualified for the available positions. Where teachers are equally qualified, seniority is the decisive variable. UFT representatives participated in these hiring committees, and were so pleased with the outcomes that the union introduced the process into contract negotiations and recommended its adoption more broadly. The contract now includes a peer selection process for teachers in all nontraditional schools, illustrating how innovation can be used as a lever to transform system policies.

In addition, in any New York school where 55% of teachers vote to do so, the school can trigger a School-Based Option that relieves it from many contract constraints and allows new arrangements to be substituted. Many innovative schools have created their own contracts for teachers which, for example, may recognize teachers' roles as advisors and acknowledge different uses of time during the day and week in return for smaller pupil loads and greater autonomy.

Rethinking Accountability. Finally, policymakers must learn new ways to manage the tension between fostering innovation and holding schools accountable to the other purposes of public education—equity, access, development of citizenship, and progress in learning. One critical aspect of the state's role is to ascertain that students are being adequately taught to become productive citizens of society. In recent years, accountability in the United States has largely come to mean tracking test scores on increasingly limited measures, rather than ensuring access to adequate and equitable learning opportunities and the achievement of a broader set of outcomes. As we have seen, the allocation of sanctions to schools based on these high-stakes measures also creates disincentives for schools to admit and keep the neediest students.

Some states, such as Nebraska and Rhode Island, have allowed schools to develop and implement broader, more ambitious assessments of student learning that are approved by the state and examined for accountability purposes along with other documented student outcomes. In New York, 31 schools in the Performance Standards Consortium, including many of those we studied, have developed their own graduation portfolio of challenging research papers and exhibitions. This collection of required products treats both academic outcomes and civic and social responsibility—the latter demonstrated through community service and contributions to the school—and is approved for use in lieu of some of the New York State Regents examinations, with the expectation that schools also track evidence of college admission and completion.

In the long run, accountability systems that provide the right incentives for school quality and equity will need to examine student growth and school progress on a range of high-quality measures, not just their status at a moment in time on one limited measure, include evidence of students' opportunities to learn as well as their outcomes, and enforce professional standards of practice that assure parents their children will be well taught, not just well tested.

CONCLUSION

A growing number of schools have disrupted the status quo by providing opportunities for low-income students of color to become critical thinkers and leaders for the future. Unless policy systems change, however, these schools will remain anomalies, rather than harbingers of the future. Creating a system that supports the learning of all students is not impossible. It will take clarity of vision and purposeful, consistent action to create a web of supportive, mutually reinforcing elements. In particular, dismantling the institutionalized inequities that feed the racial, socioeconomic, and linguistic achievement gap will require substantive policy changes in redesigning schools, developing teachers and principals, expanding our conceptions of curriculum and assessment, rethinking funding strategies, and reconceptualizing accountability. In the next chapter, I discuss the policy changes needed to create a context in which the kinds of schools described here may become the norm rather than the exception, and all students, regardless of race, income, or zip code, achieve the right to learn.

CHAPTER 9

Policy for Quality and Equality: Toward Genuine School Reform

What the best and wisest parent wants for his own child, that must the community want for all of its children. Any other ideal for our schools is narrow and unlovely; acted upon, it destroys our democracy.

—John Dewey[1]

These are all our children, and we will benefit by or pay for what they become.

—James Baldwin[2]

In 1989, then-President George H. W. Bush and the nation's governors established a set of six national goals to be accomplished by the year 2000. Among these were the goals to ensure that all students enter school healthy and ready to learn, that the high school graduation rate would increase to at least 90%, that all students would be competent in the academic disciplines—including science, foreign languages, civics, arts, history, and geography, as well as math and English—and be prepared for responsible citizenship, and that the United States would be "first in the world in mathematics and science achievement" by the year 2000.[3]

Not only were none of these goals accomplished, but as a nation, we are further away from achieving most of them then we were 2 decades ago. Although some of America's children are well supported for learning and some of our schools are among the best in the world, too many have been neglected in the 20 years since that clarion call was sounded. Clearly, we need more than a new set of national goals to mobilize a dramatically more successful educational system. We also need more than small-scale pilot projects, demonstrations, innovations, and other partial solutions. We need to take the education of poor children as seriously as we take the education of the rich, and we need to create systems that *guarantee* all of the elements of educational investment routinely to all children. This means creating systems of curriculum and assessment that point our nation toward the kind of learning our children will need for the 21st century and equalizing access to critical educational resources, including a steady supply of well-prepared and well-supported teachers to all communities and a system in which *all* school models in the system support serious teaching and learning.

How might this be done? A new paradigm for national and state education policy should be guided by twin commitments to *support meaningful learning* on the part of students, teachers, and schools and to *equalize access to educational opportunity*, making it possible for all students to profit from more productive schools. What would a well-functioning teaching and learning system look like under a federal form of government, such as the United States? As in high- and equitably achieving nations, I would argue that such a system requires five key elements:

1. *Meaningful learning goals*, including thoughtful conceptualizations of the content and skills needed for success in the 21st century—achieved by supporting the development of well-grounded common expectations of learning, developed by professional associations and curriculum experts, that are used to inform high-quality standards, curriculum, and assessments of student learning in each state. Though supported by federally developed research, development, and expert resources, the management of curriculum and assessments should remain at the state level for two reasons: First, one of the benefits of a federal system, when it creates an adequate floor for quality, is that it can learn from diverse approaches (if it is set up to do so), enabling innovation and improvement, rather than settling for the lowest common denominator. Second, curriculum and assessments need to be managed close enough to schools and teachers to support educators' engagement in development, evaluation, and ongoing improvement. As I discuss below, this is critically important to inform and improve teaching and learning, and to ensure that assessments include performance components that evaluate real abilities and support equitable curriculum, as they do in high-achieving nations.

2. *Intelligent, reciprocal accountability systems* focused on guaranteeing students competent teaching and adequate learning opportunities—what governments should be held accountable for providing to children—and means for evaluating and continually improving curriculum, teaching, and school capacity. Along with *standards of learning*, such an accountability system would include *opportunity to learn* standards that guarantee adequate and appropriate resources and professional

standards of practice that support good instruction and proper treatment for children. Supportive accountability strategies would seek to create a learning system that heightens the probability of good practice and reduces the incidence of poor practice by studying and disseminating successes and diagnosing the sources of failure, applying resources and expertise to enable improvement. Such strategies would be informed by multiple measures of student learning, school practices, and school performance to assess progress and to determine the investments and interventions needed at the school, district, and state levels.

3. *Equitable and adequate resources* that provide a level playing field for all students and an adequate opportunity to achieve the learning standards. Achieving such a playing field will require as much federal attention to opportunity-to-learn standards as to assessments of learning progress, and greater equalization of federal funding across states. It will require state funding systems that provide comparable per pupil funding, adjusted for differentials in cost-of-living and pupil needs, as well as incentives and information that can steer spending productively to maximize the likelihood of student success. Finally, an equitable and adequate system will need to address the supply of well-prepared educators—the most fundamental of all resources—by building an infrastructure that ensures high-quality preparation for all educators and the availability of well-trained educators to all students in all communities.

4. *Strong professional standards and supports* for all educators, including fully subsidized, high-quality preparation, mentoring, and professional development throughout the career, with rewards and supports for teachers and principals who devote their careers to serving high-need students. Such supports should be guided by rigorous, performance-based standards for preparation programs and for licensing, hiring, and career advancement, with performance assessments validated by their connections to teacher and leader effectiveness. Proactive recruitment systems should seek out and develop talent for teaching and leadership roles. Career development systems should support ongoing evaluation and learning, recognition of accomplished practice and a variety of contributions to student learning and school improvement, and opportunities for teachers to take on roles as mentors, master teachers, curriculum specialists, and school leaders, so that their expertise contributes to the improvement of education both within and beyond their classrooms.

5. *Schools organized for student and teacher learning,* designed to allow teams of professionals to create a coherent curriculum focused on critical content and skills, reinforced by shared norms and habits of mind, and exhibited through authentic assessments of performance that reflect the ways knowledge is used in the real world. These assessments should guide and inform teaching and learning through an ongo-

ing inquiry process at the classroom and school levels, supported by regular time for teachers to plan and learn together. These 21st-century schools should integrate new technologies for learning and create personalized structures for supporting students.

Of course, such a system needs to exist in a supportive environment that provides secure housing, food, and health care, as well as high-quality early childhood education, so that children can come to school ready to learn. And the growing number of students who earn admission to college should have guaranteed access to higher education as was the case in the 1960s and 1970s when states invested in strong public higher education systems, and federal financial aid covered the costs of attendance for those who earned admission. In the rest of this chapter, I take up each of these key elements in more detail.

MEANINGFUL LEARNING GOALS

First, it is critically important to focus the teaching and learning enterprise on the right goals. This was, as I have noted, the basic idea of standards-based reform, and President Clinton's *Goals 2000* initiative successfully launched a process in which all states established content standards for student learning, clarifying what students should know and be able to do, drawing on national standards developed by the professional associations in the disciplines—mathematics, science, reading and language arts, history and social studies, world languages, and the arts. In many states, these standards gave more focus to schools' efforts, clarified core content, incorporated more emphasis on both critical content and higher-order thinking skills, and, in the best cases, allowed states to align learning goals with financial investments, teaching standards, professional development, curriculum materials, and thoughtful assessments that improved instruction.[4]

However, as we have seen, this comprehensive approach to improving education was not pursued everywhere. In a number of states, standards and "accountability" became synonymous with student testing mandates that were detached from policies that might address the quality of teaching, the allocation of resources, or the nature of schooling. Standards became political documents, rather than curricular guideposts, proliferating objectives that create a mile-wide-and-an-inch-deep curriculum and tests that too often offer a superficial, anemic view of learning. States and districts that have relied primarily on test-based accountability emphasizing sanctions for students and schools on narrow tests have produced an impoverished version of education along with greater failure, rather than greater success, for their most educationally vulnerable students.

Evidence indicates that such test-like teaching geared primarily toward lower-order rote skills—memorizing pieces of information, conducting simple operations based on formulas or rules, and filling out short-answer and multiple-choice work-sheets—is most pronounced in urban schools serving predominantly low-income students, especially in states emphasizing high-stakes tests.[5] Students in schools that organize most of their efforts around the kinds of low-level learning represented by most widely used tests are profoundly disadvantaged when they need to engage in the extensive writing, critical thinking, and problem solving required in college and the workplace.

As Antonio Cortese and Diane Ravitch recently observed:

> We believe in the importance of preparing students to live and succeed in a global economy. We don't think that the mastery of basic skills is sufficient for this goal. What we need is an education system that teaches deep knowledge, that values creativity and originality, and that values thinking skills. This, unfortunately, is not the path on which we are now embarked.[6]

I argue here that mid-course corrections to standards-based reform should begin with thoughtful conceptualizations of the content and skills needed for success in the 21st-century—reflected in the refinement of well-grounded national standards (updating the learning standards developed in the early 1990s by national professional associations), and these should be used to inform high-quality standards, curriculum, and assessments of student learning in each state. Further, the results of these efforts should inform ongoing improvements of curriculum and teaching rather than focusing on punishing students and schools. In some states, this would result in a polishing of existing efforts that are already well designed, and in others it would mean a substantial overhaul. In this section, I describe goals for this process, including the kinds of standards, curriculum guidance, and assessments that would support stronger learning, and the reasons I believe this process must include state and local performance assessments, like those used in high-achieving nations, that both encourage and support more equitable and ambitious learning.

How Assessment Affects Learning

Many states—such as Connecticut, Delaware, Kentucky, Maine, Maryland, Nebraska, New Hampshire, New York, Oregon, Rhode Island, Vermont, and Wyoming—introduced performance assessments as part of their systems early on. Like the behind-the-wheel test given to all new drivers, these performance assessments evaluate what students can actually *do*, not just what they recognize—or guess—out of a list of choices. Students in Connecticut complete state-designed tasks to demonstrate that they can design and conduct a science experiment to answer a specific question and evaluate the resulting data. Students in Vermont and Kentucky show that they can write effectively in many genres by completing a set of commonly scored writing assignments, some analyzing great works of literature. Students in New Hampshire demonstrate how they can use computers for a variety of purposes by completing a technology portfolio illustrating their accomplishments. Just as the driving test both measures and helps improve potential drivers' skills, so performance assessments set a standard toward which everyone must work. The task and the standards are not secret: They are transparent, so students know what skills they need to develop and how they will need to be demonstrated.

Studies have found that the use of such assessments has improved teaching quality and increased student achievement, especially in areas requiring complex reasoning and problem solving.[7] However, these assessments have been difficult to sustain, especially in recent years under the annual testing requirements of No Child Left Behind, and the reluctance of the Bush administration to approve state systems that involve local schools in administering performance tasks such as writing assignments, science investigations, analyses of data, or inquiries that cannot be completed on a 2- or 3-hour test on a single day.

As discussed in Chapter 1, the NCLB approach has not raised performance on international assessments such as PISA that measure higher-order thinking skills and the ability to apply knowledge to novel problems. Over the years during which NCLB has been in force, U.S. scores and rankings declined on international assessments. On PISA, U.S. science rankings dropped from 13th to 21st out of 30 participating OECD nations between 2000 and 2006 (with a score drop from 500 to 489) and from 24th to 26th in math between 2003 to 2006, when trends could be evaluated (with a score drop from 483 to 474).[8] Of all areas tested, U.S. students scored lowest on problem solving. The PISA literacy test could not be properly scored in the U.S. tests in 2006 due to an editing problem, but on the international PIRLS assessments of reading, the United States dropped from 9th to 18th out of 28 jurisdictions between 2001 and 2006 (with a score drop from 542 to 540).[9] Meanwhile, annual gains on the U.S. National Assessment of Educational Progress (NAEP) slowed considerably after the implementation of NCLB, crawling nearly to a halt in 8th-grade reading[10] (see Figures 9.1 and 9.2).

How is it that scores have been driven upward on the state tests required by NCLB, yet they have dropped on these international measures? There are several likely reasons. First, as we have seen, attaching high-stakes to tests often causes schools to focus on the tested material and formats in ways that narrow the curriculum and do not generalize to other situations or kinds of knowledge. Second, the international PISA assessments differ significantly from the NAEP and most state tests in their focus on analyzing and applying knowledge to new situations, rather than just recalling or recognizing discrete pieces of information. This kind of

Figure 9.1. Annual Rate of Gain in Reading Achievement, Pre- and Post-NCLB, 4th and 8th Grades.

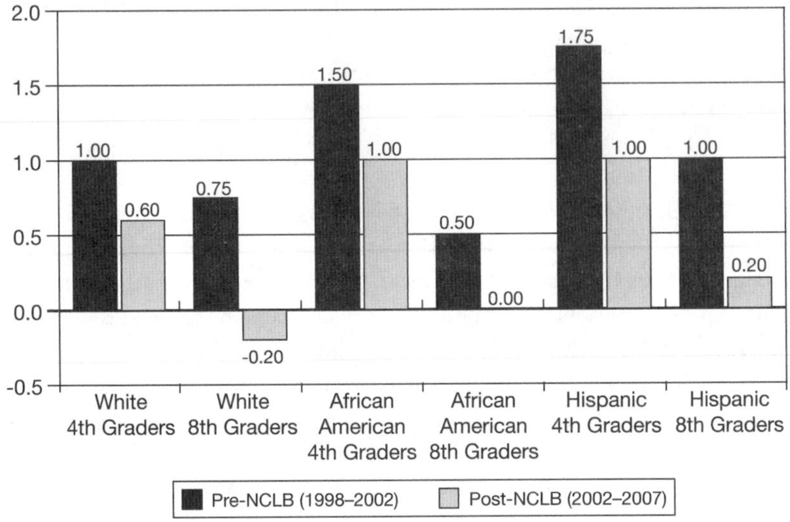

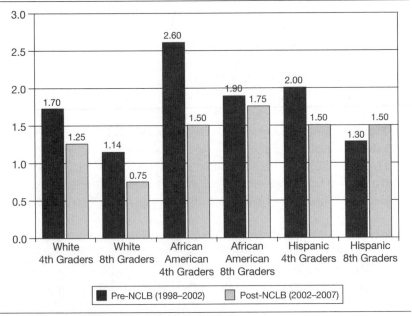

Source: Forum on Education and Democracy (2008).

Figure 9.2. Annual Rate of Gain in Mathematics Achievement, Pre- and Post-NCLB, 4th and 8th Grades.

Source: Forum on Education and Democracy (2008).

analysis is closer to the ways in which knowledge and skills are used in the world outside of school. Finally, the kind of knowledge that transfers from one situation to another is based on students' abilities to understand central principles, see connections and make distinctions, and be strategic in attacking problems and analyzing information. This is precisely the kind of learning that is less prominent in schools where multiple-choice tests of basic skills drive the curriculum.[11] Thus, the harder we try to raise scores on the narrow instruments currently used in the United States, the more likely we are to fall behind on the more sophisticated measures that are increasingly used to evaluate education around the world.

International Standards, Curriculum, and Assessments

Current policy discussions in Washington often refer to these international rankings in emphasizing the need to create more "internationally competitive" standards. Typically, this means looking at the topics that are taught at various grade levels in various countries. These analyses reveal that higher-achieving countries have much leaner standards; teach fewer topics more deeply each year; focus more on inquiry, reasoning skills, and applications of knowledge, rather than mere coverage; and have a more thoughtful sequence of expectations based on developmental learning progressions within and across domains.[12]

Smaller countries often have a system of national standards that are sometimes accompanied by national assessments that sample student performance at one or two grade levels before high school. These assessments generally include open-ended items and local performance tasks managed by teachers. Most assessment is locally managed based on curriculum frameworks or syllabi tied to the standards. Larger nations—such as Canada, Australia, and China—have state- or provincial-level standards, and their assessment systems are typically a blend of state and local assessments. Below, I discuss in some detail how these systems operate in order to open discussion about how much more productive systems could be created in the United States.

Standards and Curriculum. Whereas U.S. teachers are often asked to cover dozens or even hundreds of objectives in each subject area at each grade level, as they plow through as many as 30 textbook chapters, standards in high-achieving countries specify a small number of major concepts or topics to be covered at a given level in a given year. For example, at the 6th-grade level in the Japanese mathematics curriculum, students are to focus on four major aspects of ratio and proportion, including multiplying and dividing fractions, measurement using proportional relationships, and symmetry in figures and scale drawings, as well as the volume and surface area of solid figures, which draw on these concepts.[13] As I noted earlier, like Japan, the entire set of Finnish mathematics standards is listed in about 10 pages.

The process of developing national or state standards and curriculum is a deliberative one in which curriculum and learning experts, including practitioners, work over several years to refine sequences of expectations based on evidence from research on learning and development, as well as evidence about a range of student outcomes across the educational spectrum. These expectations are translated into curriculum frameworks, and, often, course syllabi that guide the development of more extensive curriculum and lesson materials, as well as assessments, at the school level. Highly prescriptive curricula are not used, in part because these systems believe that teachers' ability to deeply understand both the standards and student learning—and to connect the two—is developed by working with colleagues on developing curriculum plans and lessons that are "polished stones," designed and continually refined for their specific students.

Assessments. The standards and curriculum are designed to support educationally useful assessments. European and Asian nations that have steeply improved student learning have explicitly sought to create curriculum guidance and assessments that outline core knowledge in ways that focus on higher-order skills: the abilities to find and organize information to solve problems, frame and conduct investigations, analyze and synthesize data, apply learning to new situations, self-monitor and improve one's own learning and performance, communicate well in multiple forms, work in teams, and learn independently.

The Nature of Assessment Tasks. Whereas the United States now tests every child every year on tests that rely primarily on multiple-choice items that evaluate recall and recognition, most high-achieving countries use external assessments sparingly before high school—usually at only one or two grade levels—and these rely largely on open-ended tasks that require students to analyze and apply knowledge.

For example, tasks on Sweden's native language test at the upper elementary school level (grade 5—the only grade in which external tests occur before high school) often require use of many materials and production of an extended response. In a task using a travel theme, students are provided with contemporary poem, prose, and poetry extracts from a variety of authors; a practical description of how to plan a trip; and data about travel presented in a set of texts, charts, and statistical tables. Students have these materials to review a week in advance. They then have 5 hours to write an essay on one of several suggested topics. This is evaluated by teachers on specific criteria emphasized in the course syllabus. Skills assessed include using appropriate language for specific circumstances, comprehending the different purposes of language, persuasive mechanisms, presenting information, creative self-expression, word choice, and grammar.[14]

A math problem at year 5 asks students to grapple with a problem that they might have in their own lives, assessing computation along with reasoning and reflective decision making.

> Carl bikes home from school at 4 o'clock. It takes about a quarter of an hour. In the evening he's going back to school because the class is having a party. The party starts at 6 o'clock. Before the class party starts, Carl has to eat dinner. When he comes home, his grandmother, who is also his neighbor, calls. She wants him to bring in her post before he bikes over to the class party. She also wants him to take her dog for a walk, then to come in and have a chat. What does Carl have time to do before the party begins? Write and describe below how you have reasoned.[15]

The mathematics exam from the upper secondary level also frames the questions in real-world, tangible topics and formats. Students have almost 4 hours to answer 15 questions. The first 10 questions require short answers and the last 5 questions require longer answers for which students are required to show their work. A longer question asks:

> A business paid into a pension fund at the beginning of every year a sum of 15,000 kr. The fund has a yearly growth rate of 10%. The first payment was made in 1987 and the last will be in 2010. The pension fund will continue to grow until 2015. How much more will the business have in the fund at the beginning of 2015, if it pays in the same amount as above, but the rate of growth is 15%?[16]

As I describe below, these kinds of external test items, used to inform the grades that teachers give to students, are supplemented by more extensive school-based tasks and teacher observations that are part of the formal assessment system. School-based assessments, developed and scored by teachers based on guidance from curriculum documents and syllabi, are the primary tools for evaluating students and providing information about students and school progress. At the high school level, subject-matter examinations that inform university decisions are often constructed by high school and university faculty under the auspices of the Ministry of Education. These feature on-demand tests using largely open-ended items—essays and extended problem solutions—at the end of a course of study and a set of more extensive school-based tasks throughout the course—problem sets, labs, investigations, research papers, and other products—which count for 20 to 50% of the final examination grade.

In the GCE O- and A-level assessments that are used at the end of high school in England and a number of other countries, classroom-based tasks are combined with externally developed exams in each subject area assessed. Students choose the subjects in which they will sit for exams, based on their interests and areas of expertise. Most items are open-ended responses and essays. The math exam includes questions that ask students to show the reasoning behind their answers and foreign language exams require oral presentations. The International Baccalaureate (IB) program, used around the world at 11th- and 12th-grade levels, is based on a similar design. On the IB end-of-course test in English, for example, students choose the questions they will answer regarding the literature they have read. The following is a typical essay question:

> Acquiring material wealth or rejecting its attractions has often been the base upon which writers have developed interesting plots. Compare the ways the writers of two or three works you have studied have developed such motivations.[17]

A typical mathematics essay asks students to show their work and support their answers with work and explanations. It also asks students to draw any graphs they create on their graphing calculator. Students are graded on the methods they use and their reasoning, as well as the specific answers they derive. Similarly, a typical question on the Hong Kong physics examination presents information on an electrical circuitry problem—evaluating current flow in a configuration with a particular capacitor, inductor, resistor, and energy source, with multiple questions requiring open-ended responses showing work and reasoning under different circumstances as changes are made to these variables. Students are finally asked to show how they would modify the circuit to achieve a particular outcome, demonstrating how they can apply their knowledge flexibly to new problems.

In places such as England, Sweden, Hong Kong, and Australia, the local assessments that contribute to the final examination score are mapped to the standards or syllabus for the subject and are selected because they represent critical skills, topics, and concepts. They are outlined in the curriculum guide and are sometimes designed centrally, but they are administered and scored locally, based on common specifications and evaluation criteria. Whether locally or centrally developed, decisions about when to undertake these tasks are made at the classroom level, so they are used when appropriate for students' learning process and teachers can get information and provide feedback when it is needed, something that traditional standardized tests cannot do. In addition, as teachers use and evaluate these tasks, they become more knowledgeable about both the standards and their students' learning needs. Thus, the process improves the quality of teaching and learning.

An example of how this kind of system operates can be seen in Victoria, Australia, where school-based assessments are combined with centralized exams. At the high school level, the Victoria Curriculum and Assessment Authority (VCAA) establishes courses in a wide range of studies, organizes high school and university faculty to work together in developing the external examinations, and ensures the quality of the school-assessed component. The content examinations, given in grades 11 and 12, include written, oral, and performance elements scored by class-room teachers. VCAA conceptualizes assessment as "of," "for," and "as" learning. All prior year assessments are public, so that the standards and means of measuring them are as transparent as possible. Before the external examinations are given to students, teachers and academics sit and take the exams themselves, as if they were students.

At least 50% of the total examination score is comprised of classroom-based tasks that are given throughout the school year. These required classroom tasks—lab experiments and investigations on central topics as well as research papers and presentations—are designed by teachers in response to syllabus expectations. The tasks ensure that students are getting the kind of learning opportunities that prepare them for the assessments they will later take, that they are getting feedback they need to improve, and that they will be prepared to succeed not only on tests but in college and in life, where they will have to apply knowledge in more complex ways.

An example of how this blended assessment system works can be seen in the interplay between an item from the Victoria biology test, and the classroom-based tasks also evaluated for the examination score. The open-ended item describes a particular virus and how it operates, then asks students to design a drug to kill the virus and explain how the drug operates; blank pages are left for the written answer, which is to include diagrams. The next question asks students to design and describe an experiment to test the drug. In preparation for this on-demand test, students taking biology will have been assessed on six pieces of work covering specific syllabus outcomes during the term. For example, they will have conducted "practical tasks" such as using a microscope to study plant and animal cells by preparing slides of cells, staining them, and comparing them in a variety of ways, resulting in a written product with visual elements. They also will have completed and presented a research report on characteristics of pathogenic organisms and mechanisms by which organisms can defend against disease. These tasks link directly to the expectations that students will encounter on the external examination, but go well beyond what that examination can measure in terms of how students can apply their knowledge.

The tasks are graded according to criteria set out in the syllabus. The quality of the tasks assigned by teachers, the work done by students, and the appropriateness of the grades and feedback given to students are audited through an inspection system, and schools are given feedback on all of these elements. In addition, the VCAA uses statistical moderation to ensure that the same assessment standards are applied to students across schools. The external exams are used as the basis for this moderation, which adjusts the level and spread of each school's assessments of its students to match the level and spread of the same students' scores on the common external test score. The result is not only a comparable means for examining ambitious student learning, but also a richer and more equitable curriculum for students—since all students experience the labs, experiments, and research projects. Meanwhile, teachers' participation in assessment improves instruction as they come to understand the standards and how to implement them well.

The Management of School-Based Assessments. As I have noted, most assessment in high-achieving countries is school-based rather than externally designed and administered. Top-ranking Finland, for example, uses local assessments developed by teachers to evaluate its national standards and manages a voluntary national assessment on a sampling basis (like the NAEP) at only two grade levels. Systems in Sweden; Britain; Wales; Ireland; Queensland and A.C.T, Australia; and Hong Kong are similar, relying extensively on local assessments that emphasize inquiry, applications of knowledge, extensive writing, and development of problem solutions and products. These are drawn from common curriculum frameworks or syllabi and are developed and scored by teachers, with a variety of supports for consistent scoring.

For example, in Queensland, there has been no assessment system external to schools for 40 years. Until the early 1970s, a traditional "post-colonial" examination system controlled the curriculum. When it was eliminated, about the same time as in Finland and Sweden, all assessments became school-based. (As described in Chapter 6, this is also true in Finland.) School-based assessments are developed, administered, and scored by teachers in relation to the national curriculum guidelines and state syllabi (also developed by teachers), and are moderated by panels that include teachers from other schools and professors from the university system.

The syllabi spell out a small number of key concepts and skills to be learned in each course, as well as the kinds of projects or activities (including assessments) in which students should be engaged. Each school designs its program to fit the needs and experiences of its own students, choosing specific texts and topics with this in mind. At the end of the year, teachers collect a portfolio of each student's work, which includes the specific assessment tasks, and grade it on a five-point grading scale. To calibrate these grades, teachers put together a selection of portfolios from each grade level—one from each of the five score levels, plus borderline cases—and send these to a regional panel for moderation. A panel of five teachers rescores the portfolios and confers about whether the grades are warranted, making a judgment on the spread. A state panel also looks at portfolios across schools. Based on these moderation processes, the school is given instructions to adjust grades so that they are comparable to others. As in Victoria, managing assessment at the state level where it remains relatively close to the schools turns out to be an important way of enabling strong teacher participation and ensuring high-quality local assessments that can be moderated to ensure consistency in scoring.

In Britain, almost all assessment prior to the end of high school is managed by teachers with a variety of supports from the Qualifications and Curriculum Authority (QCA), which provides extensive guidance on learning progressions and how to assess and evaluate them in its Assessing Pupils' Progress program. This includes diagnostic assessment materials, evaluation rubrics, and support for the in-school moderation processes that are required to calibrate scoring. At two key stages (age 7 and 11), teachers choose from among a set of nationally developed tasks along with their locally developed assessments, student work samples, and observations to create scored profiles of their students along multiple dimensions. Among the 13 dimensions for which profile scores are developed at Key Stage 1, for example, are indicators of personal, social, and emotional development; communication, language, and literacy (e.g., language use, linking sounds and letters, reading, and writing); problem solving, reasoning, and numeracy (e.g., number sense, calculating, shape, space, and measures); knowledge and understanding of the world; physical development; and creative development. Detailed indicators are used to develop the profiles and these "standards files" are shared to create consistency as well as to inform instruction.

In Asian nations, the growing emphasis on project-based, inquiry-oriented learning has led to an increasing prominence for teacher-managed school-based tasks. In Hong Kong, for example, the assessment system is evolving from a highly centralized examination system to one that increasingly emphasizes school-based, formative assessments that expect students to analyze issues and solve problems. School-based assessments have been part of Hong Kong's examination system since 1978, but will increase in importance with the new reforms that will replace the Hong Kong Certificate of Education Examinations, for which most students sit at the end of their 5-year secondary education, with a new Hong Kong Diploma of Secondary Education that will weight classroom work and projects more heavily.

In addition, the Hong Kong Territory-wide System Assessment (TSA), which uses written, oral, and performance components to assess student performance at grades 3, 6, and 9 in Chinese, English, and mathematics, is developing an online bank of assessment tasks to enable schools to assess their students and receive feedback on their performance on their own time frames. As outlined in Hong Kong's "Learning to Learn" reform plan, the goal of the reforms is to shape curriculum and instruction around critical thinking, problem solving, self-management skills, and collaboration. A particular concern is to develop meta-cognitive thinking skills, so students may identify their strengths and the areas that need additional work.[18] The Hong Kong Education Examinations Authority explains the rationale for growing use of school-based assessments (SBA):

> Teachers know that SBA, which typically involves students in activities such as making oral presentations, developing a portfolio of work, undertaking fieldwork,

carrying out an investigation, doing practical laboratory work or completing a design project, help students to acquire important skills, knowledge and work habits
that cannot readily be assessed or promoted through paper-and-pencil testing. Not
only are they outcomes that are essential to learning within the disciplines, they are
also outcomes that are valued by tertiary institutions and by employers. Moreover,
they are activities that students find meaningful and enjoyable.[19]

Like the existing high school assessments, the new assessments are developed
by teachers with the participation of higher education faculty, and they are scored
by teachers who are trained as assessors. Tests are allocated randomly to scorers, and
essay responses are typically rated by two independent scorers.[20] Results of the new
school-based assessments are statistically moderated to ensure comparability within
the province. The assessments are internationally benchmarked, through the evaluation of sample student papers, to peg the results to those in other countries. Many of
the new assessments are also to be scored online, which the Examinations Authority
notes is now the common practice in 20 of China's mainland provinces, as well as
in the United Kingdom.

To guide the process of assessment reform, the Education Bureau has implemented a School Development and Accountability Framework that emphasizes
school self-evaluation, plus external peer evaluation, using a set of performance
indicators. The Bureau promotes the use of multiple forms of assessment in schools,
including projects, portfolios, observations, and examinations, and looks for the variety of assessments in the performance indicators used for school evaluation.[21] For
example, the performance indicators ask, "Is the school able to adopt varied modes
of assessment and effectively assess students' performance in respect of knowledge,
skills, and attitude?" and "How does the school make use of curriculum evaluation
data to inform curriculum planning?"[22] This practice of examining school practices
and the quality of assessments through an inspection or peer review process is also
used in Australia and Britain to improve teaching by using standards as a tool for
sharing knowledge and reflecting on practice.

The Uses of Assessments. Finally, the examination systems in these countries are
typically not used to rank or punish schools, nor are they used to deny diplomas
to students. Following the problems resulting from the Thatcher government's use
of test-based school rankings, which led to a narrowing of the curriculum and
widespread student exclusions from school,[23] several countries enacted legislation
precluding the use of test results for school rankings. Primary school assessments
are used to guide learning, diagnose students' needs, and inform teaching. In some
cases, they are factored into teachers' grades. High school examinations are used to
provide information for higher education, vocational training, and employment,

and students often choose the areas in which they will be examined, as a means of providing evidence of their qualifications.

The extensive school-based assessment systems are used both to evaluate student progress and to help improve teaching. The uses and benefits of such assessments are well articulated in the description of Assessing Pupils' Progress (APP), a structured approach to school-based assessment that England has recently instituted to replace its externally administered national examinations. The Department for Children, Schools, and Families notes that the APP "enables teachers to make judgments about their pupils' attainment, keyed into national standards; develops and refines teachers' understanding of progression in their subject; provides diagnostic information about the strengths and weaknesses of individual pupils and groups of pupils; enables teachers to track pupils' progress over time; informs curriculum planning; facilitates the setting of meaningful curricular targets that can be shared with pupils and parents; and promotes teaching that is matched to pupils' needs."[24]

Where systems are focused on providing information and supporting improvement rather than allocating sanctions, governments can set higher standards and work with schools to achieve them, rather than having to focus tests at a low level that pulls the system backward and deflects attention to managing the sanctions, rather than propelling schools forward.

Getting Standards, Curriculum, and Assessments Right

Creating thoughtful standards, useful curriculum guidance, and generative assessments will require a number of changes from current practice in the United States. First, to create useful standards, it will be essential to end the curriculum wars that have set U.S. schools on a zig-zag course between polarized pendulum swings that undermine both teaching and assessment. Second, it will be critical to develop standards that are well disciplined—that is, limited and carefully chosen, as well as representative of core concepts and modes of inquiry in the disciplines. Third, it will be important to develop useful curriculum guidance—the missing link in most U.S. attempts to move from standards to tests and accountability. Finally, it will be critical to develop assessment systems that prioritize the quality of information and its usefulness for teaching and learning over the quantity of tests and their deployment in driving decisions that go well beyond their capacity to support. Such assessment systems should include thoughtful school-based measures that both improve and inform practice, and that create greater equity in opportunity.

Ending the Curriculum Wars. Earlier, I discussed the many curriculum wars that have undermined teaching and learning, especially in high-need schools. Unfortunately, the first salvos in a new "content versus skills" curriculum war have recently been launched in missiles from think tanks such as the American Enterprise Institute aimed at the "21st-century skills" advocates.

Proponents of "content" fear that the "skills" people will throw away any disciplined notions of knowledge and will engage students in empty exercises at communication and collaboration that leave children chattering at one another in group work conceived without intellectual grounding and purpose, or creating projects that feature clay and toothpicks—and their 21st-century computerized equivalents—without clear curricular destinations. Diane Ravitch relayed one such concern from a teacher, directed at materials developed by the Partnership for 21st Century Skills that apparently suggest that, following a class reading of a piece of literature, students create a Claymation video enactment, rather than discussing the piece or writing an analysis that would deepen their understanding.[25]

Proponents of 21st-century skills worry that, in their concern for knowledge transmission, the "content" folks have encouraged overwhelming lists of disconnected facts that students are expected to "learn" primarily through lecture without application, to be evaluated by the multiple-choice tests upon which current accountability systems increasingly rely. Core knowledge proponent E. D. Hirsch has been caricatured as insisting on a single list of facts, out-of-sync with the rapidly changing landscape of science and technology knowledge, insensitive to the cultural contributions of people of color and non-Western nations, to be mastered by rote without a deeper understanding of how they fit together and add up, at the expense of problem solving and the production of ideas.

In fact, although the fears on both sides may have been reinforced by real events that occurred as ideas have been poorly implemented, both sets of caricatures are flawed and both groups hold valid goals. Content and skills need to be considered together, just as the teaching and practice of basic skills—decoding and arithmetic operations—need to accompany students' inquiries and applications of what they are learning in real-world contexts. For this to happen, teachers need to be well armed with the knowledge and skills that can enable them to teach in sophisticated ways that support the education of their students, rather than being treated as pawns who are the targets of competing prescriptions in the curriculum wars.

Boston teacher Liz MacDonald,[26] recognized with a Resident Teacher Award for her exemplary practices, explains how these ideological battles—embedded in mandates for teaching practice, many of them contradictory to one another and all of them impervious to the needs of students—undermine teaching. She noted that her teaching was weakest, and her students' misbehavior was greatest, when she was engaging in district-mandated classroom practices "not because I thought that they were best for my pupils, but rather because I thought that they were what I was supposed to do." MacDonald recounts that she appreciated the "child-centered, inquiry-driven practices" represented by new district mandates to use Readers and

Writers Workshop and *TERC Mathematics,* introduced by Superintendent Tom Payzant and an improvement in her view over the previous mandates that offered less opportunity to make connections to students' lives and to engage in them in interesting and ambitious thinking and production.

However, she was stymied, on the one hand, by the lack of a curriculum guide and curricular materials for Writers Workshop, which "left me somewhat uncertain as to what to teach and when" and, on the other hand, by the overprescription of content in the TERC curriculum by the district-created pacing guide "outlining which investigations (lessons) should be taught each day at each grade level throughout the district." MacDonald writes:

> Like many of my colleagues, I found that it was a challenge to keep up with the pacing guide's schedule. Other teachers in the district, like me, encountered students every day whose conceptual understanding and basic mathematical skills were so limited that more time needed to be spent with a single investigation. For example, an investigation might require pupils to solve a complex multiplication word story. When my students tried to solve such problems, I often discovered that they not only lacked proficiency in multiplication facts, but had a weak understanding of the concept of multiplication itself. At these junctures I knew that my pupils needed additional time to learn about multiplication, but the pacing guide made it difficult to take the time to remediate my struggling learners. In such instances, I usually chose to follow the pacing guide rather than dig down deeper into content, in part because my pupils were tested every four to six weeks. I believe that the times when I made that decision to follow the pacing guide coincided with a rise in students' behavioral difficulties and their learning was at its lowest level. . . .
>
> Like many teachers, I really made a good faith effort to implement my school district's curriculum and to comply with mandated reforms. I always was on the lookout for new resources to incorporate into my lessons throughout the year. Some of those resources took me far away from the Readers and Writers Workshop approach. For example, I found that some familiarity with systematic phonics provided me with a broader repertoire of teaching practices that benefited some of my struggling readers and writers. I learned that there were many sides to the literacy wars, that it went against my nature to choose one side and enter into battle with the other, and that I wanted to remain open to and inclusive of the full array of instructional approaches that different reformers advocated.
>
> What kinds of instructional practices did I want to use? In addition to my role as a facilitator of pupils' knowledge construction, as advocated by Readers and Writers Workshop and TERC, I wanted to take advantage of a wide range of practices that would allow me to share my own zest for continual learning and my enthusiasm for literature and mathematics with my pupils. I felt that I needed more structure in terms of using the Readers and Writers Workshop and wanted

to know that I was covering all of the reading skills that my children needed. I wanted children to learn several ways of conceptualizing mathematics problems, but I also wanted to make sure that they were comfortable with a certain amount of memorization in mathematics so that they were prepared for state tests when they needed to recall information about multiplication tables at a moment's notice. While I liked the emphasis on children thinking for themselves and in small groups, I believed that these activities needed to be supplemented with well-designed teacher-led instruction to make sure that the children had new knowledge on which to scaffold their extended learning activities.[27]

Like other great teachers, Liz MacDonald knows intuitively that students need both strategically managed direct instruction and opportunities for inquiry, and that they need to master basic skills in ways that ensure they can decode and multiply as well as higher-order skills that allow them to solve complex problems and produce their own knowledge and products. The either/or thinking of curriculum warriors is generally useless to teachers. MacDonald also knows that curriculum guidance is helpful to her when it incorporates professional knowledge about how students are likely to progress well through bodies of important content and the mastery of skills, but it is problematic when it represents this knowledge in rigid pacing guides that assume a level of standardization in students' prior knowledge and learning strategies that is at odds with what real children in real classrooms do and need.

Strictly enforced pacing guides, like other mandates that overly prescribe teaching, have been introduced by curriculum warriors on both sides of the battles, because they want to be sure that their assumptions about learning are strictly enforced in classrooms by teachers who, presumably, won't be able to make reasonable decisions in their use of materials. Usually, these are associated with curricula that emphasize basic skills, such as the Open Court scripted reading program, in which teachers do a lot of the talking and students read only prescribed passages and answer prescribed questions. In Liz MacDonald's case, the pacing guide was, ironically, associated with an inquiry-oriented curriculum based on a constructivist understanding of children's mathematics learning. Despite the curriculum's cognitive science base, the district's addition of the pacing guide to the TERC curriculum ignored the fact that students have different kinds of previous knowledge on which to build—and that the teacher needs time to attend to gaps in knowledge and understanding, so that students can take advantage of other experiences to come. This reality is especially true in urban districts where children are mobile, many are immigrants, and more than a few will have had poor teaching at many grade levels, leaving them with gaps in their fundamental skills that have to be made up—and will produce failure if they are ignored in the press to cover a prescribed curriculum that makes assumptions about what students already know and can do.

The Kind of Standards and Curriculum Guidance Needed. This does not mean that no curriculum guidance is useful. It is very useful to teachers to have guidance and materials that organize knowledge in sequential, meaningful ways and provide professionally well-grounded strategies for developing skills. Standards should offer a parsimonious set of expectations, derived from an understanding of what a liberal education entails and what success in the contemporary society requires. A lean, sequenced set of curriculum objectives derived from standards should be based on theoretical and empirical knowledge of how children progress in their learning within domains toward greater expertise—that is, how they learn, over time and with proper support, to read and write effectively, reason mathematically, inquire scientifically, play music, draw and paint, and understand and analyze history, geography, and social phenomena in the world around them.

While standards outline general expectations, the demands of effective teaching mean that curriculum guidance should be constructed so that teachers can use well-informed judgment as to when and how they introduce particular ideas and skills. Curriculum materials should offer enough space for teachers to meet specific needs of the very diverse learners who populate real classrooms. The demands of effective teaching also mean that curriculum should be based on a well-grounded sense of learning progressions that helps teachers understand the developmental process, so they can move students along from wherever they start. In many countries, including England, New Zealand, and some Australian states, standards and curriculum objectives are expressed in descriptions of what students can be expected to understand and do as they progress, and assessment tools allow teachers to locate students along these developmental progressions, to assist in their curriculum planning. While clarifying common learning progressions and grade level goals for learning in a content area, materials should not prescribe lesson content and pacing.

Finally, the demands of effective teaching require that curriculum guidance be *disciplined*: It should draw from the central concepts and modes of inquiry in the disciplines, and it should itself be disciplined, creating a lean and thoughtful schema of the knowledge base in a domain in ways that allow important ideas and understandings to be well constructed, not an overwhelming laundry list of facts or activities that fail to produce meaningful understanding. It should allow students to study central ideas in a content area in ways that incorporate the important modes of inquiry in that domain—scientific investigation, mathematical reasoning, social scientific inquiry, literary analysis—enabling knowledge not just to be recalled but to be applied in ways that analyze, integrate, and use understandings in transferable ways.

The importance of allowing students to learn core ideas in-depth, rather than running through a "mentioning" curriculum that can barely introduce one idea before racing off to the next has been made clear in a number of international studies, especially in mathematics.[28] When teachers in high-achieving nations take several months to ensure that students learn a given concept deeply and from many different angles, they build a strong foundation on which students can assemble solid understandings going forward. By contrast, the U.S. custom of rushing through dozens of textbook topics each year—made worse by the demands of current tests in many states—means that students "cover" topics such as fractions and decimals briefly in almost every year between third and eighth grade, yet many enter high school unable to apply these concepts easily to real problems.

A recent study of science learning reinforced the same point: Among a group of 8,310 students enrolled in introductory biology, chemistry, or physics classes in randomly selected 4-year colleges, those who had spent at least a month studying one major topic in-depth in high school earned higher college science grades than their peers who studied more topics in the same period of time. The authors pointed out that standardized tests that seek to measure broad overall knowledge in an entire discipline may not capture a student's level of mastery of science concepts, and that teachers who "teach to the test" may not be optimizing their students' chance of success in college.[29]

The Kind of Assessments Needed. Clearly, there is a need not only for leaner, more disciplined standards and more thoughtful curriculum guidance, but also for more useful assessments. A new national education policy should start by helping states develop world-class standards, curriculum, and assessments, and use them for improving teaching rather than punishing schools.

The federal government should provide support to enable states to develop systems, incorporating focused standards developed by professional subject-matter experts and associations, which provide a foundation for thoughtful curriculum guidance and useful assessments. A common American standards project, currently managed by the Council for Chief State School Officers, is working to develop a parsimonious set of standards in English language arts and mathematics that are to be internationally benchmarked and representative of student learning progressions in these subjects. If well conducted, this activity, with input from professional associations and other curriculum experts, could provide a basis for states to re-evaluate and refine their current standards and develop curriculum guidance that can inform teaching and assessment.

State and local assessments should include multiple measures of student learning, both externally developed with the involvement of school and university faculty, and school-based, evaluating those more ambitious aspects of the standards that cannot be evaluated on a single 2- or 3-hour test. Rather than being treated as black boxes, tests should be open to public scrutiny, and their quality should be evaluated in terms of the usefulness of the information they provide for supporting and informing thoughtful teaching and learning.

Periodic high-quality external assessments should include open-ended items, such as essays and problem solutions that call on students to evaluate and analyze information, and communicate and defend their ideas. These reference examinations do not need to be conducted on every child, every year in order to be useful for curriculum planning and school monitoring, and may be of higher quality if they are less frequent or conducted on a sampling basis, as is true in virtually all high-achieving nations and was true for nearly all states prior to No Child Left Behind. However frequently assessments are used, it is critical that the lure of cheap machine-scoring not trump the importance of assessments that provide insights into students' abilities to think, communicate, and explain their ideas, and that leverage intellectually demanding instruction. It matters for instruction, for example, that New York requires students to examine primary source historical documents to write essays evaluating questions of historical interpretation, and that Connecticut and Massachusetts require extended written explanations to questions about mathematics and science phenomena.

It also matters that teachers are involved in assessment development and scoring. As I have noted, the external assessments used in high-achieving jurisdictions are typically developed with and scored by teachers, which is one of the features that makes them educative for the improvement of curriculum and teaching. They are also complemented by extensive, every-year, school-based assessments based on the curriculum objectives—many of which are common across schools—that involve teachers in looking closely at student learning in systematic ways. These assessments, which require that students undertake challenging activities linked to the standards, create equitable, rich curriculum opportunities, attention to student learning, and comparability in evaluation, because of investments in teacher training and moderation.

These systems are not unlike those created in states such as Kentucky and Vermont at the start of the standards-based reform movement, which produced substantial gains in student achievement when they were being implemented. These states used periodic reference examinations in English language arts and mathematics, supplemented by writing and mathematics portfolios assembling specific kinds of work scored by teachers using common rubrics and moderation. Vermont and Connecticut have required state-designed school-based tasks such as science investigations. Maine, Minnesota, Nebraska, and Wyoming have worked with schools to create and use a range of local school-based tasks to create profiles of student performance on standards across subjects.

To encourage and better evaluate applied knowledge and higher-order skills, school-based assessments should include these kinds of tasks, plus ongoing diagnostic observation and documentation of students' developing skills—for example, mathematical understanding and reading, writing, speaking, and listening abilities in English and other languages. As in other countries, learning gains have been documented in U.S. schools that use tools such as the Developmental Reading Assessment, the Qualitative Reading Inventory, and the Primary Learning Record, which involve teachers in documentation of student learning to systematically assess and support literacy development.[30]

At the high school level, performance tasks that assess career- and college-ready performance within and across disciplines should include research papers and presentations, literary analyses, science experiments, complex mathematical problem solutions and models, uses of technology, and exhibitions of learning from the arts, community service, and internships. As in other nations, these assessments should be scored by teachers using common criteria and moderation processes, providing information that continuously improves teaching and learning, while attesting to students' accomplishments in a variety of fields. If assessments are used as they are in many high-achieving nations, students will choose the fields in which they will demonstrate their knowledge, and their performances will provide additional, rich information beyond the diploma for colleges and employers, rather than serving as graduation gatekeepers.

Portfolios of such discipline-based accomplishments—which are used for graduation by schools in the Performance Standards Consortium in New York, the Boston Pilot schools, the International High Schools Network, Envision Schools, the Asia Society schools, and states such as Rhode Island—have been found to support stronger outcomes in college and workplaces.[31] Graduates note that this is because these requirements prepare students to plan and complete major undertakings, understand an area of knowledge deeply, persevere in the face of challenges and uncertainties, frame and address problems, find and synthesize information, analyze data, evaluate and revise their work, write and speak well, and defend their ideas in public. All of these are abilities that are required to succeed in the non-multiple-choice world beyond school.

These kinds of assessment systems, if accompanied by adequate investments in teacher knowledge and skill, could both improve the overall quality of instruction and learning in American schools and leverage gains for students who will otherwise experience a low-level curriculum further impoverished by nondiagnostic teaching. Efforts to create a "thinking curriculum" for all students are critically important to individual futures and our national welfare. Such efforts are unlikely to pay off, however, unless other central changes are made in the ways tests are used and accountability systems are designed, so that new standards and assessments inform more skillful and adaptive teaching that enables more successful learning for all students.

INTELLIGENT, RECIPROCAL ACCOUNTABILITY

Standards for student learning are meaningless unless they are accompanied by the means to ensure that they can indeed be met by students in all schools. Thus, policies that ensure students' opportunities to learn are as important a part of an accountable education system as are standards for student performance.

In the currently prevailing paradigm in the United States, accountability has been defined primarily as the administration of tests and the attachment of sanctions to low test scores. Yet, from the perspective of children and parents, this approach does not ensure high-quality teaching each year, nor does it ensure that students have the courses, books, materials, supports services, and other resources they need to learn. In this paradigm, two-way accountability does not exist: Although the child and the school are accountable to the state for test performance, the state is not accountable to the child or school for providing adequate educational resources.

Furthermore, as we have seen, test-based accountability schemes have sometimes undermined education for the most vulnerable students, by narrowing curriculum and by creating incentives to exclude low-achieving students in order to boost scores. Indeed, although tests can provide some of the information needed for an accountability system, they are not the system itself. Genuine accountability should heighten the probability of good practices occurring for all students, reduce the probability of harmful practice, and ensure that there are self-corrective mechanisms in the system—feedback, assessments, and incentives—that support continual improvement.

If education is actually to improve and the system is to be accountable to students, accountability should be focused on ensuring the competence of teachers and leaders, the quality of instruction, and the adequacy of resources, as well as the capacity of the system to trigger improvements. In addition to *standards of learning* for students, which focus the system's efforts on meaningful goals, this will require *standards of practice* that can guide professional training, development, teaching, and management at the classroom, school, and system levels, and *opportunity to learn standards* that ensure appropriate resources to achieve the desired outcomes.

Alongside relevant, valid, and useful information about how individual students are doing and how schools are serving them, accountability should encompass how a school system hires, evaluates, and supports its staff; how it makes decisions; how it ensures that the best available knowledge will be acquired and used; how it evaluates its own functioning; and how it provides safeguards for student welfare.

This more complete conception is similar to what has been described as Finland's strategy of "reciprocal, intelligent accountability," in which:

> . . . schools are increasingly accountable for learning outcomes and education authorities are held accountable to schools for making expected outcomes possible. Intelligent accountability in the Finnish education context preserves and enhances trust among teachers, students, school leaders and education authorities in the accountability processes and involves them in the process, offering them a strong sense of professional responsibility and initiative. This has had a major positive impact on teaching and, hence, on student learning.[32]

If new standards are to result in greater student learning, rather than greater levels of failure, accountability policies will need to ensure that teachers and other educators have the knowledge and skills they need to teach effectively to the new standards, help schools evaluate and reshape their practices, and put safeguards in place for students who attend failing schools.

Standards of Practice: Ensuring Professional Accountability

If students are to be expected to achieve higher standards, it stands to reason that educators must meet higher standards as well. They must know how to teach in ways that enable students to master challenging content and that address the special needs of different learners. High and rigorous standards for teaching are a cornerstone of a professional accountability system focused on student learning. Professional accountability acknowledges that the only way we can ensure that students will be well taught is by making sure that they have knowledgeable and committed teachers. As Lee Shulman has stated:

> The teacher remains the key. The literature on effective schools is meaningless, debates over educational policy are moot, if the primary agents of instruction are incapable of performing their functions well. No microcomputer will replace them, no television system will clone and distribute them, no scripted lessons will direct and control them, no voucher system will bypass them.[33]

Professional accountability aims to ensure educators' competence through rigorous preparation, certification, selection, and evaluation of practitioners, as well as continuous professional learning and peer review of practice. It requires educators to make decisions on the basis of the best available professional knowledge; it also requires that they pledge their first commitment to the welfare of the client. Thus, rather than encouraging teaching that is procedure-oriented and rule-based, professional accountability seeks to create practices that are *client-oriented* and *knowledge-based*. Professional accountability seeks to ensure that all educators will have had access to profession-wide knowledge concerning best practices, not just what they picked up by themselves on the job; that they will have made a moral commitment to use this knowledge in the best interests of their students; and that they will continually seek to discover new knowledge and increasingly effective practices for themselves and their colleagues.

To achieve this, current ad hoc approaches to teacher and principal recruitment, preparation, licensing, hiring, and ongoing professional development must be reshaped so that all students will have access to teachers and school leaders who can be professionally accountable. As I describe below, this will require a serious overhaul of preparation and licensing standards so that they reflect the critical knowledge and skills for teaching, evaluated through high-quality performance assessments demonstrating that prospective teachers can actually teach effectively. It will require major investments in and greater accountability from teacher and leadership education programs, evaluated by the performance of their graduates on these assessments and other measures. It will also require more effective evaluation and professional learning systems in schools, so that tenure is earned based on demonstrated competence and ongoing assessment of practice and outcomes guides expectations and supports for professional development.

Standards for Schools: Developing Organizational Accountability

Quality teaching depends not just on teachers' knowledge and skill but on the environments in which they work. Schools need to offer a coherent curriculum focused on higher-order thinking and performance across subject areas and grades, time for teachers to work intensively with students to accomplish challenging goals, opportunities for teachers to plan with and learn from one another, and regular occasions to evaluate the outcomes of their practices.

If schools are to become more responsible and responsive, they must, like other professional organizations, make evaluation and assessment part of their everyday lives. Just as hospitals have standing committees of staff that meet regularly to look at assessment data and discuss the effectiveness of each aspect of their work—a practice reinforced by their accreditation requirements—so schools must have regular occasions to examine their practices and effectiveness.

As Richard Rothstein and colleagues describe in *Grading Education: Getting Accountability Right*,[34] school-level accountability can be supported by school inspections, like those common in many other nations, in which trained experts, usually highly respected former practitioners, evaluate schools by spending several days visiting classrooms, examining random samples of student work, and interviewing students about their understanding and their experiences, as well as looking at objective data such as test scores, graduation rates, and the like. In some cases, principals accompany the inspectors into classrooms and are asked for their own evaluations of the lessons. In this way, the inspectors are able to make judgments about the instructional and supervisory competence of principals. As described earlier, inspectors may also play a role in ensuring the quality and comparability of school-based assessments (as in England and Australia), as well as schools' internal assessment and evaluation processes (as in Hong Kong).

In most countries' inspection systems, schools are rated on the quality of instruction and other services and supports, as well as students' performance and progress on a wide range of dimensions, including and going beyond academic subject areas, such as extracurriculars, personal and social responsibility, the acquisition of workplace skills, and the extent to which students are encouraged to adopt safe practices and a healthy lifestyle. Schools are rated as to whether they pass inspection, need modest improvements, or require serious intervention, and they receive extensive feedback on what the inspectors both saw and recommend. Reports are publicly posted. Schools requiring intervention are then given more expert attention and support, and are placed on a more frequent schedule of visits. Those that persistently fail to pass may be placed under local government control and could be closed down if they are not improved.

An Americanized version of the inspectorate system, designed by former members of the British inspectorate with U.S. educators, has been piloted in several states and cities, including New York, Rhode Island, and Chicago.[35] The process has proved an extremely effective strategy for enabling schools to get an objective look at their practices, creating an evidence base that honors the broader goals of education and complements test information, and providing diagnostics and recommendations that are essential for any serious improvement ultimately to occur. When practicing educators are among the members of the teams, they also learn directly about colleagues' practices and how to evaluate education in ways that travel back with them to their own schools, creating a learning system across the state. This approach could be developed by building on these efforts or by reconceptualizing current school accreditation to focus more directly on teaching and learning, with leadership from full-time trained experts who guide the work of the volunteer participants on teams that can, thus, be more consistent and effective.

Standards for the System: Creating Safeguards for Students

An effective intervention system for diagnosing and remedying the sources of school failure is an essential component of an accountability system that works for students. If teaching and learning are to improve, federal and state accountability efforts must be structured to enhance opportunities for school learning and professional development. They should also ensure that necessary resources—ranging from qualified teachers to curriculum materials—are put in place where schools are failing.

It is critical that state and federal efforts to recognize success and remedy failure be based on thoughtful, educationally sound means for identifying schools that are succeeding or failing. We have seen that when incentives are triggered by simplistic measurements such as average school test scores, perverse incentives can be created that harm students. Measures need to be based on the growth and success of all students in the school and on educationally sound evaluations of school practices. The incentive structure must provide incentives for schools that provide high-quality education to be rewarded for opening their doors to the students who are in the greatest educational need and for supporting the spread of successful practices to other schools.

A genuinely accountable system recognizes that school problems can be caused as much by district and state policies—including unequal funding, hiring and assignment of unqualified personnel, and counterproductive curriculum policies—as they are by conditions within the school. Thus, the responsibility for correcting school failings must be shared. When there are serious shortcomings in schools' practices and outcomes, states should involve expert teams in evaluating the root causes of school failure—including the qualifications of personnel, the nature of curriculum resources, student access to high-quality teaching, administrative strategies, organizational structures, and other essential aspects of students' experiences in school—and, with the district and school, develop a plan to correct them.

If policy changes are needed to implement a remedy or to ensure that the problems experienced by the school do not recur on a regular basis (in that school or in other schools), then the state and local district should also assume responsibility for developing new policies that are more supportive of school success and that ensure the protection of students' entitlement to high-quality education. Schools should have expert technical assistance to support their efforts to change. If they cannot do so successfully, however, with infusions of resources and help, they should be redesigned or closed, and their buildings used to house new school models created by educators who can design them for greater success.

In a system of shared accountability, *states* would be responsible for providing sufficient resources, for ensuring well-qualified personnel, and for adopting standards for student learning. *School districts* would be responsible for distributing school resources equitably, hiring and supporting well-qualified teachers and administrators (and removing those who are not competent), and encouraging practices that support high-quality teaching and learning. *Schools* would be accountable for creating a productive environment for learning, assessing the effectiveness of their practices, and helping staff and parents communicate with and learn from one another. *Teachers and other staff* would be accountable for identifying and meeting the needs of individual students as well as meeting professional standards of practice. Together with colleagues, they would continually assess and revise their strategies to better meet the needs of students.

Revamping No Child Left Behind

No Child Left Behind (NCLB) will be considered for reauthorization in 2010, and will have much to do with the accountability strategies adopted by states across the country. Although problematic in its implementation, NCLB is a historic piece of legislation that has succeeded in drawing attention to the need for higher learning standards and greater equity in educational outcomes. By flagging differences in student performance by race and class, it shines a spotlight on long-standing inequalities that can trigger attention to the needs of students who are neglected in many schools. And by insisting that all students are entitled to qualified teachers, the law has stimulated important recruitment and retention efforts in states where low-income and "minority" students have experienced a revolving door of inexperienced, untrained teachers.

The goals of No Child Left Behind are the right ones; however, we have seen that the law's design and implementation have narrowed the curriculum, caused schools to abandon some successful programs, and created incentives for keeping and pushing low-achievers out of schools. In addition, its complex rules for showing "adequate yearly progress"—which require schools to meet more than 30 separate testing targets annually—have labeled many successful and improving schools as failing, while preventing adequate attention to the truly failing schools on which states should focus. Because of a number of catch-22s in the accountability formula, more than 80% of the nation's schools will have failed to "make AYP" by 2014, even if they are high-achieving or rapidly improving.

Hundreds of proposals for tweaking NCLB have been made, but a substantial paradigm shift is required if the nation's education system is to support powerful learning for all students. The Forum on Education and Accountability, a group of more than 100 education and civil rights organizations—including the National Urban League, NAACP, Aspira, and the League of United Latin American Citizens, as well as the associations representing teachers, administrators, and school boards—has argued that "the law's emphasis needs to shift from applying sanctions for failing to raise test scores to holding states and localities accountable for making the systemic changes that improve student achievement."[36]

This should include encouraging thoughtful measures of student performance that can support the kind of learning we need in schools and developing a better method for charting school progress. Although the current law calls for multiple measures and for assessing higher-order thinking skills, it currently lacks incentives to encourage better assessments. To address these problems, Congress should:

- *Fund an intensive development effort* that enables states, in collaboration with federal labs, centers, and universities, to develop, validate, and test high-quality performance assessments, and to train the field of practitioners—ranging from a new generation of state and local curriculum and assessment specialists to teachers and leaders—who can be involved in the development, administration, and scoring of these assessments in valid and reliable ways. The federal government should also fund high-quality research on the validity, reliability, instructional consequences, and equity consequences of these assessments.
- *Encourage improvements in state and local assessment practice.* To model high-quality assessment items and better measure the standards, the federal

government should move the National Assessment of Educational Practice toward a more performance-oriented assessment, as it was when it was first launched in the 1950s, with tasks that evaluate students' abilities to solve problems, explain, and defend their ideas. The new Elementary and Secondary Education Act should provide incentives and funding for states to refine their state assessments, and introduce related, high-quality, locally administered performance assessments that evaluate critical thinking and applied skills. It should also support states in making such assessments reliable, valid, and practically feasible, through teacher professional development and scorer training and moderation systems.

- *Ensure more appropriate assessment for special education students and English language learners* by underwriting efforts to develop, validate, and disseminate more appropriate assessments in the content areas for these students, and by ensuring that the law and regulations encourage assessments that are based on professional testing standards for these groups.[37] This would include helping to develop and requiring the use of tests that are language-accessible for English Language Learners and appropriate for special education students, and evaluating their gains at all points along the achievement continuum.

A new set of measures is also essential for evaluating school progress. Currently, NCLB requires states to show 100% of students reaching "proficiency" by 2014, setting separate targets every year for subgroups defined by race, ethnicity, socio-economic status, language background, and special education status, and labeling schools that miss any single target as failing to make AYP. It is impossible with the current metrics to distinguish, for example, between a school that shows little gain for its students on any of the tests and one that shows substantial gains for all groups, but had a 94% testing participation rate on one test in one subject area, rather than the required 95%.

Furthermore, under current rules, all schools that serve English language learners will eventually be declared failing, because a catch-22 provision in the law requires reaching 100% proficiency for this group, but removes students from the subgroup after they become proficient, making the target impossible to meet. Schools that serve a steady stream of new immigrants who are non–native English speakers are, by definition, unable to make adequate yearly progress under the law, no matter how successful they are in helping their students learn English over time. In addition, as we have noted, the focus on increasing test outcomes alone has created incentives for schools to boost scores by keeping or pushing out low-scoring students, especially those with special needs and English language learners. School incentives should recognize the value of keeping students in school as well as improving learning.

To address these problems, the Congress should replace the current "status model" for measuring school progress with a *Continuous Progress Index* that evaluates school progress on an index of measures that includes a range of assessments of student learning along with school progression and graduation rates. Such an index would evaluate students' growth over time, across the entire achievement continuum, thus focusing attention on progress in all students' learning, not just on those who fall at the so-called "proficiency bubble." This would recognize schools' gains with students who score well below and above a single cut score and encourage more appropriate inclusion of special education students and English language learners. The index could accommodate state and local assessments of student learning that capture more complex inquiry and problem-solving skills. It could also include assessments of subject areas beyond reading and mathematics—such as writing, science, and history—that are important in their own right and essential to develop students' knowledge and literacy skills as they are applied in the content areas.

A continuous progress index would give schools a single challenging but realistic growth target to aim for each year for each student group (rather than 30 or 40 separate targets)—one that increases more steeply for groups that are further behind, so that incentives focus both on raising the bar and closing the achievement gap. It would encourage schools' attention to all students' learning, and allow for several kinds of important evidence about progress to be considered in evaluating schools. It would also more clearly identify those that are truly failing, so that states can focus their resources for improvement where they are most needed, using a school quality review process, as described above, to diagnose school needs and to support more productive interventions.

Rather than placing all the onus of reform on the individual school, a revamped Elementary and Secondary Education Act would recognize that many of the sources of problems in failing schools are structural and systemic rather than idiosyncratic, and that failing public schools in many states are seriously underfunded and grossly understaffed. In some cases, a majority of teachers are untrained and inexperienced, due to short-sighted and unaccountable licensing and hiring practices at the state and district levels. These schools are dumping grounds for the failures of the system. They are allowed to function in this way because they serve powerless minorities and constituencies without clout, and because the system must rob some Peter in order to pay some other Paul. The solution to their problems does not lie within the schools themselves, but with major structural changes within the system as a whole. Such changes will require honesty and courage in facing the educational dirty laundry that has been allowed to accumulate across the country, as well as foresight in adopting policies that seriously address the issues of educational equity, professional accountability, and system-wide restructuring. I turn to these issues next.

EQUITABLE AND ADEQUATE RESOURCES

The onus of NCLB is on individual schools to raise test scores. However, the law does not address the profound educational inequalities that plague our nation. Despite a 3 to 1 ratio between high- and low-spending schools in most states, multiplied further by inequalities across states, neither NCLB nor other federal education policies require that states demonstrate progress toward adequate funding or equitable opportunities to learn. Furthermore, federal Title I funding gives more to states that spend more, reinforcing rather than compensating for unequal resources across states.[38] Thus, Mississippi, with its enormous concentrations of poverty, receives less federal funding per pupil than much wealthier New York, despite its greater needs.

The Federal Role

To survive and prosper, our society must finally renounce its obstinate commitment to educational inequality and embrace full and ambitious opportunities to learn for all of our children. Although education is a state responsibility, a new federal policy must finally address the deep and tenacious educational debt that holds our nation's future in hock, taking strong steps toward ensuring that every child has access to adequate school resources, facilities, and quality teachers. Federal education funding to states should be tied to each state's movement toward equitable access to education resources. Furthermore, the obvious truth—that schools alone are not responsible for student achievement—should propel attention to the provision of adequate health care and nutrition, safe and secure housing, and healthy communities for children. In addition to investing in universal health care and high-quality preschool for all low-income children, Congress should:

- *Equalize allocations of ESEA resources* across states so that high poverty states receive a greater share. Allocation formulas should use indicators of student need, with adjustments for cost-of-living differentials, rather than relying on measures of spending that disadvantage poor states.
- *Enforce comparability provisions for ensuring equally qualified teachers* to schools serving different populations of students. NCLB already requires that states develop policies and incentives to balance the qualifications of teachers across schools serving more and less advantaged students, but this aspect of the law is weakly enforced, and wide disparities continue to occur.
- *Require states to report on opportunity indicators* along with their reports of academic progress for each school, reflecting the availability of well-qualified teachers; strong curriculum opportunities; books, materials, and equipment

(such as science labs and computers); and adequate facilities. State laws should include evaluations of progress on opportunity measures in state plans and evaluations under the law, and states should be required to meet a set of opportunity-to-learn standards for schools that are identified as failing. As a condition for receiving federal funds, each state should include in its funding application for federal funds a report describing the state's demonstrated movement toward adequacy and equitable access to these education resources—and a plan for further progress.

Opportunity-to-Learn Standards

A linchpin in these efforts to secure more equitable education is the creation of opportunity-to-learn (OTL) standards that attend to the opportunity gap as well as the achievement gap. Such standards have been called for since the National Council on Education Standards and Testing issued its report in 1992 at the start of the standards-based reform movement, arguing that, just as states and localities evaluate and report on student achievement, they should report systematically on students' opportunities to learn.[39] OTL standards have been variously defined in proposals and legislation as the opportunity to learn the curriculum assessed in state standards, access to the resources needed for success in the curriculum—such as teachers who are well qualified to teach the curriculum, appropriate curriculum materials, technology, and supportive services—and access to other resources needed to succeed in school and life.

In the narrowest version, for example, if a state's curriculum frameworks and assessments outline standards for science learning that require laboratory work and computers, certain kinds of coursework, and knowledge for teaching science effectively, states and districts would be responsible for designing policies that ensure the availability of the curriculum, materials, and qualified teachers to meet these specific standards.[40] In a broader view, such as that recently advanced by the Schott Foundation in its Opportunity to Learn campaign, children's equitable access to preschool education, college preparatory coursework, effective teachers, and instructional resources are monitored, because they are elements in a more global definition of adequate education.[41] However they are configured, such standards—and the indicators used to measure them—should provide information about the nature of the teaching and learning opportunities made available to students in different schools, districts, and states across the country, and should create incentives for states and school districts to create policies that leverage access to critical resources.

Resource Equalization Strategies

Progress in equalizing resources to students will require attention to inequalities at all levels—between states, among districts, among schools within districts, and among students differentially placed in classrooms, courses, and tracks that offer substantially disparate opportunities to learn. How can policymakers tackle such a multifaceted agenda? In the past, the strategy has been to offer state aid to offset some of the core inequality resulting from locally funded education tied to the wealth of communities, and add a variety of categorical programs that give additional money for specific purposes to local districts, often with extensive strings attached. These strategies do not close the resource gap, and categorical grants have proliferated until the lowest-wealth districts must manage dozens or even hundreds of small pots of money that come and go, often inadequate to pay for their ostensible purposes, fragmenting and defusing schools' efforts and attention, requiring a panoply of administrative staff for management and reporting, and unavailable for the core work of schools—getting and supporting good teachers and leaders to focus on student learning in well-designed schools.

Aside from some large focused commitments in areas such as special education and services for English language learners that direct attention to specific students' needs, the categorical aid strategy has been inefficient and ineffective and has undermined schools' focus while doing little to improve student learning. Instead of this approach, state funding should be allocated to students based on equal dollars per student adjusted or weighted for specific student needs, such as poverty, limited English proficiency, and special education status. Establishing the per pupil base so that it represents what an adequate education to meet the standards actually costs, and determining the weights so that they accurately reflect the costs of meeting differential pupil needs is critically important for such a scheme to work well. This weighted student formula allocation should also be adjusted for cost-of-living differentials across large states, and should be supplemented with funds to address unavoidably variable costs such as transportation, which is necessarily extensive in large, sparse rural districts, and school construction, which varies by the age of buildings and changing enrollment patterns.

Developing such an equitable, reliable base of funding is critically important so that districts can maintain the foundational elements of quality education, and can make locally appropriate, strategic decisions about how to spend resources to achieve results. The reliability and availability of these funds to focus on the core work of education should reduce the wastefulness of a potpourri of startup, wind-down programs that are often created to address the shortcomings of a system that doesn't make adequate investments in strong teaching and personalized environments that would prevent students from falling through the cracks to begin with.

State efforts to rationalize resource allocations should also aim to leverage strong outcomes for the dollars that are spent. As the Public Policy Institute of California (PPIC) observed:

> Equalization policies should do more than alter growth in overall budget levels. We believe they should target the area of greatest inequality: teacher preparation.

...Traditional redistributive policies aimed at reducing variations in revenues per pupil across districts are unlikely to equalize student achievement across all schools. ...(R)esource inequality is restricted primarily to teacher training and curriculum, so that redistribution must focus on these specific characteristics of schools rather than on revenues per pupil alone.[42]

Similarly, Ron Ferguson's findings about the importance of teacher expertise for student achievement led him to recommend that investments focus on districts' capacity to hire high-quality teachers. Ferguson's conclusion—that investments in more qualified teachers lead to greater achievement gains than other uses of educational dollars—led him to recommend that states direct funding to enable even higher salaries for qualified teachers in the neediest districts:

> Equal salaries will not attract equally qualified teachers to dissimilar school districts: for any given salary, teachers prefer school districts with higher socioeconomic status and judge the attractiveness of teaching in a given district against the allure of other opportunities. This suggests that a state policy of salary differentials ... will be necessary if each district is to get its proportionate share of the best teachers.[43]

The PPIC study also argued that teacher shortages in the most heavily affected areas might be reduced through differential cost-of-education adjustments across school districts.[44]

This strategy is like that used in some countries where teachers' salaries are designed to be equivalent across districts with added stipends for those who work in harder-to-staff schools. A weighted student formula approach with an adequate base of funding would provide districts serving the neediest students with the additional funds that would allow them to support the differential salaries that Ferguson and the PPIC report call for—rather than the lower salaries they typically offer today. However, it would not ensure that districts would use the funds to hire more qualified staff or that a supply of such well-prepared staff would be available for them to recruit. This would require that the state enforce standards for teacher quality and create a strong, steady supply of effective practitioners—a job that goes beyond what districts themselves can do, even with a more stable and equitable distribution of local resources.

Both the PPIC analysis and Ferguson's underscore the importance of a strategy like Connecticut's (see Chapter 5) that ended shortages and boosted student achievement by equalizing the distribution of better-qualified teachers. Connecticut did this by offering salary aid for fully certified teachers on an equalizing basis for districts that would raise their minimum salary to a state recommended level, increasing statewide salaries above those in the region. Meanwhile, these resources and incentives were buttressed by other key state activities—strengthened preparation and licensing standards, funding for mentoring and a performance-based induction system, strengthened evaluation for teachers and school leaders, and extensive professional development. The state's strategic efforts to create an infrastructure for professional excellence allowed its increased investments to be well spent and highly effective. This agenda is critical to creating a productive system that is also cost-effective, rather than pouring money into a system that would throw much of it away.

STRONG PROFESSIONAL PRACTICE

With increased recognition that expert teachers are perhaps the most important resource for improving student learning—and the most inequitably distributed—it is imperative that the United States develop policies for recruiting, preparing, and retaining strong teachers, especially in high-need schools. Unfortunately, unlike high-achieving nations, the United States lacks a systematic approach to developing and distributing expert teachers and school leaders, or for using the skills of accomplished teachers to help improve schools.

States and the federal government have a central role to play in developing a foundation for good teaching and strong school leadership across America. As I described in Chapter 7, we know a great deal more than we once did about how to construct effective preparation, induction, and professional development programs, and we are learning much more about how to use performance-based evaluations of teaching to improve both teacher development and practice. New approaches to compensation and career development are also emerging, and there is a growing body of evidence about what incentives work to retain teachers in the profession, encourage them to teach in high-need schools, and motivate them to become more expert.

What we lack are effective policy systems for making these widespread. Although No Child Left Behind's "highly qualified teacher" requirement has reduced the hiring of utterly untrained teachers in some states, it has not included supports to make well-prepared teachers and leaders available in the neediest communities. A national supply policy like that developed in medicine is critically needed,[45] coupled with a rethinking of the teaching career so that teachers can become highly effective, have strong reasons to stay in the profession, and use their skills where they are needed most—both in communities serving the most underserved students and in capacities where they can affect whole-school reform.

Effective action can be modeled after federal investments in medicine. Since 1944, the federal government has subsidized medical training to fill shortages and build teaching hospitals and training programs in high-need areas—a commitment that has contributed significantly to America's world-renowned system of medical training and care. Intelligent, targeted incentives can ensure that all students have access to teachers who are indeed highly qualified. An aggressive Marshall Plan that would rapidly solve teacher shortages and dramatically upgrade teaching in all communities would cost $5 billion annually, far less than 1% of the cost thus far of the War in Iraq. Such a plan would:

1. *Fix teacher recruitment and retention,* so as to get and keep well-qualified teachers in every classroom. First, as it does in medicine, the federal government should maintain a substantial, sustained program of *service scholarships* that completely cover training costs in high-quality programs at the undergraduate or graduate level for high-ability candidates who prepare to teach in a high-need location or subject area, such as mathematics, science, special education, world languages, or English as a new language. As in North Carolina's successful Teaching Fellows program (see Chapter 5), scholarships for preparation can be linked to minimum service requirements of 4 years or more—the point at which most teachers have become effective and are committed to remaining in the profession. Because fully prepared novices are more than twice as likely to stay in teaching as those who lack training, shortages could be reduced rapidly if districts hire well-prepared teachers. And with lower attrition, the numbers of new recruits needed each year would decline sharply. Virtually all of the vacancies currently filled with emergency teachers could be filled with well-prepared teachers if 40,000 service scholarships of up to $25,000 each were offered annually. Although substantial, this commitment would be only a fraction of that made by high-achieving countries, which underwrite all the costs of high-quality teacher preparation for all their candidates.

Recruitment incentives could also be used *to attract and retain expert, experienced teachers* in high-need schools. As part of a broader career ladder initiative, described below, federal matching grants to states and districts could provide incentives for the design of innovative approaches to attract and keep accomplished teachers in priority low-income schools, through compensation for accomplishment and for additional responsibilities, such as mentoring and coaching, improved working conditions, and opportunities to redesign schools to make them more effective. For example, $500 million could provide $10,000 in additional compensation for 50,000 teachers annually to be allocated to expert teachers in high-need schools through innovative compensation systems that recognize teacher expertise through mechanisms such as National Board Certification, local standards-based evaluations, and carefully assembled evidence of contributions to student learning. The importance of an integrated approach to improving school settings, supporting learning, and recognizing success is described further below.

Providing *mentoring for all beginning teachers* would, research suggests, greatly reduce attrition and increase teacher competence. States should establish high-quality mentoring programs that fund regular in-classroom coaching for all beginning teachers. A federal matching grant program could help leverage such programs, ensuring support for every new teacher in the country. Based on the funding model used in California's Beginning Teacher Support and Assessment Program, a federal allocation of $3,000 for each beginning teacher, matched by states or local districts, could fund weekly in-classroom coaching for every novice in his or her first year. At 125,000 new teachers each year,[46] an investment of $500 million could ensure that every novice is coached by a trained, accomplished mentor with expertise in the relevant teaching field. If the early-career teachers who now leave teaching at high rates were to be retained, the nation would save $1 billion a year in replacement costs.[47]

Ideally, a federally funded incentive to states and districts to create strong mentoring programs would be accompanied by support for the use of beginning teacher performance assessments like those developed in California and Connecticut, which can guide teacher learning, improve mentoring and preparation, and help develop sophisticated practice as part of an ongoing career advancement process. (see Chapter 7 and the discussion below.) These assessments create a lever that not only helps teachers develop much more sophisticated skills much sooner, but also transforms preparation and mentoring so they are focused on the skills that make a difference for student and teacher success, rather than just offering disjointed advice or a buddy system.

2. Reinvent teacher preparation and professional development so that teachers can meet 21st-century learning needs and develop sophisticated skills. To transform preparation and professional development, a combination of strong pressure and supports is needed. To make expert teaching the rule rather than the exception, state and local policies need to create a continuum of professional learning for teachers based on recently developed standards that guide teacher preparation and licensing, early induction, ongoing professional development, and advanced certification.

A critical first step is for states to *make teacher education performance-based*, and require all programs—whether they are offered by universities, districts, or other providers—to demonstrate that they can enable teachers to teach effectively by meeting professional accreditation standards, and closing programs that cannot meet the standards. The two teacher education accrediting agencies—currently about to merge—have committed to making their decisions in substantial part based on evidence of graduates' performance, effectiveness, and retention in the classroom.

Development of a high-quality, nationally available *teacher performance assessment* for beginning teachers, measuring actual teaching skill in the content areas, would contribute to this effort to raise the bar dramatically on the quality of preparation. In states that have already used them, these assessments have been strong levers for improving preparation and mentoring, as well as determining teachers' competence.

They have been found not only to measure features of teaching associated with effectiveness, but actually to help develop effectiveness at the same time—not only for the participants but also for those involved in mentoring and assessing these performances (see Chapter 7). The assessments require the practices teachers need to learn to be effective with diverse students—for example, planning and teaching a curriculum unit with built-in adaptations and formative assessments for English language learners and students with disabilities, reflecting on evidence of student learning each day to revise plans for the next day, and tracking student learning growth with the goal of adapting instruction to ensure progress for all learners.[48] Thus, these approaches are particularly valuable targets for policy investments, as they offer an engine for developing teaching quality across the profession while providing a useful measure of how teachers contribute to student learning.

Federal support for the development of a nationally available performance assessment for licensing would not only provide an important tool for accountability and improvement, but it would also facilitate teacher mobility across states, if it were part of an effort to unify the current medieval system of teacher testing and licensure that has resulted in 50 separate fiefdoms across the country. This would help get teachers much more easily from the states with surpluses to those with shortages and ensure more consistency in their training. This goal is within reach: In addition to states that have already incorporated such performance assessments in the licensing process, another 10 states have recently committed to doing so and are developing a common version.

As it does in medicine, the federal government can also provide *incentives to develop successful preparation models* that focus on how to teach standards-based content to diverse learners, including students with disabilities and English Language Learner students. Successful programs like those described in Chapter 7, whose graduates are highly competent from day one and produce strong learning gains for their students, should be further documented, and their features should be incorporated in challenge grants to universities to revamp current practices. These features should also be the focus of serious accreditation reviews, creating a race to the top in teacher education, rather than the race to the bottom that we seem currently determined to win.

One thing that is clear from current studies of strong programs is that learning to practice *in* practice, with expert guidance, is essential to becoming a great teacher of students with a wide range of needs. To improve preparation, states and accreditors should require a full year of clinical training for prospective teachers, ideally undertaken in professional development schools (PDS) that, like teaching hospitals, offer yearlong residencies under the guidance of expert teachers. These PDS sites develop state-of-the-art practice and train novices in the classrooms of expert teachers while they are completing coursework that helps them learn to teach diverse learners well. These schools also engage in intensive professional learning for veteran teachers and may become hubs of professional development for their districts. Many of the more than 1,000 current sites are located in urban districts, creating a pipeline of teachers who are well prepared to teach in these districts. Highly developed models have been found to increase teacher effectiveness and raise student achievement.[49] Just as the federal government has played a major role in underwriting teaching hospitals to strengthen medical training, so a strategic initiative, partnered with states, could take this successful innovation from the margins to the mainstream.

Most important are models that can simultaneously improve teacher competence and retention and meet pressing supply needs in hard-to-staff urban and rural locations. Federal support can make a major contribution by underwriting *teacher residency programs* that place carefully screened recruits as paid apprentices in professional development school sites that offer expert mentor teachers for a year while they complete credential coursework in curriculum, teaching, and learning with local partnering universities. When they become teachers, these recruits also receive 2 years of mentoring. In exchange for this high-quality preparation, candidates pledge to spend at least 4 years in the district's schools. This model has already shown teacher retention rates of over 90% after 5 years for graduates in Chicago, Boston, and Denver. (See Chapter 7.)

Funding to develop residency programs has been included in President Obama's stimulus package, and should be continued and expanded to at least $500 million annually to support state-of-the-art training that creates a stable supply of teachers in hard-to-staff districts. Such programs can solve several problems simultaneously—creating a pipeline of committed teachers who are well prepared to engage in best practice for children in high-need schools, while developing demonstration sites that serve as models for urban and rural teaching and teacher education.

3. Encourage and reward teacher and school leader knowledge and skill to retain expert teachers and improve schools. The first order of business here is for states to develop an infrastructure for high-quality professional development by funding professional development time and organizing the multiple resources of the state—from universities, districts, and nonprofit organizations—to ensure that expertise and capacity are developed to improve teaching in the content areas and address student needs, such as support for English language learners and students with learning disabilities. As in a number of states, Teacher and Leadership Academies can play a key role in doing this, helping to organize intensive institutes and networks to support leadership learning and teaching in the content areas, training principals and teachers as mentors and coaches who can support others in districts, and providing materials and expertise to support professional learning at the school level. Districts should enable schools to tap both these external resources and the critical resource of expert teachers *within* the schools, by creating time and regular opportunities for peer coaching and collaborative learning.

Career ladder models may provide an important support for this work by recognizing, developing, and rewarding teacher expertise and providing differentiated responsibilities for accomplished teachers that feed directly back into school improvement. Existing compensation systems in teaching create a career pathway that places classroom teaching at the bottom, provides teachers with little influence in making key education decisions, and requires teachers to leave the classroom if they want greater responsibility or substantially higher pay. The message is clear: Those who work with children have the lowest status; those who do not have the highest.

A new career continuum would place teaching at the top and create a career progression that supports teachers as they become increasingly expert. Like the path from assistant professor to full professor in universities—or junior associate to partner in law firms—new pathways should recognize skill and accomplishment, enable professionals to take on roles that allow them to share their knowledge, and promote increased skill development and expertise across the profession.

Although there are indications that states, districts, and teacher associations are ready to explore changes in the single salary schedule and move beyond the factory model assumptions that teachers are merely standardized "widgets,"[50] it is important to recognize that efforts to change teacher compensation have failed many times before. Performance pay plans came and went in the 1920s, the 1950s, and, most recently, in the 1980s, when 47 states introduced versions of performance pay, all of which were gone by the early 1990s. The reasons for failure have included faulty evaluation systems, concerns about bias and discrimination, strategies that singled out individual teachers and undermined collaboration, declining morale, lack of evidence of positive effects, and lack of public will to continue increased compensation. Some newer efforts have also crashed; for example, Florida's merit pay plan, introduced by Governor Jeb Bush, paid teachers based on student test scores. The program was shanghaied by its attachment to an unpopular testing system and was viewed as unfair to teachers working in high-need schools. Some teachers burned their merit paychecks publicly before the program was repealed in the face of widespread public dissatisfaction in 2007.[51]

Merit pay that singles out individual teachers for annual bonuses has been especially problematic: It creates temporary rewards that do little for long-term salaries or retention, and has been found to be demotivating to most teachers—both to those who fail to receive it and to those who receive it one year and not the next.

Many teachers report feeling insulted by the idea that they would only work hard for children in the face of what they see as a bribe. By encouraging competition rather than collaboration, individual merit pay bonuses do little to improve teachers' collective knowledge and skills, even potentially reducing learning by discouraging sharing of ideas, lessons, and materials. As *Washington Post* writer Jay Mathews noted, leaders of effective schools are wary of the concept because "their staffs thrive on teamwork. Everyone shares lesson plans, swaps ideas and reinforces discipline to help each child." They worry that big checks to just a few members of the staff could ruin that collaboration and sense of the team.[52]

These findings mirror what researchers who look at private industry have found: Pay is generally less important for motivating employees than are well-run collegial settings, opportunities to learn, and the intrinsic rewards of becoming efficacious at one's work. Although bonuses are sometimes used in the private sector, merit pay "represent(s) a very small share of overall compensation and is generally not explicitly tied to simple measures of output."[53]

In education, innovative plans that have lasted for more than a few years have been those that allow teachers to gain greater responsibility and compensation as they gain and share expertise, which fit better with the communitarian culture of teaching. These plans build in collegial learning and allow teachers to contribute to improvement by coaching their colleagues, developing curriculum, and leading school improvement. They ensure that new teachers get support and mentoring, that all teachers get professional learning opportunities, and that teachers who demonstrate accomplished practice can advance in terms of roles and compensation without artificial quotas.

These initiatives—ranging from career ladders in cities such as Denver, Cincinnati, and Rochester to state plans in places such as Arizona and New Mexico to national models such as the Teacher Advancement Program—generally have several features in common. All combine regular, intensive evaluation based on professional teaching standards with opportunities for professional learning and advancement. Typically, serious judgments about competence—often with sizable increases in compensation—occur at several junctures as teachers move from their initial license, through a period as a novice or resident teacher under the supervision of a mentor, to designation as professional teacher after successfully passing an assessment of teaching skills. Tenure is a major step tied to a serious decision made after rigorous evaluation of performance in the first several years of teaching, incorporating administrator and peer review by expert colleagues. Lead or master teacher status—which triggers additional compensation and access to differentiated roles—may be determined by advanced certification from the National Board for Professional Teaching Standards or other evidence of performance through standards-based evaluation systems, which typically include evidence about contributions to student learning.

Multiple measures of practice and student outcomes are used for evaluation, including systematic collection of evidence about teacher planning and instruction, work with parents and students, and contributions to the school; performance on teaching assessments such as the National Board or local standards-based instruments; and contributions to student learning from classroom assessments and documentation about student performance, growth, and accomplishments, as well as standardized test evidence, when appropriate. Evaluations trigger continuous goal-setting for areas teachers want to work on, specific professional development supports and coaching, as well as recognition and compensation. Good systems are designed so that teachers are not penalized for teaching the students who have the greatest educational needs. They explicitly seek to provide incentives that recognize and reward teachers who work with challenging students.

A career continuum based on standards of professional practice must also remove individuals from the profession when they do not, after receiving assistance, meet professional standards. In some school districts, career pathways have incorporated peer review and assistance from lead teachers who provide intensive support for beginning teachers and for veterans who are having difficulty. These systems—collaborations between unions and school boards that build in due process—have proven more effective than traditional evaluation systems at both effectively improving and efficiently dismissing teachers without union grievances. (See Chapter 7.)

The best systems create high-quality professional learning opportunities, including time for teachers to work and learn together during the school day. New approaches could include additional incentives for teachers recognized as accomplished to take on mentor and master teacher roles in high-need schools, and even, as part of a group of teachers, to take on redesigning and reconstituting failing schools so that they become more effective.

Combining Incentives with Teacher Learning and School Improvement

The combination of professional learning, support, and incentives is critical to improving school performance. Indeed, getting good teachers and leaders to restructure high-need schools—and developing greater competence from within, with strong leadership and coaching support—has been found repeatedly to be more effective than offering bonuses for teachers to go to dysfunctional schools that are structured to remain that way. One recent summary of the literature notes:

(S)chool districts have tried offering additional pay for high-needs schools without much positive result, even when substantial bonuses are awarded. In 2004, Palm

Beach, Florida eliminated its $7,500 high-needs school stipend after few teachers took the offer. Dallas's offer of $6,000 to accomplished teachers to move to challenging schools also failed to generate much interest. . . . A decade ago, South Carolina set out to recruit "teacher specialists" to work in the state's weakest schools. Despite the offer of an $18,000 bonus, the state attracted only 20 percent of the 500 teachers they needed in the first year of the program, and only 40 percent after three years.[54]

Although money can help, teachers are primarily attracted by principals who are good instructional leaders, by like-minded colleagues who are committed to the same goals, by having the instructional materials they need readily available, and by having learning supports that enable them to be efficacious. A recent poll by the Public Agenda Foundation found that almost 80% of teachers would choose to teach in a school where administrators supported them, as opposed to only about 20% at one where there were significantly higher salaries.[55] As one National Board Certified teacher noted in a discussion of what would attract him to a high-needs school:

I would move [to a low-performing school], but I would want to see social services for parents and children, accomplished leadership, adequate resources and facilities, and flexibility, freedom and time. . . . One of the single greatest factors in school success is principal leadership. Effective administrators are magnets for accomplished teachers. In addition, it is amazing to me that attention is being paid to teaching quality in hard-to-staff schools when little is done to address the sometimes appalling conditions in which teachers are forced to work and students are forced to learn. . . . Finally, as an accomplished teacher, my greatest fear is being assigned to a hard-to-staff school and not being given the time and the flexibility to make the changes that I believe are necessary to bring about student achievement.[56]

Transforming schools so that they can recruit good teachers and support strong learning requires attention to all of these factors and more. A good case in point is the turnaround story of nine of Tennessee's lowest-performing schools in Chattanooga's Hamilton County School District where, on average, only 12% of third graders could read at grade level at the start of the initiative. With the help of the Benwood Foundation and the Public Education Foundation, a comprehensive strategy was forged, which began with but was not limited to financial incentives.

Bonuses of $5,000 were offered to recruit teachers with high value-added student scores to the nine schools. Some of these teachers were willing to transfer, but not nearly enough. For those who did, the greater attraction was often the opportunity to work with visionary principals and to engage in collegial professional learning communities. The school district replaced many of the previous principals, created a leadership program for teachers, and funded teacher-coaches, while transforming professional development from one-shot workshops to job-embedded activities led by teachers. Teachers were also supported to pursue a specialized master's degree in urban education.

This comprehensive support raised 3rd-grade reading proficiency levels to 74% and 5th-grade scores to 80% of students by 2005. Comparable improvements occurred in math. At the end of the day, it turned out that the largest student gains were produced not by the teachers who had been imported with bonuses but by existing staff who had become much more effective. An Education Sector report concluded: "The Benwood Initiative was about much more than pay incentives and reconstitution; the district invested heavily in programs to train teachers, in additional staff to support curriculum and instruction, and in stronger and more collaborative leadership at the school level."[57]

Similarly, the turnaround from failure to success at Mitchell Elementary School in Phoenix relied on the use of incentives as learning supports, rather than bonuses. The strategy was to grow teacher expertise from within through an intensive commitment to the National Board certification process, which can earn teachers greater compensation, while also strengthening their skills. In this low-income Latino community where most students are English language learners, more than 60% of the teachers—most of whom are from the community and reflect their student population—are either National Board Certified or in the process of earning certification. Not only has the school's achievement dramatically improved, but teacher turnover is no longer a problem.[58] Mitchell teachers claim that the National Board process has transformed the school, as they have worked collectively to better understand their teaching as it directly impacts student achievement, focusing in on teaching students with special needs, among other critical areas. As district associate superintendent Suzanne Zentner noted, "We believe in the National Board Certification process as an alternative approach to improving student performance and closing the achievement gaps."[59]

The experiences of Mitchell Elementary and other improving schools illustrate the claims of organizational experts such as W. Edwards Deming and Peter Senge: that organizational learning is created by developing and sharing knowledge widely among employees about the nature of the work and its outcomes, developing teams that can collaborate effectively, collecting and using information to inform decisions, and engaging in an ongoing learning process to be ever more diagnostic and responsive to clients and changing needs.[60]

Developing Leadership

Educational leaders who understand how to create effective, equitable learning for students, teachers, and organizations are central to this kind of inside-out school improvement. Indeed, the quality of school-level leaders and the specific practices in which they engage are second only to teachers' influence in predicting student achievement.[61] Their work enables teachers to be effective—as it is not just the traits that teachers bring but their ability to use what they know in a high-functioning organization that produces student success. As we have seen, the number-one reason for teachers' decisions about whether to go to or stay in a school is the quality of administrative support.

Despite the obvious importance of school leaders and growing reports of shortages, especially in urban areas,[62] only a few states and districts have developed pathways to recruit dynamic teacher leaders into high-quality training programs for the principalship. Although some initiatives have been extremely successful in transforming the quality of leadership and the performance of schools,[63] they are not yet supported by stable policies to ensure a strong supply of able leaders, especially in the communities where they are most needed. Furthermore, these leaders need to know how to design and create the schools of the future, not just administer the schools of the past. This is a new mission for leadership development that will require dramatic changes in past practices, which have often offered intellectually weak programs, disconnected from the practical work of school reform, to whomever shows up for a credential program.

To develop visionary and effective leadership on a wide scale, state and local career ladders should include pathways for a subset of expert teachers to receive high-quality training for roles as principals, as well as mentors and curriculum leaders, as nations like Singapore do (see Chapter 6). In addition, the federal government should offer matching grant funding and technical assistance to states to develop competitive service scholarship programs, like the North Carolina Principal Fellows program (see Chapter 5), and high-quality program models that proactively recruit talented candidates who combine teaching expertise and leadership potential and who want to work in high-need communities. In exchange for at least 4 years of leadership service in public schools, the initiative would underwrite the cost of a full-year internship under the wing of an expert principal who has succeeding in reforming schools in high-need communities, while the prospective principals are studying instructional leadership, organizational improvement, and change management in high-quality programs tightly connected to schools.

As in teaching, these programs—and the credentialing decision—should be guided by rigorous performance assessments like those developed in Connecticut (see Chapter 5) that ascertain that principals know how to evaluate teaching, organize professional development, and manage school improvement. The federal government should support the development of a nationally available administrator performance assessment that can set a high bar for essential knowledge and skills, facilitate a national labor market for excellent principals, and leverage major program improvements.

To develop knowledge and set a standard for developing a cadre of expert leaders who know how to develop quality teaching and schooling in diverse communities, the federal government should join hands with private philanthropists to create a West Point for educational leaders—a National Leadership Academy where the most talented educators in the country can be developed into top leaders, capable of leading reform in the highest-need communities, and deployed both to turning around struggling schools and systems, and later to becoming the coaches and trainers of the next generation of principals and superintendents.

Federal challenge grants should also be available to create and further enhance State Leadership Academies in every state. These academies, located in universities, state agencies, or nonprofit organizations, can serve as centers where each state's top educational leaders gather to share practices and help create and coordinate the professional development infrastructure in their states. Like existing successful academies, these can serve as hubs to develop institutes, coaching and mentoring supports, and principal and superintendent networks that address the unique challenges encountered by leaders in diverse kinds of schools. The federal government should also launch a line of research about the effectiveness of these various approaches to leadership development so that future investments can be guided by evidence about what best supports leaders' capacities to develop high-performing school organizations.

SCHOOLS ORGANIZED FOR
STUDENT AND TEACHER LEARNING

Finally, leaders will need the vision, capacity, and policy support to create much more productive schools. Schools have to be places that support good teaching, and the work that students and teachers are asked to do needs to be work worth doing. As we have seen, instead of the isolated, egg-crate classrooms offered by the factory-model schools developed in the United States, schools in most other high-achieving countries ensure that teachers have time for collaboration, collective planning, lesson study, peer coaching, developing curriculum and assessments, and joint examination of student work. In addition to working in teams so that they can be more effective, these teachers generally stay with their students for longer blocks of time, so that they come to know their learners well. They also engage in teaching and assessment that requires and enables students to construct and organize knowledge, consider alternatives, apply what they are learning, use new technologies, and present and defend their ideas, supporting powerful learning that is reinforced across the school.

As described in Chapter 8, U.S. schools that have been redesigned around these principles have been more successful, especially with high-need students for whom a personalized, intellectually challenging, and meaningful experience at school is most essential if they are to succeed. Such schools are also much more able to attract and retain well-qualified teachers, as they are satisfying places to learn and work. Ultimately, teachers and students want most of all to be efficacious, which is why supportive teaching and learning conditions are so important to retention and, ultimately, effectiveness for both.

In high-need communities, redesign efforts should also enable schools to meet the challenges they face in serving their students and families.[64] Initiatives like the Harlem Children's Zone offer not only new approaches to schools for students in low-income communities, but also to the integration of early childhood education, parent education, social services, and health care as well.[65] Community Schools, like those developed by the Children's Aid Society, and new schools initiatives, like New York City's Julia Richman Education Complex (see Chapter 8), have been successful by creating strong schools with wraparound services in many communities. In Ohio, the Knowledge Works Foundation, in collaboration with the superintendents and teacher union presidents from the eight largest urban school districts, has sought to create full-service schools, or Hubs that "create a fully aligned P–20 education system, from prenatal care for mothers, to baby colleges for prospective parents, to early childhood education through college and workforce development, along with lifelong learning opportunities for everyone in the community."[66]

The challenge of getting to scale with good educational practice[67] is one of developing widespread educational leadership and expert teaching, on the one hand, and encouraging the design of effective organizations on a system-wide scale, on the other. In addition to the human capital investments described above, at least three major levers are needed:

First, states and districts both should encourage more productive school designs as a general rule, rather than as exceptions to the rule, and remove current barriers to these changes. Current school organizations are a highly institutionalized vestige of the 1920s Taylor model of management, in which roles are fragmented and highly specialized, hierarchies are long, staff work in silos, and many resources are spent on nonteaching staff to run or support a plethora of programs, rather than on the core work of classroom teaching. Changing this will require changes in policy as well as practice. States need to unearth the geological dig of regulations that hold current designs in place, and systematically remove obstacles to new approaches, ranging from categorical programs and other mandates prescribing staffing patterns and specific instructional approaches, to Carnegie units and seat time requirements, to specifications for the design of facilities and roles that keep the egg-crate classroom and the assembly-line model firmly in place.

To achieve more personalized school settings in which students do not fall through the cracks and teachers have adequate time to create strong instruction together, states and districts must also flatten administrative hierarchies and restructure time and staffing so that teachers have regular time to work with one another in every school—at least 10 hours a week for joint planning and collaborative learning (which is two to three times what most U.S. teachers now have available, but only half of the time set aside for most teachers abroad). This will require more focused investments in teachers: Most high-achieving nations invest 70% or more of their staff resources in teachers. We should aim for no less. These commitments should be accompanied by investments in technology that extend the capacity of every teacher and child to connect with an infinite variety of resources and tools for learning, and in new assessment systems that value students' abilities to use these tools to solve real-world problems.

Second, federal and state governments can sponsor research and offer incentives for the development and dissemination of effective school designs, as well as for the development of more productive ways of organizing districts to support schools. Initiatives like Maine's Innovative Educational Grants, Iowa's School Improvement Program, and Ohio's Venture Capital Fund have triggered reforms by supporting staff learning aimed explicitly at systemic change. Successful incentives have offered funding for staffs to evaluate both their own organizations and to examine successful models elsewhere in order to plan strategic changes with help from the top in clearing the regulatory brush and providing professional development resources. Governments can also award grants to successful schools to further develop, document, and share their practices with others.

It is critical to remember, too, that effective strategies can travel only if the receiving organizations have both the freedom and the capacity to incorporate new practices. Many innovative initiatives are doomed to marginalization where they exist in a protected waiver zone—as many charters and alternative schools do—while the rest of the system is increasingly overregulated, held in a stranglehold that prevents schools from adopting the practices that are successful elsewhere. Thus, policymakers need to take responsibility for their role in creating a context that enables the adoption of successful practices throughout the system.

Finally, to transform systems, incentives must be structured to promote collaboration and knowledge-sharing across organizations, rather than competition. This is needed to develop not only learning organizations but a learning-oriented system of education. This has been the primary strategy for improvement in Finland, where ongoing evaluation and inquiry into practice are stimulated within and across classrooms, across schools partnered within regions, and within the system as a whole (see Chapter 6).

Also key is the creation of networks that allow teachers, leaders, schools, and districts to learn from one another, like those described in Chapters 7 and 8. Andy Hargreaves describes an initiative in England in which 300 schools that were declining in performance were networked with one another, provided with technical assistance and support from mentor schools, and given a small discretionary budget that they could spend to support their efforts. Schools were also given a practitioner-generated list of strategies that had produced short-, medium-, and long-range improvements. More than two-thirds of these "exceptionally energized" schools experienced gains over the next 2 years at rates double the national average, "without," the researchers noted, "the characteristic mandates and prescriptions that had characterized English reforms before this point."[68] An initiative in Ontario, Canada, used similar school-to-school networking strategies and leveraged them further by identifying positive exemplars that schools could visit to see what successful reforms looked like in action. Hargreaves notes, "Lateral support across schools is wedded to positive peer pressure as schools push each other to higher and higher standards of performance."[69]

Although it would be romantic to assume that massive change can come exclusively from school-to-school networking, the power of learning systems has proven to be stronger than the power of mandates to transform schools. As Milbrey McLaughlin has noted, governments cannot mandate what matters most.[70] Organizations cannot be flogged into excellence. Both top-down support and bottom-up reform are needed, orchestrated in a call-and-response that builds capacity by providing resources and leveraging genuine accountability for student learning.

CONCLUSION

Creating schools that enable all children to learn requires the development of systems that enable all educators and schools to learn. At heart, this is a capacity-building enterprise leveraged by clear, meaningful learning goals and intelligent, reciprocal accountability systems that guarantee skillful teaching in well-designed, adequately resourced schools for all learners. It is not only possible but imperative that America close the achievement gap among its children by addressing the yawning opportunity gap that denies these fundamental rights. Given the critical importance of education for individual and societal success in the flat world we now inhabit, inequality in the provision of education is an antiquated tradition the United States can no longer afford. If "no child left behind" is to be anything more than empty rhetoric, we will need a policy strategy that creates a 21st-century curriculum for all students and supports it with thoughtful assessments, access to knowledgeable, well-supported teachers, and equal access to school resources.

For the United States to make progress on its long-standing inequalities, we will need to make the case to one another that none of us benefits by keeping any of us ignorant, and, as a society, all of us profit from the full development of one another's abilities. As Martin Luther King observed in 1968:

> I said to my children, "I'm going to work and do everything that I can do to see that you get a good education. I don't ever want you to forget that there are millions of God's children who will not and cannot get a good education, and I don't want you feeling that you are better than they are. For you will never be what you ought to be until they are what they ought to be."[71]

Now more than ever, high-quality education for all is a public good that is essential for the good of the public. Smart, equitable investments will, in the long run, save far more than they cost. The savings will include the more than $200 billion we now lose in wages, taxes, and social costs annually due to dropouts; the $50 billion we pay for lost wages and prison costs for incarceration tied to illiteracy and school failure; and the many tens of billions wasted each year on reforms that fail, fads that don't stick, unnecessary teacher turnover, avoidable special education placements, remedial education, grade retention, summer school, lost productivity, and jobs that move overseas.[72]

As the fate of individuals and nations is increasingly interdependent, the quest for access to an equitable, empowering education for all people has become a critical issue for the American nation as a whole. As a country, we can and must enter a new era. No society can thrive in a technological, knowledge-based economy by depriving large segments of its population of learning. The path to our mutual well-being is built on educational opportunity. Central to our collective future is the recognition that our capacity to survive and thrive ultimately depends on ensuring to all of our people what should be an unquestioned entitlement—a rich and inalienable right to learn.

Notes

Chapter 1

1. Drucker (1994); Wagner (2008).
2. U.S. Department of Labor (2006).
3. Gunderson, Jones, & Scanland (2004).
4. Douglas (2006); OECD (2008).
5. U.S. Census Bureau (2008).
6. Prison nation (2008).
7. Darling-Hammond & Schnur (2008).
8. Friedman (2005).
9. Karmarkar & Apte (2007) and Apte, Karmarkar, & Nath (2008), cited in Partnership for 21st Century Skills (2008), p. 2.
10. Varian & Lyman (2003).
11. Jukes & McCain (2002).
12. Tyack (1974).
13. Finnish National Board of Education (2007, November 12); Lavonen, (2008).
14. Sahlberg (2009).
15. OECD (2006).
16. Borja (2004).
17. http://nces.ed.gov/timss/TIMSS03Tables.asp?Quest=3&Figure=5
18. Singapore Ministry of Education (2007).
19. Nan Chiau Primary School (2007).
20. *Williams et al. v. State of California* (2000), pp. 22–23.
21. Organisation for Economic Co-operation and Development (2007).
22. Stage (2005).
23. Stage (2005).
24. OECD (2007). Vol. 1, pp. 180–191; chart p. 184. Vol 2, pp 123–124; and U.S. Country note briefings. Retrieved on 3/31/08 from http://www.oecd.org/dataoecd/16/28/39722597.pdf.
25. ETS (1991); Kozol (2005).
26. For a recent summary of the research on mathematics teaching, see Schoenfeld (2008).
27. Stigler & Hiebert (1999); Stevenson, 1992.
28. Schmidt, Wang, & McKnight (2005).
29. Stigler & Hiebert (1999); see also Tsuneyoshi (2005).
30. Mullis et al. (2007).
31. Kate Walsh (2001) has argued, for example, against Maryland's requirements for preparation to teach reading as a barrier to entry for alternatively certified candidates.
32. Gamse et al. (2008).
33. Organisation for Economic Cooperation and Development (2008).
34. Barton (2005).
35. Douglass (2006).
36. Organisation for Economic Cooperation and Development (2008).
37. Douglass (2006); U.S. Bureau of the Census (2005); KEDI (2006).
38. U.S. Census Bureau, Ibid.
39. Orfield (2001).
40. Kozol (2005).
41. Organisation for Economic Cooperation and Development (2007).
42. OECD (2005).
43. "Boost value of Pell grants" (2006).
44. National Science Foundation (2008).
45. Krieger (2008), p. 15A.
46. Oakes (2004).
47. U.S. Bureau of the Census (2006).
48. National Center for Education Statistics (2004).
49. Kozol (1991), pp. 63–65.
50. Metz (1990); Orfield & Lee (2005); Rothstein (2004).
51. Kozol (2005), pp. 321–324.
52. ETS (1991); Kozol (2005).
53. Darling-Hammond (2004a).
54. Oakes (2004).
55. Kozol (1991), p. 104.
56. Kozol (1991), p. 104.
57. Bureau of Labor Statistics (2009), Table 6.
58. Barton & Coley.
59. Gemignani (1994).
60. Bonstingl (2004).
61. U.S. Bureau of the Census (1996), table numbers 281 and 354, pp. 181 and 221.
62. Pew Center on the States (2008).
63. Western, Schiraldi, & Ziedenberg, (2003).
64. Pew Center on the States (2008), pp. 15–16.

65. Schweinhard et al. (2005).
66. Pew Center on the States (2008), p. 16.
67. Rumberger (2007) estimates costs due to dropouts of $46.8 billion for California, which represents approximately 10% of the nation's population. Estimates from Belfield & Levin (2007), p. 194, place costs from lost wages and taxes, crime, and welfare for each cohort of dropouts at $147 billion. Levin, by personal communication, indicates that a complete tallying of economic costs would exceed $200 billion annually.

Chapter 2

1. Jefferson (1786; 1817).
2. DuBois ([1949], 1970), pp. 230–231.
3. Darling-Hammond, Williamson, & Hyler (2007).
4. Ladson-Billings (2006).
5. Cremin (1970), pp. 411–412.
6. Tyack (1974), pp. 109–125; Kluger (1976); Meier, Stewart, & England (1989); Schofield (1992).
7. Tyack (1974). p. 110.
8. Tyack (1974), p. 119.
9. Conant (1961).
10. Kozol (1991), p. 225.
11. New America Foundation (2008). Data are from the U.S. Census Bureau Annual Survey of Government Finances for the 2003–04 school year.
12. Liu (2003).
13. See, for example, Herrnstein & Murray (1994).
14. DeNavas-Walt, Proctor, & Lee (2005); U.S. Census Bureau (2006).
15. Bell, Bernstein, & Greenberg (2008); Corak (2005).
16. U.S. Department of Agriculture (2004).
17. Neault, Cook, Morris, & Frank (2005).
18. Children's Sentinel Nutrition Assessment Program (C-SNAP) (2004, July).
19. U.S. Conference of Mayors (2004).
20. Census Bureau (2006), p. 25.
21. UNICEF (2001), p. 3.
22. Zigler, Gilliam, and Jones (2006), p. 23.
23. See, e.g., Hart & Risley, 1995.
24. Denton & West (2002).
25. Heckman (2008), p. 49.
26. Heckman (2008), pp. 52, 53.
27. Reynolds & Temple (2006), p. 50.
28. Bueno, Darling-Hammond, & Gonzales (2009).
29. Children's Defense Fund calculations based on data from U.S. Census Bureau (June 2001).
30. Children's Defense Fund calculations, based on data from U.S. Bureau of the Census (2001)
31. Heckman (2008), p. 52.
32. Rumberger & Palardy (2005).
33. Schofield (1995), p. 336.
34. Orfield, Monfort, & Aaron (1989), cited in Schofield (1995), p. 336.
35. Clotfelter, Ladd, & Vigdor (2005).
36. *Parents Involved in Community Schools v. Seattle School District No. 1 and Meredith v. Jefferson County Board of Education* (2007).
37. American Educational Research Association (2006).
38. Orfield (2001).
39. James Coleman et al. (1966), p. 325. For a recent review of this evidence, see Richard Kahlenberg (2001).
40. National Center for Education Statistics (2003), p. 11.
41. Rumberger & Palardy, 2005.
42. Schofield (1995); Anyon (1997); Dawkins & Braddock (1994); Natriello & McDill (1990).
43. Lee (2004); Horn (2002).
44. Garofano, Sable, & Hoffman (2008).
45. Silard & Goldstein (1974), p. 324.
46. Kaufman & Rosenbaum (1992).
47. Roza & Hill (2004).
48. Education Trust-West (2005).
49. New America Foundation (2008b).
50. Kozol, 2005, pp. 142–145.
51. Mont & Rees (1996); Loeb, Darling-Hammond, & Luczak (2005).
52. *Rodriguez et al. v. Los Angeles Unified School District* (1992).
53. Shields et al. (2001).
54. Merrow (1999).
55. Darling-Hammond (2004).
56. Analyses of teacher distribution data conducted by the author.
57. NCES (1997); Lankford, Loeb, & Wyckoff (2002).
58. Oakes (1990).

59. Haycock (2000), p. 11.
60. See, e.g., Betts, Reuben, & Dannenberg (2000); Boyd et al. (2006); Clotfelter, Ladd & Vigdor, (2007); Darling-Hammond (2000); Darling-Hammond, Holtzman, Gatlin, & Heilig (2005); Ferguson (1991); Felter (1999); Goe (2002); Hawk, Coble, & Swanson (1985); Goldhaber & Brewer (2000); Monk (1994); Strauss & Sawyer (1986).
61. Motoko Akiba, Gerald LeTendre & Jay Scribner (2007).
62. Clotfelter, Ladd, & Vigdor (2007).
63. Boys, Lankford, Loeb, Rockoff, & Wyckoff (2008).
64. See, for example, National Commission on Teaching and America's Future (1996).
65. NCTAF (1996).
66. Constantine et al. (2009).
67. Darling-Hammond (2009).
68. Boyd, Grossman, Lankford, Loeb, & Wyckoff (2006); Darling-Hammond, Holtzman, Gatlin, & Heilig (2005); Kane, Rockoff, & Staiger (2006).
69. Laczko-Kerr & Berliner (2002); Darling-Hammond et al. (2005).
70. Henke et al. (2000).
71. National Commission on Teaching for America's Future (2003).
72. Shapiro, Who will teach for America?
73. Hegarty (2001).
74. Darling-Hammond (2003), p. 128.
75. Sanders and Rivers (1996).
76. Betts, Reuben, & Dannenberg (2000); Darling-Hammond (2000); Fetler (1999); Fuller (1998, 2000); Goe (2002); Strauss & Sawyer (1986).
77. Shields et al. (2001).
78. Dreeben (1987), p. 34.
79. College Board (1985); Pelavin & Kane, (1990); Oakes (2005).
80. Oakes et al. (2006).
81. California Postsecondary Education Commission (2007).
82. Oakes (1992).
83. Pelavin & Kane (1990).
84. Korea Institute of Curriculum & Evaluation (2006); Stevenson & Lee (1998); Eckstein & Noah (1993).
85. Cubberley (1909), pp. 15–16, 18–19.
86. Terman et al. (1922), pp. 27–28.
87. Pillsbury (1921), p. 71.
88. McKnight et al. (1987); Usem (1990); Wheelock (1992).
89. Wagner (2008), p. 8.
90. Alexander & McDill (1976); Gamoran (1990); Gamoran & Berends (1987); Gamoran & Hannigan (2000); Gamoran & Mare (1989); Oakes (1985, 1990).
91. Peterson (1989), cited in Levin (1992).
92. Oakes, 2005, pp. 236–238; see also Hallinan & Kubitschek (1999).
93. Resnick (1987); Braddock & McPartland (1993); Garcia (1993); Wenglinsky (2002).
94. Eckstrom & Villegas (1991); Oakes (2005).
95. Good & Brophy (1987).
96. Oakes (2005); Cooper & Sherk (1989).
97. Oakes (2005), pp. 80–83.
98. Oakes (2005), pp. 86–89.
99. Haycock (2000), p. 1.
100. Kozol (1991), p. 97.
101. Fine (2002).
102. Gamoran (1992); Oakes (1992); Useem (1990); Mickelson (2001).
103. Oakes (1993).
104. Oakes (2005); Hoffer (1992); Kulik & Kulik (1982); Slavin (1990).
105. Oakes (1986); Finley (1984); Talbert (1990); NCTAF (1996).
106. Olsen (1997), pp. 156–157.
107. Olsen (1997), p. 167.
118. Dewey (1916), p. 87.
109. Dewey (1916), p. 84.
110. Darling-Hammond (1997).
111. Carrajat (1996).
112. Poplin & Weeres (1992), p. 11.
113. Poplin & Weeres (1992), p. 23.
114. Poplin & Weeres (1992), pp. 21–22.
115. For a review, see Darling-Hammond, Ross, & Milliken (2007).
116. Darling-Hammond, Ancess, & Ort (2002); Fine (1994); Fine, Stoudt, & Futch (2005); Howley & Harmon (2000); Wasley et al. (2000).
117. Darling-Hammond, Ross, & Milliken (2007).
118. Irvine (1990).
119. Fine (1991); Nieto (1992); Carter & Goodwin (1994).
120. Fordham (1988); Spring (1997).
121. Blackwell, Trzesniewski, & Dweck (2007).
122. Steele, Spencer, & Aronson (2003).

Chapter 3

1. Wolfe (1987, pp. 130–131), quoted in Madaus, Russell, & Higgins (2009).
2. Vasquez Heilig & Darling-Hammond (2008).
3. Wald & Losen (2003).
4. O'Day and Smith (1993).
5. DeBard & Kubow (2002); Ladd & Zelli (2002); Woody et al. (2004).
6. Herman et al. (2000), see also reviews by Linn (2000); Shepard (2000).
7. For a discussion of several of these states' approaches, see Darling-Hammond (2000; 2004a).
8. For a review see Darling-Hammond & Rustique-Forrester (2005).
9. See, for example, Darling-Hammond & Ancess (1994); Falk & Ort (1997); Goldberg & Rosewell (2000); Murnane & Levy (1996).
10. See, for example, Madaus et al. (1992).
11. Newmann, Marks, & Gamoran (1995)
12. Lee, Smith, & Croninger (1995).
13. Darling-Hammond, Barron, et al. (2008).
14. Darling-Hammond, (2000).
15. Baron (1999); National Education Goals Panel (1999); see also Wilson, Darling-Hammond, & Berry (2001).
16. Bransford, Cocking, & Brown, *How people learn* (1999).
17. Herman (2002) notes
18. Darling-Hammond (2004).
19. Klein et al. (2000); Koretz & Barron (1998); Koretz, Barron, et al. (1996); Koretz et al. (1991); Linn (2000); Linn, Graue, & Sanders (1990); Stecher et al. (2000).
20. Brown (1992); Haney (2000); Jones et al. (1999); Jones & Egley (2004); Popham (1999); Smith (1991).
21. Center on Education Policy (2007).
22. *Education Week* (2001).
23. Hoffman, Assaf, & Paris, 2001.
24. Pedulla et al. (2003).
25. Russell & Abrams (2004).
26. Pedulla et al. (2003).
27. Southeast Center for Teaching Quality (2003), p. 15.
28. McKnight et al. (1987).
29. Amrein & Berliner (2002); Klein, Hamilton, McCaffrey, & Stecher (2000).

30. Haney (2000), part 6, p. 10.
31. Koretz, Mitchell, Barron, & Keith (1996); Stecher et al. (1998).
32. Pedulla et al. (2003).
33. Corbett & Wilson (1991); Firestone & Mayrowetz (2000); Anagnostopoulous (2003).
34. Jennifer O'Day (2002), p. 5.
35. NCEST (1992), pp. E12–E13.
36. Wald & Losen (2003).
37. Griffin & Heidorn (1996); Orfield & Ashkinaze (1991); Haney (2000); Vasquez Heilig & Darling-Hammond (2008); Jacob (2002).
38. Center on Education Policy (2004).
39. Carnoy and Loeb (2002).
40. Hanushek & Raymond (2003).
41. Lee & Wong (2004).
42. Amrein & Berliner (2002, 2003).
43. Lilliard & DeCicca (2001); Clarke, Haney, & Madaus (2000); Roderick (1999); Wheelock (2003).
44. Jacobs (2001).
45. Roderick, Bryk, Jacob, Easton, & Allensworth (1999).
46. Roderick et al. (1999), pp. 55–56.
47. Roderick et al. (1999), p. 57.
48. New York City Division of Assessment and Accountability (2001).
49. Wasserman (1999).
50. New York City Division of Assessment and Accountability (2001), p. 1.
51. Advocates for Children, 2002.
52. Arenson (2004).
53. High School Graduates 1997–98 as a percentage of average enrollment grades 7 to 9 1994–95 in the 100 largest districts. National Center for Education Statistics (1998).
54. Orfield and Ashkinaze (1991), p. 139.
55. Heubert & Hauser (1999). For additional reviews, see Baenen (1988); Holmes & Matthews (1984); Illinois Fair Schools Coalition (1985); Labaree (1984); Meisels (1992); Oakes & Lipton (1990); Ostrowski (1987); Shephard & Smith (1986).
56. Rumberger & Larson (1998); see also Jimerson, Anderson, & Whipple (2002); Hess (1986); Hess, Ells, Prindle, Liffman, & Kaplan (1987); Safer (1986); Smith & Shepard (1987).

57. Hauser (1999), p. 3.
58. Smith & Shepard (1987).
59. NCES (2003). After 2001, NCES changed its method of calculating graduation rates, so data now available for 2002 and 2003 cannot be directly compared to the previous years.
60. Becker & Watters (2007).
61. Kozol (2005), p. 282.
62. Noguera (2008), pp. 175–176.
63. Noguera (2008), p. 176.
64. DeVise (1999); Fischer (1999).
65. Clotfelter, Ladd, Vigdor, & Diaz (2004).
66. Clotfleter, Ladd, & Vigdor (2007).
67. Darling-Hammond (2000).
68. Clotfelter, Ladd, Vigdor, & Diaz (2004), p. 272.
69. DeBray, Parson, & Woodworth (2001); Diamond & Spillane (2004); Mintrop (2003); Rustique-Forrester (2005).
70. Rustique-Forrester (2005).
71. Haney (2000); Gordon & Reese (1997); Hoffman et al. (2001); Klein et al. (2000); Stotsky (1998).
72. Klein et al. (2000). A later RAND Corporation study also found a much larger achievement gap on the NAEP than the TAAS tests. See McCombs et al. (2005).
73. Haney (2000); Intercultural Development Research Association (1996).
74. Vasquez Heilig & Darling-Hammond (2008). Colleagues involved in interviews included Elle Rustique-Forrester at Stanford University, and Eileen Coppola, Linda McNeil, and Judy Radigan at Rice University.
75. All quotes from teachers and students in this section are from Vasquez Heilig & Darling-Hammond (2008), pp. 97–99.
76. Texas State Board of Educator Certification data, analyzed by Ed Fuller.
77. Wheelock (2003).
78. Noguera (2008), p. 177.
79. Bernstein (2004).
80. Springfield Education Association (2006).
81. Hancock v. Driscoll (2002), pp. 172–173.

Chapter 4

1. Hanushek (2003), p. 4.
2. *Edgewood v. Kirby* cited in Wise & Gendler (1989), p. 16.
3. Downes & Pogue (1994); Duncombe, Ruggiero, & Yinger (1996).
4. Coleman et al. (1966); cited in Ferguson (1991), p. 467.
5. See, for example, MacPhail-Wilcox & King (1986).
6. See, for example, Darling-Hammond, Ross, & Milliken (2007); Ferguson (1991); Greenwald, Hedges, & Laine (1996); Grissmer et al. (2000); Krueger (2000).
7. *Wall Street Journal,* June 27, 1989, cited in Kozol (1991), p. 133.
8. Hanushek (2003), p. 4.
9. For methodological critiques, see, for example, Greenwald, Hedges, & Laine (1996b); Hedges, Laine, & Greenwald (1994); Kruger (2003); Rebell (2007); Taylor (1997). In addition, courts have raised concerns. In an Alabama fiscal adequacy case, for example, the Court criticized Hanushek's failure to control for "variables that could affect student scores[,] such as race, socio-economic status, and parental education" and failures to use actual rather than average test scores. *Opinion of the Justices,* 624 So. 2d 107, 140 (Ala. 1993). When Hanushek's data were reanalyzed using actual scores "[there was] *a statistically significant positive correlation* between expenditures and achievement." *Id.* at 140 n. 34 (emphasis added).
10. NCES (2000), p. 15.
11. NCES (2000), p. 17.
12. Wise (1979).
13. Wise (1965).
14. *San Antonion Independent School District v. Rodriguez,* 411 U.S. 1 1973.
15. Taylor & Piche (1991), p. 67.
16. Taylor & Piche (1991), pp. xi–xii.
17. McUsic (1991), p. 307.
18. Nelson & Weinbaum (2006), p. 67.
19. See "Bennett Assailed on Education Cuts," *New York Times* (15 January 1987).
20. Ferguson (1991).
21. Ferguson (1991), p. 490.
22. Glass et al. (1982); Walberg (1982); Centra & Potter (1980); Education Research Service (1980).
23. Mosteller (1995); Krueger (2003).
24. Greenwald, Hedges, & Laine (1996a); Darling-Hammond (2000).

25. Greenwald, Hedges, & Laine (1996a).

26. Strauss and Sawyer (1986), p. 47.

27. Levin (2007) estimates the costs per dropout at $209,000 in lost wages and taxes, plus health and social service costs. With at least 1 million dropouts annually, these costs exceed $209 billion per year, before adding incarceration costs of over $50 billion annually. Capriccioso (2005) reports that deficits in basic skills for high school graduates are estimated to cost students, businesses, and colleges up to $16 billion annually for remediation and in loss of productivity.

28. Milanowski & Odden (2007); Benner (2000).

29. Rivkin, Hanushek, & Kain (2000); Kain & Singleton (1996).

30. Benner (2000), p. 2.

31. Vasudeva, Darling-Hammond, Newton, & Montgomery (2009).

32. Fullan (2007); Smith (2008).

33. Luczak, (2004); NCTAF (1996).

34. Baugh & Stone (1982); Brewer (1996); Mont & Rees (1996); Murnane et al. (1989); Theobald (1990); Theobald et al. (1996). Hanushek et al. (1999); Gritz & Theobald (1996).

35. Murnane & Olsen (1990).

36. Loeb, Darling-Hammond, & Luczak (2005).

37. Leithwood, Seashore-Louis, Anderson, & Wahlstrom (2004); Darling-Hammond, Meyerson, LaPointe, & Orr (in press).

38. National Access Network (2009).

39. Card & Payne (2002).

40. Goertz & Weiss (2007); Guryan (2001).

41. Deke (2003).

42. Petition of Harry Briggs (1949).

43. *Abbeville County School District v. State,* 515 S.E.2d 535 (S.C. 1999).

44. http://www/corridorofshame.com/reflections.php

45. Access Quality Education (2008).

46. Guryan (2001), p. 1.

47. Berger & McLynch (2006).

48. *Richland County v. Campbell,* 364 S.E.2d 470 (S.C. 1888).

49. *Abbeville County School District v. State,* 515 S.E.2d 535 (S.C. 1999).

50. Access Quality Education (2008).

51. In South Carolina, African American students are the overwhelming majority of students of color, so "percent African American" is the variable we used. In Massachusetts, there are also relatively large proportions of Hispanic and Asian American students, who are included, along with Native American students, in the "minority" student category. In Massachusetts, we also included the proportion of students whose first language is not English, as there are a substantial number of nonnative English speakers in some districts.

52. School resource data available in Massachusetts were much sparser than those available in South Carolina. One might expect even greater predictive power with a more complete data set.

53. Teachers on substandard certificates include all of those in a variety of certification categories who lack a full standard certificate noting that they have the requisite subject-matter background and teacher training. This variable has a strong positive correlation with students scoring below basic on the state tests. Teachers who are certified but teaching at least part of the time on an "out-of-field" permit are a subset of those on substandard certificates. These are the more qualified individuals in the substandard credential pool, as they have met teacher preparation requirements in one field, but not in every field that they teach. The negative coefficient on this variable means that fewer students score poorly in districts where a greater share of the substandard credentials were granted to already certified teachers.

54. *Flores v. Arizona,* Pet. App. 108a. *Amicus Curiae* Brief of Education Policy Scholars in Support of Petitioners, filed February 26, 2009, p. 3.

55. Brief of education policy scholars as *Amicus Curiae* in support of petitioners in *Horne v. Flores,* filed with U.S. Supreme Court, February 26, 2009.

56. Brief *Amici Curiae* of 30 recognized leaders of education research in support of neither party, filed with U.S. Supreme Court, March 25, 2009.

57. *Horne v. Flores* (2009).
58. NCES (undated).
59. NCES (2007b).
60. NCES (2007a).
61. Anyon (1997), p. 136; Centolanza (1986), p. 524.
62. *Star Ledger*, April 2, 1976.
63. Anyon (1997), p. 136.
64. ETS (1991), p. 9.
65. *Abbott v. Burke*, 1990, 376.
66. *Abbott v. Burke*, 1990, 364.
67. New Jersey State Department of Education (1994b), pp. 43–44, 66. Cited in Jean Anyon (1997), pp. 144–145.
68. Education Trust (1996), p. 143. Cited in Jean Anyon, p. 146.
69. Burns (2003).
70. *Abbott v. Burke*, 748 A.2d 82 (2000) (*Abbott VI*).
71. MacInnes (2009), p. 58.
72. MacInnes (2009), pp. 61–62.
73. Doolan & Peters (2007); see also MacInnes (2009).
74. Bueno, Darling-Hammond, & Gonzales (in press); MacInnes (2009), p. 47.
75. Frede et al. (2007).
76. MacInnes (2009), p. 48.
77. Ryan & Ackerman (2004).
78. MacInnes, p. 68.
79. MacInnes, p. 78.
80. New Jersey Department of Education (2006).

Chapter 5

1. Between 1992 and 2000, for example, Massachusetts Black students' achievement scores on NAEP rose at rates twice those of Whites (18 points v. 8 at the 4th-grade level, and 15 points v. 7 at the 8th-grade level), whereas between 2003 and 2007, Black scores just kept pace for fourth graders and fell much further behind at the 8th-grade level (4 points v. 13 for whites). NAEP Data Explorer, found at http://nces.ed.gov/nationsreportcard/nde/viewresults.asp.
2. In the fall of 1999, Connecticut had 30% students of color, including the 12th-largest Hispanic enrollment in the nation, and in 2002, 36% of students attended Title I schools. In the same years, North Carolina had 38% students of color, including the 8th-largest enrollment of African Americans, and 38% of students attended Title I schools (NCES, 2001, table 42; NAEP State Data, 2002, retrieved from http://nces.ed.gov/nationsreportcard/statedata). In 2007, 34% of students in Connecticut were members of minority groups, as were 43% in North Carolina. NAEP state data, retrieved on 4/1/09 from http://nces.ed.gov/nationsreportcard/states/.
3. National Education Goals Panel (1999).
4. NEGP (1999).
5. Baron (1999).
6. *Horton v. Meskill*, 376 A.2d 359 (1977).
7. *Sheff v. O'Neill*, 678 A.2d 1267 (1996).
8. Baron (1999).
9. Connecticut State Department of Education (1990).
10. Connecticut State Board of Education (1992), p. 3.
11. National Education Goals Panel (1998).
12. NAEP Analysis (2001).
13. Darling-Hammond, Meyerson, LaPointe, & Orr (in press).
14. Darling-Hammond, Meyerson, LaPointe, & Orr (in press).
15. Baron (1999).
16. Baron (1999).
17. Personal communication, 1995.
18. NCTAF (1996).
19. National Education Goals Panel (1998).
20. See for example, Bond, Smith, Baker, & Hattie (2000); Cavaluzzo, L. (2004); Goldhaber & Anthony (2005); Smith, Gordon, Colby, & Wang (2005); Vandevoort, Amrein-Beardsley, & Berliner (2004).
21. See, for example, Haynes (1995); Bradley (1994); Areglado (1999); Buday & Kelly (1996).
22. Clotfelter, Ladd, & Vigdor (2007).
23. Darling-Hammond, Meyerson, LaPointe, & Orr (in press).
24. Darling-Hammond, Meyerson, LaPointe, & Orr (in press).
25. Bryant, Maxwell, Taylor, Poe, Peisner-Feinberg, & Bernier (2003).

26. NAEP Analysis (2001).
27. NAEP Data trends, State profiles. Retrieved on 4/4/09 from http://nces.ed.gov/nationsreportcard/states/.
28. Clotfelter, Ladd, Vigdor, & Diaz (2004).
29. Clotfelter, Ladd, & Vigdor (2007).
30. *Hoke County v. North Carolina* (2004), 95 CVS 1158, pp. 109–110.
31. National Access Network, North Carolina litigation. Retrieved on 4/4/09 from http://www.schoolfunding.info/states/nc/lit_nc.php3.
32. Sonstelie et al. (2000).
33. Merrow (2004).
34. Ed Source (2001), pp. 3, 4, 6.
35. Here and elsewhere, "underqualified" refers to teachers who lack a preliminary or clear credential in their teaching field, the standard credential recognized by the state of California as reflecting full attainment of its standards for beginning and veteran teachers.
36. EdSource (2001).
37. Loeb, Grissom, & Strunk (2007).
38. These figures are from data downloaded on 4/29/03 from the Ed Data website's district fiscal reports. http://www.ed-data.k12.ca.us/Navigation/fsTwoPanel.asp?bottom=%2Fprofile %2Easp %3Flevel %3D06%26reportNumber%3D16.
39. Loeb, Darling-Hammond, & Luczak (2005).
40. Pogodzinski (2000).
41. Shields et al. (2001), p. 37.
42. Shields et al. (2001).
43. Schrag (1999).
44. Sonstelie et al. (2000), pp. 131–137; Carroll et al. (2000).
45. PACE (2000).
46. Rogers (2007)
47. Eddin, Macallair, & Schiraldi (1999).
48. Strupp (2009).
49. The California prison disaster (2008).
50. Baldassare & Hanak (2005), p. 14.
51. Oakes (2003), pp. 13–14.
52. Oakes (2003).
53. Fine (2002), p. 20.
54. Fine (2002), p. 29.
55. Raymond (2003), p. 2.
56. Hanushek (2003), p. 17.
57. Oakes (2003).
58. Betts et al. (2000); Fetler (1999); Goe (2002); Los Angeles County Office of Education (1999).
59. Betts, Rueben, & Dannenberg (2000), p. xxii.
60. The term *aggressive neglect* has been used by Gloria Ladson-Billings (2006) in her discussion of African-American education in New Orleans and other U.S. cities.
61. Analyses conducted by Susanna Loeb, and reported in L. Darling-Hammond (2003b).
62. The state created a set of Cal-T Grants, Governors Fellowships, and APLE loans that made a substantial dent in teacher shortages by enabling candidates to afford preparation and giving them incentives to serve in high-need schools.
63. The Teachers as a Priority Program offered a set of incentives for increasing the share of qualified teachers in low-income schools.
64. Center for the Future of Teaching and Learning (CFTL) (2006).
65. Darling-Hammond (2003a); CFTL (2006).
66. Bohrnstedt & Stecher (2002).
67. Bohrnstedt & Stecher (2002).
68. Darling-Hammond (2003a).
69. Oakes (2003), p. 41.
70. See, for example, Pearson (2004) and Moustaffa & Land (2002) on debates regarding reading curriculum; Schoenfeld (2004) regarding mathematics curriculum; and Woolf (2005) regarding science curriculum.
71. Sciences Education Foundation (2004).
72. Letter to the California State Board of Education (2004).
73. NAEP (2007a), pp. 16, 32.
74. NAEP (2007b), pp. 16, 34, The Nation's Report Card: Reading, 2007.
75. NCES (2006), pp. 16, 28.
76. Oakes (2003), pp. 47–49.
77. Little Hoover Commission (2000), p. vi.
78. Governor's veto message to the legislature, October 10, 1999.
79. Oakes (2003), p. 53.
80. See, for example, Darling-Hammond & Bransford (2005).
81. Gamoran & Berends (1987); Oakes (2005).
82. Lee & Smith (1995); Newmann & Wehlage (1995).

Chapter 6

1. Finland Ministry of Education (2009).
2. Kim (2002), p. 30.
3. Hean (2001).
4. OECD (2007)
5. Sahlberg (2009), p. 2.
6. Statistics Finland (2007).
7. OECD (2007a).
8. Sahlberg (2009); OECD (2001, 2005, 2007b).
9. Sahlberg (2007), p. 49.
10. Foreigners in Finland (2009).
11. Sahlberg (2007), p. 148.
12. Sahlberg (2007), p. 148.
13. Sahlberg (2009), p. 7.
14. Laukkanen (2008), p. 319. See also Buchberger & Buchberger (2003), pp. 222–237.
15. Sahlberg (2009), p. 22.
16. Sahlberg, p. 10.
17. Sahlberg (2007).
18. Eckstein & Noah (1993), p. 84.
19. Sahlberg (2009), p. 20.
20. Sahlberg (2007).
21. The Finnish Matriculation Examination (2008).
22. Kaftandjieva & Takala (2002).
23. Lavonen (2008); Finnish National Board of Education (2007).
24. Finnish National Board of Education (June 2008).
25. Finnish National Board of Education (June 2008).
26. Korpela (2004).
27. Lavonen (2008).
28. Sahlberg (2007), p. 152.
29. Westbury et al. (2005).
30. Buchberger & Buchberger, p. 9.
31. Buchberger & Buchberger, p. 10.
32. Buchberger & Buchberger, p. 16.
33. R. Laukkanen (2008), p. 319. See also Buchberger & Buchberger (2003).
34. OECD (2004).
35. Gonnie van Amelsvoort & Scheerens (1996).
36. Sahlberg (2007), p. 155.
37. Fullan (2005).
38. Sahlberg (2007), p. 167.
39. Laukkanen (2008).
40. Korean Educational Development Institute (KEDI) (2007a).

41. Lee (2005), pp. 30–31, citing OECD PISA 2003 database, Table 4.3a.
42. Lee (2005).
43. Korean Educational Development Institute (KEDI) (2007b).
44. Lee (2005), pp. 25–26.
45. KEDI (2006).
46. Huh (2007), p. 15.
47. KEDI (2004) lists class sizes of 32.9 at the primary level, 35.1 at the middle school level, 33.8 in general high schools, and 30.2 in vocational high schools.
48. Huh (2007), p. 15.
49. Huh (2007).
50. Huh (2007), pp. 41–44.
51. Huh (2007), p. 46.
52. Seth (2005), p. 9.
53. Hwang (2000), p. 396. See also Huh (2007), p. 80.
54. Kan & Hong (2008).
55. Y. Kim & Lee (2002).
56. Y. Kim & Lee (2002).
57. Lee (2005), p. 35.
58. Huh (2007), p. 35.
59. Kang & Hong (2008), p. 202.
60. Kang & Hong (2008), p. 203.
61. Kang & Hong (2008).
62. Korea Education and Research Information Service.
63. Kang & Hong (2008), p. 203.
64. Dixon (2005).
65. Dixon (2005).
66. Ministry of Education (2007, June).
67. Lepoer (1989).
68. Gopinathan (2007); Goh & Gopinathan (2008); Lepoer (1989).
69. Lepoer (1989).
70. Ministry of Education (2007, June).
71. Stevenson (1992).
72. See also Tsuneyoshi (2005).
73. Ng (2008), p. 6.
74. Tsuneyoshi (2005).
75. Lee (2004).
76. Tharman (2005a).
77. Thurman (2005b), cited in Ng (2008), p. 7.
78. Tsuneyoshi (2005), p. 46.
79. Singapore Examinations and Assessment Board (2006), p. 2.
80. Singapore Examinations and Assessment Board (2006), p. 9.
81. Kaur (2005).

82. Kaur (2005).
83. Goh & Gopinathan (2008).
84. Chuan, G. K. & Gopinathan, S. (2005).
85. Tripp (2004); Salleh (2006).
86. Tripp (2004).
87. Barber & Mourshed (2007).

Chapter 7

1. Barber & Mourshed (2007).
2. Elmore & Fuhrman (1993), p. 86.
3. Ballou & Podgursky (1997); Walsh (2001); Walsh & Podgursky (2001); USDOE (2002); Thomas B. Fordham Foundation (1999).
4. See, for example, the National Research Council report on learning by Bransford, Brown, & Cocking (1999), and the National Academy of Education report on teaching by Darling-Hammond & Bransford (2005).
5. Flexner & Pritchett (1910), p. x.
6. This section draws on Darling-Hammond (2005) and Wei, Andree, & Darling-Hammond (2009).
7. Britton (2006); Clement (2000).
8. Barber & Mourshed (2007).
9. OECD (2005).
10. OECD (2005).
11. Barber & Mourshed (2007).
12. Stansbury & Zimmerman (2000).
13. Mikkola (2001).
14. Buchberger & Buchberger (2004), p. 10.
15. Sahlberg (2009).
16. OECD (2004).
17. Cochran-Smith & Lytle (1993).
18. OECD (2004).
19. OECD (2005).
20. Barber & Mourshed (2007).
21. Fernandez (2002); Pang (2006); Barber & Mourshed (2007).
22. Fernandez (2002).
23. Stigler & Stevenson (1991), p. 46.
24. OECD (2007).
25. Barber & Mourshed (2007).
26. Fullan (2007); Earl et al. (2002).
27. Earl et al. (2002).
28. Fullan (2007).
29. Skilbeck & Connell (2003); Atelier Learning Solutions (2005).
30. Meiers, Ingvarson, Beavis, Hogan, & Kleinhenz (2006).

31. Meiers, Ingvarson, Beavis, Hogan, & Kleinhenz (2006); Ingvarson (2005).
32. Meiers, Ingvarson, Beavis, Hogan, & Kleinhenz (2006).
33. Darling-Hammond, Wei, Richardson, Andree, & Orphanos (2009).
34. Darling-Hammond, Wei, Richardson, Andree, & Orphanos (2009).
35. Darling-Hammond, Wei, Richardson, Andree, & Orphanos (2009).
36. Yoon et al. (2007).
37. Boyd, Grossman, Lankford, Loeb, & Wyckoff (2008); Darling-Hammond (2006).
38. Boyd, Grossman, et al. (2006) found that, on average, holding student and school characteristics equal, beginning teachers who came through college pre-service programs produced stronger achievement gains than those who entered through alternative programs and temporary licenses. In 2008, the same team examined the contributions to student learning gains of graduates from these pre-service programs and identified the features of programs whose graduates produced the strongest value-added gains.
39. Darling-Hammond & Bransford (2005); Darling-Hammond (2006).
40. For a fuller treatment of the design of a national teacher supply policy, see Darling-Hammond & Sykes (2003).
41. Anyon (1997); Cooper & Sherk (1989).
42. Fine (1991); Nieto (1992); Carter & Goodwin (1994); Irvine (1990).
43. Names of teachers in this chapter are pseudonyms.
44. Futernick (2005).
45. Shapiro (1993), p. 89.
46. Darling-Hammond & Bransford (2005).
47. Carter & Doyle (1987); Doyle (1986).
48. Cooper & Sherk (1989), p. 318.
49. Cooper & Sherk (1989); see also Resnick (1987); Bowman (1993); Braddock & McPartland (1993); Garcia (1993).
50. Strickland (1985).
51. The seven were Alverno College in Milwaukee, Wisconsin; Bank Street College in New York City; Trinity College in San Antonio, Texas; University of California at Berkeley; University of Southern Maine; University of Virginia;

and Wheelock College in Boston, Massachusetts. See Darling-Hammond (2006).

52. Adapted from Snyder (2000), pp. 101–105.

53. Darling-Hammond (2006).

54. Irvine (1992), Ladson-Billings (1992), and Eugene Garcia (1993); Nieto & Rolon (1996); Strickland (1995).

55. Darling-Hammond (2006).

56. The concept of adaptive expertise and how it is acquired is described in Darling-Hammond & Bransford (2005).

57. Ball & Cohen (1999); Hammerness, Darling-Hammond, & Shulman (2002).

58. Moll, Amanti, Neff, & Gonzalez, 1992.

59. Gallego (2001), p. 314.

60. Abdal-Haqq (1998), pp. 13–14; Darling-Hammond (2005); Trachtman (1996).

61. See, e.g., Darling-Hammond (2005); Guadarrama, Ramsey, & Nath (2002).

62. For a summary, see Darling-Hammond & Bransford (2005), pp. 415–416.

63. Keller (2006).

64. Ingersoll & Kralik (2004); Cheng & Brown (1992); Odell & Ferraro (1992); Spuhler & Zetler (1995); Fuller (2003).

65. Bartell (1995); Smith & Ingersoll (2004); Olebe (2001); Wang, Odell, & Schwille (2008)

66. For reviews of research on these issues, see Braun (2005); Darling-Hammond (2007).

67. Braun (2005), p. 17.

68. Darling-Hammond, Wise, & Klein (1999); Thompson & Zeuli (1999).

69. Elmore & Fuhrman (1993), p. 86.

70. See, for example, Bond, Smith, Baker, & Hattie (2000); Cavaluzzo (2004); Goldhaber & Anthony (2005); Smith, Gordon, Colby, & Wang (2005); Vandevoort, Amrein-Beardsley, & Berliner (2004).

71. Athanases (1994).

72. Chittenden & Jones (1997); Sato (2000); Sato, Wei, & Darling-Hammond (2008).

73. Areglado, N. (1999); Bradley (1994); Buday, M., & Kelly, J. (1996); Haynes (1995).

74. Haynes, p. 60.

75. Darling-Hammond et al. (2006).

76. Wilson, M., & Hallum, P. J. (2006). Using Student Achievement Test Scores as Evidence of External Validity for Indicators of Teacher Quality: Connecticut's *Beginning*

Educator Support and Training Program. Berkeley, CA: University of California at Berkeley.

77. Darling-Hammond (2007), p. 8.

78. Darling-Hammond (2006), pp. 326–327.

79. Milanowski, Kimball, & White (2004).

80. See, for example, NCTAF (1996); Van Lier (2008).

81. The teacher responsibility rubrics were designed based on several teacher accountability systems currently in use, including the Rochester (New York) Career in Teaching Program, Douglas County (Colorado) *Teacher's Performance Pay Plan*, Vaughn Next Century Charter School (Los Angeles, CA) Performance Pay Plan, and Rolla (Missouri) School District Professional Based Teacher Evaluation.

82. Solomon, White, Cohen & Woo (2007).

83. Agam, Reifsneider, & Wardell (2006).

84. For more detail about the Denver Procomp system, see http:// denverprocomp.org.

85. Packard & Dereshiwsky (1991).

86. Hassell (2002).

87. Darling-Hammond, Wei, Richardson, Andree, & Orphanos (2009).

88. Darling-Hammond & McLaughlin (1995), p. 598.

89. Carpenter et al. (1989); Cohen & Hill (2001); Lieberman & Wood (2002); Merek & Methven (1991); Saxe, Gearhart & Nasir (2001); Wenglinsky (2000).

90. Garet et al. (2001); Snow-Renner & Lauer (2005); Carpenter et al. (1989); Cohen & Hill (2001); Garet et al. (2001); Desimone et al. (2002); Penuel, Fishman, Yamaguchi, & Gallagher (2007); Saxe, Gearhart & Nasir (2001); Supovitz, Mayer & Kahle (2000).

91. Blank, de las Alas & Smith (2007); Carpenter et al. (1989); Cohen & Hill (2001); Lieberman & Wood (2002); Merek & Methven (1991); Saxe, Gearhart & Nasir (2001); Wenglinsky (2000); McGill-Franzen et al. (1999).

92. Merek & Methven (1991).

93. Cohen & Hill (2001).

94. Saxe, Gearhart, & Nasir (2001).

95. Ball & Cohen, 1999; Dunne, Nave & Lewis, 2000; Little, 2003.

96. See, for example, Strahan (2003).
97. Garet et al. (2001); Cohen & Hill (2001); Supovitz, Mayer, & Kahle (2000).
98. Hord (1997); Joyce & Calhoun (1996); Louis, Marks, & Kruse (1996); McLaughlin & Talbert (2001); Newman & Wehlage (1997); Friedlander & Darling-Hammond (2007).
99. Newman & Wehlage (1997).
100. Bryk et al. (1999); Calkins, Guenther, Belfiore, & Lash (2007); Goddard, Goddard, & Tschannen-Moran (2007); Louis & Marks (1998); Supovitz & Christman (2003).
101. Dunne, Nave, & Lewis (2000).
102. Louis, Marks, & Kruse (1996).
103. This section draws from Elmore & Burney (1999).
104. Darling-Hammond, Hightower, et al. (2005).
105. Elmore & Burney (1999); Darling-Hammond, Hightower et al. (2005).
106. Elmore & Burney (1999).
107. Elmore & Burney (1999), p. 268.
108. LaPointe, Darling-Hammond, & Meyerson (2007), p. 36.

Chapter 8

1. Darling-Hammond, Ancess, & Ort (2002).
2. Darling-Hammond, Ancess, & Ort (2002); Fine, Stoudt, & Futch (2005); Friedlaender & Darling-Hammond et al. (2007); Wasley et al. (2000).
3. Darling-Hammond, Ancess, & Ort (2002); Bosman (2007).
4. Ravitch (2009).
5. Ravitch (2002).
6. Darling-Hammond, Ancess, & Ort (2002); Fine, Stoudt, & Futch (2005); Lee, Bryk, & Smith (1993); Newmann & Wehlage (1995); Wasley et al. (2000).
7. Kearns (1988).
8. Deming (2000); Senge (1990).
9. Braddock & McPartland (1993); Gottfredson & Daiger (1979); Lee, Bryk & Smith (1993); Wehlage et al. (1989).
10. Lee & Smith (1995).
11. For reviews, see Lee, Bryk, & Smith (1993); Newmann & Wehlage (1995).
12. Newmann, Marks, & Gamoran (1995).
13. Lee, Smith, & Croninger (1995); see also Darling-Hammond, Barron, et al. (2008).
14. Friedlaender & Darling-Hammond et al. (2007).
15. The state graduation rate calculation in 2007 and preceding years used a formula from the National Center for Education Statistics, which adjusts for transfers in and out of schools. In 2008, the state adopted a different graduation rate calculation proposed by the National Governors Association.
16. Friedlaender & Darling-Hammond et al. (2007).
17. Darling-Hammond, Ancess, & Ort (2002).
18. See Ancess (1995); Bensman (1987, 1994, 1999); Darling-Hammond (1997); Darling-Hammond, Ancess, & Falk (1995).
19. The 4-year graduation rate reflects the proportion of a class of students who began as ninth graders in a school and have, within 4 years, graduated from that school or any other in New York City or have received a GED. Data are from New York City Public Schools (1994).
20. Darling-Hammond, Ancess, & Ort (2002).
21. Fine, Stoudt, & Futch (2005).
22. See, for example, Wasley et al.'s (2000) analysis of more than 50 Chicago new small high schools, which found much lower dropout rates, higher grade point averages, stronger reading achievement, and comparable math achievement for students in the new smaller schools as compared to peers in larger schools, controlling for student characteristics and prior achievement and Fine's (1994) study of small school units, called charters, in Philadelphia high schools, with similar outcomes. Both identify small size, personalizing structures, teacher collaboration, project-based learning and performance assessment as critical features of the more successful schools. French (2008) documents much stronger achievement for Boston's Pilot Schools than other city schools serving comparable students, attributing the differences to personalizing structures that produce lower student-teacher loads, wraparound student support (including advisory structures), substantial time for staff collaboration (285 minutes per week plus 6 professional development days versus 29 minutes per week and 3 professional development days in other BPS schools), and authentic instruction and assessment

through internships, research projects and demonstrations, exhibitions, portfolios, and performance assessments.

23. The following section draws on Darling-Hammond, Ancess, & Ort (2002) and Friedlaender, Darling-Hammond et al. (2007) and includes quotations originally published in these sources.

24. Darling-Hammond, Ross, & Milliken (2007).

25. For a review, see Darling-Hammond, Ross, & Milliken (2007).

26. Howley & Howley (2004) found that optimal school size varies by student socioeconomic status, with schools in the smallest decile nationally maximizing the achievement of the lowest-income students. They observe that achievement equity in mathematics is maximized in high schools enrolling fewer than 300 students, and equity in reading is maximized in schools enrolling 300–600 students; inequity is greatest in schools enrolling more than 1,500 students. Another group of studies conducted by Friedkin & Necochea (1998) in California and replicated by Howley & Bickel (1999) across six other states also found the relationship between school size and student achievement to be related to the socioeconomic status of the community, with smaller schools appearing to be most beneficial in low-income communities.

27. Howley (1995), p. 2.

28. Howley (1995).

29. Verlinden, Hersen, & Thomas (2000).

30. Lee et al. (2000).

31. Lee, Bryk, & Smith (1993).

32. Powell, Ferrar, & Cohen (1985).

33. Miles & Darling-Hammond (1998).

34. Bryk, Lee, & Holland (1993); Lee, Croninger, & Smith (1997).

35. Black, Harrison, Lee, Marshall, & Wiliam (2003).

36. Glaser (1990), pp. 16–17.

37. Newman et al. (1996).

38. Little (1982); McLaughlin & Talbert (2001).

39. Newmann, Marks, & Gamoran, "Authentic Pedagogy and Student Performance."

40. Darling-Hammond, Ancess & Ort (2002); Lee & Loeb, School Size in Chicago Elementary Schools; Wasley et al. (2000); Bryk, Camburn, & Louis (1999).

41. Edmonds (1979).

42. For a review, see Levine & Lezotte (1990).

43. Eight-year study

44. Erkstine (2002).

45. Robinson (1984).

46. Cremin (1961).

47. Hill (2006).

48. Gates Foundation (2005), p. 3.

49. French (2008).

50. Young et al. (2009).

51. Imberman (2007); Miron & Nelson (2001), p. 36.

52. CREDO (2009).

53. Carnoy et al. (2005).

54. Institute on Race and Poverty (2008).

55. Miron, Coryn et al. (2007). For a review of charter school governance issues and outcomes, see Darling-Hammond & Montgomery (2008).

56. General Accounting Office (2001).

57. Council for Great City Schools (2008).

58. Data on Milwaukee schools achievement trends, which include district schools, instrumentality charters, noninstrumentality charters, and partnership schools, are from Milwaukee Public Schools District Report Card 2007–08 and the Wisconsin Department of Public Instruction web page; retrieved on 5/8/09 from http://data.dpi.state.wi.us/data/.

59. Jennings & Pallas (2009); Advocates for Children (2009).

60. NCTAF (1996); Darling-Hammond (1997).

61. NCTAF (1996).

62. Japanese statistics are for elementary and lower secondary schools, as reported in Japanese Ministry of Education, Culture, Sports, Science, and Technology (2004); U.S. statistics are from National Center for Education Statistics (2005a), Table 79.

Chapter 9

1. Dewey (1900), p. 3.

2. James Baldwin, in a concert program to benefit the Wiltwyck School for Boys.

3. Swanson (1991).

4. For a summary, see Darling-Hammond & Rustique-Forrester (2005).

5. Darling-Hammond & Rustique-Forrester (2005).

6. Cortese & Ravitch (2008), p. 4.

7. Darling-Hammond & Rustique-Forrester (2005).
8. Institute for Education Sciences (2007).
9. Mullis, Martin, Kennedy, & Foy (2007).
10. Forum on Education and Democracy (2008).
11. See Darling-Hammond & Rustique-Forrester (2005).
12. See, for example, Schmidt, Wang, & McKnight (2005); Valverde & Schmidt (2000); Fensham (1994).
13. Takahashi, Watanabe, & Yoshida (2004).
14. Eckstein and Noah (1993), p. 119.
15. Pettersson (2008).
16. Eckstein & Noah (1993).
17. International Baccalaureate Organization (2005).
18. Chan, J. K., Kennedy, K. J., Yu, F. W., & Fok, P. (2008).
19. Hong Kong Examinations Assessment Authority (2009).
20. Dowling, M. (undated).
21. Chan et al. (2008); Quality Assurance Division of the Education Bureau (2008).
22. Quality Assurance Division of the Education Bureau (2008).
23. Rustique-Forrester (2005).
24. Department for Children, Schools, and Families (2009).
25. Ravitch (2009).
26. MacDonald & Shirley (2009, in press).
27. MacDonald & Shirley (2009, in press).
28. Schmidt, Wang, & McKnight (2005).
29. Schwartz, M. S., Sadler, P. M., Sonnert, G., & Tai, R. H. (2008).
30. Darling-Hammond, Ancess, & Falk (2005).
31. Evidence on success beyond high school.
32. Sahlberg (2007).
33. Shulman (1983), p. 504.
34. Rothstein, R., Jacobsen, R., & Wilder, T. (2008).
35. Ancess (1996); Wilson (1996).
36. Forum on Educational Accountability (2004).
37. American Educational Research Association (1999).
38. Liu (2008).
39. National Council on Education, Standards, and Testing (1992).
40. Darling-Hammond (1992–93).
41. Schott Foundation (2009).
42. Betts, Rueben, & Danenberg (2000), pp. xxix–xxx.
43. Ferguson (1991), p. 489.
44. Betts, Rueben, & Danenberg, 2000, p. xxiv.
45. For a fuller treatment of the design of a national teacher supply policy, see Darling-Hammond & Sykes (2003).
46. About 250,000 teachers are hired each year, but typically only 40–60% of them are new to teaching. The others are experienced teachers changing schools or returning teachers who are re-entering the labor force.
47. Current attrition rates result in the loss of about 50,000 teachers with less than 3 years of experience in each cohort of new teachers. At replacement costs of $20,000 per recruit, this costs the nation approximately $1billion annually, not counting the costs of other turnover.
48. Pecheone & Chung (2006).
49. Darling-Hammond & Bransford (2005), pp. 415–416.
50. New Teacher Project (2009).
51. Bush merit pay repeal.
52. Mathews, J. (2008, October 6).
53. Allegretto, S., Mishel, L., & Corcoran, S. P. (2008).
54. Berry, B. (2009).
55. Rochkind, J., Ott, A., Immerwahr, J., Doble, J., & Johnson, J. (2007).
56. Berry, B. (2009).
57. Silva, E. (2008).
58. Berry, B. (2009).
59. Zentner, S. M., & Wiebke, K. (2009, May 11).
60. Senge, P. (1990); Deming, W. E. (1986).
61. Leithwood, K., & Jantzi, D. (2005); see also Leithwood, K., Seashore-Louis, K., Anderson, S., & Wahlstrom, K. (2004).
62. Darling-Hammond, Meyerson, et al. (in press).
63. For descriptions of successful programs, see Darling-Hammond, Meyerson, et al. (in press).
64. Berry (2009).
65. Harlem Children's Zone (2008).
66. Lefkowits, L., & Diamond, B. (2009).
67. Elmore, R. (1996).
68. Hargreaves, A. (2008).
69. Hargreaves (2008), p. 25.
70. McLaughlin (1991), p. 147.
71. King, M. L. Jr. (1968, January 7).
72. Levin (2008); Western, Schiraldi, & Ziedenberg (2003).

References

Abbeville County School District v. State, 515 S.E.2d 535 (S.C. 1999).

Abdal-Haqq, I. (1998). *Professional development schools: Weighing the evidence.* Thousand Oaks, CA: Corwin Press.

Access Quality Education. (2008). South Carolina litigation history. Retrieved August 9, 2008, from http://www.schoolfunding.info/states/sc/lit_sc.php3

Advocates for Children. (2002). *Pushing out at-risk students: An analysis of high school discharge figures—a joint report by AFC and the Public Advocate.* Retrieved June 3, 2009, from http://www.advocatesforchildren.org/pubs/pushout-11-20-02.html

Agam, K., Reifsneider, D., & Wardell, D. (2006). *The Teacher Advancement Program (TAP): National teacher attitudes.* Washington, DC: The Teacher Advancement Program Evaluation.

Akiba, G. L., & Scriber, J. (2007). Teacher quality, opportunity gap, and national achievement in 46 countries. *Educational Researcher, 36*, 369–387.

Alexander, K. L., & McDill, E. L. (1976). Selection and allocation within schools: Some causes and consequences of curriculum placement. *American Sociological Review, 41*, 963–980.

Allegretto, S., Mishel, L., & Corcoran, S. P. (2008). *The teaching penalty: Teacher pay losing ground.* Washington, DC: Economic Policy Institute.

Allington, R., & McGill-Franzen, A. (1992). Unintended effects of educational reform in New York. *Educational Policy, 6*(4), 397–414.

American Educational Research Association. (1999). *Standards for educational and psychological testing.* Washington, DC: American Educational Research Association, American Psychological Association, and National Council on Measurement in Education.

American Educational Research Association. (2006). Brief amicus curiae filed in *Parents Involved in Community Schools v. Seattle School District No. 1.* 127 S. Ct. 2738 (2007).

Amrein, A., & Berliner, D. (2002). High-stakes testing, uncertainty, and student learning. *Educational Policy and Analysis Archives, 10*(8). Retrieved November 21, 2003, from http://www.epaa.asu.edu/epaa/v10n18

Amrein-Beardsley, A. A., & Berliner, D. C. (2003). Re-analysis of NAEP math and reading scores in states with and without high-stakes tests: Response to Rosenshine. *Education Policy Analysis Archives, 11*(25). Retrieved November 16, 2003, from http://epaa.asu.edu/epaa/v11n25/

Anagnostopoulos, D. (2003). The new accountability, student failure, and teachers' work in urban high schools. *Educational Policy, 17*(3), 291–316.

Ancess, J. (1995). *An inquiry high school: Learner-centered accountability at the Urban Academy.* New York: National Center for Restructuring Education, Schools, and Teaching, Teachers College, Columbia University.

Ancess, J. (1996). *Outside/inside, inside/outside: Developing and implementing the school quality review.* New York: National Center for Restructuring Education, Schools, and Teaching, Teachers College, Columbia University.

Anyon, J. (1997). *Ghetto schooling: A political economy of urban educational reform.* New York: Teachers College Press.

Apte, U. M., Karmarkar, U.S., & Nath, H. (2008, Spring). Information services in the U.S. economy: Value, jobs, and management implications. *California Management Review, 50*(3). Available
online at http://ssrn.com/abstract=1265809

Areglado, N. (1999). "I became convinced": How a certification program revitalized an educator.
Journal of Staff Development, 20(1), 35–37.

Arenson, K. W. (2004, May 15). More youths opt for G.E.D., skirting high-school hurdle. *New York
Times*. Retrieved March 16, 2009, from http://www.nytimes.com/2004/05/15/us/more-
youths-opt-for-ged-tests-skirting-the-hurdle-of-high-school.html

Ashton, P., & Crocker, L. (1987, May–June). Systematic study of planned variations: The essential
focus of teacher education reform. *Journal of Teacher Education, 38*, 2–8.

Atelier Learning Solutions Ltd. (2005). *An evaluation of the Australian Government Quality Teacher Programme, 1999 to 2004*. Canberra, Australia: Department of Education, Science and Training.

Athanases, S. (1994). Teachers' reports of the effects of preparing portfolios of literacy instruction.
Elementary School Journal, 94(4), 421–439.

Baenen, N. (1988, April). *A perspective after five years: Has grade retention passed or failed?* Paper presented at the Annual Meeting of the American Educational Research Association, New Orleans, LA.

Baldassare, M., & Hanak, E. (2005). *California 2025: It's your choice*. San Francisco: Public Policy
Institute of California.

Ball, D., & Cohen, D. (1999). Developing practice, developing practitioners: Toward a practice-
based theory of professional education. In L. Darling-Hammond & G. Sykes (Eds.), *Teaching
as the learning profession: Handbook of policy and practice* (pp. 3–32). San Francisco: Jossey-Bass.

Ballou, D., & Podgursky, M. (1997). Reforming teacher training & recruitment. *Government Union
Review, 17*(4), 1–47.

Barber, M., & Mourshed, M. (2007) *How the world's best-performing school systems come out on top*.
London: McKinsey and Company.

Baron, J. B. (1999). *Exploring high and improving reading achievement in Connecticut: Lessons from the
states*. Washington, DC: National Educational Goals Panel.

Barr, R., & Dreeben, R. (1983). *How schools work*. Chicago: University of Chicago Press.

Bartell, C. (1995). Shaping teacher induction policy in California. *Teacher Education Quarterly, 22*(4),
27–43.

Barton, P. E. (2005). *One-third of a nation: Rising dropout rates and declining opportunities. Policy information report*. Princeton, NJ: Educational Testing Service.

Barton, P. E., & Coley, R. J. (1996). *Captive Students: Education and training in America's prisons*.
Princeton, NJ: Educational Testing Service.

Baugh, W. H., & Stone, J. A. (1982). Mobility and wage equilibration in the educator labor market.
Economics of Education Review, 2(3), 253–274.

Becker, D. E., & Watters, C. (2007). *Independent evaluation of the California high school exit examination
(CAHSEE): 2007 evaluation report*. Alexandria, VA: Human Resources Research Organization
(HumRRO).

Belfield, C., & Levin, H. (2007). *The price we pay: Economic and social consequences of inadequate education*. Washington, DC: Brookings Institution.

Bell, K., Bernstein, J., & Greenberg, M. (2008). Lessons for the United States from other advanced
economies in tackling child poverty. In *Big ideas for children: Investing in our nation's future* (pp.
81–92). Washington, DC: First Focus.

Benner, A. D. (2000). *The cost of teacher turnover*. Austin: Texas Center for Educational Research.

Bensman, D. (1987). *Quality education in the inner city: The story of the Central Park East schools*. Report to the New York Community Trust.

Bensman, D. (1994). *Lives of the graduates of Central Park East elementary school: Where have they gone?
What did they really learn?* New York: National Center for Restructuring Education, Schools,
and Teaching, Teachers College, Columbia University.

Bensman, D. (1995). *Learning to think well: Central Park East secondary school graduates reflect on their high school and college experiences.* New York: National Center for Restructuring Education, Schools, and Teaching, Teachers College, Columbia University.

Berger, N., & McLynch, J. (2006). *Public school funding in Massachusetts: Where we are, what has changed, and options ahead.* Boston: Massachusetts Budget and Policy Center.

Bernstein, D. S. (2004, June 11). Achievement gap: This is improvement? *The Boston Phoenix.* Retrieved January 2, 2005, from http://www.bostonphoenix.com/boston/news_features/this_just_in/documents/03902591.asp

Berry, B. (1995). *Keeping talented teachers: Lessons learned from the North Carolina teaching fellows.* Report commissioned by the North Carolina Teaching Fellows Commission. Raleigh, NC: Public School Forum.

Berry, B. (2009). *Keeping the promise: Recruiting, retaining, and growing effective teachers for high-needs schools.* Raleigh, NC: Center for Teaching Quality.

Betts, J. R., Rueben, K. S., & Danenberg, A. (2000). *Equal resources, equal outcomes? The distribution of school resources and student achievement in California.* San Francisco: Public Policy Institute of California.

Black, P. J., Harrison, C., Lee, C., Marshall, B., & Wiliam, D. (2003). *Assessment for learning: Putting it into practice.* Maidenhead, England: Open University Press.

Blackwell, L. S., Trzesniewski, K. H., & Dweck, C. S. (2007). Implicit theories of intelligence predict achievement across an adolescent transition: A longitudinal study and an intervention. *Child Development, 78*(1), 246–263.

Blank, R. K., de las Alas, N., & Smith, C. (2007). *Analysis of the quality of professional development programs for mathematics and science teachers: Findings from a cross-state study.* Washington, DC: CCSSO.

Bohrnstedt, G. W., & Stecher, B. M. (2002, September). *What we have learned about class size reduction in California.* Sacramento: California Department of Education.

Bond, L., Smith, T., Baker, W., & Hattie, J. (2000). *The certification system of the National Board for Professional Teaching Standards: A construct and consequential validity study.* Greensboro, NC: Center for Educational Research and Evaluation.

Bonstingl, J. J. (2004). Expanding learning potential for all students. *Leadership Magazine.* Retrieved March 31, 2008, from http://www.acsa.org/publications/pub_detail.cfm?leadershipPubID=1415

Boost value of Pell grants. (2006, December 18). *The Ledger,* p. A12. Retrieved on January 15, 2009, from http://www.theledger.com/apps/pbcs.dll/article?AID=/20061218/NEWS/612180334/1036

Borja, R. (2004, May 6). Singapore's digital path. Technology Counts. *Education Week.*

Bosman, J. (2007, June 30). Small schools are ahead in graduation. *New York Times.* Retrieved May 14, 2009, from http://query.nytimes.com/gst/fullpage.html?res=9C06E1D8173EF933A05755C0A9619C8B63&sec=&spon=&pagewanted=1

Bowman, B. (1993). Early childhood education. In L. Darling-Hammond (Ed.), *Review of research in education* (Vol. 19, pp. 101–134). Washington, DC: American Educational Research Association.

Boyd, D., Grossman, P., Lankford, H., Loeb, S., & Wyckoff, J. (2006). How changes in entry requirements alter the teacher workforce and affect student achievement. *Education Finance & Policy, 1*(2), 176–216.

Boyd, D., Grossman, P., Lankford, H., Loeb, S., & Wyckoff, J. (2008). Teacher preparation and student achievement. NBER Working Paper No. W14314. National Bureau of Economic Research. Retrieved September 21, 2009, from http://ssrn.com/abstract=1264576

Boyd, D., Lankford, H., Loeb, S., Rockoff, J., & Wyckoff, J. (2008, June). *The narrowing gap in New York City teacher qualifications and its implications for student achievement in high-poverty schools.* NBER Working Paper No. 14021. Cambridge, MA: NBER.

Braddock, J., & McPartland, J. M. (1993). Education of early adolescents. In L. Darling-Hammond (Ed.), *Review of research in education* (Vol. 19, pp. 135–170). Washington, DC: American Educational Research Association.

Bradley, A. (1994, April 20). Pioneers in professionalism. *Education Week, 13*, 18–21.

Bransford, J. D., Brown, A. L., & Cocking, R. R. (Eds.). (1999). *How people learn: Brain, mind, experience, and school.* Washington, DC: National Research Council.

Braun, H. (2005). *Using student progress to evaluate teachers: A primer on value-added mode* (p. 17). Princeton, NJ: Educational Testing Service.

Brewer, D. J. (1996). Career paths and quit decisions: Evidence from teaching. *Journal of Labor Economics, 14*(2), 313–339.

Britton, T. (2006). Mentoring in the induction system of five countries: A sum is greater than its parts. In C. Cullingford (Ed.), *Mentoring in education: An international perspective* (pp. 110–123). Aldershot, England: Ashgate Publishing.

Brown, D. F. (1992, April). *Altering curricula through state-mandated testing: Perceptions of teachers and principals.* Paper presented at the annual meeting of the American Educational Research Association, San Francisco, CA.

Bryant, D., Maxwell, K., Taylor, K., Poe, M., Peisner-Feinberg, E., & Bernier, K. (2003). *Smart start and preschool child care quality in NC: Change over time and relation to children's readiness.* Chapel Hill, NC: FPG Child Development Institute.

Bryk, A., Camburn, E., & Louis, K. (1999). Professional community in Chicago elementary schools: Facilitating factors and organizational consequences. *Educational Administration Quarterly, 35*(5), 751–781.

Bryk, A., Lee, V., & Holland, P. (1993). *Catholic schools and the common good.* Cambridge, MA: Harvard University Press.

Buchberger, F., & Buchberger, I. (2004). Problem-solving capacity of a teacher education system as a condition of success? An analysis of the "Finnish Case." In F. Buchberger & S. Berghammer (Eds.), *Education policy analysis in a comparative perspective* (pp. 222–237). Linz, Austria: Trauner.

Buday, M., & Kelly, J. (1996). National board certification and the teaching profession's commitment to quality assurance. *Phi Delta Kappan, 78*(3), 215–219.

Bueno, M., Darling-Hammond, L, & Danielle Gonzales, D. (2009). *Pre-k 101: Preparing teachers for the Pre-k classroom.* Washington, DC: PreK Now.

Bureau of Labor Statistics. (2009, January 23). *America's youth at 21: School enrollment, training, and employment transitions between ages 20 and 21.* Washington, DC: U.S. Department of Labor. Retrieved January 25, 2009, from http://www.bls.gov/news.release/pdf/ nlsyth.pdf

Burns, P. (2003). Regime theory, state government, and a takeover of urban education. *Journal of Urban Affairs, 25*(3), 285–303.

California Postsecondary Education Commission. (2007). *College-going rates: A performance measure in California's higher education accountability framework* (Commission Report No. 07-04). Sacramento, CA: Author.

Calkins, A., Guenther, W., Belfiore, G., & Lash, D. (2007). *The turnaround challenge: Why America's best opportunity to dramatically improve student achievement lies in our worst-performing schools.* Boston: Mass Insight Education & Research Institute.

Capriccioso, R. (2005, November 3). High schools and high college costs. *Inside Higher Ed.* Retrieved March 31, 2008, from http://www.insidehighered.com/news/2005/11/03/costs

Card, D., & Payne, A. (2002). School finance reform, the distribution of school spending, and the distribution of student test scores, *Journal of Public Economics, 83*, 49–80.

Carnoy, M., Jacobsen, R., Mishel, L., & Rothstein, R. (2005). *The charter school dust-up: Examining the evidence on enrollment and achievement.* Washington, DC: Economic Policy Institute.

Carnoy, M., & Loeb, S. (2002). Does external accountability affect student outcomes? A cross-state analysis. *Education Evaluation and Policy Analysis, 24*(4), 305–332.

Carpenter, T., Fennema, E., Peterson, P., Chiang, C., & Loef, M. (1989). Using knowledge of children's mathematical thinking in classroom teaching: An experimental study. *American Educational Research Journal, 26,* 499–532.

Carrajat, M. A. (1996). *Why do academically able Puerto Rican males drop out of high school?* Unpublished doctoral dissertation, Teachers College, Columbia University, New York, NY.

Carroll, S., Reichardt, R., & Guarino, C. (2000). *The distribution of teachers among California's school districts and schools.* Santa Monica, CA: RAND Corporation.

Carter, K., & Doyle, W. (1987). Teachers' knowledge structures and comprehension processes. In J. Calderhead (Ed.), *Exploring teacher thinking* (pp. 147–160). London: Cassell.

Carter, R., & Goodwin, L. (1994). Racial identity and education. In L. Darling-Hammond (Ed.), *Review of research in education (Vol. 20).* Washington, DC: American Educational Research Association.

Cavaluzzo, L. (2004). *Is national board certification an effective signal of teacher quality?* (National Science Foundation No. REC-0107014). Alexandria, VA: The CNA Corporation.

Center for the Future of Teaching and Learning (2006). *California's teaching force: Key issues and trends.* Santa Cruz, CA: Author.

Center on Education Policy. (2004). *State exit exams: A maturing reform.* Washington, DC: Author.

Center on Education Policy. (2007, July). *Choices, changes, and challenges: curriculum and instruction in the NCLB Era.* Washington, DC: Author.

Chan, J. K., Kennedy, K. J., Yu, F. W., & Fok, P. (2008). Assessment policy in Hong Kong: Implementation issues for new forms of assessment. *The Hong Kong Institute of Education.* Retrieved September 12, 2008, from http://www.iaea.info/papers.aspx?id=68

Children's Sentinel Nutrition Assessment Program (C-SNAP). (2004, July). *The safety net in action: Protecting the health and nutrition of young american children.* Boston: C-SNAP. Retrieved August 22, 2005, from http://dcc2.bumc.bu.edu/csnappublic/CSNAP2004.pdf

Centra, J. A., & Potter, D. A. (1980). School and teacher effects: An interrelational model. *Review of Educational Research, 50*(2), 273–291.

Cheng, M., & Brown, R. S. (1992). *A two-year evaluation of the peer support pilot project: 1990–1992.* Toronto, Ontario, Canada: Toronto Board of Education, Research Department.

Chittenden, E., & Jones, J. (1997, April). *An observational study of national board candidates as they progress through the certification process.* Paper presented at the annual meeting of the American Educational Research Association, Chicago, IL.

Clarke, M., Haney, W., & Madaus, G. (2000). High stakes testing and high school completion. *The national board on educational testing and public policy statements, 1*(3). Chestnut Hill, MA: Boston College, Center for the Study of Testing.

Clement, M. (2000). Making time for teacher induction: A lesson from the New Zealand model. *The Clearing House, 73*(6), 329–330.

Clotfelter, C. T., Ladd, H. F., & Vigdor, J. L. (2005). Classroom-level segregation and resegregation in North Carolina. In J. C. Boger & G. Orfield (Eds.), *School resegregation: Must the South turn back?* (pp. 127–147). Chapel Hill: University of North Carolina Press.

Clotfelter, C. T., Ladd, H. F., & Vigdor, J. L. (2007). *How and why do teacher credentials matter for student achievement?* (NBER Working Paper 12828). Cambridge, MA: National Bureau of Economic Research.

Clotfelter, C. T., Ladd, H. F., Vigdor, J. L., & Diaz, R. A. (2004). Do school accountability systems make it more difficult for low performing schools to attract and retain high quality teachers? *Journal of Policy and Management, 23*(2), 251–272.

Cochran-Smith, M., & Lytle, S. (1993). *Inside/outside: Teacher research and knowledge.* New York: Teachers College Press.

Cohen, D., et al. (1990). Case studies of curriculum implementation. *Educational Evaluation and Policy Analysis,* 12(3).

Cohen, D. K., & Hill, H. C. (2001). *Learning policy.* New Haven, CT: Yale University Press.

College Board. (1985). *Equality and excellence: The educational status of Black Americans.* New York: College Entrance Examination Board.

College Board. (2003). *Advanced placement summary reports.* New York: The College Board.

Coleman, J. S., Campbell, E. Q., Hobson, C. J., McPartland, J., Mood, A. M., Weinfeld, F. D., & York, R. L. (1966). *Equality of educational opportunity.* Washington, DC: U.S. Government Printing Office.

Commission on Chapter 1. (1992). *High performance schools: No exceptions, no excuses.* Washington, DC: Author.

Conant, J. B. (1961). *Slums and suburbs.* New York: McGraw-Hill.

Connecticut State Department of Education. (1990). Impact of Education Enhancement Act. *Research Bulletin,* School Year 1990, No. 1.

Connecticut State Board of Education. (1992). *The other side of the equation: Impact of the teacher standards provisions of the Education Enhancement Act.* Hartford, CT: Author.

Constantine, J., Player, D., Silva, T., Hallgren, K., Grider, M., & Deke, J. (2009). *An evaluation of teachers trained through different routes to certification, final report* (NCEE 2009-4043). Washington, DC: National Center for Education Evaluation and Regional Assistance, Institute of Education Sciences, U.S. Department of Education.

Cooper, E., & Sherk, J. (1989). Addressing urban school reform: Issues and alliances. *Journal of Negro Education,* 58(3), 315–331.

Corak, M. (2005). *Principles and practicalities in measuring child poverty for the rich countries* (Working Paper 2005–01). Florence, Italy: Innocenti Research Center.

Corbett, H., & Wilson, B. (1991). The central office role in instructional improvement. *School Effectiveness and School Improvement, 3*(1), 45–68.

Cortese, A., & Ravitch, D. (2008). Preface. In *Still at risk: What students don't know, even now.* Washington, DC: Common Core.

Council for Great City Schools. (2008). Beating the odds: Assessment results from the 2006–2007 school year: Individual district profiles. Retrieved June 3, 2009, from http://www.cgcs.org/pdfs/BTO_8_Combined.pdf

Cremin, L. (1961). *The transformation of the school: Progressivism in American education, 1876–1957.* New York: Vintage Books.

Cremin, L. (1970). *American education: The colonial experience 1607–1783.* New York: Harper & Row.

Cubberley, E. P. (1909). *Changing conceptualizations of education.* Boston: Houghton Mifflin.

Darling-Hammond, L. (1990a). Teacher quality and equality. In J. Goodlad & P. Keating (Eds.), *Access to knowledge: An agenda for our nation's schools* (pp. 237–258). New York: College Entrance Examination Board.

Darling-Hammond, L. (1990b). Instructional policy into practice: "The power of the bottom over the top." *Educational Evaluation and Policy Analysis, 12*(3), pp. 233–242.

Darling-Hammond, L. (1991). The implications of testing policy for quality and equality. *Phi Delta Kappan, 73*(3), 220–225.

Darling-Hammond, L. (1992–93, Winter). Creating standards of practice and delivery for learner-centered schools. *Stanford Law and Policy Review, 4,* pp. 37–52.

Darling-Hammond, L. (1997). *The right to learn: A blueprint for creating schools that work.* San Francisco: Jossey-Bass.

Darling-Hammond, L. (2000, January). Teacher quality and student achievement: A review of state policy evidence. *Educational Policy Analysis Archives, 8*(1). Retrieved August 14, 2009, from http://epaa.asu.edu/epaa/v8n1.

Darling-Hammond, L. (2003a). Access to quality teaching: An analysis of inequality in California's public schools, *Santa Clara Law Review, 43*, pp. 101–239.

Darling-Hammond, L. (2003b). *Testimony responding to the state's expert reports with respect to questions of resource equity and teacher quality in* Williams v. California. Retrieved March 20, 2009, from http://www.decentschools.org/expert_reports/ldh_rebuttal.pdf

Darling-Hammond, L. (2004a). Standards, accountability, and school reform. *Teachers College Record, 106*(6), 1047–1085.

Darling-Hammond, L. (2004). The color line in American education: Race, resources, and student achievement. *W.E.B. DuBois Review: Social Science Research on Race, 1*(2), 213–246.

Darling-Hammond, L. (2005). Teaching as a profession: Lessons in teacher preparation and professional development, *Phi Delta Kappan, 87*(3), pp. 237–240.

Darling-Hammond, L. (2006). *Powerful teacher education: Lessons from exemplary programs.* San Francisco: Jossey-Bass.

Darling-Hammond, L. (2007). *Recognizing and enhancing teacher effectiveness: A policy maker's guide.* Washington, DC: Council for Chief State School Officers.

Darling-Hammond, L. (2009). *Educational opportunity and alternative certification: New evidence and new questions.* Stanford, CA: Stanford Center for Opportunity Policy in Education.

Darling-Hammond, L., & Ancess, J. (1994). *Authentic assessment and school development.* New York: National Center for Restructuring Education, Schools, and Teaching, Teachers College, Columbia University.

Darling-Hammond, L., Ancess, J., & Falk, B. (1995). *Authentic assessment in action: Studies of schools and students at work.* New York: Teachers College Press.

Darling-Hammond, L., Ancess, J., & Ort, S. (2002). Reinventing high school: Outcomes of the coalition campus schools project. *American Educational Research Journal, 39*(3), 39–73.

Darling-Hammond, L., Barron, B., Pearson, P. D., Schoenfeld, A., Stage, E. K., Zimmerman, T. D., Cervetti, G. N., & Tilson, J. L. (2008). *Powerful learning: What we know about teaching for understanding.* San Francisco: Jossey-Bass.

Darling-Hammond, L., & Bransford, J. (2005). *Preparing teachers for a changing world: What teachers Should learn and be able to do.* San Francisco: Jossey-Bass.

Darling-Hammond, L., Hightower, A. M., Husbands, J. L., LaFors, J. R., Young, V. M., & Christopher, C. (2005). *Instructional leadership for systemic change: The story of San Diego's reform.* Lanham, MD: Scarecrow Education Press.

Darling-Hammond, L., & McLaughlin, M. W. (1995). Policies that support professional development in an era of reform. *Phi Delta Kappan, 76*(8), 597–604.

Darling-Hammond, L., & Rustique-Forrester, E. (2005). The consequences of student testing for teaching and teacher quality. In J. Herman & E. Haertel (Eds.), *The uses and misuses of data in accountability testing. The 104th yearbook of the National Society for the Study of Education, part II* (pp. 289–319). Malden, MA: Blackwell.

Darling-Hammond, L., Holtzman, D., Gatlin, S. J., & Heilig, J. V. (2005). Does teacher preparation matter? Evidence about teacher certification, Teach for America, and teacher effectiveness. *Education Policy Analysis Archives, 13*(42). Retrieved June 4, 2009, from http://epaa.asu.edu/epaa/v13n42/

Darling-Hammond, L., Meyerson, D., LaPointe, M., & Orr, M. (2009, in press). *Preparing principals for a changing world: Lessons from effective school leadership programs.* San Francisco: Jossey-Bass.

Darling-Hammond, L., & Montgomery, K. (2008). Keeping the promise: The role of policy in reform. In L. Dingerson, B. Miner, B. Peterson, & S. Waters (Eds.), *Keeping the promise? The debate over charter schools* (pp. 91–110). Milwaukee, WI: Rethinking Schools.

Darling-Hammond, L., Ross, P., & Milliken, M. (2007). High school size, organization, and content: What matters for student success? In F. Hess (Ed.), *Brookings papers on education policy 2006/07* (pp. 163–204). Washington, DC: Brookings Institution.

Darling-Hammond, L., & Schnur, J. (2008, November 4). The economic bailout is not enough: The case for Obama, education, and the longer view. *Huffington Post*. Retrieved June 4, 2009, from http://www.huffingtonpost.com/martin-carnoy/the-economic-bailout-is-n_b_140285.html

Darling-Hammond, L., & Sykes, G. (2003). Wanted: A national teacher supply policy for education: The right way to meet the "highly qualified teacher" challenge. *Educational Policy Analysis Archives, 11*(33). Retrieved June 4, 2009, from http://epaa.asu.edu/epaa/v11n33/

Darling-Hammond, L., Wei, R. C., Richardson, N., Andree, A., & Orphanos, S. (2009). *Professional learning in the learning profession: A status report on teacher development in the U.S. and abroad.* Washington, DC: National Staff Development Council.

Darling-Hammond, L., Williamson, J., & Hyler, M. (2007). Securing the right to learn: The quest for an empowering curriculum for African American citizens. *Journal of Negro Education, 76*(3), pp. 281–296.

Darling-Hammond, L., Wise, A., & Klein, S. (1999). *A license to teach: Building a profession for 21st century schools.* San Francisco: Jossey-Bass.

Dawkins, M. P., & Braddock J. H. (1994). The continuing significance of desegregation: School racial composition and African American inclusion in American society. *Journal of Negro Education, 63*(3), 394–405.

Davis, D. G. (1986, April). *A pilot study to assess equity in selected curricular offerings across three diverse schools in a large urban school district.* Paper presented at the Annual Meeting of the American Educational Research Association, San Francisco.

DeBard, R., & Kubow, P. K. (2002). From compliance to commitment: The need for constituent discourse in implementing testing policy. *Education Policy, 16*(3), 387–405.

DeBray, E., Parson, G., & Woodworth, K. (2001). Patterns of response in four high schools under state accountability policies in Vermont and New York. In S. Fuhrman (Ed.), *From capitol to the classroom: Standards-based reform in the states. The annual yearbook of the National Society for the Study of Education* (Vol. 2, pp. 170–192). Chicago: National Society for the Study of Education.

Deke, J. (2003). A study of the impact of public school spending on postsecondary educational attainment using statewide school district financing in Kansas. *Economics of Education Review, 22*(3), 275–284.

Delors, J. (1996). Learning evaluation report on the Regional Network of Educational Innovation for Development. Bangkok, Thailand: UNESCO.

Deming, W. E. (1986). *Out of the crisis.* Cambridge: Massachusetts Institute of Technology, Center for Advanced Engineering Study.

Deming, W. E. (2000). *The new economics for industry, government, education* (2nd ed.). Cambridge: MIT Press.

Denton, K., & West, J. (2002). Children's reading and mathematics achievement in kindergarten and first grade (NCES 2002–125). *Education Statistics Quarterly, 44*(1). Retrieved March 14, 2009, from http://nces.ed.gov/programs/quarterly/Vol_4/4_1/q3-1.asp

DeNavas-Walt, C., Proctor, B. D., & Lee, C. H. (2006). Income, poverty, and health insurance coverage in the United States: 2005. *Current Population Reports.* Washington, DC: U.S. Department of Commerce.

Department for Children, Schools, and Families. (2009). *Getting to grips with assessing pupils' progress.* London: Crown.

Desimone, L., Porter, A., Garet, M., Yoon, K., & Birman, B. (2002). Effects of professional development on teachers' instruction: Results from a three-year longitudinal study. *Education Evaluation and Policy Analysis, 24*(2), 81–112.

DeVise, D. (1999, November 5). A+ plan prompts teacher exodus in Broward County. *Miami Herald*, p. 1B.

Dewey, J. (1900). *The school and society.* Chicago: University of Chicago Press.

Dewey, J. (1916). *Democracy and education*. New York: Macmillan.

Diamond, J., & Spillane, J. (2002). *High stakes accountability in urban elementary schools: Challenging or reproducing inequality?* Working paper for the Northwestern University Institute for Policy Research, Evanston, IL.

Dixon, Q. L. (2005). Bilingual education policy in Singapore: An analysis of its sociohistorical roots and current academic outcomes. *International Journal of Bilingual Education and Bilingualism, 8*(1), 25–47.

Doyle, W. (1986). Content representation in teachers' definitions of academic work. *Journal of Curriculum Studies, 18,* 365–379.

Doolan, J., & Peters, T. (2007, October 17). *NAEP 2007: Reading and mathematics, grades 4 and 8.* Presentation to the New Jersey State Board of Education.

Douglass, J. A. (2006). *The waning of America's higher education advantage.* Paper CSHE-9-06. Berkeley: Center for Studies in Higher Education, University of California at Berkeley.

Dowling, M. (undated). *Examining the exams.* Retrieved September 14, 2008, from http://www.hkeaa.edu.hk/files/pdf/markdowling_e.pdf

Downes T. A., & Pogue, T. F. (1994). Adjusting school aid formulas for the higher cost of educating disadvantaged students. *National Tax Journal, 47*(1), 89–110.

Doyle, W. (1986). Content representation in teachers' definitions of academic work. *Journal of Curriculum Studies, 18,* 365–379.

Duncombe, W., Ruggiero, J., & Yinger, J. (1996). Alternative approaches to measuring the cost of education. In H. F. Ladd (Ed.), *Holding schools accountable: Performance-based reform in education* (pp. 327–356). Washington, DC: Brookings Institution.

Dreeben, R. (1987, Winter). Closing the divide: What teachers and administrators can do to help Black students reach their reading potential, *American Educator, 11*(4), pp. 28–35.

Dreeben, R., & Gamoran, A. (1986). Race, instruction, and learning. *American Sociological Review, 51*(5), pp. 660–669.

Dreeben, R., & Barr, R. (1987, April). *Class composition and the design of instruction.* Paper presented at the Annual Meeting of the American Education Research Association, Washington, DC.

Drucker, P. F. (1994, November). The age of social transformation. *Atlantic Monthly, 274*(5), pp. 53–80.

DuBois, W.E.B. (1970). The freedom to learn. In P. S. Foner (Ed.), *W.E.B. DuBois speaks* (pp. 230–231). New York: Pathfinder.

Dunne, F., Nave, B., & Lewis, A. (2000). Critical friends: Teachers helping to improve student learning. *Phi Delta Kappa International Research Bulletin (CEDR), 28,* 9–12. Retrieved September 11, 2008, from http://www.pdkintl.org/edres/resbul28.htm

Earl, L., Watson, N., & Torrance, N. (2002). Front row seats: What we've learned from the National Literacy and Numeracy Strategies in England. *Journal of Educational Change, 3*(1), 35–53.

Ebmeier, H., Twombly, S., & Teeter, D. (1990). The comparability and adequacy of financial support for schools of education. *Journal of Teacher Education, 42*(3), 226–235.

Eckstein, M. A., & Noah, H. J. (1993). *Secondary school examinations: International perspectives on policies and practice.* New Haven, CT: Yale University Press.

Eckstrom, R., & Villegas, A. M. (1991). Ability grouping in middle grade mathematics: Process and consequences. *Research in Middle Level Education, 15*(1), pp. 1–20.

Eddin, K. T., Macallair, D., & Schiraldi, V. (1999). *Class dismissed: Higher education vs. corrections during the Wilson years.* San Francisco: Justice Policy Institute.

Edmonds, R. (1979). Effective schools for the urban poor. *Educational Leadership, 37*(1), 15–18, 20–24.

EdSource. (2001, October). *How California ranks: A comparison of education expenditures.* Palo Alto, CA: Author.

Education Trust. (2004). *EdWatch online: 2004 state summary reports.* Retrieved June 4, 2009, from www.edtrust.org

Education Trust-West. (2005). *California's hidden teacher spending gap: How state and district budgeting practices shortchange poor and minority students and their schools.* Oakland, CA: Author. Retrieved January 29, 2009, from http://www.hiddengap.org/resources/report031105.pdf

Educational Research Service. (1980). *Class size: A summary of research.* Reston, VA: Author.

Educational Testing Service. (1991). *The state of inequality.* Princeton, NJ: Author.

Elmore, R. (1996). Getting to scale with good educational practice. *Harvard Educational Review, 66*(1), 1–26.

Elmore, R., & Burney, D. (1999). Investing in teacher learning: Staff development and instructional improvement in community school district #2, New York City. In L. Darling-Hammond & G. Sykes (Eds.), *Teaching as the learning profession.* San Francisco: Jossey-Bass.

Elmore, R., & Fuhrman, S. (1993). Opportunity to learn and the state role in education. In *The debate on opportunity-to-learn standards: Commissioned papers.* Washington, DC: National Governors Association.

Erskine, R. (2002, February). *Statement on school reform and the Seattle contract.* Society for the Advancement of Excellence in Education. Retrieved June 9, 2009, from http://www.saee.ca/index.php?option=com_content&task=view&id=319&Itemid=90

Falk, B., & Ort, S. (1997, April). *Sitting down to score: Teacher learning through assessment.* Presentation at the annual meeting of the American Educational Research Association. Chicago.

Fensham, P. (1994). Progression in school science curriculum: A rational prospect or a chimera? *Research in Science Education, 24*(1), 76–82.

Ferguson, R. F. (1991, Summer). Paying for public education: New evidence on how and why money matters. *Harvard Journal on Legislation, 28*(2), pp. 465–498.

Ferguson, R. F., & Ladd, H. F. (1996). How and why money matters: An analysis of Alabama schools. In H. Ladd (Ed.), *Holding schools accountable* (pp. 265–298). Washington, DC: Brookings Institution.

Fernandez, C. (2002). Learning from Japanese approaches to professional development: The case of lesson study. *Journal of Teacher Education, 53*(5), 393–405.

Fetler, M. (1999). High school staff characteristics and mathematics test results. *Education Policy Analysis Archives, 7*(9). Retrieved June 4, 2009, from http://epaa.asu.edu/epaa/v7n9.html

Figlio, D. N., & Getzler, L. S. (2002, April). *Accountability, ability, and disability: Gaming the system?* Cambridge, MA: National Bureau of Economic Research.

Fine, M. (1991). *Framing dropouts: Notes on the politics of an urban public school.* Albany: State University of New York Press.

Fine, M. (1994). *Charting urban school reform: Reflections on public high schools in the midst of change.* New York: Teachers College Press.

Fine (2002). Expert report in *Williams v. California.* Retrieved July 30, 2008, from http://www.decentschools.org/expert_reports/fine_report.pdf

Fine, M. (2002). The psychological and academic effects on children and adolescents of structural facilities' problems, exposure to high levels of under-credentialed teachers, substantial teacher turnover, and inadequate books and materials. Report prepared for *Williams v. California.* Retrieved March 20, 2009, from http://www.decentschools.org/expert_reports/fine_report.pdf

Fine, M., Stoudt, B., & Futch, V. (2005). *The internationals network for public schools: A quantitative and qualitative cohort analysis of graduation and dropout rates.* New York: City University of New York, Graduate Center.

Finland Ministry of Education. (2009). Education policy: Objectives and programmes. Retrieved April 6, 2009, from http://www.minedu.fi/OPM/Koulutus/koulutuspolitiikka/linjaukset_ohjelmat_ja_hankkeet/?lang=en

Finley, M. K. (1984). Teachers and tracking in a comprehensive high school. *Sociology of Education, 57*, pp. 233–243.

Finnish National Board of Education. (2007, November 12). Background for Finnish PISA success. Retrieved August 25, 2008, from www.oph.fi/english/SubPage.asp?path=447,65535,77331

Firestone, W., & Mayrowetz, D. (2000). Rethinking "high stakes": Lessons from the United States and England and Wales. *Teachers College Record, 102*(4), 724–49.

Flexner, A., & Pritchett, H. S. (1910). *Medical education in the United States and Canada: A report to the Carnegie Foundation for the Advancement of Teaching.* New York: Carnegie Foundation for the Advancement of Teaching.

Flores v. Arizona, Pet. App. 108a. *Amicus Curiae* Brief of Education Policy Scholars in Support of Petitioners, filed February 26, 2009.

Fordham, S. (1988). Racelessness as a factor in Black students' school success: Pragmatic strategy or pyrrhic victory? *Harvard Educational Review, 58*, 54–84.

Forum on Educational Accountability. (2004, October 21). Joint organizational statement on No Child Left Behind (NCLB) Act. Retrieved May 30, 2009, from http://www.edaccountability.org/Joint_Statement.html

Frede, E., Jung, K., Barnett, W. S., Lamy, C. E., & Figueras, A. (2007). *The Abbott Preschool Program longitudinal effects study.* New Brunswick, NJ: Early Learning Improvement Consortium and New Jersey Department of Education.

French, D. (2008). Boston's pilot schools: An alternative to charter schools. In L. Dingerson, B. Miner, B. Peterson, & S. Walters (Eds.), *Keeping the promise? The debate over charter schools* (pp. 67–80). Milwaukee, WI: Rethinking Schools.

Friedkin, N., & Necochea, J. (1998). School system size and performance: A contingency perspective. *Educational Evaluation and Policy Analysis, 10*(3), 237–249.

Friedlaender, D., & Darling-Hammond, L., with Andree, A., Lewis-Charp, H., McCloskey, L., Richardson, N., & Vasudeva, A. (2007). *High schools for equity: Policy supports for student learning in communities of color.* Stanford, CA: School Redesign Network at Stanford University. Retrieved June 4, 2009, from http://www.srnleads.org/resources/publications/hsfe.html

Friedman, T. L. (2005). *The world is flat: A brief history of the twenty-first century.* New York: Picador.

Fullan, M. (2005). *Leadership and sustainability: System thinkers in action.* Thousand Oaks, CA: Corwin.

Fullan, M. (2007). *The new meaning of educational change* (4th ed.). New York: Teachers College Press.

Fuller, E. (1998, November). *Do properly certified teachers matter? A comparison of elementary school performance on the TAAS in 1997 between schools with high and low percentages of properly certified regular education teachers.* Austin: The Charles A. Dana Center, University of Texas at Austin.

Fuller, E. (2000, April). *Do properly certified teachers matter? Properly certified algebra teachers and Algebra I achievement in Texas.* Paper presented at the annual meeting of the American Educational Research Association. New Orleans, LA.

Fuller, E. (2003). *Beginning teacher retention rates for TxBESS and non-TxBESS teachers.* Unpublished paper. State Board for Educator Certification, Texas.

Fuller, E. (2008, October). *Secondary mathematics and science teachers in Texas: Supply, demand, and quality.* Austin: Department of Educational Administration, University Council for Educational Administration, The University of Texas at Austin.

Futernick, K. (2001, April). *A district-by-district analysis of the distribution of teachers in California and an overview of the Teacher Qualification Index (TQI).* Sacramento: California State University.

Gallego, M. A. (2001). Is experience the best teacher? The potential of coupling classroom and community-based field experiences. *Journal of Teacher Education, 52*(4), 312–325.

Gamoran, A. (1992). Access to excellence: Assignment to honors English classes in the transition from middle to high school. *Educational Evaluation and Policy Analysis, 14*(3), 185–204.

Gamoran, A. (1990, April). *The consequences of track-related instructional differences for student achievement.* Paper presented at the Annual Meeting of the American Educational Research Association, Boston.

Gamoran, A., & Berends, M. (1987). The effects of stratification in secondary schools: Synthesis of survey and ethnographic research. *Review of Educational Research, 57*, 415–436.

Gamoran, A., & Hannigan, E. C. (2000). Algebra for everyone? Benefits of college-preparatory mathematics for students with diverse abilities in early secondary school. *Educational Evaluation and Policy Analysis, 22*, 241–254.

Gamoran, A., & Mare, R. (1989). Secondary school tracking and educational inequality: Compensation, reinforcement or neutrality? *American Journal of Sociology, 94*, 1146–1183.

Gamse, B. C., Jacob, R. T., Horst, M., Boulay, B., & Unlu, F. (2008). *Reading First impact study final report* (NCEE 2009-4038). Washington, DC: National Center for Education Evaluation and Regional Assistance, Institute of Education Sciences, U.S. Department of Education.

Garcia, E. (1993). Language, culture, and education. In L. Darling-Hammond (Ed.), *Review of research in education* (Vol. 19, pp. 51–98). Washington, DC: American Educational Research Association.

Garet, M., Porter, A., Desimone, L., Birman, B., & Yoon, K. S. (2001). What makes professional development effective? Results from a national sample of teachers. *American Educational Research Journal, 38*(4), 915–945.

Garofano, A., Sable, J., & Hoffman, L. (2008). *Characteristics of the 100 largest public elementary and secondary school districts in the United States: 2004–05*. U.S. Department of Education, National Center for Education Statistics. Washington, DC: U.S. Government Printing Office.

Gates Foundation. (2005). *High performing schools districts: Challenge, support, alignment, and choice.* Seattle: Bill and Melinda Gates Foundation.

Gemignani, R. J. (1994, October). Juvenile correctional education: A time for change. Update on research. *Juvenile Justice Bulletin.* Washington, DC: U.S. Department of Justice, Office of Juvenile Justice and Delinquency Prevention.

General Accounting Office. (2001). *School vouchers: Publicly funded programs in Cleveland and Milwaukee.* Washington, DC: Author.

Glaser, R. (1981). The future of testing: A research agenda for cognitive psychology and psychometrics. *American Psychologist, 39*(9), 923–936.

Glaser, R. (1990). *Testing and assessment: O Tempora! O Mores!* Pittsburgh, PA: University of Pittsburgh, Learning Research and Development Center.

Glass, G. V., Cahen, L. S., Smith, M. L, & Filby, N. N. (1982). *School class size: Research and policy.* Beverly Hills, CA: Sage.

Goddard, Y. L., Goddard, R. D., & Tschannen-Moran, M. (2007). Theoretical and empirical investigation of teacher collaboration for school improvement and student achievement in public elementary schools. *Teachers College Record, 109*(4), 877–896.

Goe, L. (2002). *Legislating equity: The distribution of emergency permit teachers in California.* Berkeley: Graduate School of Education, University of California, Berkeley.

Goe, L. (2002). Legislating equity: The distribution of emergency permit teachers in California. *Educational Policy Analysis Archives, 10*(42). Retrieved June 4, 2009, from http://epaa.asu.edu/epaa/v10n42/

Goertz, M. E., & Weiss, M. (2007, November 12). *Assessing success in school finance litigation: The case of New Jersey.* Paper for Columbia University, Teachers College, Symposium: Equal Educational Opportunity: What Now? Retrieved June 4, 2009, from http://devweb.tc.columbia.edu/manager/symposium/Files/111_goertz_NJ_case_study_draft%20_10.04.07_.pdf

Goldberg, G. L., & Rosewell, B. S. (2000). From perception to practice: The impact of teachers' scoring experience on the performance based instruction and classroom practice. *Educational Assessment, 6*, 257–290.

Goldhaber, D., & Anthony, E. (2005). *Can teacher quality be effectively assessed?* Seattle: University of Washington and the Urban Institute.

Goldhaber, D. D., & Brewer, D. J. (2000). Does teacher certification matter? High school certification status and student achievement. *Educational Evaluation and Policy Analysis, 22*, 129–145.

Gonnie van Amelsvoort, H.W.C., & Scheerens, J. (1996). International comparative indicators on teachers. *International Journal of Educational Research, 25*(3), 267–277.

Good, T. L., & Brophy, J. (1987). *Looking in classrooms.* New York: Harper and Row.

Gordon, S. P., & Reese, M. (1997, July). High stakes testing. Worth the price? *Journal of School Leadership, 7,* 345–368.

Gottfredson, G. D., & Daiger, D. C. (1979). *Disruption in 600 schools.* Baltimore: The Johns Hopkins University, Center for Social Organization of Schools.

Grant, C. A. (1989, June). Urban teachers: Their new colleagues and curriculum. *Phi Delta Kappan, 70*(10), 764–770.

Greenwald, R., Hedges, L. V., & Laine, R. D. (1996a). The effect of school resources on student achievement. *Review of Educational Research, 66*(1), 361–396.

Greenwald, R., Hedges, L. V., & Laine, R. D. (1996b). Interpreting research on school resources and student achievement: A rejoinder to Hanushek. *Review of Educational Research, 66*(3), 411–416.

Griffin, B., & Heidorn, M. (1996). An examination of the relationship between MCT performance and dropping out of high school. *Educational Evaluation and Policy Analysis, 18:* 243–251.

Grissmer, D. W., Flanagan, A., Kawata, J., & Williamson, S. (2000). *Improving student achievement: What NAEP state test scores tell us.* Santa Monica, CA: RAND Report. Retrieved June 4, 2009, from http://www.rand.org/publications/MR/MR924

Gritz, R. M., & Theobald, N. D. (1996). The effects of school district spending priorities on length of stay in teaching. *Journal of Human Resources, 31*(3), 477–512.

Guadarrama, I. N., Ramsey, J., & Nath, J. L. (Eds.). *Forging alliances in community and thought: Research in professional development schools.* Greenwich, CT: Information Age Publishing.

Gunderson, S., Jones, R., & Scanland, K. (2004). *The jobs revolution: Changing how America works.* Austin, TX: Copywriters, Inc.

Guryan, J. (2001). *Does money matter? Regression-discontinuity estimates from education finance reform in Massachusetts.* NBER Working Paper 8269. Cambridge, MA: National Bureau of Economic Research.

Hallinan, M. T. & Kubitschek, W. N. (1999). Curriculum differentiation and high school achievement. *Social Psychology of Education, 3,* 41–62.

Hammerness, K., Darling-Hammond, L., & Shulman, L. (2002). Toward expert thinking: How curriculum case writing prompts the development of theory-based professional knowledge in student teachers. *Teaching Education, 13*(2), 221–245.

Hancock v. Driscoll. (2002). Superior Court Civil Action No. 02-2978.

Haney, W. (2000). The myth of the Texas miracle in education. *Educational Policy Analysis Archives, 8*(41). Retrieved June 9, 2009, from http://epaa.asu.edu/epaa/v8n41/

Hanushek, E. (2003). The structure of analysis and argument in plaintiff expert reports for *Williams v. State of California.* Retrieved March 20, 2009, from http://www.decentschools.org/expert_reports/hanushek_report.pdf

Hanushek, E. (2003). *The structure of analysis and argument in plaintiff expert reports for* Williams v. State of California. Retrieved April 19, 2004, from http://www.mofo.com/decentschools/expert_reports/hanushek_report.pdf

Hanushek, E. A., Kain, J. F., & Rivkin, S. G. (1999). *Do higher salaries buy better teachers?* Working Paper 7082. Cambridge, MA: National Bureau of Economic Research.

Hanushek, E., & Raymond, M. (2003). Improving educational quality: How best to evaluate our schools? In Y. Kodrzycki (Ed.), *Education in the 21st Century: Meeting the Challenges of a Changing World.* Boston: Federal Reserve Bank of Boston.

Hargreaves, A. (2008). The coming of post-standardization: Three weddings and a funeral. In C. Sugrue (Ed.), *The future of educational change: International perspectives* (pp 15–33). New York: Routledge.

Harlem Children's Zone. (2008). Home page. Retrieved May 29, 2009, from http://www.hcz.org/

Hart, B., & Risley, T. (1995). *Meaningful differences in the everyday experience of young American children.* Baltimore: Brookes Publishing.

Hassell, B. C. (2002). *Better pay for better teaching: Making teacher compensation pay off in the age of accountability.* Progressive Policy Institute 21st Century Schools Project. Retrieved November 18, 2004, from http://www.broadfoundation.org/investments/education-net.shtml

Hauser, R. (1999, October). *Should we end social promotion? Truth and consequences.* CDE Paper 96-04. Madison: The University of Wisconsin-Madison, Center for Demography and Ecology.

Hawk, P., Coble, C. R., & Swanson, M. (1985). Certification: It does matter. *Journal of Teacher Education, 36*(3), 13–15.

Haycock, K. (2000, Spring). Honor in the boxcar: Equalizing teacher quality. *Thinking K–16, 4*(1), 1.

Haycock, K. (2000, Spring). No more settling for less. *Thinking K–16, 4*(1), 11.

Haynes, D. (1995). One teacher's experience with National Board assessment. *Educational Leadership, 52*(8), 58–60.

Hean, T. C. (2001, October 23). Leading innovation in education. Speech given at the LEP Graduation Ceremony at Grand Copthorne Waterfront Hotel, Singapore.

Heckman, J. J. (2008). The case for investing in disadvantaged young children. In *Big ideas for children: Investing in our nation's future* (pp. 49–66). Washington, DC: First Focus.

Hedges, L. V., Laine, R. D., & Greenwald, R. (1994). Does money matter? A meta-analysis of studies of the effects of differential school inputs on student outcomes. *Educational Research, 23*(3), 5–14.

Hegarty, S. (2001, January 21). Newcomers find toll of teaching is too high: Among those quitting are non-education majors thrust into challenging classrooms. *St. Petersburg Times.*

Henke, R. R., Chen, X., Geis, S., & Knepper, P. (2000). *Progress through the teacher pipeline: 1992–93 college graduates and elementary/secondary school teaching as of 1997.* NCES 2000-152. Washington, DC: National Center for Education Statistics.

Herman, J. L., & Golan, S. (1993). Effects of standardized testing on teaching and schools. *Educational Measurement: Issues and Practice, 12*(4): 20–25, 41–42.

Herman, J. L. (2002). *Black-white-other test score gap: Academic achievement among mixed race adolescents.* Institute for Policy Research Working Paper. Evanston, IL: Northwestern University Institute for Policy Research.

Herman, J. L., Brown, R. S., & Baker, E. L. (2000). *Student assessment and student achievement in the California public school system.* Retrieved November 18, 2004, from cresst96.cse.ucla.edu/CRESST/Reports/TECH519.pdf

Herrnstein, R. J., and Murray, C. (1994). *The bell curve: Intelligence and class structure in American life.* New York: Free Press.

Hess, A. (1986). Educational triage in an urban school setting. *Metropolitan Education, 2,* pp. 39–52.

Hess, G. A., Ells, E., Prindle, C., Liffman, P., & Kaplan, B. (1987). Where's room 185? How schools can reduce their dropout problem. *Education and Urban Society, 19*(3), 330–355.

Heubert, J., and Hauser, R. (Eds.). (1999). *High stakes: Testing for tracking, promotion, and graduation.* A report of the National Research Council. Washington, DC: National Academy Press.

Hill, P. (2006). *Put learning first: A portfolio approach to public schools.* Washington, DC: Progressive Policy Institute.

Hoffer, T. B. (1992). Middle school ability grouping and student achievement in science and mathematics. *Educational Evaluation and Policy Analysis, 14*(3), 205–227.

Hoffman, J. V., Assaf, L. C., & Paris, S. G. (2001). High stakes testing in reading: Today in Texas, tomorrow? *The Reading Teacher, 54*(5), 482–492.

Holmes, T., & Matthews, K. (1984). *The effects of nonpromotion on elementary and junior high pupils: A meta-analysis. Review of Educational Research,* Vol. 54, pp. 225–236.

Hord, S. (1997). *Professional learning communities: Communities of continuous inquiry and improvement.* Austin, TX: Southwest Educational Development Laboratory.

Horn, C. (2002). The intersection of race, class and English learner status. Working Paper. Prepared for National Research Council.

Howard, R., Hitz, R., & Baker, L. (1997). Comparative study of expenditures per student credit hour of education programs to programs of other disciplines and professions. Montana State University–Bozeman.

Howley, C. (1995). The Matthew principle: A West Virginia replication? *Education Policy Analysis Archives* 3, no. 18.

Howley, C. B., & Bickel, R. (1999). *The Matthew project: National report.* Charleston, WV: Appalachia Educational Laboratory.

Howley, C. B., & Harmon, H. L. (2000). *Small high schools that flourish: Rural context, case studies, and resources.* Charleston, WV: Appalachia Educational Laboratory.

Howley, C., & Howley, A. (2004). School size and the influence of socioeconomic status on student achievement: Confronting the threat of size bias in national data sets. *Education Policy Analysis Archives* 12, no. 52.

Illinois Fair Schools Coalition. (1985). *Holding students back: An expensive reform that doesn't work.* Chicago: Author.

Huh, Kyung-chul. (2007). *Understanding Korean education, volume 1: School curriculum in Korea.* Seoul: Korean Educational Development Institute.

Imberman, S. (2007). Achievement and behavior in charter schools: Drawing a more complete picture occasional paper 142. New York: National Center for the Study of Privatizations in Education.

Ingersoll, R., & Kralik, J. M. (2004). *The impact of mentoring on teacher retention: What the research says.* Denver: Education Commission of the States.

Ingvarson, L. (2005). Getting professional development right. In Australian Council for Educational Research *Annual Conference Proceedings 2005—Getting Data to Support Learning Conference* (pp. 63–71). Retrieved June 28, 2008, from http://www.acer.edu.au/documents/RC2005_Ingvarson.pdf

Institute for Education Sciences. (2007). *Highlights from PISA 2006: Performance of U.S. 15-year-old students in science and mathematics literacy in an international context.* Washington, DC: U.S. Department of Education. Retrieved April 1, 2008 from http://nces.ed.gov/surveys/pisa/index.asp

Institute on Race and Poverty. (2008). *Failed promises: Assessing charter schools in the Twin Cities.* Minneapolis: University of Minnesota, Institute on Race and Poverty.

Intercultural Development Research Association. (1996, October). *Texas school survey project: A summary of findings.* San Antonio, TX: Intercultural Development Research Association.

International Baccalaureate Organization. (2005, November). *IB diploma programme: English A1—higher level—Paper 2.* Retrieved May 31, 2008, from http://www.ibo.org/diploma/curriculum/examples/samplepapers/documents/gp1_englisha1hl2.pdf

Irvine, J. J. (1990). *Black students and school failure: Policies, practices, and prescriptions.* New York: Praeger.

Irvine, J. J. (1992). Making teacher education culturally responsive. In M. E. Dilworth (Ed.), *Diversity in teacher education* (pp. 79–92). San Francisco: Jossey-Bass.

Jacob, B. A. (2002). *The impact of high-stakes testing on student achievement: Evidence from Chicago.* Working Paper. Harvard University.

Jacobs, B. A. (2001). Getting tough? The impact of high school graduation exams. *Educational Evaluation and Policy Analysis, 23*(2), 99–122.

Japanese Ministry of Education, Culture, Sports, Science, and Technology. (2004). *Japan's education at a glance, 2004, School education.* Tokyo, Japan: Author.

Jefferson, T. (1786). Thomas Jefferson to George Wythe, ME 5:396.

Jefferson, T. (1817). Thomas Jefferson: Elementary School Act, 1817. ME 17:440.

Jimerson, S. R., Anderson, G. E., & Whipple, A. D. (2002). Winning the battle and losing the war: Examining the relationship between grade retention and dropping out of high school. *Psychology in the Schools, 39*(4), pp. 441–457.

Jones, B. D., & Egley, R. J. (2004). Voices from the frontlines: Teachers' perceptions of high-stakes testing. *Education Policy Analysis Archives, 12*(39). Retrieved August 10, 2004, from http://epaa.asu.edu/epaa/v12n39/

Jones, L. V. (1984). White-Black achievement differences: The narrowing gap. *American Psychologist, 39*, pp. 1207–1213.

Jones, L. V., Burton, N. W., & Davenport, E. C. (1984). Monitoring the achievement of Black students. *Journal for Research in Mathematics Education, 15*, pp. 154–164.

Jones, M. G., Jones, B. D., Hardin, B., Chapman, L., & Yarbrough, T. M. (1999). The impact of high-stakes testing on teachers and students in North Carolina. *Phi Delta Kappan, 81*(3), 199–203.

Joyce, B., & Calhoun, E. (1996). *Learning experiences in school renewal: An exploration of five successful programs.* Eugene, OR: ERIC Clearinghouse on Educational Management.

Jukes, I., & McCain, T. (2002, June 18). *Living on the future edge.* InfoSavvy Group and Cyster.

Justice Policy Institute. (2005). *Cellblocks or classrooms?* Retrieved September 22, 2007, from http://www.justicepolicy.org/article.php?id=14

Kahlenberg, R. (2001). *All together now.* Washington, DC: Brookings Institution Press.

Kain, J. F., & Singleton, K. (1996). Equality of educational opportunity revisited. *New England Economic Review,* May–June, 87–111.

Kang, N. H., & Hong, M. (2008). Achieving excellence in teacher workforce and equity in learning opportunities in South Korea. *Educational Researcher, 37*(4), 200–207.

Karmarkar, U.S., & Apte, U. M. (2007, March). Operations management in the information economy: Information products, processes, and chains. *Journal of Operations Management.*

Kaufman, J. E., & Rosenbaum, J. E. (1992). Education and employment of low-income Black youth in White suburbs. *Educational Evaluation and Policy Analysis, 14*(3), pp. 229–240.

Kearns, D. (1988). A business perspective on American schooling. *Education Week.* Retrieved June 14, 2009, from http://www.edweek.org/login.html?source=http://www.edweek.org/ew/articles/1988/04/20/30kearns.h07.html&destination=http://www.edweek.org/ew/articles/1988/04/20/30kearns.h07.html&levelId=2100

Kim, G. J. (2002). Education policies and reform in South Korea. In *Secondary Education in Africa: Strategies for Renewal, World Bank Africa Region ed.* (p. 30). Washington, DC: World Bank.

Kim, Y., & Lee, S. (2002). *Adapting education to the information age: A white paper.* Seoul, Korea: Ministry of Education and Human Resources Development.

Klein, S. P., Hamilton, L. S., McCaffrey, D. F., & Stetcher, B. M. (2000). *What do test scores in Texas tell us?* Santa Monica, CA: The RAND Corporation.

Kluger, R. (1976). *Simple justice.* New York: Alfred A. Knopf.

Knapp, M. S. (Ed.). (1995). *Teaching for meaning in high-poverty classrooms.* New York: Teachers College Press.

Korea Education and Research Information Service. *Adapting ICT to elementary and secondary schools.* Retrieved March 29, 2007, from http://www.keris.or.kr/english/pages/sub_04_2.html

Korea Institute of Curriculum & Evaluation. (nd.) *National curriculum and evaluation.* Retrieved November 16, 2006, from http://www.kice.re.kr/kice/eng/info/info.2.jsp

Korean Educational Development Institute (KEDI). (2004). *Statistical yearbook of education, 2004.* Seoul, Korea: KEDI.

Korean Educational Development Institute (KEDI). (2006). *Statistical yearbook of education, 2006.* Seoul, Korea: KEDI.

Korean Educational Development Institute (KEDI). (2007a). *Understanding Korean education, vol. 3: School education in Korea.* Seoul, Korea: Author.

Korean Educational Development Institute (KEDI). (2007b). *Understanding Korean education, vol. 5: Education and Korea's development.* Seoul, Korea: Author.

Koretz, D., & Barron, S. I. (1998). *The validity of gains on the Kentucky Instructional Results Information System (KIRIS).* Santa Monica, CA: RAND, MR-1014-EDU.

Koretz, D., Linn, R. L., Dunbar, S. B., & Shepard, L. A. (1991, April). The effects of high-stakes testing: Preliminary evidence about generalization across tests. In R. L. Linn (chair), *The effects of high stakes testing.* Symposium presented at the annual meetings of the American Educational Research Association and the National Council on Measurement in Education, Chicago.

Koretz, D., Mitchell, K. J., Barron, S. I., & Keith, S. (1996). *Final report: Perceived effects of the Maryland school performance assessment program.* CSE Technical Report. Los Angeles: UCLA National Center for Research on Evaluation, Standards, and Student Testing.

Kozol, J. (1991). *Savage inequalities.* New York: Crown.

Kozol, J. (2005). *The shame of a nation.* New York: Crown.

Krieger, L. M. (2008, July 18). In this contest, China beats UC-Berkeley. *San Jose Mercury News,* pp. 1A, 15A.

Krueger, A. B. (2000). Economic considerations and class size, Paper 447. Princeton University, Industrial Relations Section. Retrieved on May 30, 2007, from www.irs.princeton.edu/pubs/working_papers.html

Krueger, A. B. (2003). Economic considerations and class size. *The Economic Journal, 113*(485), F34–F63.

Kulik, C. C., & Kulik, J. A. (1982). Effects of ability grouping on secondary school students: A meta-analysis of evaluation findings. *American Education Research Journal, 19,* pp. 415–428.

Labaree, D. F. (1984). Setting the standard: Alternative policies for student promotion. *Harvard Educational Review, 54*(1): 67–87.

Laczko-Kerr, I., & Berliner, D. (2002). The effectiveness of Teach for America and other undercertified teachers on student academic achievement: A case of harmful public policy. *Education Policy Analysis Archives, 10*(37). Retrieved August 14, 2009, from http://epaa.asu.edu/epaa/v10n37

Ladd, H. F. & Zelli, A. (2002). School-based accountability in North Carolina: The responses of school principals. *Educational Administration Quarterly, 38*(4), 494–529.

Ladson-Billings, G. (1992). Culturally relevant teaching. In C. A. Grant (Ed.), *Research and multicultural education: From the margins to the mainstream* (pp. 106–121). Washington, DC: Falmer Press.

Ladson-Billings, G. (2006). Equity after Katrina. *Voices in urban education, 10.* Providence, RI: Annenberg Institute for School Reform. Retrieved March 20, 2009 from http://www.annenberginstitute.org/VUE/winter06/Billings.php.

Ladson-Billings, G. (2006). From the achievement gap to the education debt: Understanding achievement in U.S. schools. *Educational Researcher, 35*(10), pp. 3–12.

Lankford, H., Loeb, S., & Wyckoff, J. (2002). Teacher sorting and the plight of urban schools: A descriptive analysis. *Education Evaluation and Policy Analysis, 24*(1), 37–62.

Lavonen, J. (2008). *Reasons behind Finnish students' success in the PISA scientific literacy assessment.* Helsinki, Finland: University of Helsinki. Retrieved August 25, 2008 from www.oph.fi/info/finlandinpisastudies/conference2008/science_results_and_reasons.pdf

Lee, C. (2004). *Racial segregation and educational outcomes in metropolitan Boston.* Cambridge, MA: The Civil Rights Project at Harvard University.

Lee, C. J. (2005). Korean model of secondary education development: Approaches, outcomes and emerging tasks. In M. Kaneko (Ed.), *Core academic competences: Policy issues and educational reform.* Tokyo: University of Tokyo, Center for Research of Core academic competences.

Lee, J., & Wong, K (2004). The impact of accountability on racial and socioeconomic equity: Considering both school resources and achievement outcomes. *American Educational Research Journal, 41*(4).

Lee, V., et al. (2000). Inside large and small high schools: Curriculum and social relations. *Educational Evaluation and Policy Analysis, 22*(2), 147–71.

Lee, V., & Bryk, A. (1988). Curriculum tracking as mediating the social distribution of high school achievement. *Sociology of Education, 61*, pp. 78–94.

Lee, V., Bryk, A., & Smith, J. (1993). The organization of effective secondary schools. In Linda Darling-Hammond (Ed.), *Review of research in education*. Washington, DC: American Educational Research Association.

Lee, V., Croninger, R., & Smith, J. (1997). Course-taking, equity, and mathematics learning: Testing the constrained curriculum hypothesis in U.S. secondary schools. *Educational Evaluation and Policy Analysis, 19*(2), 99–121.

Lee, V., & Loeb, S. (2000). "School size in Chicago elementary schools: Effects on teachers' attitudes and students' achievement." *American Educational Research Journal, 37*(1), 3–31.

Lee, V. E., & Smith, J. B. (1995). Effects of high school restructuring and size on early gains in achievement and engagement. *Sociology of Education, 68*(4), 241–270.

Lee, V. E., Smith, J. B., & Croninger, R. G. (1995, Fall). Another look at high school restructuring: More evidence that it improves student achievement and more insight into why. *Issues in Restructuring Schools.* Issue report no. 9, pp. 1–9. Madison: Center on the Organization and Restructuring of Schools, University of Wisconsin.

Lefkowits, L., & Diamond, B. (2009). *Transforming urban education: Implications for state policymakers.* Knowledgeworks Foundation. Retrieved May 29, 2009, from http://www.futureofed.org/pdf/taking-action/PolicyBrief1.pdf

Leithwood, K., & Jantzi, D. (2005). A review of transformational school leadership research 1996–2005. Paper presented at the annual meeting of the American Educational Research Association. Montreal, Canada.

Leithwood, K., Seashore-Louis, K., Anderson, S., & Wahlstrom, K. (2004). *How leadership influences student learning.* Center for Applied Research and Educational Improvement and Ontario Institute for Studies in Education. New York: The Wallace Foundation. Retrieved August 14, 2009, from http://www.wallacefoundation.org/wf/KnowledgeCenter/KnowledgeTopics/EducationLeadership/

Lepoer, B. L. (1989). *Singapore: A country study.* Washington, DC: Government Printing Office for the Library of Congress.

Letter to the California State Board of Education from leading scientists, CEOs, and university presidents. (2004, March 5). Retrieved March 20, 2009, from http://www.sci-ed-ga.org/standards/Final-Board-Letter.pdf

Levin, H. M. (1992). The necessary and sufficient conditions for achieving educational equity. In R. Berne (Ed.), *New York equity study.* Report of the Equity Study Group. Albany: New York State Education Department.

Levin, H. M. (2007). *The costs and benefits of an excellent education.* New York: Teachers College, Columbia University.

Levine, D., & Lezotte, L. (1990). *Unusually effective schools: A review and analysis of research and practice.* Madison, WI: The National Center for Effective Schools Research & Development.

Lieberman, A., & Wood, D. (2002). From network learning to classroom teaching. *Journal of Educational Change, 3*, 315–337.

Lilliard, D., & DeCicca, P. (2001). Higher standards, more dropouts? Evidence within and across time. *Economics of Education Review, 20*(5), 459–473.

Linn, R. L. (2000). Assessments and accountability. *Educational Researcher, 29*(2), 4–16.

Linn, R. L., Graue, M. E., & Sanders, N. M. (1990). Comparing state and district test results to national norms: The validity of claims that "everyone is above average." *Educational Measurement: Issues and Practice, 9*, 5–14.

Little Hoover Commission. (2000). *To build a better school.* Sacramento: Author.

Little, J. W. (1982). Norms of collegiality and experimentation: Workplace conditions of school success. *American Educational Research Journal, 19*(3), 325–340.

Little, J. W. (2003). Inside teacher community: Representations of classroom practice. *Teachers College Record, 105*(6), 913–945.

Liu, G. (2008). Improving Title I funding equity across states, districts, and schools. *Iowa Law Review, 93*(3), 973–1013.

Loeb, S., Darling-Hammond, L., & Luczak, J. (2005). How teaching conditions predict teacher turnover in California schools. *Peabody Journal of Education, 80*(3), pp. 44–70.

Loeb, S., Grissom, J., & Strunk, K. (2007). *District dollars: Painting a picture of revenues and expenditures in California's school districts.* Stanford, CA: Stanford University Institute for Research on Education Policy and Practice.

Los Angeles County Office of Education. (1999, May). Teacher quality and early reading achievement in Los Angeles County public schools. *Trends: Policy issues facing Los Angeles County public schools, 6*(2).

Louis, K. S., Marks, H. M., & Kruse, S. (1996). Professional community in restructuring schools. *American Educational Research Journal, 33*(4), 757–798.

Louis, K. S., & Marks, H. M. (1998). Does professional learning community affect the classroom? Teachers' work and student experiences in restructuring schools. *American Journal of Education, 106*(4), 532–575.

MacDonald, E., & Shirley, D. (2009). *The mindful teacher.* New York: Teachers College Press.

MacInnes, G. (2009). *In plain sight: Simple, difficult lessons from New Jersey's expensive effort to close the achievement gap.* New York: The Century Foundation.

MacPhail-Wilcox, B., & King, R. A. (1986). Resource allocation studies: Implications for school improvement and school finance research. *Journal of Education Finance, 11*, pp. 416–432.

Madaus, G., Russell, M., & Higgins, J. (2009). *The paradoxes of high stakes testing.* Charlotte, NC: Information Age Publishing.

Madaus, G., West, M. M., Harmond, M. C., Lomax, R. G., & Vator, K. A. (1992). *The influence of testing on teaching math and science in grades 4–12.* Chestnut Hill, MA: Center of Study of Testing, Evaluation, and Educational Policy, Boston College.

Massachusetts Department of Education. (2004). Dropout Rates for 2002–03. Retrieved June 30, 2007, from http://www.doe.mass.edu/infoservices/reports/dropout/0203/dropouts.pdf

Mathews, J. (2008, October 6). Merit pay could ruin teamwork. *Washington Post.* P. B02.

Matthews, W. (1984). Influences on the learning and participation of minorities in mathematics. *Journal for Research in Mathematics Education, 15*, pp. 84–95.

McCombs, J. S., Kirby, S. N., Barney, H., Darilek, H., & Magee, S. (2005). *Achieving state and national literacy goals: A long uphill road.* Santa Monica, CA: RAND Corporation.

McGill-Franzen, A., Allington, R. L., Yokio, L., & Brooks, G. (1999). Putting books in the classroom seems necessary but not sufficient. *The Journal of Educational Research, 93*(2), 67–74.

McKnight, C. C., Crosswhite, J. A., Dossey, J. A., Kifer, E., Swafford, S. O., Travers, K. J., & Cooney, T. J. (1987). *The underachieving curriculum: Assessing U.S. School mathematics from an international perspective.* Champaign, IL: Stipes Publishing.

McLaughlin, M. W., & Talbert, J. E. (2001). *Professional communities and the work of high school teaching.* Chicago: University of Chicago Press.

McUsic, M. (1991, Summer). The use of education clauses in school finance reform litigation. *Harvard Journal on Legislation 28*(2), pp. 307–340.

Meier, K. J., Stuart, J., Jr., & England, R. E. (1989). *Race, class and education: The politics of second-generation discrimination.* Madison: University of Wisconsin Press.

Meiers, M., Ingvarson, L, Beavis, A., Hogan, J., & Kleinhenz, E. (2006). *An evaluation of the Getting it Right: Literacy and numeracy strategy in western Australian schools.* Victoria: Australian Council for Educational Research.

Meisels, S. (1992, June). Doing harm by doing good: Iatrogenic effects of early childhood enrollment and promotion policies. *Early Childhood Research Quarterly, 7*(2), 155–174.

Merek E., & Methven, S. (1991). Effects of the learning cycle upon student and classroom teacher performance. *Journal of Research in Science Teaching, 28*(1), 41–53.

Merrow, J. (1999). *Teacher shortage: False alarm?* Video production. New York: Merrow Reports.

Merrow, J. (2004). *From first to worst.* Retrieved March 20, 2009, from http://www.pbs.org/merrow/tv/ftw/

Metz, M. (1990). How social class differences shape teachers' work. In M.W. McLaughlin, J. E. Talbert, & N. Bascia (Eds.), *The contexts of teaching in secondary schools.* New York: Teachers College Press.

Meyer, L. (2002, January 18). The state of the states. *Education Week.* Washington, DC: Editorial Projects in Education.

Mickelson, R. A. (2001). Subverting Swann: First- and second-generation segregation in the Charlotte-Mecklenburg Schools. *American Educational Research Journal, 38,* 215–252.

Mikkola, A. (2000). Teacher education in Finland. In B. Campos Paiva (Ed.), *Teacher education policies in the European Union* (pp. 179–193). Lisbon, Portugal: INAFOP.

Milanowski, A. T., Kimball, S. M., & White, B. (2004). *The relationship between standards-based teacher evaluation scores and student achievement.* Madison: University of Wisconsin–Madison, Consortium for Policy Research in Education.

Miles, K. H., & Darling-Hammond, L. (1998). Rethinking the allocation of teaching resources: Some lessons from high-performing schools. *Educational Evaluation and Policy Analysis, 20*(1), 9–29.

Miller, J. G. (1997, June). African American males in the criminal justice system. *Phi Delta Kappan,* K1–K12.

Ministry of Education. (2007, June). *Overview of the Singapore education system.* Singapore: Author.

Mintrop, H. (2003). The limits of sanctions in low-performing schools: A study of Maryland and Kentucky schools on probation. *Education Policy Analysis Archives, 11*(3). Retrieved November 8, 2004, from http://epaa.asua.edu/epaa/v11n3.htm

Miron, G., Coryn, C., & Mackety, D. M. (2007). *Evaluating the impact of charter schools on student achievement: A longitudinal look at the Great Lakes states.* East Lansing, MI: The Great Lakes Center for Education Research and Practice.

Miron, G., & Nelson, C. (2001). Student achievement in charter schools: What we know and why we know so little. Occasional Paper No. 41. New York: Teachers College, Columbia University, National Center for the Study of Privatization in Education.

Monk, D. H. (1994). Subject matter preparation of secondary mathematics and science teachers and student achievement. *Economics of Education Review, 13*(2), 125–145.

Mont, D., & Rees, D. I. (1996). The influence of classroom characteristics on high school teacher turnover. *Economic Inquiry, 34,* 152.

Moore, D., & Davenport, S. (1988). *The new improved sorting machine.* Madison, WI: National Center on Effective Secondary Schools.

Moore, E. G., & Smith, A. W. (1985). Mathematics aptitude: Effects of coursework, household language, and ethnic differences. *Urban Education, 20,* 273–294.

Mosteller, F. (1995). The Tennessee study of class size in the early school grades. *The Future of Children, 5*(2), 113–127.

Mullis, I.V.S., Martin, M. O., Kennedy, A. M., & Foy, P. (2007). *PIRLS 2006 International Report: IEA's Progress in international reading literacy study in primary schools in 40 countries.* Boston: TIMSS & PIRLS International Study Center, Lynch School of Education, Boston College.

Murnane, R., & Levy, F. (1996). *Teaching the new basic skills.* New York: The Free Press.

Murnane, R., and Olsen, R. J. (1990). The effects of salaries and opportunity costs on length of stay in teaching: Evidence from North Carolina. *The Journal of Human Resources 25*(1), 106–124.

Murnane, R., & Phillips, B. R. (1981, Fall). Learning by doing, vintage, and selection: Three pieces of the puzzle relating teaching experience and teaching performance. *Economics of Education Review, 1*(4), 453–465.

Murnane, R., Singer, J. D., & Willett, J. B. (1989). The influences of salaries and opportunity costs on teachers' career choices: Evidence from North Carolina. *Harvard Educational Review, 59*(3), 325–346.

NAEP Analysis reveals details on states beyond simple scores. (2001, May). *National Education Goals Panel Monthly, 2*(25), 1–8.

Nan Chiau Primary School. (2007). *Curriculum Innovations* brochure. Singapore: Author.

National Center for Education and the Economy. (2007). *Tough choices or tough times. Executive summary.* Washington, DC: Author.

National Center for Education Statistics (NCES). (Undated). *Top four states in closing achievement gap.* Retrieved August 2, 2008, from http://www.fldoe.org/asp/naep/pdf/Top-4-states.pdf

National Center for Education Statistics (NCES). (1985). *The condition of education, 1985.* Washington, DC: U.S. Department of Education.

National Center for Education Statistics (NCES). (1994). *Digest of education statistics, 1994.* Washington, DC: U.S. Department of Education.

National Center for Education Statistics (NCES). (1997). *America's teachers: Profile of a profession, 1993–94.* Washington, DC: U.S. Department of Education.

National Center for Education Statistics (NCES). (1998a). *Characteristics of the 100 largest public elementary and secondary school districts in the United States,* NCES 98-214, Washington, DC: U.S. Department of Education.

National Center for Education Statistics (NCES). (1998b). *The condition of education, 1998.* Washington, DC: U.S. Department of Education.

National Center for Education Statistics (NCES). (2000). *Digest of education statistics, 1999.* Washington, DC: U.S. Department of Education.

National Center for Education Statistics (NCES). (2002). *The condition of education, 2002.* Washington, DC: U.S. Department of Education.

National Center for Education Statistics (NCES). (2003). *The condition of education, 2003.* Washington, DC: U.S. Department of Education.

National Center for Education Statistics (NCES). (2003). *Trends in international mathematics and science study: 2003 results.* Washington, DC: Institute of Educational Sciences, U.S. Department of Education. Retrieved July 12, 2008, from http://nces.ed.gov/timss/TIMSS03Tables.asp?Quest=3&Figure=5

National Center for Education Statistics (NCES). (2004). *Trends in average mathematics scale scores by race/ethnicity.* Retrieved June 13, 2008, from http://nces.ed.gov/nationsreportcard/ltt/results2004/sub-math-race.asp

National Center for Education Statistics (NCES). (2005a). *Digest of education statistics, 2005,* Table 79. Washington, DC: U.S. Department of Education. Retrieved May 16, 2009, from http://nces.ed.gov/programs/digest/d05/tables/dt05_079.asp?referrer=list

National Center for Education Statistics (NCES). (2005b). *NAEP trends on-line.* Washington, DC: U.S. Department of Education, National Assessment of Educational Progress.

National Center for Education Statistics (NCES). (2006). *The nation's report card: Science, 2005.* Washington, DC: U.S. Department of Education.

National Center for Education Statistics (NCES). (2007a). *The nation's report card: Mathematics, 2007.* Washington, DC: U.S. Department of Education. Retrieved August 2, 2008, from http://nces.ed.gov/nationsreportcard/pdf/main2007/2007494.pdf

National Center for Education Statistics (NCES). (2007b). *The nation's report card: Reading, 2007.* Washington, DC: U.S. Department of Education. Retrieved August 2, 2008, from http://nces.ed.gov/nationsreportcard/pdf/main2007/

National Commission on Teaching and America's Future (NCTAF). (1996). *What matters most: Teaching for America's future.* New York: Author.

National Commission on Teaching and America's Future (NCTAF). (1997). Unpublished tabulations from the 1993–94 Schools and Staffing Surveys.

National Commission on Teaching and America's Future (NCTAF). (2003). *No dream denied: A pledge to America's children.* New York: Author.

National Council on Education Standards and Testing (NCEST). (1992). *Raising standards for American education.* Washington, DC: Government Printing Office.

National Education Goals Panel (NEGP). (1998). *The National Education Goals report: Building a nation of learners, 1998.* Washington, DC: U.S. Government Printing Office.

National Education Goals Panel (NEGP). (1999). *Reading achievement state by state, 1999.* Washington, DC: U.S. Government Printing Office.

National Science Foundation. (2008). *Survey of earned doctorates.* Washington, DC: Author.

Natriello, G., McDill, E. L., & Pallas, A. M. (1990). *Schooling disadvantaged children: Racing against catastrophe.* New York: Teachers College Press.

Neault, N., Cook, J. T., Morris, V., & Frank, D. A. (2005, August). *The real cost of a healthy diet: Healthful foods are out of reach for low-income families in Boston, Massachusetts.* Boston: Boston Medical Center, Department of Pediatrics.

Nelson, N., & Weinbaum, E. (2006). *Federal education policy and the states, 1945–2004: A brief synopsis.* Albany: New York State Archives.

New America Foundation. (2008). *Federal education budget project.* Retrieved January 25, 2009, http://www.newamerica.net/education_budget_project/state_per_pupil_expenditures

New America Foundation. (2008b). Within District Comparability Requirement. Retrieved January 29, 2009, from http://www.newamerica.net/programs/education_policy#

New Jersey Department of Education. (2006, July 7). *New Jersey's plan for meeting the highly qualified teacher goal.* Submitted to the U.S. Department of Education. Retrieved August 20, 2008, from http://liberty.state.nj.us/education/data/hqt/06/plan.pdf

New Teacher Project. (2009). *The widget effect: Our national failure to acknowledge and act on differences in teacher effectiveness.* New York: Author.

New York City Division of Assessment and Accountability. (2001). *An examination of the relationship between higher standards and students dropping out.* Flash research report #5. New York: Author.

New York City Public Schools. (1994, February 22). *School profile and school performance in relation to minimum standards, 1992–1993.* New York: New York City Public Schools.

Newmann, F. M., Marks, H. M., & Gamoran, A. (1995). Authentic pedagogy: Standards that boost performance. *American Journal of Education, 104*(4), 280–312.

Newmann, F. M., & Wehlage, G. G. (1995). *Successful school restructuring: A report to the public and educators.* Madison, WI: Center on Organization and Restructuring of Schools.

Newmann, F. M., & Wehlage, G. G. (1997). *Successful school restructuring: A report to the public and educators by the Center on Organization and Restructuring of Schools.* Madison, WI: Document Service, Wisconsin Center for Education Research.

Ng, P. T. (2008). Educational reform in Singapore: From quantity to quality. *Education Research on Policy and Practice, 7*, 5–15.

Nieto, S. (1992). *Affirming diversity.* New York: Longman.

Nieto, S., & Rolon, C. (1996). The preparation and professional development of teachers: A perspective from two Latinas. In J. J. Irvine (Ed.), *Defining the knowledge base for urban teacher education.* Atlanta, GA: CULTURES, Emory University.

Noguera, P. (2008). *The trouble with black boys . . . and other reflections on race, equity, and the future of public education.* San Francisco: Jossey-Bass.

Oakes, J. (1992). Can tracking research inform practice? Technical, normative, and political considerations. *Educational Researcher, 21*(4), pp. 12–21.

Oakes, J. (1990). *Multiplying inequalities: The effects of race, social class, and tracking on opportunities to learn mathematics and science.* Santa Monica, CA: The RAND Corporation.

Oakes, J. (1986). Tracking in secondary schools: A contextual perspective. *Educational Psychologist, 22,* 129–154.

Oakes, J. (1985). *Keeping track.* New Haven: Yale University Press.

Oakes, J. (1993). *Ability grouping, tracking, and within-school segregation in the San Jose Unified School District.* Los Angeles: UCLA.

Oakes, J. (2003). *Education inadequacy, inequality, and failed state policy: A synthesis of expert reports prepared for* Williams v. State of California. Retrieved July 30, 2008, from http://www.decentschools.org/expert_reports/oakes_report.pdf

Oakes, J. (2004). Investigating the claims in *Williams v. State of California:* An unconstitutional denial of education's basic tools? *Teachers College Record, 106*(10), 1889–1906.

Oakes, J. (2005). *Keeping track: How schools structure inequality* (2nd ed). New Haven, CT: Yale University Press.

Oakes, J., and Lipton, M. (1990). *Making the best of schools: A handbook for parents, teachers, and policy-makers.* New Haven, CT: Yale University Press.

Oakes, J., Rogers, J., Silver, D., Valladares, S., Terriquez, V., McDonough, P., Renée, M., & Lipton, M. (2006). *Removing the roadblocks: Fair college opportunities for all California students.* Los Angeles: University of California/All Campus Consortium for Research Diversity & UCLA Institute for Democracy, Education, and Access.

O'Day, J. A. (2002). Complexity, accountability, and school improvement. *Harvard Educational Review, 72*(3), 5, 293–329.

O'Day, J. A., & Smith, M. S. (1993). Systemic school reform and educational opportunity. In S. Fuhrman (Ed.), *Designing coherent education policy: Improving the system.* San Francisco: Jossey-Bass.

Odell, S. J., & Ferraro, D. P. (1992). Teacher mentoring and teacher retention. *Journal of Teacher Education, 43*(3), 200–204.

Olebe, M. (2001). A decade of policy support for California's new teachers: The beginning teacher support and assessment program. *Teacher Education Quarterly, 10*(2), 9–21.

Olsen, L. (1997). *Made in America: Immigrant students in our public schools.* New York: New Press.

Olson, L. (2001). Quality counts 2001: A better balance. *Education Week, 20*(16), 3.

Orfield, G. (2001). *Schools more separate: Consequences of a decade of resegregation.* Cambridge, MA: The Civil Rights Project, Harvard University.

Orfield, G., & Ashkinaze C. (1991). *The closing door: Conservative policy and Black opportunity* (p. 139). Chicago: University of Chicago Press.

Orfield, G., & Lee, C. (2005). *Why segregation matters: Poverty and educational inequality.* Cambridge, MA: The Civil Rights Project, Harvard University.

Orfield, G. F., Monfort, F., & Aaron, M. (1989). *Status of school desegregation: 1968–1986.* Alexandria, VA: National School Boards Association.

Organisation for Economic Cooperation and Development (OECD). (2004). *Completing the foundation for lifelong learning: An OECD survey of upper secondary schools.* Paris: Author.

Organisation for Economic Cooperation and Development (OECD). (2005). *Education at a glance: OECD indicators, 2005.* Paris: Author.

Organisation for Economic Cooperation and Development (OECD). (2006). *Education at a glance: OECD indicators, 2006.* Paris: Author.

Organisation for Economic Cooperation and Development (OECD). (2008). *Education at a glance: OECD indicators, 2007.* Paris: Author.

Organisation for Economic Cooperation and Development (OECD). (2007). *Programme for International Student Assessment 2006: Science competencies for tomorrow's world.* Paris: Author. Retrieved August 14, 2009, from: http://nces.ed.gov/surveys/pisa/index.asp

Ostrowski, P. (1987, November). *Twice in one grade—A false solution. A review of the pedagogical practice of grade retention in elementary schools: What do we know? Should the practice continue?* ERIC # ED300119.

Packard, R., & Dereshiwsky, M. (1991). *Final quantitative assessment of the Arizona career ladder pilot-test project.* Flagstaff: Northern Arizona University.

Pang, M. (2006). The use of learning study to enhance teacher professional learning in Hong Kong. *Teaching Education, 17*(1), 27–42.

Parents Involved in Community Schools v. Seattle School District No. 1 (2007). 127 S. Ct. 2738 (June 28, 2007), decided together with *Meredith v. Jefferson County Board of Education.*

Partnership for 21st Century Skills. (2008). *Twenty-first century skills, education, and competitiveness: A resource and policy guide.* Tucson, AZ: Author.

Paterson Institute. (1996). *The African American data book.* Reston, VA: Paterson Institute.

Pearson, P. D. (2004). The reading wars. *Educational Policy, 18*(1), 216–252.

Pecheone, R. L., & Chung, R. R. (2006). Evidence in teacher education: The performance assessment for California teachers (PACT). *Journal of Teacher Education, 57*(1), 22–36.

Pelavin, S. H., & Kane, M. (1990). *Changing the odds: Factors increasing access to college.* New York: College Entrance Examination Board.

Pedulla, J. J., Abrams, L. M., Madaus, G. F., Russell, M. K., Ramos, M. A., & Miao, J. (2003). *Perceived effects of state-mandated testing programs on teaching and learning: Findings from a national survey of teachers.* Boston: National Board on Testing and Public Policy, Boston College.

Penuel, W., Fishman, B., Yamaguchi, R., & Gallagher, L. (2007, December). What makes professional development effective? Strategies that foster curriculum implementation. *American Educational Research Journal, 44*(4), 921–958.

Peterson, P. (1989). Remediation is no remedy. *Educational Leadership, 46*(60), 24–25.

Petterson, A. (2008). *The National Tests and National Assessment in Sweden.* Stockholm, Sweden: Stockholm Institute for Education. PRIM gruppen. Retrieved May 31, 2008, from http://www.prim.su.se/artiklar/pdf/Sw_test_ICME.pdf

Petition of Harry Briggs et al. to Board of Trustees of School District #22, Clarendon County, November 11, 1949. Retrieved February 10, 2009, from http://www.palmettohistory.org/exhibits/briggs/pages/Briggs4.htm

Pew Center on the States. (2008). *One in 100: Behind bars in America 2008.* Washington, DC: Pew Charitable Trusts.

Pillsbury, W. B. (1921, January). Selection—An unnoticed function of education. *Scientific Monthly, 12,* p. 71.

Pogodzinski, J. M. (2000). *The teacher shortage: Causes and recommendations for change.* San Jose, CA: Department of Economics, San Jose State University.

Policy Analysis for California Education (PACE). (2000). *Crucial issues in California education 2000: Are the reform pieces fitting together?* Berkeley: University of California at Berkeley, PACE.

Popham, W. J. (1999). Why standardized test scores don't measure educational quality. *Educational Leadership, 56*(6), 8–15.

Poplin, M., & Weeres, J. (1992). *Voices from the inside: A report on schooling from inside the classroom.* Claremont, CA: The Institute for Education in Transformation, Claremont Graduate School.

Powell, A. G., Farrar, E., & Cohen, D. K. (1985). *The shopping mall high school.* Boston: Houghton Mifflin.

Prison nation. (2008, March). *New York Times.* Editorial. Retrieved March 28, 2008, from http://www.nytimes.com/2008/03/10/opinion/10mon1.html?_r=1&scp=1&sq=%22prison+nation%22&st=nyt&oref=slogin

Quality Assurance Division of the Education Bureau. (2008). *Performance indicators for Hong Kong schools, 2008, with evidence of performance.* Retrieved September 12, 2008, from http://www.edb.gov.hk/FileManager/EN/Content_6456/pi2008%20eng%205_5.pdf

Ravitch, D. (2002, August 12). *A visit to a core knowledge school.* Retrieved May 12, 2009, from http://www.hoover.org/pubaffairs/dailyreport/archive/2856501.html

Ravitch, D. (2009). What about 21st-century skills? *Education Week*. Retrieved May 9, 2009, from htpp://blog.edweek.org/edweek/Bridging-Differences/2009/03/what_about_21st_century_skills.html

Raymond, M. (2003). Expert report filed in *Williams v. California*. Retrieved March 20, 2009, from http://www.decentschools.org/expert_reports/raymond_report.pdf

Rebell, M. A. (2007). Poverty, "meaningful" educational opportunity, and the necessary role of the courts. *North Carolina Law Review, 85,* 1467–1480.

Resnick, L. B. (1987). *Education and learning to think.* Washington, DC: National Academy Press.

Reynolds, A., & Temple, J. (2006). Economic returns of investments in preschool education. In E. Zigler, W. S. Gilliam, & S. M. Jones. (Eds.), *A vision for universal preschool education* (pp. 37–68). New York: Cambridge University Press.

Richland County v. Campbell, 364 S.E.2d 470 (S.C. 1888).

Rivkin, S. G., Hanushek, E. A., & Kain, J. F. (2000). Teachers, schools, and academic achievement. Cambridge, MA: National Bureau of Economic Research, Working Paper No. 6691 (revised).

Robinson, H. S. (1984). The M Street School, Records of the Columbia Historical Society of Washington, D.C., Vol. LI (1984), 122. In Thomas Sowell, *The education of minority children.* Retrieved August 10, 2008, from http://www.tsowell.com/speducat.html#copy

Rochkind, J., Ott, A., Immerwahr, J., Doble, J., & Johnson, J. (2007). *Lessons learned: New teachers talk about their jobs, challenges, and long-range plans: A report from the National Comprehensive Center for Teacher Quality and Public Agenda.* New York: Public Agenda.

Rock, D. A., Hilton, T. L., Pollack, J., Ekstrom, R. B., & Goertz, M. E. (1985). *A study of excellence in high school education: Educational policies, school quality, and student outcomes.* Washington, DC: National Center for Education Statistics.

Roderick, M., Bryk, A., Jacob, B., Easton, J., & Allensworth, E. (1999). *Ending social promotion: Results from the first two years.* Chicago: Consortium on Chicago School Research.

Rodriguez et al. v. Los Angeles Unified School District, Superior Court of the County of Los Angeles #C611358. Consent decree filed August 12, 1992.

Rogers, J. (2007). Constructing success: Accountability, public reporting, and the California high school exit exam. *Santa Clara Law Review, 47,* 755–780.

Rosenbaum, J. (1976). *Making inequality: The hidden curriculum of high school tracking.* New York: Wiley.

Rothstein, R. (2004). *Class and schools: Using social, economic and educational reform to close the Black-White achievement gap.* Washington, DC: Economic Policy Institute.

Rothstein, R., Jacobsen, R., & Wilder, T. (2008). *Grading education: Getting accountability right.* New York: Teachers College Press.

Roza, M., & Hill, P. T. (2004). How within-district spending inequities help some schools to fail. *Brookings papers on education policy.* Washington, DC: Brookings Institution.

Rumberger, R. W. (2007, July 12). Seeking solutions to dropout crisis. *Sacramento Bee,* Editorials Section, p. B7. Retrieved April 1, 2008, from http://www.sacbee.com/110/story/268222.html.

Rumberger, R. W., & Larson, K. A. (1998). Student mobility and the increased risk of high school dropout. *American Journal of Education, 107*(1), 1–35.

Rumberger, R. W., & Palardy, G. J. (2005). Does resegregation matter? The impact of social composition on academic achievement in Southern high schools. In John Charles Boger & Gary Orfield (Eds.), *School resegregation: Must the South turn back?* (pp. 127–147). Chapel Hill: The University of North Carolina Press.

Russell, M., & Abrams, L. (2004). Instructional uses of computers for writing: The impact of state testing programs. *Teachers College Record, 106*(6), 1332–1357.

Rustique-Forrester, E. (2005). Accountability and the pressures to exclude: A cautionary tale from England. *Education Policy Analysis Archives.* Retrieved August 14, 2009, from http://epaa.edu/epaa/v13n26/

Ryan, S., & Ackerman, D. (2004). *Creating a qualified preschool teaching workforce, part 1: Getting qualified: A report on the efforts of preschool teachers in New Jersey's Abbott districts to improve their qualifications.* New Brunswick, NJ: National Institute for Early Education Research.

Sable, J., & Hoffman, L. (2005). *Characteristics of the 100 largest public elementary and secondary school districts in the United States: 2002–03.* U.S. Department of Education, National Center for Education Statistics. Washington, DC: U.S. Government Printing Office.

Safer, D. (1986). The stress of secondary school for vulnerable students. *Journal of Youth and Adolescence, 15*(5), 405–417.

Sahlberg, P. (2007). Education policies for raising student learning: The Finnish approach. *Journal of Education Policy, 22*(2), 147–171.

Sahlberg, P. (2009). Educational change in Finland. In A. Hargreaves, M. Fullan, A. Lieberman, & D. Hopkins (Eds.), *International Handbook of Educational Change* (pp. 1–28). The Netherlands: Kluwer Academic Publishers.

Salleh, H. (2006). Action research in Singapore education: constraints and sustainability. *Educational Action Research, 14*(4), 513–523.

San Antonio Independent School District v. Rodriguez. 411 U.S. 1 1973.

Sanders, W. L., & Rivers, J. C. (1996). *Cumulative and residual effects of teachers on future academic achievement.* Knoxville: University of Tennessee Value-Added Research and Assessment Center.

Sato, M. (2000, April). The National Board for Professional Teaching Standards: Teacher learning through the assessment process. Paper presented at the Annual Meeting of American Educational Research Association. New Orleans, LA.

Sato, M., Wei, R. C., & Darling-Hammond, L. (2008). Improving teachers' assessment practices through professional development: The case of national board certification. *American Educational Research Journal, 45*, pp. 669–700.

Saxe, G., Gearhart, M., & Nasir, N. S. (2001). Enhancing students' understanding of mathematics: A study of three contrasting approaches to professional support. *Journal of Mathematics Teacher Education, 4*, 55–79.

Schmidt, W. H., Wang, H. C., & McKnight, C. (2005). Curriculum coherence: An examination of U.S. mathematics and science content standards from an international perspective. *Journal of Curriculum Studies, 37*(5), 525–559.

Schoenfeld, A. (2004). The math wars. *Educational Policy, 18*(1), 253–286.

Schoenfeld, A. (2008). Teaching mathematics for understanding. In L. Darling-Hammond (Ed.), *Powerful learning: What we know about teaching for understanding.* San Francisco: Jossey-Bass.

Schott Foundation. (2009). National Opportunity to Learn campaign. Boston: Author. Retrieved May 30, 2009, from http://www.schottfoundation.org/funds/otl

Schrag, P. (1999). *Paradise lost: California's experience, America's future.* Berkeley: University of California Press.

Schwartz, M. S., Sadler, P. M., Sonnert, G., & Tai, R. H. (2009). Depth versus breadth: How content coverage in high school science courses relates to later success in college science coursework. *Science Education.* Retrieved March 11, 2009, from http://www.interscience.wiley.com

Schweinhart, L. J., Montie, J., Xiang, Z., Barnett, W. S., Belfield, C. R., & Nores, M. (2005). *Lifetime effects: The High/Scope Perry Preschool study through age 40.* (Monographs of the High/Scope Educational Research Foundation, 14). Ypsilanti, MI: High/Scope Press.

Sciences Education Foundation. (2004). Briefing regarding the January 16, 2004 draft criteria for evaluating K–8 instructional materials for California's students. Retrieved March 22, 2009, from http://www.sci-ed-ga.org/standards/9page-briefing.doc

Senge, P. M. (1990). *The fifth discipline: The art and practice of the learning organization.* New York: Doubleday.

Seth, M. (2005). *Korean education: A philosophical and historical perspective.* In Kim-Renaud, Y., Grinker, R., & Larsen K. (Eds.), *Korean education.* Washington, DC: The George Washington University.

Shapiro, M. (1993). *Who will teach for America?* Washington, DC: Farragut Publishing.

Shepard, L. A. (2000). The role of assessment in a learning culture. *Educational Researcher, 29*(7), 4–14.

Shephard, L., & Smith, M. L. (1986). Synthesis of research on school readiness and kindergarten retention. *Educational Leadership, 44*(3), 86.

Shields, P. M., Humphrey, D. C., Wechsler, M. E., Riel, L. M., Tiffany-Morales, J., Woodworth, K., Youg, V. M., & Price, T. (2001). *The status of the teaching profession 2001.* Santa Cruz, CA: The Center for the Future of Teaching and Learning.

Shulman, L. S. (1983). Autonomy and obligation: The remote control of teaching. In L. S. Shulman & G. Sykes (Eds.), *Handbook of teaching and policy.* New York: Longman.

Schofield, J. W. (1995). Review of research on school desegregation's impact on elementary and secondary school students. In J. A. Banks & C. A. M. Banks (Eds.), *Handbook of research on multicultural education* (pp. 799–812). New York: Simon & Schuster Macmillan.

Silard, J., & Goldstein, B. (1974, July). Toward abolition of local funding in public education. *Journal of Law and Education, 3,* p. 324.

Silva, E. (2008). *The Benwood Plan: A lesson in comprehensive teacher reform.* Washington, DC: Education Sector.

Singapore Examinations and Assessment Board. (2006). *2006 A-level examination.* Singapore: Author.

Singapore Ministry of Education. (2007). Mission statement from the Ministry of Education website. Retrieved August 25, 2008, from http://www.moe.gov.sg/corpora/mission_statement.htm

Skilbeck, M., & Connell, H. (2003). *Attracting, developing and retaining effective teachers: Australian country background report.* Canberra: Commonwealth of Australia.

Slavin, R. E. (1990). Achievement effects of ability grouping in secondary schools: A best evidence synthesis. *Review of Educational Research, 60* (3), 471–500.

Smith, F. (1986). *High school admission and the improvement of schooling.* New York: New York City Board of Education.

Smith, L. (2008). *Schools that change: Evidence-based improvement and effective change leadership.* Thousand Oaks, CA: Corwin Press.

Smith, M. L. (1991). Put to the test: The effects of external testing on teachers. *Educational Researcher, 20*(5), 8–11.

Smith, M. L., & Shepard, L. A. (1987). What doesn't work: Explaining policies of retention in the early grades. *Phi Delta Kappan, 69*(2), 129–134.

Smith, T., Gordon, B., Colby, S., & Wang, J. (2005). *An examination of the relationship of the depth of student learning and National Board Certification status.* Boone, NC: Office for Research on Teaching, Appalachian State University.

Smith, T. M., & Ingersoll, R. M. (2004). What are the effects of induction and mentoring on beginning teacher turnover? *American Educational Research Journal, 41*(3), 681–714.

Snow-Renner, R., & Lauer, P. (2005). *Professional development analysis.* Denver: Mid-Content Research for Education and Learning.

Snyder, J. (2000). Knowing children, understanding teaching: The Developmental Teacher Education Program at the University of California–Berkeley. In L. Darling-Hammond (Ed.), *Studies of excellence in teacher education: Preparation at the graduate level* (pp. 97–172). Washington, DC: American Association of Colleges for Teacher Education.

Solomon, L., White, J. T., Cohen, D., & Woo, D. (2007). *The effectiveness of the Teacher Advancement Program.* National Institute for Excellence in Teaching.

Spuhler, L., & Zetler, A. (1995). *Montana beginning teacher support program: Final report.* Helena: Montana State Board of Education.

Sonstelie, J., Brunner, E., & Ardon, K. (2000). *For better or for worse? School finance reform in California.* San Francisco: Public Policy Institute of California.

Southeast Center for Teaching Quality. (2003, December 3–5). *Teacher Leaders Network conversation: No Child Left Behind.* Retrieved July 25, 2007, from http://www.teacherleaders.org/old_site/Conversations/NCLB_chat_full.pdf

Southeast Center for Teacher Quality. (2004). High-stakes accountability in California: A view from the teacher's desk. *Teaching Quality RESEARCH MATTERS, 12,* 1–2. Retrieved September 2, 2004, from http://www.teachingquality.org/ResearchMatters/issues/2004/issue12-Aug2004.pdf

Spring, J. (1997). *Deculturalization and the struggle for equity* (2nd ed.). New York: McGraw-Hill.

Springfield Education Association and Springfield Finance Control Board/Springfield School Committee (2006, October 10). Ch. 71, Sec. 38 Arbitration decision in Arbitration over Teacher Performance Standards.

Stage, E. K. (2005, Winter). Why do we need these assessments? *Natural Selection: Journal of the BSCS,* 11–13.

Stansbury, K., & Zimmerman, J. (2000), *Lifelines to the classroom: Designing support for beginning teachers.* San Francisco: WestEd.

Statistics Finland. (2007). *Education.* Retrieved December 30, 2007, from http://www.stat.fi/til/kou_en.html

Stecher, B., Baron, S., Chun, T., & Ross, K. (2000). *The effects of the Washington state education reform on schools and classroom* (CSE Technical Report). Los Angeles: UCLA National Center for Research on Evaluation, Standards, and Student Testing.

Stecher, B. M., Barron, S., Kaganoff, T., & Goodwin, J. (1998). The effects of standards-based assessment on classroom practices: Results of the 1996–97 RAND Survey of Kentucky Teachers of Mathematics and Writing (CSE Technical Report 482). Los Angeles: Center for Research on Evaluation, Standards, and Student Testing.

Steele, C. M., Spencer, S., & Aronson, J. (2003). Contending with group image: The psychology of stereotype and social identity threat. In M. Zanna (Ed.), *Advances in experimental social psychology* (Vol. 34, pp. 379–440). New York: Academic Press.

Stevens, R. J., & Slavin, R. E. (1995). The cooperative elementary school: Effects on students' achievement, attitudes, and social relations. *American Educational Research Journal, 32,* 321–351.

Stevenson, H., & Lee, S. Y. (1998). *The educational system in Japan: Case study findings.* Washington, DC: Office of Educational Research and Improvement, U.S. Department of Education. Retrieved June 27, 2008, from http://www.ed.gov/pubs/JapanCaseStudy/title.html

Stevenson, H. W. (1992, December). Learning from Asian schools. *Scientific American, 267,* 66, 70–76.

Stigler, J. W., & Hiebert, J. (1999). *The teaching gap: The best ideas from the world's teachers for improving education in the classroom.* New York: Free Press.

Stigler, J. W., & Stevenson, H. W. (1991, Spring). How Asian teachers polish each lesson to perfection. *American Educator,* pp. 12–20, 43–47.

Stotsky, S. (1998). Analysis of Texas reading tests, grades 4, 8, and 10, 1995–1998. Report prepared for the Tax Research Association. Retrieved September 21, 2009, from http://www.educationnews.org/analysis_of_the_texas_reading_te.htm

Strahan, D. (2003). Promoting a collaborative professional culture in three elementary schools that have beaten the odds. *The Elementary School Journal, 104*(2), 127–133.

Strauss, R. P. and Sawyer, E. A. (1986). Some new evidence on teacher and student competencies. *Economics of Education Review, 5*(1), 41–48.

Strickland, D. S. (1985). Early childhood development and reading instruction. In C. Brooks (Ed.), *Tapping potential: English and language arts for the black learner* (pp. 88–101). Washington, DC: National Council of Teachers of English.

Strickland, D. S. (1995). Reinventing our literacy programs: Books, basics, balance. *Reading Teacher, 48*(4), 294–302.

Strupp, H. (2009, March 27). Solving California's prison crisis requires smarter approach. *New America Media,* Commentary. Retrieved April 4, 2009, from http://news.newamericamedia.org/news/view_article.html?article_id=4fe07cee4026189e000b3ba688db867d&from=rss

Supovitz, J. A., & Christman, J. B. (2003, November). *Developing communities of instructional practice: Lessons from Cincinnati and Philadelphia* (CPRE Policy Briefs RB-39). Philadelphia: University of Pennsylvania, Graduate School of Education.

Supovitz, J. A., Mayer, D. P., & Kahle, J. B. (2000). Promoting inquiry based instructional practice: The longitudinal impact of professional development in the context of systemic reform. *Educational Policy, 14*(3), 331–356.

Swanson, Beverly B. (1991). An overview of the six national education goals. *Eric Digest,* ED334714. Retrieved May 21, 2009, from http://www.ericdigests.org/pre-9220/six.htm

Takahashi, A., Watanabe, T., & Yoshida, M. (2004). *Elementary school teaching guide for the Japanese course of study: Arithmetic (Grades 1–6).* Madison, NJ: Global Education Resources.

Talbert, J. E. (1990). *Teacher tracking: Exacerbating inequalities in the high school.* Stanford, CA: Center for Research on the Context of Secondary Teaching, Stanford University.

Taylor, C. (1997). Does money matter? An empirical study introducing resource costs and student needs to educational production function analysis. In *Developments in School Finance.* Washington, DC: U.S. Department of Education. Retrieved on August 14, 2009, from http://nces.ed.gov/pubs98/dev97/98212g.asp

Taylor, W. L., & Piche, D. M. (1991). *A report on shortchanging children: The impact of fiscal inequity on the education of students at risk.* Prepared for the Committee on Education and Labor, US House of Representatives. Washington, DC: U.S. Government Printing Office.

Terman, L. M., Dickson, Virgil E., Sutherland, A. H., Franzen, Raymond H., Tupper, C. R., & Fernald, Grace. (1922). *Intelligence tests and school reorganization.* Yonkers, NY: World Book.

Tharman, S. (2005a). Parliamentary reply by Mr. Tharman Shanmugaratnam, Minister for Education, at the Singapore Parliament, 9 March.

Tharman, S. (2005b). Achieving quality: Bottom up initiative, top down support. Speech by Mr. Tharman Shanmugaratnam, Minister for Education, at the MOE Work Plan Seminar 2005 at the Ngee Ann Polytechnic Convention Centre, Singapore.

The California prison disaster. (2008, October 28). *New York Times.* Retrieved April 4, 2009, from http://www.nytimes.com/2008/10/25/opinion/25sat1.html

Theobald, N. D. (1990). An examination of the influences of personal, professional, and school district characteristics on public school teacher retention. *Economics of Education Review, 9*(3), 241–250.

Theobald, N. D., & Gritz, R. M. (1996). The effects of school district spending priorities on the exit paths of beginning teachers leaving the district. *Economics of Education Rreview, 15*(1), 11–22.

Thompson, C. L. & Zeuli, J. S. (1999). The frame and the tapestry: Standards-based reform and professional development. In L. Darling-Hammond and G. Sykes (Eds.), *Teaching as the learning profession: A handbook of policy and practice* (pp. 341–375). San Francisco: Jossey-Bass.

Trimble, K., & Sinclair, R. L. (1986). *Ability grouping and differing conditions for learning: An analysis of content and instruction in ability-grouped classes.* Paper presented at the annual meeting of the American Educational Research Association, San Francisco.

Tripp, D. (2004). Teachers' networks: a new approach to the professional development of teachers in Singapore. In C. Day & J. Sachsm (Eds.), *International handbook on the continuing professional development of teachers* (pp. 191–214). Maidenhead, UK: Open University Press.

Tsuneyoshi, R. (2005). Teaching for "thinking" in four nations: Singapore, China, the United States, and Japan. In M. Kaneko (Ed.), *Core academic competences: Policy issues and educational reform.* Tokyo: University of Tokyo, Center for Research of Core Academic Competences.

Tyack, D. B. (1974). *The one best system: A history of American urban education.* Cambridge, MA: Harvard University Press.

UNICEF. (2001). *A league table of child deaths by injury in rich nations. Innocenti Report Card 2.* Florence: UNICEF, Innocenti Research Centre.

U.S. Bureau of the Census. (1992). *Statistical abstract of the United States: 1992* (112th ed.). Washington, DC: U.S. Department of Commerce.

U.S. Bureau of the Census. (1996). *Statistical abstract of the United States: 1996* (116th ed.). Washington, DC: U.S. Department of Commerce.

U.S. Bureau of the Census. (2001). *School enrollment—Social and economic characteristics of students: October 2000* (Current Population Reports P20-533). Retrieved June 10, 2008, from http://www.census.gov/population/www/socdemo/school.html

U.S. Bureau of the Census. (2004). *Statistical abstract of the United States: 1992* (112th ed.). Washington, DC: U.S. Department of Commerce.

U.S. Bureau of the Census. (2005). *Current population reports*, Series P-20; Current Population Survey, March 1990 through March 2005. Washington, DC: U.S. Department of Commerce.

U.S. Bureau of the Census. (2006). *Poverty status of people, by age, race, and Hispanic origin: 1959–2006*. Washington, DC: U.S. Department of Commerce.

U.S. Conference of Mayors. (2004). *Status on hunger and homelessness in America's cities*. Washington, DC: Author.

U.S. Department of Agriculture (2004). *Hunger and homelessness fact sheet*. Retrieved August 14, 2009, from http://www.fsuhabitat.org/hunger.html

U.S. Department of Education. (2002, June). *Meeting the highly qualified teachers challenge: The secretary's annual report on teacher quality*. Washington, DC: U.S. Department of Education, Office of Postsecondary Education.

U.S. Department of Education. (2003). *2000 Elementary and secondary school civil rights*. Washington, DC: Author.

U.S. Department of Labor. (2006). *Number of jobs held, labor market activity, and earnings growth among the youngest baby boomers: Results from a longitudinal survey*. Washington, DC: Bureau of Labor Statistics. Retrieved September 22, 2007, from http://www.bls.gov/news.release/pdf/nlsoy.pdf

Useem, E. L. (1990). You're good, but you're not good enough: Tracking students out of advanced mathematics. *American Educator, 14*(3), 24–27, 43–46.

Usiskin, Z. (1987). Why elementary algebra can, should, and must be an eighth grade course for average students. *Mathematics Teacher*, 80, pp. 428–438.

Valverde, G. A., & Schmidt, W. H. (2000). Greater expectations: Learning from other nations in the quest for "world-class standards" in U.S. school mathematics and science. *Journal of Curriculum Studies, 32*(5), 651–687.

Vandevoort, L. G., Amrein-Beardsley, A., & Berliner, D. C. (2004). National Board Certified teachers and their students' achievement. *Education Policy Analysis Archives, 12*(46), 117.

Van Lier, P. (2008). *Learning from Ohio's best teachers*. Cleveland, OH: Policy Matters.

Varian, H., & Lyman, P. (2003). *How much information?* UC Berkeley School of Information Management & Systems (SIMS). Retrieved September 22, 2007, from www2.sims.berkely.edu/research/projects/how-much-info-2003/printable_report.pdf.

Vasudeva, A., Darling-Hammond, L., Newton, S., & Montgomery, K. (2009). *Oakland unified school district: New small schools initiative evaluation*. Stanford, CA: School Redesign Network at Stanford University.

Verlinden, S., Hersen, M., & Thomas, J. (2000). Risk factors in school shootings. *Clinical Psychology Review, 20*(1), 3–56.

Wagner, T. (2008). *The global achievement gap*. New York: Basic Books.

Walberg, H. (1982). What makes schooling effective. *Contemporary Education: A Journal of Review*, 1, 22–34.

Wald, M., & Losen, D. (2003). *Deconstructing the school to prison pipeline*. San Francisco: Jossey-Bass.

Walsh, K. (2001). *Teacher certification reconsidered: Stumbling for quality*. Baltimore: Abell Foundation. Retrieved October 15, 2001, from: www.abellfoundation.org

Walsh, K., & Podgursky, M. (2001, November). *Teacher certification reconsidered: Stumbling for quality, A rejoinder.* Baltimore: Abell Foundation.

Wasley, P. A., Fine, M., Gladden, M., Holland, N. E., King, S. P., Mosak, E., & Powell, L. C. (2000). *Small schools: Great strides; a study of new small schools in Chicago.* New York: Bank Street College of Education.

Wasserman, J. (1999, September 2). 21,000 kids left back: Record number to repeat; social promotion ends. *New York Daily News.*

Watson, B. C. (1996). *Testing: Its origins, use and misuse.* Philadelphia: Urban League of Philadelphia.

Wehlage, G., Smith, G., Rutter, R., & Lesko, N. (1989). *Reducing the risk: Schools as communities of support.* New York: Falmer Press.

Wei, R. C., Andree, A., & Darling-Hammond, L. (2009). How nations invest in teachers, *Educational Leadership, 66*(5), 28–33.

Wenglinsky, H. (2000). *Teaching the teachers: Different settings, different results.* Princeton, NJ: Policy Information Center, Educational Testing Service.

Wenglinsky, H. (2002). How schools matter: The link between teacher classroom practices and student academic performance. *Education Policy Analysis Archives, 10*(12). Retrieved August 14, 2009, http://epaa.asu.edu/epaa/v10n12/

Westbury, I., Hansen, S.-E., Kansanen, P., & Björkvist, O. (2005). Teacher education for research-based practice in expanded roles: Finland's experience. *Scandinavian Journal of Educational Research, 49*(5), 475–485.

Western, B., Schiraldi, V., & Ziedenberg, J. (2003). *Education & incarceration.* Washington, DC: Justice Policy Institute. Retrieved March 28, 2008, from http://www.justicepolicy.org/images/upload/0308_REP_EducationIncarceration_AC-BB.pdf

Wheelock, A. (1992). *Crossing the tracks.* New York: The New Press.

Wheelock, A. (2003). *School awards programs and accountability in Massachusetts: Misusing MCAS scores to assess school quality.* Retrieved May 30, 2005, from http://www.fairtest.org/arn/Alert%20June02/Alert%20Full%20Report.html

Williams et al. v. State of California. (2000). Superior Court of the State of California, complaint filed June, 2000.

Wilson, M., & Hallum, P. J. (2006). *Using student achievement test scores as evidence of external validity for indicators of teacher quality: Connecticut's Beginning Educator Support and Training Program.* Berkeley, CA: University of California at Berkeley.

Wilson, S. (1990). A conflict of interests: Constraints that affect teaching and change. *Educational Evaluation and Policy Analysis, 12*(3), pp. 309–326.

Wilson, S. M., Darling-Hammond, L., & Berry, B. (2001). *Teaching policy: Connecticut's long-term efforts to improve teaching and learning.* Seattle: Center for the Study of Teaching and Policy, University of Washington.

Wilson, M., & Hallum, P. J. (2006). Using student achievement test scores as evidence of external validity for indicators of teacher quality: Connecticut's Beginning Educator Support and Training Program. Berkeley, CA: University of California at Berkeley.

Wise, A. E. (1968). *Rich schools, poor schools: The promise of equal educational opportunity.* Chicago: University of Chicago Press.

Wise, A. E. (1979). *Legislated learning.* Berkeley: University of California Press.

Wise, A. E., & Gendler, T. (1989). Rich schools, poor schools: The persistence of unequal education. *College Board Review, 151,* 12–17, 36–37.

Wolfe, T. (1987). *The bonfire of the vanities.* New York: Bantam Books.

Woody, E., Buttles, M., Kafka, J., Park, S., & Russell, J. (2004, February). *Voices from the field: Educators respond to accountability.* Retrieved November 19, 2004, from pace.berkeley.edu/ERAP_Report-WEB.pdf

Woolf, L. (2005). California Political Science Education. Forum on Education of the American Physical Society, Summer 2005 Newsletter. Retrieved March 20, 2009, from http://www.aps.org/units/fed/newsletters/summer2005/woolf.html

Yoon, K. S., Duncan, T., Lee, S.W.-Y., Scarloss, B., & Shapley, K. (2007). *Reviewing the evidence on how teacher professional development affects student achievement* (Issues & Answers Report, REL 2007–No. 033). Retrieved October 15, 2008, from http://ies.ed.gov/ncee/edlabs/regions/southwest/pdf/REL_2007033.pdf

Young, V. M., Humphrey, D. C., Wang, H., Bosetti, K. R., Cassidy, L., Wechsler, M. E., Rivera, E., Murray, S., & Schanzenbach, D. W. (2009). *Renaissance schools fund-supported schools: Early outcomes, challenges, and opportunities*. Menlo Park, CA: Stanford Research International and Chicago: Consortium on Chicago School Research. Retrieved May 21, 2009, from http://ccsr.uchicago.edu/publications/RSF%20FINAL%20April%2015.pdf

Zentner, S. M., & Wiebke, K. (2009, May 11). Using NBCT as a springboard to schoolwide teaching excellence. *Inside the School*. Retrieved May 29, 2009, from http://www.insidetheschool.com/using-nbct-as-a-springboard-to-school-wide-teaching-excellence

Zigler, E., Gilliam, W. S., & Jones, S. M. (2006). *A vision for universal preschool education*. New York: Cambridge University Press.

Index

About the Author

Dr. Linda Darling-Hammond is currently Charles E. Ducommun professor of education at Stanford University, where she founded and oversees the School Redesign Network. The program works across the nation to transform schools to teach 21st-century skills and support student success through innovations in district and school redesign, as well as in curriculum, teaching, and assessment. She also founded and co-directs the Stanford Center for Opportunity Policy in Education, which conducts research and policy analysis on issues affecting educational equity and opportunity. Recently, Darling-Hammond was named one of the nation's ten most influential people affecting educational policy over the past decade, and she served as the leader of President Barack Obama's education policy transition team.

Darling-Hammond has conducted research on a wide range of policy issues affecting teaching and schooling and has advised policymakers at all levels of government. From 1994–2001, she was executive director of the National Commission on Teaching and America's Future, whose 1996 report, *What Matters Most: Teaching for America's Future*, led to sweeping policy changes affecting teaching and schooling and was named one of the most influential reports affecting U.S. education.

She began her career as a public school teacher and has co-founded a preschool and day care center as well as a charter public high school. She has worked with countless schools and districts on studying, developing, and scaling up new model schools and has advised many states on creating policies to support educational quality and equity.

Darling-Hammond is past president of the American Educational Research Association, a two-term member of the National Board for Professional Teaching Standards, and a member of the National Academy of Education. She served on the White House Advisory Panel's Resource Group for the National Education Goals, the National Academy's Panel on the Future of Educational Research, the Academy's Committee on Teacher Education, and on the boards of the Carnegie Foundation for the Advancement of Teaching, the Spencer Foundation, the National Foundation for the Improvement of Education, the Center for Teaching

Quality, the Alliance for Excellent Education, and the National Council for Educating Black Children.

Among Darling-Hammond's more than 300 publications are *Preparing Teachers for a Changing World: What Teachers Should Learn and Be Able to Do* (with John Bransford, for the National Academy of Education, winner of the Pomeroy Award from AACTE), *Powerful Teacher Education: Lessons from Exemplary Programs*, *Teaching as the Learning Profession* (co-edited with Gary Sykes, awarded the National Staff Development Council's Outstanding Book Award for 2000), *Authentic Assessment in Action* (with Jacqueline Ancess and Beverly Falk), *Learning to Teach for Social Justice* (with Jennifer French and Silvia Paloma Garcia-Lopez), and *The Right to Learn* (recipient of AERA's Outstanding Book Award for 1998).

Darling-Hammond received her B.A. (magna cum laude) from Yale University in 1973, and her Ed.D. in urban education (with highest distinction) from Temple University in 1978. She holds honorary degrees from many universities in the United States and abroad and has received numerous awards for her research contributions.